Turkish Odyssey

A Cultural Guide to Turkey

http://www.turkishodyssey.com

Şerif Yenen

Third Edition, İstanbul 2001
Copyright © 1997, 1998, 2001 Şerif Yenen

Contact address:
PK 14 Acıbadem
81020 İSTANBUL / TURKEY

Web Site:	http://www.turkishodyssey.com
E-mail:	yenen@turkishodyssey.com
Phone:	+90 (216) 340 4383 - 369 9874
Fax:	+90 (216) 326 6456 - 357 5287

ISBN 975-94638-0-6
Published by Şerif Yenen, Meander Publishing
Color separations and prepress by Ebru Grafik ve Mat. A.Ş.
Printed in İstanbul by Şan Ofset

Cover photo: Temple of Athena, 6C BC, Assos
For inset pictures in the cover, see pages 432, 270, 375, 176 and 184

Special Sales:
"**Turkish Odyssey**" is available at special discount for bulk purchases (100 copies or more) for promotions or premiums. Special editions, including personalized covers, excerpts, and corparate imprints, can be created for special needs. For more information, contact **Şerif Yenen**.

"Everything flows and nothing stays."

Heraclitus,
Philosopher of Ephesus
(c.540-480 BC)

MUSTAFA KEMAL ATATÜRK (1881-1938)
Founder of the Turkish Republic

"We Turks!

European or Asian?
Shamanistic, Moslem or secular?
Settled villagers or nomadic Turkomans?
The grandchildren of Mehmet the Conqueror or
children of Atatürk?
Sword of Islam or the lash of Christianity?
Ottoman orphans or Turkish citizens?
The conquerors or the conquered?
Fighting soldiers or peaceful civilians?
An army, a tribe or a nation?
Member of the West or outpost guard of the West?
A contemporary society or a historical bridge?
Do we belong to the East, to Anatolia or to the West?
Who are we?"

Bozkurt Güvenç[1]

[1] Güvenç Bozkurt,
Türk Kimliği, (Turkish Identity)
Kültür Bakanlığı, 1993

CONTENTS

CONTENTS

CONTENTS

The land of the ancient Asia Minor or Anatolia is today's Turkey.

Although Turkey is predominantly an Islamic country, it is a secular, democratic republic and people have freedom of religion and belief.

Turkey is an extension and homeland of many great civilizations of the world heritage, such as Hattians, Hittites, Phrygians, Urartians, Lydians, Ionians, Carians, Lycians, Persians, Hellenistic people, Romans, Seljuks, Ottomans and finally the people of the modern republic.

The earliest landscape painting in history exists on a wall of a Çatalhöyük house dating from 6200 BC. It shows the eruption of a volcano, probably that of Hasandağ's.

The Neolithic culture had its origin in Turkey and the peoples of Anatolia played a leading part in the Neolithic Revolution.

The first recorded international treaty in the world was the Treaty of Kadesh between the Hittite and Egyptian Empires, Hattusilis III and Ramses II, in 1284 BC.

Homer's birthplace İzmir (Smyrna) and his mythological city Troy are located in Anatolia.

The world's first beauty contest was held on Mount Ida (Kaz Dağı). The contestants were Aphrodite, Hera and Athena under the judgment of Paris.

Many city names in different parts of the world such as Philadelphia, Paris, Antioch, Troy or the continental name "Europe" originate in Anatolia.

The oldest known shipwreck on earth was excavated by a team headed by Don Frey in Ulu Burun near Kaş.

DID YOU KNOW?

In 640 BC, for the first time in history, coins made of electrum were used by the Lydians in Sardis (Sart).

The Persian Royal Road of the 6C BC ran from Sardis, western Anatolia, to Susa.

Aesop, teller of animal fables, was an Anatolian.

King Midas was an Anatolian.

Alexander the Great cut the Gordian knot near Ankara. The double knot in Turkish carpets is called "Gördes Düğümü" which is the Turkish expression for the Gordian knot.

Alexander's tutor, Aristotle, virtually invented the life sciences while he stayed in Assos (Behramkale) for three years.

Between 7 and 5C BC, Miletus was the home of Thales (one of the Seven Sages), of Anaximander and Anaximenes (natural philosophers), Hippodamus (philosopher and the earliest town planner) and Hecataeus (geographer).

Historian Herodotus, physician Galen, mathematician Apollonius, philosophers Anaxagoras, Scopelianus, Cleanthes and many more were all Anatolians.

Two of the Seven Wonders of the World stood in Anatolia: **the Temple of Artemis** at Ephesus and **the Mausoleum at Halicarnassus**. The others are the Pyramids of Egypt, the Hanging Gardens of Babylon, the Statue of Zeus at Olympia, the Colossus of Rhodes and, the Pharos of Alexandria.

The words of Julius Caesar "Veni, vidi, vici (I came, I saw, I conquered)" were said in Amasya, east of Ankara when he went to Anatolia in 47 BC.

*W*hen the Egyptians prohibited the export of papyrus, the King of Pergamum ordered that a new material be found. The new discovery was "parchment", a fine material from sheep or goat skin, which is highly polished with pumice stone and slit into sheets. The name, Pergamum, has been perpetuated and seen as synonymous with the word "parchment".

*A*natolia was the first major stronghold of Christianity.

The Garden of Eden in the Book of Genesis was said to be watered by a river which separated into four streams as it left the garden; two of them the Tigris (Dicle) and Euphrates (Fırat) rise in the mountains of eastern Turkey.

*M*ount Ararat (Ağrı Dağı) is in Anatolia. According to tradition, Ararat is the place where Noah's Ark landed. Ararat is the Hebrew form for Urartu, the Assyrian name for a kingdom that existed in the region from the 11C to the 7C BC.

*E*arly Christians escaping from Roman persecution sheltered in Cappadocia.

*S*t. Paul was born in Tarsus (southern Turkey). He undertook most of his missionary journeys and wrote most of his biblical epistles to early Christians in Anatolia.

*T*he Seven Churches of Asia mentioned in the Revelation of John are all located in Anatolia; Ephesus (Efes), Smyrna (İzmir), Laodicea ad Lycum (Denizli, Goncalı), Sardis (Sart), Pergamum (Bergama), Philadelphia (Alaşehir) and Thyatira (Akhisar).

*S*t. Nicholas, known as Santa Claus today was born and lived as bishop of Myra in Demre. According to legend, he secretly bestowed dowries upon the daughters of a poor citizen. This originated the custom of giving presents on the eve of the feast of St. Nicholas, a tradition later transferred to Christmas Day.

All of the 7 Ecumenical Councils which are accepted by both the Orthodox and the Catholic Churches were held in Anatolia.

Istanbul houses the Greek Orthodox Ecumenical Patriarchate in Fener and the Armenian Patriarchate in Kumkapı.

The huge building of the Hagia Sophia, which was for many centuries the largest church in Christendom, is still standing in İstanbul.

For the first time in history, Seljuks created state insurance for the losses of tradesmen.

Sultan Bayezit II dispatched the Ottoman Navy to bring the Jewish people who were expelled from Spain. They were brought safely to the Ottoman lands in 1492.

Tulips were introduced to Holland from Anatolia by Ogier Ghiselin de Busbecq He was ambassador of Charles V to Süleyman the Magnificent in 1554.

The first man ever to fly was Turkish. Using two wings Hezarfen Ahmet Çelebi flew from the Galata Tower over the Bosphorus to land in Üsküdar in the 17C.

Istanbul houses the historical building of Sirkeci Train Station. This served as the last stop of the **Simplon-Orient Express** *"king of trains and the train of kings"* between Paris and İstanbul from 1883 to 1977. It still lives on in the pages of **Stamboul Train** by Graham Greene, 1932, **Murder on the Orient Express** by Agatha Christie, 1934 and **From Russia with Love** by Ian Fleming, 1957.

Indo-European languages derive from Anatolia not the Russian Plains.[2]

[2] *See Renfrew's argument on page 34*

DID YOU KNOW?

*M*any words in English language such as **angora, bulgur, byzantine, caique, divan, kiosk, mausoleum, meander, parchment, sherbet, turban, turquoise** and **yoghurt** derive from Anatolia.[3]

*T*urkish women were far ahead of many European women when they obtained the right to vote at municipal level in 1930.

*T*urkey provided homes for 313,000 Bulgarian refugees of Turkish origin in 1989.

*T*urkey welcomed nearly half a million Kurds from Northern Iraq who fled from Saddam Hussein during the Gulf War in 1991.

*T*he number of species of flowers in Turkey is approximately 9,000, of which 3,000 are endemic. In Europe for instance there are 11,500 species.

*T*urkey is one of only 8 countries in the world which consistently produces surplus food and cattle for export.

*M*any valuable finds from Anatolia can also be seen in museums all over the world. The Pergamum Museum of Berlin contains the Zeus Altar, Gateway to the Sanctuary of Athena from Pergamum, Statues from Priene and the great Market Gate from Miletus. The British Museum has become the adopted home for the Temple of Artemis from Ephesus, the Mausoleum of Halicarnassus, and the Harpy Tomb from Xanthos.

For the present-day traveler, the fact that Western excavators were often working for institutions back home means that some of the better sculpture and architecture has left the country. This has made it difficult to study the overall effect of architecture and sculpture together.

[3] See Anatolia's contribution to English on page 142

Note on spelling and pronunciation

All the Anatolian proper nouns and place names, either in Turkish or in former Anatolian languages, have been given in their original spelling or familiar Latin forms unless they have synonyms in English. Therefore, if you want to read Turkish words correctly, it is recommended that you take a look at **Characteristics of Turkish** in Appendix 3 on page 520 before starting to read this book.

Abbreviations

b.   born
C   century
c.   circa, approximately (with dates)
Ç.   çay (river)
d.   died
.E   east
F   French
fl.   flourished
G.   göl (lake)
Gr.   Ancient Greek (language)
Ir.   ırmak (river)
L   Latin (language)
N.   nehir (river)
N   north
NE   northeast
Per.   Persian (language)
r.   reigned
sq.   square
Tr.   Turkish (language)

FOREWORD

*Ever since man has learned to stand on his own feet
Anatolia has been a crossroads, a way station and a meeting
point. This bare reality has been embedded and enriched by
so many cultures; on a remote and lonely mountain of
central Anatolia, a Hittite may whisper into your ear how
proud he was when they sat down to sign the first Peace
Treaty of human history with the Egyptians; a Phrygian may
give away their national secret of their King, Midas's long
donkey ears; a sorrowful Trojan may explain on a bright coast
of the Dardanelles, why they lost the war; Anatolian born
St. Paul may let you follow his footsteps to the heart of his
painful mission; an Ottoman may explain at the entrance of
the Hagia Sophia how they were so impressed by this magical
masterpiece when they captured the city; and finally you may
encounter a modern Turkey whose citizens are proud of the
miraculous revolution that has created a new nation out of
the subjects of a dying monarch.*

Mustafa Özcan

Writer, tour guide

PREFACE

So far, nearly all the guidebooks about Turkey have been written by foreigners. We, the Anatolians, have something to say about our land as well.

Türkiye, meaning "the land of Turks" in the Turkish language, is the name of the secular modern republic which is based on the heritage of all the Anatolian civilizations. Nomadic Turks came to Anatolia as Seljuks in the 11C AD, during the Byzantine period. In the Ottoman Empire, different people from different ethnic origins including the pre-existing people of Anatolia were unified under the domination of the Ottoman Sultan. At that time, except by Europeans, people did not call themselves "Turks"; they were simply "Ottomans".

Each nation is a society but each society is not a nation. It was necessary to be a nation to survive. And it was only after the big defeat of World War I that, parallel to all nationalistic movements in Europe, a group of people under the leadership of Mustafa Kemal Atatürk fought a war of survival and formed a nation for the first time, by trying to unify all the people under the biggest ethnic group's identity; Turks. Even though it was obvious that people of Anatolia were not ethnically homogeneous, they came from different ethnic origins, Mustafa Kemal's

ŞERİF YENEN
b. 1963, Ödemiş, İzmir

motto was "So happy is the man who says he is a Turk". Here, at this point, being a Turk played an important role in uniting the nation and creating the feeling of Turkish identity.

The Turkish Revolution was not an awakening but a birth.

The roots of the Turks, their existence and the Turkish culture can be summarized as follows:

♦ Anatolian civilizations, cultures and people before the Turks.

♦ Central Asian Turkish tribes before their arrival in Anatolia.

♦ The nomadic Moslem Turkomans who came to Anatolia.

♦ The conquered people of Anatolia who converted to Islam and became Turks.

♦ The western, contemporary and secular Turks.

Throughout history, Anatolia has undergone two different kinds of attacks. Firstly, by those people who wanted to plunder and capture the land like the Persians, Alexander the Great, the Romans or the Allied Forces during World War I. Secondly, by those who wanted to live and create their home here like the Hittites, Phrygians, Urartians, Seljuks, or Ottomans each of whom enriched the indigenous culture with his own.

Anatolians of today are unified to form a mosaic which is enriched by different people from different cultures and ethnic origins. Nobody is pure in Anatolia, neither in culture nor in race.

As Bozkurt Güvenç points out "Variety in unity, unity in variety".

Şerif Yenen

Philologist, teacher and tour guide

Acıbadem, İstanbul

ACKNOWLEDGMENTS

The author wishes to thank the following people for their support and assistance:

Ahmet Memiş, Ahmet Turgut, Atilla Türkoğlu, Aydın Kudu, Bozkurt Güvenç, Coşkun Beşler, Dee Stuart, Fatma Çakıroğlu, Feza Solaklar, Hami Fidanoğlu, Hulusi Oran, İlhan Kesken, Jale Boğa, Janet-David Humprey, Julie Harris, Kenan Özdemir, Matthew Boylan, Maureen Arnold, Mehmet Aktürk, Mustafa Özcan, Necdet Aydın, Nejat Demirkollu, Nigar Aksu, Nural Ercan, Orhan Coplu, Özcan Doğan, Sabri Mandıracı, Sandra Gutmann, Serdar Aslım, Şaban Civelek, Şafak Özhan, Tine Çatak, Turgay Erol, Yıldız Özalp

Special thanks to Mehmet Çatak, Vicki King and Sinan Torunoğlu

Photographs by Yusuf Tuvi

Cover Photo (inset), 18, 19, 20, 22-3, 25-8, 36-7, 40, 44, 51, 63, 65, 69, 134, 210, 256 and 290

Photographs by Nejat Demirkollu

24, 43, 47, 70, 74, 162, 169, 178, 190, 191, 193-5, 216-8, 220-1, 225, 232, 234, 244, 245 and 248

Photographs by Şerif Yenen

Cover Photo, 1, 3, 17, 21, 26-B, 29, 34-5, 41-2, 45-6, 48-9, 50, 52-8, 60, 68, 71-2, 75, 77 A-E, 78, 79 A-E, 80, 82-6, 88, 93, 95, 97-9, 102-5, 107, 111, 118-9, 121, 123-33, 135-138, 138-A, 140, 144-5, 147-9, 152, 160-1, 163, 165, 167-8, 174-6, 180, 182, 183 A-B, 184-6, 188-9, 192, 197-9, 200-8, 211-5, 219, 222-4, 226-31, 235-43, 246-7, 249-55, 258-60, 263-74, 276, 278-83, 285, 291, 294-8 and 299

Photographs from Ministry of Tourism

64, 101, 120, 181, 209, 233, 257 and 262

Photograph by Mustafa Özcan

59

Ebru (Marbled Paper) by Sabri Mandıracı

94

Caricature by Orhan Coplu

62

3D-Reconstruction Drawings by Coşkun Beşler

108, 146, 150, 164, 166, 170-3, 177, 179, 196 and 284

Design & Maps by Sinan Torunoğlu
Proofread by Graham Pritchard

Turkey (Türkiye in Turkish) is a country located at a point where the 3 continents of the old world (Asia, Africa and Europe) are closest to each other and where Asia and Europe meet.

Because of its geographical location, Anatolia has always been important throughout history and is the birthplace of many great civilizations.

The surface area of Turkey including the lakes is 814,578 km^2 / 314,503 sq miles. It is much larger than many European countries or even Texas (18%) in the US. Out of the total land, 97% is in Asia and this part is called Anatolia[4] or Asia Minor[5]; 3% is in Europe which is called Thrace[6].

Although 97% of Turkey is located in Asia, in many respects it is accepted as a European country and as a result, Turkey takes its place in nearly all European contests and associations.

Turkey is rectangular in shape with a length of 1,660 km / 1,031 miles and a width of 550 km / 341 miles.

Turkey is the 36th largest country in the World.

European border		
Bulgaria	269 km	167 miles
Greece	212 km	131 miles
Asian border		
The Commonwealth of Independent States (Georgia, Armenia, Azerbaijan)	610 km	380 miles
Iran	454 km	280 miles
Iraq	331 km	205 miles
Syria	877 km	540 miles

(opposite page)
GALATA QUARTER
viewed from the Galata Tower [1]

[4] ANADOLU (in Turkish) which comes from Greek, meaning **East, the Land of Sunrise.**

[5] Peninsula of Anatolia is so isolated from the rest of the continent that it is sometimes known as Asia Minor.

[6] TRAKYA (in Turkish)

HISTORY

When discussing history it is always difficult to know from which period to actually begin. The earlier civilizations of Anatolia cannot be ignored. Some historians take the advent of the Turks into Anatolia in the 11C as the "beginning". If this were to be the case then history is limited to dating from the nomadic Turks.

It has to be noted that civilizations are never built without foundations. Just like a wall made of bricks, they are all established upon former civilizations. Therefore it is quite possible to see traces of the very earliest cultures inherent in those that followed.

If we want to speak about Turkey, we have to begin by going back to the very early ages as the present country is an extension and mixture of people who come from various origins.

ÇATALHÖYÜK HOUSES,
6000 BC, Neolithic period [2]

THE PALEOLITHIC AGE

Paleolithic Period (Old Stone Age) 600000-10000 BC	
600000-200000	Lower Paleolithic
200000-40000	Middle Paleolithic
40000-10000	Upper Paleolithic
?-8000	Cave dwellings at Karain; primitive stone implements and weapons

(opposite page)
MEDUSA RELIEF, *2C AD, Didyma* [3]

Neanderthal man appeared in the middle Paleolithic age. *Homo Sapiens*, the ancestor of modern man, were first seen in the upper Paleolithic age.

Life, generally in this age, was perilous and at best uncertain. Survival depended largely on successful hunting, but the hunt often brought sudden and violent death. Social organization rather than bravery shaped subsequent success. Therefore man learned to hunt in

MURAL FROM ÇATALHÖYÜK DEPICTING A HUNTING SCENE, *Neolithic period, Museum of Anatolian Civilizations, Ankara* [4]

groups. In the earlier periods rough stone tools were used but later, tools were refined. Flint hand-axes, scrapers, cutters, and chisels are artifacts which served their specific needs.

Edible plants were gathered. They moved on whenever food resources became scarce. Home for the Paleolithic people also varied according to the environment. In cold regions they sought refuge in caves from the weather, predatory animals and other people.

Early art was produced by decorating cave walls with details of everyday lives especially depicting activities relating to hunting.

The most important Paleolithic places in Anatolia are in *Yarımburgaz* near İstanbul and *Karain* near Antalya. Karain is the only cave known in Anatolia where all the phases of the Paleolithic age are represented without interruption. It contains a number of habitation levels of this age. Teeth and bone pieces of Neanderthal man and Homo Sapiens have been unearthed in this cave.

THE NEOLITHIC AGE

Neolithic Period (New Stone Age) 8000-5500 BC	
7040	First settlement at Hacılar; earliest evidence of agriculture in Anatolia
6500-5500	Çatalhöyük becomes first cultural center in Anatolia; earliest known religious shrines, pottery, statuettes and frescoes
6200	Earliest landscape painting in Çatalhöyük

The term Neolithic, from the ancient Greek neos "new" and lithos "stone", was adopted. This age begins with man taking advantage of his environment by cultivating plants and domesticating animals. This is the age in which agriculture started. People did not need to move now as they began to control their conditions. As a result, town life started.

Neolithic farmers usually raised more food than they could consume and their surpluses permitted larger, healthier populations. The surplus of food had two other momentous consequences. First, grain became an article of commerce. The farming community traded surplus grain for items it could not produce itself. The community obtained raw materials such as precious gems and metals. Second, agricultural surplus made the division of labor possible. It freed some members of the community from the necessity of cultivating food. Artisans and craftsmen devoted their attention to making new stone tools for farming, shaping clay into pottery vessels and weaving textiles.

Neolithic farmers domesticated bigger and stronger animals such as the bull and the horse to work for them.

In Anatolia, the earliest evidence of agricultural life was found in Hacılar 25 km / 15 miles SE of Burdur, 7040 BC. Wheat, barley and lentils as well as the bones of goats, sheep and horned cattle were found in the houses of Hacılar. The

STATUETTE OF A SEATED NUDE FROM ÇATALHÖYÜK, *one of the earliest examples representing the Mother Goddess, Neolithic period, Museum of Anatolian Civilizations, Ankara* [5]

The earliest landscape painting in history exists on a wall of a Çatalhöyük house dating from 6200 BC. It shows the eruption of a volcano, probably that of Hasandağ's.

dog appeared to be the only household animal.

This settlement is best known for its clay female figurines, represented alone or with animals and children.

The most advanced Neolithic center in the Near East is Çatalhöyük, located 50 km / 30 miles SE of Konya and prominent between 6500-5500 BC. Çatalhöyük is a town consisting of rectangular, single-storied houses built of mudbricks supported by wooden beams and buttresses from the inside. The houses had flat roofs and were built around courtyards. Entrances were through the roofs using ladders. The flat roofs were for defense and provided a working space and passageways from house to house. The houses had the same layout; a living room, a storage room and a kitchen. The floor was raised and in one corner stood a bench under which dead people were buried after the removal of the flesh from their bodies.

The walls of Neolithic houses were decorated with colored murals, repeatedly repainted after replastering. The designs closely resembled the cave paintings of the Paleolithic era. These paintings give information about early man's activities, appearance, dress and even religion. Some scenes depicted death, hunting, dancing, and images of flowers, butterflies and bees.

Other arts and crafts were well attested. Human and animal figurines were carved in stone or modeled in clay. Bone was used for tools and implements, sometimes with finely carved ornamentation. Weapons included polished maces, arrows and lances with tanged obsidian heads. Impressions of mats and baskets were found, as well as implements used in spinning and weaving. Miraculously, preserved fragments of actual textiles were also recovered.

Besides animal figures representing fertility, there was also the cult of the mother goddess generally shown with her leopards which was to be repeated many times throughout later Anatolian civilizations.

"Generally speaking, nothing suggests that this precocious culture had its origin exclusively elsewhere than in Turkey and the peoples of the Anatolian plateau may well have played a leading part in the Neolithic Revolution." [7]

THE CHALCOLITHIC AGE

Chalcolithic Period (Copper Stone Age) 5500-3000 BC	
5500	Sophisticated painted pottery and figurines at Hacılar and Çatalhöyük
5000-3000	Settlements at Hacılar and Çatalhöyük continue; new settlements at Alacahöyük, Alişar, Canhasan, Beycesultan and Aphrodisias

As copper started to be used in addition to stones, this period is called the Chalcolithic age which means Copper Stone Age. Man in this age cultivated crops, herded livestock, lived in brick houses, made vessels of clay, stone, wood or basket work and fashioned weapons of bone or flint. He traded for the raw materials to manufacture his weapons and personal ornaments and his religious beliefs found expression in sculpture and painting. The figure of the Mother Goddess continued, but was domesticated and found in nearly all houses.

Hacılar is the most advanced example of the Chalcolithic culture in Anatolia. The difference of the houses of this age is the number of the floors. They become two storied with

[7] *Encyclopedia Britannica*, 1995

an entrance at ground level. The most distinguishing feature of Hacılar is its handmade painted pottery decorated with geometric motifs in reddish brown on a pinkish yellow background.

In Hacılar, a pot shaped in the form of a woman's head might indicate that there had been the basis of a belief which continued until Hittite culture. Hittites believed and wrote in their tablets that drinking from god-shaped pots enabled unification with God.[8]

With the increase of the metal industry, trade developed eastwards with Syria and Mesopotamia and westwards with the Balkans and Mediterranean regions.

Canhasan, 13 km / 8 miles NE of Karaman in the province of Konya, is an important Chalcolithic center together with Beycesultan, Alişar and Alacahöyük.

Although densely populated in this age, Anatolia lacked a cultural uniformity due to the limitations imposed by its natural geography.

THE BRONZE AGE

Bronze Age (3000-1200 BC)	
3000-2500	Early Bronze, Troy I
2500-2000	Middle Bronze
?-2000	The Hattian Culture
2500-2200	Troy II
2200-2050	Troy III
2050-1900	Troy IV
2000-1750	Early Hittite Period
2000-1200	Late Bronze
1950	Assyrian traders at Kültepe; first written records in Anatolia; transition from prehistory to history

[8] Akyıldız Erhan, *Taş Çağı'ndan Osmanlı'ya Anadolu*, Milliyet, 1990

THE BRONZE AGE

1900	Founding of Hattusha by Hittites
1900-1800	Troy V
1800-1300	Troy VI
1700-1450	Old Hittite Kingdom
1450-1200	Hittite Empire
1300-1260	Troy VII
1284	Treaty of Kadesh between Hittites and Egyptians
1260	Fall of Troy
1200	Fall of Hattusha

[9] Tuncer Ömer, *İşte Anadolu*, Arkeoloji ve Sanat Yayınları, 1993

[10] Turfan Naim, *Blue Guide Turkey*, A & C Black, 1989

STAG STATUETTE FROM ALACAHÖYÜK, *Bronze Age, Museum of Anatolian Civilizations, Ankara* [6]

The Bronze Age in Anatolia starts with the use of bronze, a mixture of tin and copper. The people of this age made all their weapons, utensils and ornaments from this alloy. In addition to bronze they also used copper, gold, silver and electron; an alloy of gold and silver.

A great advance in metallurgy is notable during this age, especially from the rich finds of gold, silver, bronze and copper excavated. Various vessels, jewelry, bull and stag statuettes, ritual standards, sun-dials (as symbols of the universe)[9] and musical instruments were discovered in the burial chambers of Alacahöyük. The bull figure plays an important role as a link between the Neolithic and the Hittite religions. Thus, the roots of Hatti and later Hittite religious belief may be inferred as extending as far back as the Neolithic Age in Anatolia.[10]

Men were buried with weapons, women with ornaments and toiletry articles as well as domestic vessels and utensils, many of them in precious metals. The tombs themselves were rectangular pits enclosed by rough stone walls and roofed with timber.

HATTIANS

The Hatti or Hattians were a race of indigenous people who lived in Central Anatolia. As they lived in the prehistoric age before writing was introduced to Anatolia their name has come through Hittite sources. The Hatti gave their name to Anatolia, which was then called *the land of the Hatti*. Even the Hittites called their own kingdom the land of the Hatti.

The influence of the Hatti civilization is apparent in Hittite religious rites, state and court ceremonies and their mythology. Although they lacked a native written tradition, these people had reached an advanced intellectual level; a richness and sophistication of their own Anatolian culture. They developed true polychrome pottery and also monumental architecture; for example, the 60-room ground level palace at the Kültepe site. The bronze Hatti sun-disc, with its radial lobes representing the planets, shows the complexity of their cosmic views.

ASSYRIAN MERCHANTS IN THEIR KARUM IN KANİŞ, *20C BC, Kültepe* [7]

ASSYRIAN TRADERS

This period is also known as the Middle Bronze Age during which the old Assyrian state in Mesopotamia established a trading system with Anatolia. In this period Anatolia was divided into feudal city states ruled by indigenous Hattians. They established markets out of cities each of which was called *"karum"*. There were 20 of these karums ruled by one central market, *Kaniş,* located in

CYLINDER SEAL FROM KARAHÖYÜK REPRESENTING A RELIGIOUS CEREMONY, *18C BC, Early Hittite period, Konya Museum* [8]

Kültepe. They paid tax and rent and in return, security was granted by local rulers. Caravans were employed which generally brought tin, perfumes and ornaments in exchange for goods made of silver and gold.

Written history started in Anatolia with the introduction of the Assyrian language, the cuneiform script and the use of cylinder seals by the Assyrian traders.

The tablets which date back to this period are written in cuneiform script in the language of old Assyria. They are written, baked, put into envelopes and then sealed by rebaking; an example of the first use of envelopes in the world.[11] Most of the tablets are about trading activities with some about private lives of people of this age.

"The figurative symbolism has been one of the most revealing aspects of the finds at Kültepe, because it emphasizes the existence of an authentic and indigenous Anatolian culture persisting through the vicissitudes of migration and political change. A fully developed Anatolian iconography persisted into later centuries, reappearing almost unchanged in the art of the Hittites." [12]

HITTITES

The Hittites are a people mentioned frequently in the Bible (Old Testament). They were immigrant people who arrived in Anatolia in 2000 BC. It took them 250 years to establish

[11] Tuncer Ömer, *İşte Anadolu*, Arkeoloji ve Sanat Yayınları, 1993

[12] *Encyclopedia Britannica*, 1995

a kingdom in central Anatolia after 1750 BC and their powerful Empire flourished in the 14-13C BC until it was destroyed in 1200 BC by the Sea Peoples.[13]

When the Hittites, who lived north of the Black Sea, migrated into Anatolia that region was already occupied by native people, the Hattians. Their arrival and diffusion had been peaceful and accompanied by intermarriage and alliance with the natives. So well did the Hittites integrate themselves into the local culture of central Anatolia that they even adopted the worship of several native deities.

KADESH BATTLE
between the Hittites and Egyptians on the Orontes River, c.1286 BC [9]

Hittites named their own state as *the land of the Hatti.* As Naim Turfan[14] argues, this does not show the tolerance of the conquering Hittites, but their meeting of a much higher level of civilization than their own. For approximately 600 years they continued this habit of borrowing from wherever it suited them.

Another argument by language archeologist, Renfrew claims in 1987 that Indo-European languages derived not from the Russian plains but from Anatolia. The Neolithic people of Anatolia carried their languages together with their plows to Europe and India. In this case the language of the Hittites did not need to come from somewhere, on the contrary, Hittites spoke Anatolian languages. So far Renfrew's argument has been undisputed.[15]

It is generally accepted that Anitta founded the Hittite State in the 18C BC. Hattusilis I established his capital in the fortress city of Hattusha (Boğazköy), which remained the prin-

[13] See Phrygians on page 41

[14] Donagh Bernard Mc, *Blue Guide Turkey,* A & C Black, 1989

[15] Güvenç Bozkurt, *Türk Kimliği,* Kültür Bakanlığı, 1993

cipal Hittite administrative center. From a strategic point, Hattusha formed an easily defensible mountain stronghold. Hattusilis I's campaigns were into northwestern Syria and eastward across the Euphrates River to Mesopotamia. Control of that region was to become a permanent objective of the Hittites in order to increase their economic power.

It remained for Suppiluliumas I (1380-1346 BC), an energetic and successful campaigner, to restore Hittite control in Anatolia and effectively extend the borders of his kingdom to the south and east. His major accomplishments were the defeat of Mitanni and conquests in Syria, including the capture of the powerful city-state of Kargamış. His period saw the Empire at its peak, but even so during that time the Hittite Empire was never a single, political unit. Hittite penetration into Syria brought the newly revived state into conflict with Egypt. A major battle between the Hittites under Muwattalis and the Egyptian King Ramses II was fought at Kadesh on the Orontes River c.1286 BC with victory going to the Hittites. They were realistic enough to recognize the limits of their power and far-sighted enough to appreciate the value of peace and an alliance with Egypt. Although there was no real victor in this battle, each side claimed to have won.

The battle was one of the first in history of which a tactical description has survived. The Hittite specialist O. R. Gurney summarizes the Egyptian text as follows:

"The Hittite army based on Kadesh succeeded in completely concealing its position from the Egyptian scouts and as the unsuspecting Egyptians advanced in marching order towards the city and started to pitch their camp, a strong detachment of Hittite chariotry passed round unnoticed behind the city, crossed the river Orontes and fell upon the center of the Egyptian column with shattering force. The Egyptian army would have been annihilated, had not a detached Egyptian regiment arrived most opportunely from another direction and caught the Hittites unawares as they were pillaging the camp. This lucky chance enabled the Egyptian king to save the remainder of his forces and to represent the battle as a great victory."[16]

THE TABLET OF THE KADESH PEACE TREATY *signed by the Hittites and the Egyptians after the Battle of Kadesh, 1284 BC. It is written in the Akkadian language in Hittite cuneiform.* [10]

Their rapid adoption of a new cuneiform script made the Hittites the first known literate civilization of Anatolia.

[16] O. R. Gurney, *The Hittites,* Penguin Books, 1952

The Peace Treaty of Kadesh between Hattusilis III and Ramses II insured peace between the Hittites and Egypt on the southern border of the Empire (1284 BC). It is accepted as the first recorded international treaty in the world. The ratification of the treaty was followed by a cordial exchange of letters, not only between the two kings but also from one queen to another. Thirteen years later a daughter of Hattusilis was married to the Egyptian Pharaoh.

In Anatolia, the old pattern of unrest and revolt presented continuing dangers for the Hittite state, as vassals sought to reassert their independence. Beset by both internal and external pressures, the Hittites were unable to resist the onslaught of the Sea Peoples, who overran Anatolia about 1200 BC.

Hittite Culture

In addition to the cuneiform script imported from Mesopotamia, the Hittites also used a picture writing form (hieroglyphs) which can be seen on their seals and public monuments.

Hittite culture was an amalgamation of native Anatolian and Hurrian elements in religion, literature and art. The scribes of imperial Hattusha were familiar with Sumerian, Assyrian and Babylonian texts and perhaps to some extent with Egyptian materials as well. Hittite culture thus drew to itself a representative sampling of the cosmopolitan perspectives of the ancient Near East. This is reflected in the thousands of cuneiform tablets uncovered in the ruins of the Hittite capital.

The pantheon of Hittite religion included thousands of deities—many of them associated with various Anatolian localities. The state cult was dominated by an Anatolian deity called the Sun-goddess *Arinna*, protectress of the royal dynasty. Her consort was the Weather god *Hatti*. In the later empire, strong Hurrian influence in Hittite religion appeared with the introduction of the goddess, *Hepat*, identified with the Sun-goddess and with *Teshub*, who became identified with the Weather-god. "Zeus's wife Hera and Adam's wife Eve are the extensions of Hittite goddess Hepat."[17]

RELIEF OF WARRIOR GOD *from the King's Gate in Boğazköy, 14-13C BC, Museum of Anatolian Civilizations, Ankara* [11]

Hittite literature includes historical annals, royal testaments as well as a number of myths and legends. Many of the latter appear to be of Hurrian origin.

They created the best military architecture of the Near East. Their system of offensive defense works, handed down from the Old Kingdom, grew into a unique type of fortification under the Empire.

The major characteristic of Hittite architecture is its completely asymmetrical ground plan. They employed square piers as supports and had neither columns nor capitals.

Outstanding among examples of Hittite art are the Sphinx Gate of Alacahöyük and the rock reliefs of Yazılıkaya, an outdoor religious shrine in the form of a rock gallery located

[17] Tuncer Ömer, *İşte Anadolu*, Arkeoloji ve Sanat Yayınları, 1993

outside the walls of Hattusha, where two converging lines of male and female deities strikingly depict the major gods of the Hittite Empire.

First seen in a relief of 12 gods in Yazılıkaya, the number twelve has been repeated often throughout historic and prehistoric times with 12 Gods of Olympus, 12 Apostles, 12 İmams in Islamic mysticism, 12 in a dozen and 12 months in a year.[18]

Finally, a significant feature of Hittite culture is to be observed in the Hittite Law Code, which appears to be more humane than others in the ancient Near East and in the Hittite practice of treaty relations with allies and vassals during the empire period.

A number of major Anatolian sites have now been excavated that have yielded objects or inscriptions of the Hittite period. Among these, in addition to Hattusha, are Alişar, Alacahöyük and Kültepe, all in the central Anatolian plateau; Karahöyük, near Konya in the southwest; and Tarsus and Mersin in the Cilician plain of southern Anatolia.

There is no certain typical tradition with regards to their burial customs, but cremation and inhumation can be seen together. What is interesting is that people were buried with their animals, mostly horses.

Hittite Society

At the head of Hittite society sat the king and queen. The king was supreme commander of the army, chief judge and supreme priest. He carried out all diplomatic dealings with

[18] Tuncer Ömer, *İşte Anadolu,* Arkeoloji ve Sanat Yayınları, 1993

foreign powers and in times of war personally led the army into the field. The queen, who was highly regarded, held a strong, independent position. She had important religious duties to perform and some queens even engaged in diplomatic correspondence with foreign queens.

Below the king and queen was the aristocracy. The relatives of the king constituted a privileged group.

In contrast to earlier periods of Anatolian culture, where the place of women was high, in the Hittite period the importance of men increased.

Society was divided into two levels; the free people and the slaves. Free citizens were farmers, artisans, tradesmen and petty officials. Slaves could be bought and sold, but they had rights of property and marriage.

It was the Hittites who domesticated horses for the first time. They used them for their war chariots and also realized that they could be ridden. It is probable that centaurs of the Aegean legends are images of those people who saw the Hittite people on horseback.

THE IRON AGE

Iron Age (1200-700 BC)	
1200-650	Neo-Hittites
1100-1000	Migration of Aeolians and Ionians to Aegean coast of Anatolia
860-580	Urartians
800	Foundation of Panionic League and rise of Ionian culture in Anatolia
c.800	Birth of Homer in Smyrna
750-300	Phrygians
717	Kargamış and other Neo-Hittite states fall to the Assyrians

The Iron Age marks the period of the development of technology, when the working of iron came into general use, replacing bronze as the basic material for implements and weapons. It is the last stage of the archaeological sequence known as the three-age system; Stone Age, Bronze Age and Iron Age.

NEO-HITTITES

Following the collapse of Hittite power, Anatolia entered a dark age, not to recover substantially until about 800 BC. The territories previously held by the Hittites in Syria were also pillaged and burned by invaders, but they quickly recovered and reorganized into more than a dozen small independent kingdoms, with a Hittite culture modified by Syrian-Semitic influences. These are known as the *Neo-Hittite* states. Many of their inhabitants were probably refugees or descendants of refugees from the Hittite homeland. These Neo-Hittites are the Hittites, or "Sons of Heth," referred to in the Bible. The Neo-Hittite states—among them Aleppo, Kargamış, Arpad and Maraş—were absorbed into the Assyrian Empire by the late 8C BC.

ORTHOSTAT RELIEF FROM KARGAMIŞ DEPICTING A CHARIOT BATTLE, *Neo-Hittite period, Museum of Anatolian Civilizations, Ankara* [13]

URARTIANS

The Urartians established a state around Lake Van in 1000 BC. They were the descendants of the Hurrians who were contemporary to the Hittites in the east and southeast Anatolia. Tushpa near Lake Van, was the capital, with the massive fortress of Van as the citadel.

For about 300 years, from 860-580 BC until the invasion of the Medes from the north,

Urartu was a formidable regional power. Assyria in Mesopotamia competed with the Assyrian foe for complete hegemony over eastern and south-eastern Anatolia.

PHRYGIANS

The Phrygians were among those migrating peoples known as the "Sea Peoples" who were responsible for the final destruction of the Hittite Empire.

ORTHOSTAT RELIEF FROM ASLANTEPE-MALATYA DEPICTING THE KING OFFERING LIBATION TO THE SKY-GOD, *Neo-Hittite period, Museum of Anatolian Civilizations, Ankara* [14]

During the period of Midas (8C BC), they rose to be a powerful kingdom and dominated central and southeastern Anatolia. Actually, for the Hellenistic people, this Midas period is the subject of mythology. Midas's name was perpetuated in epics; for example, the stories of how he became king and how his Gordian knot was cut through and also how his ears were transformed into those of an ass.

Gordian Knot[19]

The Gordian knot was the name given to an intricate knot used by Gordius to secure his oxcart. According to legend, Gordius, who was a poor peasant, arrived with his wife in a public square of Phrygia in an oxcart where an oracle had informed the populace that their future king would come riding in a wagon. Seeing Gordius, the people made him king. In gratitude, Gordius dedicated his oxcart to Zeus, tying it up with a peculiar knot. An oracle foretold that he who untied the knot would rule all of Asia. According to a later legend, Alexander the Great cut the knot with his sword. From that time, "cutting the Gordian knot" came to mean solving a difficult problem.

[19] *Grolier* Electronic Publishing, Inc., 1993

Midas's Ears

When Midas was asked to decide on the winner of a musical contest between Marsyas and Apollo, he insisted that Marsyas (or Pan) was a better musician than Apollo, after which Apollo gave Midas the ears of an ass. He concealed the ears under a turban, permitting no one but his barber to see them. The barber, sworn to silence, whispered the secret into a hole in the ground and then filled in the hole, but reeds grew from the hole and whispered Midas's secret in the wind.

In the beginning of the 7C BC, the Phrygians declined with the invasion of the Cimmerians.

The most important finds are from Gordion, the Phrygian capital and at some other Phrygian centers such as Alişar, Boğazköy, Alaca and Ankara. The most imposing of Phrygian monuments is the Midas rock-cut cult monument or Yazılıkaya near Eskişehir.

The Phrygian nobles were buried either in rock-carved graves or in rooms under tumuli; a type of grave formed by making piles from soil. These rooms were not typical for Anatolia and were probably taken from Macedonia or Thrace. The dead were laid on benches in rooms with many gifts. After the walls were covered with colorful and ornamented fabrics, the rooms were heaped over with soil. The more important the noble in the grave, then the higher the tumulus.

Phrygians excelled in metallurgy, weaving and the production of timber. Their bronze vessels, fibulae and ladles were famous as far away as Assyria in the east and Greece in the west. Their furniture was made without the use of nails. They also used geometrical designs in their wooden works. Their *phyales*—used for pouring libations to the mother goddess, Kubile— are identical to today's *hamam tası* used in bathing. For the Phrygians, Kubile was the goddess of nature or even revered as nature itself.

IONIANS

From the 11C BC to the 6 BC, three Hellenic tribes of Hellas Ionians, Dors and Aeolians faced with a growing population that could not be fed from the hinterland or the sea, sent out colonies to western Anatolia and some Aegean islands. Out of these three colonies, Ionians became prominent by developing important cities under the influence of the preexisting Anatolian culture.

The term Ionia refers strictly to the central part of the west coast of Anatolia where Ionic Greek was spoken, although the term is usually applied to the entire west coast. Many Mycenaean Greeks emigrated to Ionia in order to escape the invading Dorians (c.1100 BC). Their close contact with the more advanced civilizations of Anatolia; Lydians, Carians, Lycians, Phrygians, even Hittites and Urartians, quickly raised the level of their culture. Trade along with the arts and sciences flourished in Ionia, especially in Miletus.

In 800 BC, a league of religious and cultural organization; *Panionium* was established among 12 principal Ionian cities: *Miletus, Myus, Priene, Samos, Ephesus, Colophon, Lebedos, Teos, Erythrae, Chios, Clozomenae and Phocaea.*

The Ionians were subjugated by Croesus, ruler of the expanding Kingdom of Lydia, to the north of Ionia. In turn, the Persian King Cyrus the Great conquered Croesus by 546 BC, which resulted in the subjugation of the Ionians. They attempted a revolt against Darius I in 499-494, but they were defeated and Miletus was destroyed.

When the Ionian cities fell under the domination of the Persians, all the philosophers and artists migrated to Athens and Italy. Thus, as Professor Ekrem Akurgal argues, the Ionian golden age passed from Anatolia to Athens.[20] In other words, the foundations of the highly admired Greek Civilization were built much before in Anatolia. The first steps of democracy which had been taken in Ionia, were later established in Athens in 508 BC.

The Ionians regained their freedom by becoming members of the Delian League.

Alexander the Great's conquest of the Persian Empire (334-325) freed Ionia, but its cities soon became the prey of contending Hellenistic monarchs. When one of them, Attalus III of Pergamum, died in 133 BC, he bequeathed his kingdom to Rome. Pergamum became the province of Asia and the Ionians became Roman subjects. The Ionian cities continued to be important economic and cultural centers.

THE DARK AGE

Anatolia's Dark Age (700-490 BC)	
680-546	Lydians
667	Foundation of Byzantium by colonists from Megara led by Byzas
650	Cimmerians destroy most cities in western and central Anatolia
640	First use of coinage in Anatolia
c.600	Carians
561-546	Reign of King Croesus of Lydia
546	Fall of Sardis; Croesus defeated by King Cyrus II of Persia; Anatolia under Persian domination
545-333	Persian period
512	Byzantium taken by Darius

[20]Akurgal Ekrem, *Anadolu Uygarlıkları*, Net, 1987

508	Democracy established in Athens
499	Ionian cities revolt against Persia
494	Ionians defeated at Battle of Lade and revolt against Persia crushed
484	Herodotus was born at Halicarnassus
480	Xerxes crosses Hellespont and invades Greece; Persians defeated at Salamis
479	Persians defeated at Plataea and Mycale; Persians evacuate Greece and Ionian cities regain their freedom

After 2,000 years of great civilizations, the eastern world fell into the dark ages in the 8C BC. This was the time that civilizations passed to the western world. At this turning point of world history, the civilized eastern world was represented by the Egyptians, Hittites, Phoenicians, Babylonians, Assyrians and Urartians. The Urartians were the last civilization of this age.

LYDIANS

In ancient times Lydia was the name of a fertile and geologically wealthy region of western Anatolia. It extended from Caria in the south to Mysia in the north and was bound by Phrygia in the east and by the Aegean in the west. Lydia first achieved prominence under the rule of the Mermnad in 680 BC. They underwent some Cimmerian attacks on several occasions. During the reign of Croesus, powerful King of Lydia (560-546 BC), the borders of the state in the east reached as far as Halys (Kızılırmak River). In 546, Croesus was defeated by the Persian King Cyrus and Lydia was dominated by the Persians until Alexander the Great. The country passed to the Romans in 133 AD.

The most important city in Lydia was Sardis (Sart), N of Mount Tmolos (Bozdağ), where the Pactolos River (Sartçay) passed through to reach the Hermos River (Gediz). The rich gold deposits of the Pactolos Valley were very important for Lydia's economy. This wealth was obtained from the alluviums of the mythological Pactolos River.

The Golden Touch of Midas

According to mythology Midas, a Phrygian king, turned everything to gold with his touch. Dionysus gave Midas the gift of a golden touch as a reward for a favor. After a brief period, during which his food, drink and daughter were all turned into gold, Midas regretted his wish and asked that it be withdrawn. He was allowed to wash his hands in the Pactolos River and ever after the sands of that river were gold.

Lydians claimed to have invented games like knucklebones and dice which they passed on to their Greek neighbors and through them to the rest of the world.[21]

In 640 BC, the first time in history, coins made of electrum (a natural mixture of gold and silver) were used in exchange for goods and facilitated regularization of commercial transactions by the Lydians. This was Lydia's most significant contribution to human history.

CARIANS

The Carians, from the hinterland of Miletus and Halicarnassus, enter history as mercenaries in the service of the Egyptian king along with their Ionian neighbors in the 7C BC.

In the 5C BC, Caria was ruled by tyrants and princes, some of whom chose the Persian side at the time of the Ionian insurrection. At the end of the 5C BC Caria belonged to

[21] Donagh Bernard Mc, *Blue Guide Turkey*, A & C Black, 1995

the Delian League. It seems to have been constituted as a separate Persian Satrapy. The Carian Satrap Mausolus took part in the great insurrection of the western satraps but later changed sides and conquered Phaselis and western Lycia for the Persian King. Mausolus made Halicarnassus the metropolis of Caria. The architecture of the city included the Satrap's tomb and the Mausoleum (another of the Seven Wonders of the World). The Mausoleum was planned by Mausolus himself but was actually built by his wife and successor, Artemisia.

THE CLASSICAL AGE

Classical Period (479-300 BC)	
478	Ionian cities join the Delian Confederacy
401	Xenophon and Ten Thousand begin their expedition
386	Ionia subjugated once more by Persia
377-353	Reign of Mausolus
356	Birth of Alexander the Great
353-351	Reign of Artemisia
336	Accession of Alexander the Great
334	Alexander the Great crosses the Hellespont and defeats the Persians at the Battle of Granicus and takes control of Anatolia, liberating Ionia, Caria and Lycia
333	Alexander conquers western Asia Minor, the Persian army defeated at Issus (İskenderun)
323	Death of Alexander
323	Outbreak of war between the Diadochi, Alexander's successors

The rise of Philip II of Macedonia and his son, Alexander the Great, initiated a victorious Pan-Hellenic crusade that destroyed the Persian Empire.

ALEXANDER THE GREAT (356-323 BC)

Alexander the Great, King of Macedonia, is one of history's foremost military leaders who established an Empire that extended from Greece to India.

Alexander III, who became the king of Macedonia at the age of 20, the first king to be called "the Great", conquered the Persian Empire and annexed it to Macedonia. He was taught for a time by Aristotle and acquired a love of Homer and an infatuation with the heroic age. The war horse of Alexander the Great was named Bucephalus.

In 334 BC his army moved onto Asia Minor. After defeating a Persian army at the Granicus River, he marched through Asia Minor with little opposition, then defeated a large Persian army under Darius III at Issus (near modern İskenderun) in 333 BC. He occupied Syria and then entered Egypt, where he was accepted as pharaoh. After organizing Egypt and founding Alexandria, Alexander crossed the Eastern Desert, the Euphrates and Tigris Rivers and in the autumn of 331 BC defeated Darius's grand army at Gaugamela (near modern Erbil, Iraq). Later he reached the Indian Ocean. In the spring of 324 BC, Alexander held a great victory celebration at Susa. He returned to Babylon, where he prepared an expedition for the conquest of Arabia. He died in June 323 BC without designating a successor. His death opened the anarchic age of the Diadochi, meaning "successors" in ancient Greek and his burial place is a matter of dispute. The cultural policy of Alexander the Great was very respectful and tolerant towards the Eastern World and he contributed to the unification between East and West. The suffixes *-assus* and *-nd-* are those used for hellenization of pre-Hellenic Anatolian ancient city names.

ALEXANDER THE GREAT ON A COIN
minted by Lysimachus, British Museum [15]

THE HELLENISTIC AGE

Hellenistic Period (300-133 BC)	
318-317	Antigonus controls Asia Minor
301	Battle of Ipsus and death of Antigonus; Lysimachus rules Anatolia and Seleucus gains northern Syria
281	Seleucus defeats Lysimachus and occupies Anatolia; assassination of Seleucus
276-275	Gauls invade Anatolia and are defeated by Antiochus
261-141	Reign of Eumenes I and rise of Pergamum
230	Alliance of Rome and Pergamum; Attalus I defeats the Gauls
223-187	Reign of Antiochus III, the Great
189	Antiochus defeated by Romans and Pergamenes at the Battle of Magnesia
188	Treaty of Apamea ends Seleucid Rule in Anatolia; expansion of Pergamum
133	Death of Attalus III of Pergamum; Rome inherits his kingdom

The period between Alexander's death and the Roman conquest of Anatolia is called the Hellenistic age. The mixture of Greek and Anatolian cultures resulted in a new civilization, the Hellenistic.

After Alexander's death three major monarchies emerged out of the wars of the Diadochi; Macedonia under the rule of Antigonus, Egypt under that of Ptolemy and Anatolia under that of Seleucus.

Then followed the rise of a number of independent states in Anatolia—among them Bithynia, Cappadocia, Pergamum and Pontus—all of which were eventually absorbed by the Roman Empire in the 1C BC.

The Kingdom of Pergamum, under the rule of Attalids, became the most prominent and continued until Attalus III bequeathed his kingdom and treasury to Rome on his death in 133 AD.

THE ROMAN AGE

Roman Period (133 BC-395 AD)	
129	Becomes a Roman Province of Asia Minor
88	Mithridates, King of Pontus, begins his first revolt against Rome; slaughter of Roman colonists in Asia Minor
83	End of Seleucid Empire
74	Rome inherits Bithynia
64	End of Mithridatic Wars; Romans control most of Asia Minor
40	Antony and Cleopatra marry in Antioch
34	Octavius defeats Antony and Cleopatra at the Battle of Actium
27	Octavius becomes Augustus
AD	
14	Death of Augustus
44-56	Missionary journeys of St. Paul; establish ment of first Christian churches in Anatolia
117-38	Reign of Hadrian
263-70	Goths invade Asia Minor
324	Constantine defeats Licinius and becomes sole ruler of the Roman Empire; begins to build new capital at Byzantium
330	Christianity declared official religion of the Roman Empire; Constantinople dedicated as capital of the Roman Empire by Constantine

The Kingdoms of Pergamum and Bithynia were bequeathed to Rome, and Pontus and Cappadocia were conquered. Cilicia also fell under Roman domination. A Roman administrative reorganization took place in Anatolia which brought

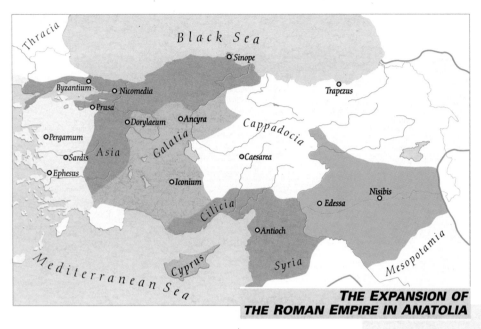

THE EXPANSION OF THE ROMAN EMPIRE IN ANATOLIA

	Until 133 BC
	103-64 BC
	65-25 BC
	18-117 AD
	211 AD

the Roman culture to Anatolia. At this point according to Naim Turfan Anatolia "hellenized" Rome while Rome colonized her, for she possessed a creative and well-developed culture, the roots of which stretched back thousands of years.[22]

CHRISTIANITY

St. Paul of Tarsus (c.1-67 AD)

Also called Saul in Hebrew and leader of the early Christian movement, was instrumental in the spreading of Christianity throughout the Greco-Roman world. He was born a Jew in Tarsus of Cilicia in Anatolia probably between 1-10 AD.

Thirteen New Testament letters have been attributed to him, many of which show him adjusting Jewish ideas and traditions to new circumstances and measuring Old Testament laws by their relevance to Jesus Christ.

[22]Turfan Naim, *Blue Guide Turkey,* A & C Black, 1989

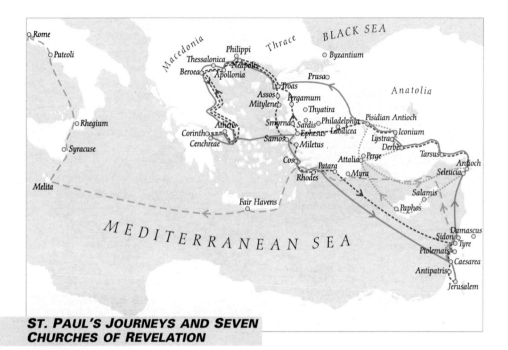

ST. PAUL'S JOURNEYS AND SEVEN CHURCHES OF REVELATION

■ **1st Journey**
from Antioch
(Acts 13:4 - 14:28)
47-49 AD

■ **2nd Journey**
from Antioch
(Acts 15:36 - 18:22)
50-53 AD

■ **3rd Journey**
from Antioch
(Acts 18:23 - 21:17)
53-57 AD

■ **Journey to Rome**
from Caesarea
(Acts 27:1 - 28:15)
59-60 AD

The New Testament records how he actively tried to suppress the early Christian movement through persecution until he was converted to Christianity by a visionary encounter with the risen Jesus while on the road to Damascus in about 36 AD. Because of this vision, Paul held that he, too, had met Jesus and was therefore qualified to be called an apostle. After being instructed and receiving Christian baptism in Damascus, Paul went to "Arabia" for a short time. He then returned to Damascus for 3 years until he was driven out and back to Tarsus, probably in 40 AD. Several years later Barnabas brought Paul to Antioch in Syria, where they ministered together for a year.

Paul spent the following 10 years on 3 lengthy missionary journeys to Anatolia and Greece. The second journey included an 18-month stay in Corinth and the third, 2-3 years in Ephesus. During this time Paul wrote letters to churches he had previously founded and could not visit in person. Some of these letters have been preserved in the New Testament. Paul was especially concerned that he protect his understanding of the life and teachings of Jesus from alteration toward Jewish practices or toward Hellenistic religious and philosophical ideas. He instructed the Christian communities he founded in ethical behavior by correcting their failings and offering advice. The Book of Acts describes the typical pattern of Paul's ministry: he began by preaching in a synagogue but was soon expelled as a rabble-rouser; then, with a small number of Jewish adherents, Paul turned to the Gentiles, converting large numbers but occasionally encountering trouble with the civil authorities.

The different accounts of Paul's visit to Jerusalem to settle the controversy over how much of the Jewish Law Gentile Christians were required to keep, have never been fully reconciled. Years later (c.58 AD), Paul brought a collection to Jerusalem for the city's poor Christians, but he was arrested. After 2 years in prison he used his right as a Roman citizen to appeal to the emperor and was sent to Rome for trial.

The Book of Acts ends with Paul under house arrest (c.63 AD), still preaching about Jesus. Clement of Rome and Eusebius of Caesarea report that Paul was eventually acquitted before traveling to Spain where he was arrested again and subsequently martyred in Rome under Nero, c.67 AD. Feast day: June 29 (with Saint Peter).

Seven Churches of Revelation

The Seven Churches of Asia are all located in Anatolia; Ephesus (Efes), Smyrna (İzmir), Laodicea ad Lycum (Goncalı), Sardis (Sart), Pergamum (Bergama), Philadelphia (Alaşehir) and Thyatira (Akhisar).

These churches are associated both with Saint Paul and with Revelations (the Apocalypse); letters written in c.95 AD to the Seven Churches by John. For some people John is a visionary who lived on the island of Patmos. But some people say he is the Apostle John.

There should have been more than seven cities with major Christian congregations in Anatolia at the time that John wrote and it is unknown why he addressed only these seven. These were possibly the most important ones at that time or letters to other churches were lost.

These churches were not church buildings as such but congregations. These early congregations had their meetings in private homes as there had been no original church buildings until the 3C AD. St. Paul possibly founded some of the Seven Churches on his missionary journeys between 47-57 AD, as he was thought to have visited all seven cities.

Constantine the Great (280-337 AD)

He was the first Roman emperor to adopt Christianity. Before 312 AD Constantine seems to have been a tolerant pagan, willing to accumulate heavenly patrons but not committed to any one deity. However, between 312-324 AD he gradually adopted the Christian God as his protector and on several occasions granted special privileges to individual churches and bishops.

Soon after his victory over Licinius at Chrysopolis in 324 AD, Constantine openly embraced Christianity and became more directly involved in the affairs of the church. Christianity spread fastest among the urban populations while people who lived in villages continued to worship different deities. The early Christians called non-Christians pagans because *pagani* in Latin means "country-dwellers".

THE BYZANTINE PERIOD

Byzantine Period (395-1453 AD) İstanbul	
392	Edict of Theodosius I banned paganism
395	Division of the Roman Empire into Eastern and Western by Theodosius I
524-65	Reign of Justinian the Great; zenith of Byzantine power
531	Nika Revolt against Justinian
616	Sardis and other cities in western Asia Minor sacked by the Persians
632	Mohammed dies at Medina in Arabia, Ebubekir becomes his first successor, or Caliph and Islam spreads throughout Arabia.
636	Arabs defeat Byzantines at the battle of Yarmuk and penetrate deep into Anatolia
677	Arab fleet attacks Constantinople
717-18	Arabs besiege Constantinople
813	Bulgarians besiege Constantinople
1096	Beginning of First Crusade; Latin armies enter Anatolia for the first time
1203	Beginning of the Fourth Crusade; Latins attack Constantinople
1204	Latins take Constantinople; dismemberment of the Byzantine Empire
1242	Mongols defeat Seljuks at Kösedağ and destroy their power in Anatolia

The Byzantine Empire is one of the longest-lasting empires in world history. Its name, which is derived from the name of the city of *Byzantium*, was given by 19C historians. Byzantines always called and regarded themselves as Romans. In 330 AD Constantine made Byzantium Rome's second capital, naming it Constantinople which meant "city of Constantine".

In 395 AD Theodosius I divided the Roman Empire into

two, Eastern and Western. Culturally, the Western part was Latin and the Eastern part was Hellenistic. Soon after, in 476 AD, the Western Roman Empire collapsed and the Eastern Empire survived. The Eastern Romans were Christians and changed their language from Latin to Greek.

Justinian I's successful efforts to reconquer the West followed in the early Byzantine period.

The Middle Byzantine period (610-1081 AD) began with the triumph of Heraclius over the Persians and his subsequent defeat by the Arabs. After 634 AD Arabs seized Palestine, Syria and Egypt and raided deep into Anatolia.

In the 11C, a struggle started between the generals who were great landowners and the bureaucrats. Distracted by this struggle, the emperors were unable to resist the Seljuks, who began conquering Anatolia.

In 1204 AD the Fourth Crusade seized and brutally sacked the capital and established the Latin Empire of Constantinople.

In 1261 AD the ruler of Nicaea regained Constantinople and refounded the Byzantine Empire which had to face threats from Westerners and from Turks in the East. Gradually reduced in area, the Empire finally succumbed in 1453 AD to the Ottoman Turks, who pronounced Constantinople to be the capital of the Ottoman Empire.

In this final period, the landed aristocracy dominated all provincial and central administrative positions of the Byzantine Empire. The army consisted of mercenaries and a "feudal" levy based on government properties awarded to great landlords in return for military service. The Byzantine emperors repeatedly tried to reunify the Orthodox and Catholic churches in return for Western aid against the Turks, but their efforts proved futile.

PRE-ANATOLIAN TURKS

Turks, or Turkic peoples, are the principal descendants of large bands of nomads who roamed in the Altai Mountains (and thus are also called the Altaic peoples) in northern Mongolia and on the steppes of Central Asia during the early centuries of the Christian era. Their language is a branch of the Ural-Altaic family. Physically, most of the Turkic peoples resemble the Mongols, although those of the West have been so mixed with native peoples that they cannot be distinguished from other Mediterranean ethnic groups.

The original Central Asian Turkic nomads established their first great empire in the 6C AD, a nomadic confederation that they called *Göktürk* meaning "Sky Turk".

Shamanistic in religion and tribal in organization, Göktürks broke up in the 7C. The Eastern part of the confederation became assimilated with the Chinese civilization and gave rise to the Mongols. The Western part contracted and was ultimately influenced by the Islamic civilization of the Middle East.

The *Uighur* remained in northern Mongolia and the *Kırgız* wandered in the steppes to the north. The *Oğuz* Turks, called the *Türkmen* (Turkoman) in Europe, dominated the area between Mongolia and Transoxiania, where contacts with Moslem missionaries, merchants and warriors led to further assimilation.

Under the leadership of the Seljuk warrior family, the Oğuz tribes entered Iran and then other parts of the Middle East. They went as raiders and mercenaries in service of the weakening Abbasid caliphs and also were hired by many towns to provide defenses against the anarchical conditions of the time.

In the meantime, in Central Asia the Kırgız pushed the

Uighur out of Mongolia in the late 9C. The Uighur moved south, into northern China and west into Transoxiania. The Kırgız also moved, finally settling in the mountains of what is now the Commonwealth of Independent States, where they remain today. The Mongols of northern China were formed into a powerful military confederation under the leadership of Genghis Khan about 1200 AD. They conquered China and the Asian steppes between northern China and Transoxiania and by the middle of the 13C had invaded and conquered the Seljuk-Abbasid Middle East as well as Anatolia. The Mongols brought substantial devastation while at the same time, however, they introduced Christian and Buddhist elements from Central Asia and established trade and cultural relations between the Middle East and China.

THE SELJUK PERIOD

Seljuk Turks Period (1071-1243 AD)	
1040	Dandanakan Battle and establishment of Great Seljuk Empire
1071	Byzantines defeated by Seljuks at the Battle of Manzikert (Malazgirt); Turks overrun Anatolia
1075-1076	First İznik and then Konya becomes capital
1219-1237	The golden age of the Anatolian Seljuks
1240	Ottoman Turks make first appearance in western Anatolia as minor vassals of Seljuks; Mongols invade eastern Anatolia
1243	Mongols defeat Seljuks at Kösedağ, it becomes a province of the Mongol Empire and gradually disintegrates into a number of principalities

The Oğuz Turks, under the leadership of Tuğrul Bey and Çağrı Bey, (the grandsons of Selçuk), subdued Horasan and defeated the Ghaznavids in the Dandanakan Battle and established the Great Seljuk Empire in 1040 AD. In 1071

Alparslan defeated the Byzantine emperor in the Battle of Manzikert which marked the beginning of the period of Turks and that of Islam in Anatolia. It was following this date that the Turks fully conquered the whole of Anatolia and established the Anatolian Seljuk State as part of the Great Seljuk Empire.

The Turks were the first people who invaded Anatolia completely. The previous invading peoples captured only parts of Anatolia. Although Persians and Romans invaded completely, they kept it under their political control rather than settling.

Turks came to Anatolia in migrations. Before coming they were Moslems and mixed with those of the local people who accepted being Moslem.

It is wrong to believe, as many have, that the pursuance of an Islamic policy and of conquest in Anatolia led the Seljuks to persecute the Christians. Inside the Seljuk Empire, as soon as order was restored, the lot of Christians was much the same as it had been before: the crusaders, who thought it must be otherwise, were judging conditions in Jerusalem by those prevailing in Anatolia.[23]

After 1150 AD Seljuk weakness enabled various Turkoman leaders to establish their own principalities along the fringes of the Empire. They acted as *gazis*, or fighters for the faith of Islam against the infidels. The Great Seljuks defended Syria and Palestine against incursions during the Crusades, limiting the domination of the Crusaders to the coastal areas. Contact between Islam and the crusading representatives of Christianity was largely limited to military matters and trade.

The Seljuks understood the importance of transit trade and adjusted their military and economic policies accordingly. It

[23] *Encyclopedia Britannica*, 1995

was very interesting that, for the first time in history, Seljuks created state insurance for the losses of tradesmen. For the caravans, they developed the *kervansaray* (caravansary) which was designed to meet the needs of any trader on the account of the state.

Parallel to well-organized international trade, cities in this period developed in wealth and population. That period also recorded universal teachings of enlightened sages like Mevlana Celaleddin Rumi[24] or Yunus Emre.[25] They taught about unity with God through devotion.

The Arabic language was used by scholars, Persian was the state language and Turkish was the daily or business language. Seljuk art blended those of Central Asia, Islamic Middle East and Anatolia.

The shamanistic Göktürks, before burying their dead, mummified and kept them in a tent for six months. This Central Asian tradition gave way to the rise of domed tombs, *türbe*, in Anatolia.

Lions and bulls, double-headed eagles, dragons, astrological motifs like planets and the Tree of Life were common in Seljuk decorative arts. These symbols come from Anatolian culture or perhaps from pre-Islamic shamanism.

Another innovation and artistic achievement was the production of tiles.

THE CRUSADES

The Crusades were Christian military expeditions undertaken between the 11C and 14C to recapture the Holy Land from the Moslems. The word crusade, which is derived from the Latin *crux* "cross", is a reference to the biblical injunction that Christians carry their crosses. Crusaders wore a red cloth cross sewn on their tunics to indicate that they had

[24] See page 466

[25] See page 219

assumed the cross and were soldiers of Christ.

Causes

The Crusaders continued the older tradition of Pilgrimage to the Holy Land, which was often imposed as a penance; however, they also assumed a dual role as pilgrims and warriors. Such an armed pilgrimage was regarded as a justifiable war, because it was fought to recapture the places sacred to Christians.

For Christians, the very name of Jerusalem evoked visions of the end of time and of the heavenly city. To help rescue the Holy Land would fulfill the ideal of the Christian knight. Papal encouragement, the hope of eternal merit and the offer of indulgences motivated thousands to enroll in the cause.

Political considerations were also important. The Crusades were a response to appeals for help from the Byzantine Empire, threatened by the advance of the Seljuk Turks. The year 1071 AD had seen both the capture of Jerusalem and the decisive defeat of the Byzantine army at Manzikert, creating fear of further Turkish victories. In addition, the hopes of the Papacy for the reunification of East and West, the nobility's hunger for land at a time of insufficient crop, population pressure in the West and an alternative to warfare at home were major factors.

Equally, the Crusades were a result of economic circumstances. Many participants were lured by the fabulous riches of the East; a campaign abroad appealed as a means of escaping from the pressures of feudal society, in which the younger sons in a family often lacked economic opportunities. On a larger scale, the major European powers and the rising Italian cities (Genoa, Pisa and Venice) saw the Crusades as a means of establishing and extending trade routes.

Campaigns

Out of all of the Crusades the first and the forth are the most important from an Anatolian point of view. In general, the others were not as successful as these two. Some of them came out to be the Children's Crusade (1212 AD), in which thousands of children perished from hunger and disease or were sold into slavery on their way to the Mediterranean.

The First Crusade

(1096-99 AD) The main army, mostly French and Norman knights assembled at Constantinople and proceeded on a long, arduous march through Anatolia. They captured Antioch (June 3, 1098) and finally Jerusalem (July 15, 1099) in savage battles.

The Fourth Crusade

(1202-04 AD) The Crusaders first attacked the Christian city of Zara in Dalmatia. Then, they sailed on to lay siege to Constantinople. The Byzantine capital fell on April 13, 1204; it was looted, particularly for its treasures and relics and made the residence of a Latin emperor, with Baldwin, Count of Flanders, as the first incumbent. A Greek army, almost casually, recaptured the city in 1261 AD.

The sacking of the wealthy city of Constantinople in three days by this fourth crusade was so tragic that a Christian high official declared, "it would be better to see the royal turban of the Turks in the midst of the city than the Latin miter".

Consequences

The results of the Crusades are difficult to assess. In religious terms, they hardened Moslem attitudes toward Christians. At the same time, doubts were raised among Christians about God's will, the church's authority and the role of the papacy. Religious fervor yielded to disinterest, skepticism and a growing legalism although the Crusades did stimulate religious enthusiasm on a broad scale. Knowledge, through contact with the Moslem world, replaced ignorance about other cultures and religions, and earned them a certain respect. The idea of religious conversion by force gave way to a new emphasis on apologetics and mission. The Koran was translated into Latin in 1143 AD.

Politically, the Crusades did not effect much change. The Crusader states and the Latin Empire of Constantinople were short-lived. The almost endless quarrels among rival lords in the Levant exposed a fatal weakness of the West and strengthened the Moslem conviction that the war could be carried farther west. In this sense, the Crusades led directly to the Turkish wars of later centuries, in which the Ottoman Empire expanded into the Balkans and threatened the very heart of Europe. Today, only the ruins of Crusader castles remain as evidence of the knights' presence in the East during which more than 100 castles and fortresses were built.

Through the Crusades, Islamic science, philosophy and medicine deeply influenced intellectual life in the West.

THE BEYLİKS (PRINCIPALITIES) PERIOD

Political unity in Anatolia was disrupted with the collapse of the Anatolian Seljuk state at the beginning of the 14C. As a result, some regions fell under the domination of Beyliks (Principalities) until the beginning of the 16C.

The Ottoman Empire is an extension of one of these principalities.

THE OTTOMAN PERIOD

Ottoman Turks Period (1299-1923)	
1299	Establishment of the Ottoman Principality by Osman Bey in Söğüt and Domaniç (east of Bursa)
1326-1362	Orhan Bey period. Accepted as the real founder of the Ottoman State by his military and administrative organization and forming the *divan*. The first ruler to use the title of sultan.
1326	Ottomans under Sultan Orhan take Bursa and establish their first capital there
1336	Karesi Principality conquered by Sultan Orhan; the Troad becomes part of the Ottoman realm
1353	Crossing the Hellespont and establishing the first Turkish foothold in Europe
1364	Turks under Sultan Murat I capture Adrianople (Edirne) and establish Ottoman capital there
1389	Murat I wins the Kosova I Battle; He establishes the Janissary Corps
1396	Ottoman force led by Bayezit I defeats Crusader army at Nicopolis (Niğbolu)
1397	First Ottoman siege of Constantinople
1402	Tamerlane defeats Ottomans under Bayezit I at Ankara; the Sultan is captured and eventually commits suicide. Mongols overrun Anatolia, and Ottoman power in the subcontinent is temporarily crushed
1403-1413	Interregnum in the Ottoman Empire
1413-1421	Reign of Mehmet I; revival of Ottoman power in Anatolia
1421-1451	Reign of Murat II; Ottoman armies sweep through the Balkans and also regain lost territory in Anatolia
1451-1481	Reign of Mehmet II, the Conqueror
1452	He builds the Rumeli Fortress on the Bosphorus
1453 (May 29)	Turks under Mehmet II conquer Constantinople, which becomes the fourth and last Ottoman

	capital under the name of İstanbul; he is entitled as the conqueror
1453-1579	Rise in the Ottoman Empire
1481-1512	Reign of Bayezit II
1512-1520	Reign of Selim I; Battles of Çaldıran, Mercidabık, Ridaniye
1517	Selim I captures Cairo and adds the title of caliph to that of sultan
1520-1566	Reign of Süleyman the Magnificent (the longest in the Ottoman Empire; 46 years); zenith of Ottoman power
	Because he organizes the state by making new laws, he is called *Kanuni* meaning law-giver
	The Mediterranean Sea becomes a Turkish lake with many captures
1526	Battle of Mohacs (Mohaç) and the conquest of Buda and Pest (Peşte)
1529	First and unsuccessful Siege of Vienna
1534-1535	Süleyman the Magnificient's expedition into Iran and Iraq
1538	Preveze naval battle, Barbaros Hayrettin Paşa (Barbarossa) becomes *Kaptan-ı Derya* (Commander in chief of the fleet)
1566-1574	Reign of Selim II
1569	The great fire of İstanbul
1571	At Lepanto naval battle allied fleet defeat the Ottomans except one squadron of Kılıç Ali Paşa.
1588	Death of Sinan
1579-1699	The rule of women. Ineffectual sultans give up control of Ottoman Empire to their women and grand viziers; Reforms and Renaissance in Europe
1607	Celali uprisings, rebellions against the land tenure system of the provincial fief-holding cavalry
1638	Murat IV captures Baghdad
1648	Great earthquake of İstanbul

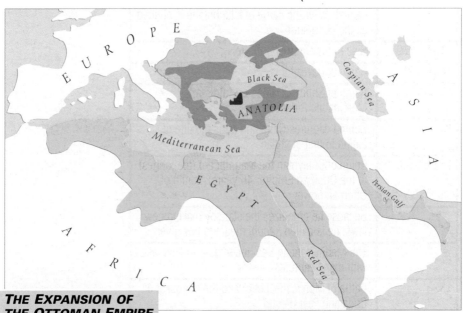

THE EXPANSION OF THE OTTOMAN EMPIRE UNTIL 17C

- ■ Early 14C
- 14C
- ■ 15C
- 17C

1661	Another great fire in İstanbul
1666-1812	Period of intermittent wars between Turks and European powers; Ottoman Empire loses much power in southern Europe
1683	Second and unsuccessful Siege of Vienna by Grand Vizier Kara Mustafa Paşa of Merzifon
1686	Ottomans are forced to evacuate Hungary
1699	Treaty of Karlowitz (*Karlofça*); the first loss of territory by the Ottoman Empire
1699-1792	Decline of the Ottoman Empire
1711	Grand Vizier Baltacı Mehmet Paşa's battle of Pruth against Russians. According to a spicy tradition, Paşa surrounded Peter the Great's army but then let him avoid humiliation because he was persuaded by a secret nocturnal visit to his tent by the czar's mistress (later empress) Catherine
1718-1774	Treaties of Passarowitz (Pasarofça) and Belgrade with Austrians, Küçük Kaynarca with Russians
1718-1730	Tulip period

	İstanbul is decorated with beautiful palaces and gardens; the first printing house in İstanbul and the first paper factory in Yalova are set up
1750	Another great fire in İstanbul
1754	Major earthquake in İstanbul
1782	Fire in İstanbul
1789-1807	Recovery period; Selim III
	Education becomes obligatory, reform in the army; *Nizam-ı Cedit* (organized army)
1790	Ottoman-Prussian alliance against Austria and Russia
1808-1839	Mahmut II period
1826	Mahmut II abolishes the Janissary Corps; Medical and military schools are opened; General Post Office is set up; Ministries are established instead of the Divan; Government officers obliged to wear trousers
1839-76	The Tanzimat Period; Mahmut II puts the westernizing Imperial Reform Decree of the Tanzimat into operation
	Abdülmecit and Mustafa Reşit Paşa prepare a new program of reform: laws are made instead of sultan's orders; equal rights for everybody; equal taxes according to incomes; no punishment without trials
1856	Paris Treaty: Ottoman Empire to be accepted as a European state
1876-1909	Reign of Abdülhamit II
1876-1877	Short-lived first Constitutional Regime
1876	First Constitution is prepared by Young Turks and the first Turkish Parliament is established
1877	Parliament is dissolved by Abdülhamit II
1877-1908	Autocracy of Abdülhamit II
1881	Birth of Mustafa Kemal in Salonika
1908	Constitutional Regime II
1908	Abdülhamit is forced to accept constitutional rule; parliament restored

1909	Abdülhamit deposed; Young Turks take power
1912-13	Balkan Wars; Turks lose Macedonia and part of Thrace
1914	Ottoman Empire enters World War I as an ally of Germany
1915	Turks, led by Mustafa Kemal, repel Allied landings on Gallipoli Peninsula
1918	Turks surrender to Allies; İstanbul occupied by Anglo-French Army
1919-1922	War of Independence
1919	Sivas Congress; Atatürk leads Turkish Nationalists to start the struggle for national sovereignty; Greek army lands at Smyrna
1920	Treaty of Sévres; Ottoman Empire dissolved
1920	Establishment of the Grand National Assembly of Turkey with Atatürk as the president
1922	Turks defeat Greeks and drive them out of Asia Minor; sultanate abolished
1923	Treaty of Lausanne establishes sovereignty of modern Turkey, defines its frontiers and arranges for exchange of minorities between Greece and Turkey; Turkish Republic is proclaimed, Mustafa Kemal is elected president, Ankara replaces İstanbul as the capital

The Ottoman Empire was a Moslem Turkish state that encompassed Anatolia, Southeastern Europe, the Arab Middle East and North Africa from the 14C to the early 20C.

The Ottoman Empire succeeded both the Byzantine Empire (1453) and the Arab Caliphate, the mantle of descent from Mohammed after the conquest of Egypt (1517).

Expansion of the Ottoman Empire

The Ottoman Turks were descendants of Turkoman nomads who entered Anatolia in the 11C as mercenary soldiers for the Seljuks. At the end of the 13C, Osman I (from whom the name Ottoman is derived) asserted the independence of his small principality in Söğüt near Bursa, which adjoined the decadent Byzantine Empire.

Gazis from all over Anatolia hitched themselves to Osman's rising star, following the usual custom of adopting the name of their leader and thus calling themselves *Osmanlı.* Their fight for their religion, holy war, was called *gaza,* and was intended not to destroy but to subjugate the non-Moslem world.

Within a century the Osman Dynasty had extended its domains into an Empire stretching from the Danube to the Euphrates. In Bosnia, Bulgaria, Greece and Serbia the conquered Christian princes were restored to their lands as vassals, while the subjects were left free to follow their own religions in return for loyalty. The Ottomans accepted submissive local nobility and military commanders into their service, along with their troops, instead of killing them.

The empire was temporarily disrupted by the invasion of the Tatar conqueror Timur, who defeated and captured the Ottoman Sultan Bayezit I at the Battle of Ankara (1402). However, Mehmet I (1389-1421), the Restorer, succeeded in reuniting much of the Empire and it was reconstituted by Murat II and Mehmet II. In 1453, Mehmet II conquered Constantinople, the last Byzantine stronghold.

During the reigns of Murat II and Mehmet II the *devşirme* system of recruiting young Christians for conversion to Islam and service in the Ottoman army and administration was developed. The Christians in the army were organized into the elite infantry corps called the *Janissaries.* Urban families, those with particular skills vital to the local economy, or families with only one son were excluded in this devşirme system. From the poor families' point of view, it was a great chance for their sons to be offered a high level of education especially in the palace which would provide good future prospects.

The empire reached its peak in the 16C. Sultan Selim I (r. 1512-20) conquered Egypt and Syria, gained control of the Arabian Peninsula and beat back the Safavid rulers of Iran at the Battle of Çaldıran (1514). He was succeeded by Süleyman I (the Magnificent, r. 1520-66), who took Iraq, Hungary and Albania and established Ottoman naval supremacy in the Mediterranean. Süleyman codified and institutionalized the classic structure of the Ottoman state and society, making his dominions into one of the great powers of Europe.

Decline of the Ottoman Empire

The decline of the empire began late in the 16C. It was caused by a myriad of interdependent factors, among which the most important were the flight of the Turco-Islamic aristocracy and degeneration of the ability and honesty both of the sultans and of their ruling class. The *devşirme* divided into many political parties and fought for power, manipulated sultans and used the government for their own benefit. Corruption, nepotism, inefficiency and misrule spread.

Reform Attempts

Sultan Selim III (r. 1789-1807) attempted to reform the Ottoman system by destroying the Janissary corps and replacing it with the *Nizam-ı Cedit* (new order) army modeled after the new military institutions being developed in the West. This attempt so angered the Janissaries and others with a vested interest in the old ways that they overthrew him and massacred most of the reform leaders. Defeats at the hands of Russia and Austria, the success of national revolutions in Serbia and Greece and the rise of the powerful independent Ottoman governor of Egypt, Mohammed Ali, so discredited the Janissaries, however, that Sultan Mahmut II was able to massacre and destroy them in 1826.

Mahmut then inaugurated a new series of modern reforms, which involved the abolition of the traditional institutions and their replacement with new ones imported from the West. This affected every area of Ottoman life, not just the military. These reforms were continued and brought to their culmination during the Tanzimat reform era (1839-76) and the reign of Abdülhamit II (1876-1909). The scope of government was extended and centralized as reforms were made in administration, finance, education, justice, economy, communications and army.

Financial mismanagement and incompetence, along with national revolts in the Balkans and eastern Anatolia, the French occupation of Algeria and Tunisia, the takeover by the British in Egypt and the Italians in Libya, threatened to end the very existence of the Empire, let alone its reforms. By this time the Ottoman Sultanate was known as the "Sick Man of Europe," and European diplomacy focused on the so-called Eastern Question—how to dispose of the Sick Man's territories without upsetting the European balance of power. Abdülhamit II, however, rescued the empire, at least temporarily, by reforming the Ottoman financial system, manipulating the rivalries of the European powers and developing the pan-Islamic and pan-Turkic movements to undermine the empires of his enemies. The sultan granted a constitution and parliament in 1876, but he soon abandoned them and ruled autocratically so as to achieve his objectives as rapidly and efficiently as possible. He became so despotic that liberal opposition arose under the leadership of the Young Turks, many of whom had to leave the country from Abdülhamit's police.

Overthrow of the Ottoman Empire

In 1908 a revolution led by the Young Turks forced Abdülhamit to restore the parliament and constitution. After a few months of constitutional rule, however, a counter-revolutionary effort to restore the sultan's autocracy led the Young Turks to dethrone Abdülhamit completely in 1909. He was replaced by Mehmet (Reşit) V (r. 1909-18), who was only a puppet of those controlling the government.

Rapid modernization continued during the Young Turk era (1908-18), with particular attention given to urbanization, agriculture, industry, communications, secularization of the state and the emancipation of women.

The empire was involved in World War I to take sides with Germany and Austria-Hungary. The defeat of these Central Powers led to the breakup and foreign occupation of the Ottoman Empire.

The Administration

The head of the empire was the sultan and the sultanate passed from father to son. The orders of the sultan were accepted as laws. His three major duties were commanding the army, appointing the statesmen and supervising the **Divan,** today's Cabinet. Members of the Divan were the **chief vizier** (prime minister), **viziers** (state ministers), **kazasker** (minister responsible for the military), two **defterdars** (finance ministers), **nişancı** (general secretary), **şeyhülislam** (authorized head of the religious matters) and **kaptan-ı derya** (Commander in chief of the fleet).

The functions of the ruling class were limited to exploiting the resources of the empire, largely for their own benefit; expanding and defending the state and maintaining order and preserving the faith and practice of Islam as well as the religions of all the subjects of the sultan.

The vast class of subjects were left to carry out all other functions of the state through autonomous religious communities, artisans' guilds, popular mystic orders and confederations, which together formed a substratum of popular society.

The Use of Land

In the Ottoman Empire the lands belonged to the state. The right to use the land was given to people and some revenue from the income received was given to the state. However, when people failed to use their land effectively for three consecutive years it had to be returned.

The lands in general were divided into two categories; **Vakıf** and **Dirlik.** Vakıf estates were spared for charity institutions and public use like mosques, hospitals, caravansaries and suchlike. Dirlik (fief) lands were given to statesmen according to their incomes; each of these lands was classified as **Has**, **Zeamet**, or **Tımar**. Owners used some part of them for themselves and spared other parts for the expenses of a certain number of soldiers. With this system, the state had a powerful army without costs.

The Army

The Ottoman army was mainly divided into three classes:

a) Kapıkulu soldiers were professionals who acted directly under the strict command of the sultan. They were not even allowed to marry. They did not have any connection to the land holding system as they worked for salaries. **Ulufe** was

the name given to their salaries which they received every 3 months. The majority of these Kapıkulu soldiers consisted of janissaries. There were both foot-soldiers and cavalrymen.

b) Eyalet soldiers were Dirlik-holding soldiers. The majority of the Ottoman army were Eyalet soldiers. They were the front line soldiers and like Kapıkulu soldiers they were divided into both foot-soldiers and cavalrymen.

c) Reinforcements were soldiers who came from annexed rulers.

Education

The two main arteries of education were **Enderun** and **Medrese**.

Enderun was a royal school with a very high level of education. The aim of this school was to educate statesmen. Students were treated with considerable discipline and by the age of 30 approximately, they finished their schooling and attained their posts.

Although the medrese was originally a theological school, in the Ottoman period, education in the medrese was conducted in four faculties; *1*-religion and law, *2*-language and literature, *3*-philosophy, *4*-basic sciences. The language of education was Arabic. There was no set period, students had to finish particular books rather than years. Students lived in cells, ate in *imarets* (kitchens for the public, generally the poor) and received some pocketmoney from the school Foundations.

THE REPUBLIC PERIOD

Modern Turkish Period (1923-Present)	
1923	Establishment of the Turkish Republic with Atatürk as its first president
1924	Abolition of Caliphate
1925-38	Atatürk's program of reforms to modernize Turkey
1938	Death of Atatürk; İsmet İnönü becomes the Republic's second president
1939-45	Despite the alliance with Britain and France, Turkey remains neutral during World War II
1946	Turkey becomes a charter member of United Nations; change into a multi-party system
1950	Turkey enters Korean War as a part of United Nations force; Celal Bayar becomes the third president
1952	Joins the North Atlantic Treaty Organization (NATO)

The attempt of the victorious Allies to control the Anatolian territory led to the Turkish War of Independence (1918-23).

Following the occupation of İstanbul in 1920 by the British, Italian and French, a Greek army advanced from İzmir deep into Anatolia.

While the sultan offered no resistance, under the leadership of Kemal Atatürk, the Turkish Nationalists overturned the postwar settlement embodied in the Treaty of Sévres (1920) and established the Republic of Turkey, formally recognized by the Treaty of Lausanne in 1923.

Mustafa Kemal retired his military uniform and inspired the people to an even greater task: Transformation of the country into the democratic, secular Republic of Turkey.

(opposite page)
MINIATURE DEPICTING
OTTOMAN ARMY [16]

Mustafa Kemal Atatürk

1881	Birth of Mustafa in Salonika
1893	Enters Military Secondary School where he is given the name of Kemal
1899	Enters War College in Constantinople
1902	Graduates as lieutenant
1905	Posted to 5th Army in Damascus
1907	Posted to 3rd Army in Salonika
1908	"Young Turk" Revolution in Salonika
1911	Posted to General Staff in Constantinople; goes to Tobruk and Derna with Turkish Forces, promoted to Major
1912	Balkan War; severe defeat, returns home
1913	Appointed Military Attaché in Sofia
1914	Promoted Lieutenant-Colonel; Turkey signs secret alliance with Germany; Russia, Britain and France declare war on Turkey
1915	Appointed to reorganize 9th Division, in Thrace; unsuccessful allied naval attack on Dardanelles; allied military landing at Arıburnu (Anzac); promoted to colonel; appointed to command 16th Army Corps
1916	Allied evacuation of Gallipoli Peninsula; transferred to Caucasus front; promoted to General and Paşa
1917	Returns to Constantinople
1919	Appointed Inspector-General in Anatolia; lands in Samsun; issues "Declaration of Independence" at Amasya; ordered by Government to return; resigns from the army; Nationalist Congress at Sivas and Erzurum; National Pact; new parliament elected; headquarters at Angora
1920	(April 23) First Turkish Grand National Assembly (TGNA) at Ankara
1921	Consecutive battles against different enemies; given title of Gazi and rank of Marshal by TGNA

1922	İzmir is retaken; proclaims abolition of Sultanate
1923	Treaty of Lausanne; People's Party; Second GNA; Angora (Ankara) becomes capital; proclamation of the Republic; becomes President; marries Latife in İzmir
1925	Divorces Latife
1938	Death of Atatürk; succession of İsmet İnönü as President of the Republic

Thousands of his statues or busts and millions of his photos have been erected or hung all over the country. His name has been given to countless institutions, buildings, streets, parks and suchlike.

Foreigners unaware of his accomplishments might think that the Turks are a bit obsessed with a man now dead for approximately 60 years.

No other nation on earth has loved a leader as much as the Turkish nation loves Mustafa Kemal Atatürk.

"Mustafa Kemal Atatürk differed from the dictators of his age in two significant respects; his foreign policy was based not on expansion but on retraction of frontiers; his home policy on the foundation of a political system which could survive his own time. It was in this realistic spirit that he regenerated his country, transforming the old sprawling Ottoman Empire into a compact new Turkish Republic.

> ....I don't act for public opinion. I act for the nation and for my own satisfaction.....

It was a restless mind, nurtured on those principles of Western civilization which had influenced Turkish liberal thought since the nineteenth century; continually refueled by the ideas of others, which he adapted and adopted as his own; but always grounded in a common sense mistrustful of theory..."[26]

[26] Kinross Lord, *Atatürk, The Rebirth of a Nation*, Rustem, 1990

His life

He was born in Salonika in 1881 and named Mustafa. Kemal was a nickname meaning "perfection" given by a tutor. He was a good student and did well at the military academy.

He was one of the early members of the Young Turks movement and a front-runner in the revolution which demanded a constitutional government for the Ottoman Empire.

During the First World War, he fought on many fronts. In 1915, then a Lieutenant Colonel, Mustafa Kemal was commanding a division of troops on the Gallipoli Peninsula. His actions in the Dardanelles as a soldier of determination, bravery and brilliance gave him great standing amongst the soldiers. His successes against the Allies were well received by the civilian population and he was acclaimed as the "Hero of Gallipoli".

This man, a military genius, soon showed himself as a great statesman too. After calling national congresses, he was elected President of the Turkish Grand National Assembly in April 1920. From then until his death in 1938, he remained in power in Turkey.

In 1934 everyone had to take a surname and Mustafa Kemal received the surname ATATÜRK which means "Father of the Turks". With all that he did for his country, he really deserved this title.

Reforms

1924	Abolition of the Caliphate
1925	Abolition of the fez; suppression of religious brotherhoods; closing of sacred tombs as places of worship
1926	Adoption of new Civil Law code
1928	Introduction of Latin alphabet

1934	Kemal takes name of Atatürk when a new law required Turks to adopt surnames; women made eligible to vote in elections and to become members of Parliament

Mustafa Kemal Atatürk's reforms can be summarized as follows:

♦ Abolition of the Sultanate and Caliphate; establishment of the Republic.

♦ Implementation of secularism nationwide.

♦ Abolition of the religious courts.

♦ Suppression of religious brotherhoods; closing of sacred tombs as places of worship.

♦ Replacement of traditional clothing by Western styles; abolition of the fez.

♦ Abolition of *Medreses*, unification of education, renovations of school programs according to contemporary and national needs, opening of new universities.

♦ Adoption of new Civil Law code.

♦ Adoption of the solar calendar and changing of the Moslem holy day of the week, Friday, into a weekday with Sunday becoming the official day of rest.

♦ Introduction of Latin alphabet.

♦ Purification of Turkish language from foreign words.

♦ Implementation of *"Peace at home, Peace in the world"* as Turkish foreign policy.

İsmet İnönü

The statesman and career military officer İsmet İnönü, (1884-1973), became the principal lieutenant of Kemal Atatürk in the post-World War I struggle for Turkish independence. İnönü was the Turkish representative at the Lausanne Conference which overturned the wartime settlement and established the Turkish Republic in 1923.

He was twice prime minister during Atatürk's presidency. As the second president (1938-50), İnönü kept Turkey neutral during World War II and prepared the country for democratic elections, which resulted in the removal of his Republican People's party from power (1950). He then led the opposition to the Democratic party's regime until its overthrow by a coup in 1960.

The military coup of 1960 [27]

Relatively neglected from 1923 to 1939, the army during the war had undergone a rapid expansion and a considerable modernization subsequently with the aid of US advisers. Many officers feared that the Democratic Peak (DP) threatened the principles of the secular, progressive Kemalist state. Some younger officers saw the army as the direct instrument of unity and reform. On May 3, 1960, the commander of the land forces, General Cemal Gürsel, demanded political reforms and resigned when they were refused. On May 27 the army acted; an almost bloodless coup was carried out by officers and cadets from the İstanbul and Ankara War colleges. The leaders established a 38-man "National Unity Committee" with Gürsel as chairman. The Democrat Party leaders were imprisoned. Most of the senior officers wanted to withdraw the army from politics as soon as possible and in November 1960 the decision was taken. The main work of the National Unity Committee was to destroy the DP and to prepare a new constitution. The DP was abolished and many Democrats were brought to trial on charges of corruption, unconstitutional rule and high treason. Three former ministers, including Menderes, were executed; 12 others, including Bayar, had their death sentences commuted to life imprisonment. The new constitution was

[27] Encyclopedia Britannica, *1995*

completed and approved by 61% of the votes at a referendum. The first elections were held in October 1961. The army then withdrew from direct political involvement.

The military coup of 1980

In 1980 the military, which had watched the growing violence and the government's ineffectiveness with alarm, intervened, precipitating a bloodless coup on September 12. A National Security Council composed of the military high command took over governmental duties, naming General Kenan Evren head of state, quickly dissolved the Assembly, political parties and the trade unions. The constitution was suspended and martial law imposed. In November 1982 a new constitution won overwhelming approval in a national referendum. In April 1983 the National Security Council lifted its ban on political parties and the following November it transferred power to an elected unicameral parliament.

In 1989 Turgut Özal was elected by parliament to succeed Evren. In 1993, Süleyman Demirel succeeded Özal after his death. Since then coalition governments have been effective in the Turkish Grand National Assembly.

GEOGRAPHY

REGIONS

Anatolia is divided into 7 geographical regions:

The Black Sea Region is a mountainous area in the north. This region is approximately 1/6 of Turkey's total land mass. It has a steep and rocky coast and rivers cascade through the gorges of the coastal ranges. As the Northern Anatolian Mountains run parallel to the coastline access inland from the coast is limited to a few narrow valleys, so the coast therefore has always been isolated from inland areas. It is densely wooded, comprising more than one-fourth of Turkey's forested areas. The region is mainly agricultural, corn being the dominant field crop. Tea is grown in the eastern coastal strip, hazelnuts around Giresun and Ordu and tobacco in Samsun and Trabzon.

The Marmara Region covers the European part as well as the northwest of the Anatolian plain. It comprises a central plain of rolling terrain surrounded by mountains of moderate height. Although it is the smallest region after Southeastern Anatolia, it has the highest population density. The Marmara region is economically the most developed area of Turkey. Its agriculture is varied, including tobacco, wheat, rice, sunflower, corn, olives, grapes and natural silk. On the straits and coasts of the Marmara Sea fishing is well developed.

The Aegean Region extends from the Aegean coast to the inner parts of Western Anatolia. Forest lands and fertile

(opposite page)
DÜDEN RIVER [17]

plains carrying the same names as its rivers are dominant. The lowlands of the Aegean and Marmara Regions contain about half of the country's agricultural wealth in the broad, cultivated valleys, the most important of which are the İzmit Valley, the Bursa Plains and the Plains of Troy. Its wealth rests on the production of several export crops, including tobacco (more than 50% of Turkey's total production), cotton (30% of the total), high-quality grapes suitable for drying, olives (more than 50% of the Turkish output) and figs.

The Mediterranean Region is located in the south of Anatolia. The western and central Taurus Mountains suddenly rise up behind the coastline. Forest lands are dominant here like the Aegean and the Black Sea regions. The region has several subregions: the sparsely populated limestone plateaus of Taşeli in the middle; the lake district in the west with its continental climate, where grain is grown; and the intensively cultivated, densely populated coastal plains. The coastal areas produce cotton (60 percent of Turkey's output), sesame, citrus fruits (more than 90 percent of the country's production), early vegetables and bananas. The higher elevations have relatively little arable land; grain and livestock are produced and there is pastoral nomadism among the Yörüks.

The Central Anatolia Region is exactly in the middle of Turkey and is less mountainous when compared to the other regions. This region varies in altitude from 600-1,200 m (1,970-3,940 ft) west to east. Steppes are common. Geologically young volcanic features characterize the landscape. For the most part, the region is bare and monotonous and is used for grazing. But overgrazing has caused soil erosion on the plateau and during frequent summer dust storms a fine yellow powder blows across the plains. One-third of Turkey's

Geographical Regions of Turkey

sheep and three-quarters of its Angora goats are raised there.

The Eastern Anatolia Region is Anatolia's largest and highest region. Nearly all of the area has an average altitude of 1,500-2,000 m / 4,920-6,560 ft. Anatolia's highest peak Mount Ararat is located in this region. This is the most thinly populated region of the country. Farming is difficult because of the long, severe winters, steep slopes and eroded soil. Grain, chiefly summer wheat and barley, is the dominant crop. In the humid northeast, beef and dairy cattle are raised whilst in the south there are pastoral nomads who raise sheep and goats.

The Southeastern Anatolia Region is notable for the uniformity of its landscape. Vast stretches of this region consist only of wild or barren wasteland. Agriculture is confined mainly to irrigated valleys and basins (wheat, rice, vegetables, grapes). Much of the population is nomadic or seminomadic. Turkey's principal oil fields are here.

SOILS

Anatolia has a variety of soil types. Nearly 40% of the land, including the Black Sea coast and most of the northeast, is covered by red and gray brown podzols and by brown forest soils. The Aegean and Mediterranean coasts are characterized by mountain soils: Brown forest, terra rossa and rendzina. Chestnut and desert soils are found in Central Anatolia. The southeast has rich chernozems and chestnut-type soils.

COASTLINES

Turkey is surrounded by sea on three sides; the **Black Sea** in the north, the **Mediterranean** in the south and the **Aegean Sea** in the west. In the northwest there is also an important internal sea; the **Marmara Sea**, between the straits of the **Dardanelles** and the **Bosphorus.**

The name of The Marmara Sea comes from the Marmara Island which is known for the high grade of marble from its quarries.

The Black Sea coastline is 1,595 km / 990 mi long and the Mediterranean is nearly the same: at 1,577 km / 980 miles. Because the mountains reach the sea perpendicularly, the Aegean coastline has many curves and is much longer measuring 2,800 km / 1,740 miles.

The Marmara Sea occupies an area of 11,350 km² / 4,381 sq miles and the coastline is about 1,000 km / 621 miles long.

Salinity of the Seas	
The Black Sea	1.7%
The Marmara Sea	2.2%
The Mediterranean Sea	3.8%
The Aegean Sea	3.8%

As a country surrounded by seas on 3 sides, Turkey has 159 **islands** most of which are not even known or inhabited. 109 of these islands are in the Aegean Sea, 26 in the Mediterranean, 23 in the Marmara Sea with only one in the Black Sea.

LAKES

With more than 300 natural and 130 artificial, Turkey is indeed a country of lakes. The total area of the lakes is around 9,250 km² / 3,570 sq miles and nearly 50 of them occupy areas larger than 10 km² / 3.8 sq miles each.

There are also many smaller lakes which are usually not shown on maps.

Some lakes are fed by rivers whilst others form rivers by dispersing their excess water. Lakes which lose water predominantly by evaporation develop a build up of mineral salts which make them saltwater.

The freshwater lakes are used for irrigation when their altitudes are higher than the plateaus around them. Lake Beyşehir on the Konya plateau is an example of this.

The lakes of Anatolia are not similar to each other either in size or formation. They can be divided roughly into 2 categories.

> The largest, Lake Van is 3,713 km² / 1,433 sq miles and 100 m / 328 ft deep.

Natural lakes

a)Tectonic lakes

These lakes were formed during the deformation of the earth's crust. More than 20 of the major lakes in Turkey are of the tectonic formation. Because many of the roads or railways pass by these tectonic lakes it is possible to see many of them while traveling around Turkey.

b)Crater lakes

These volcanic lakes were formed when the bowl-shaped depressions around the orifices of volcanoes were filled with water after the eruptions. Since roads rarely pass through areas of volcanic formation, it is unlikely that many crater lakes of Anatolia are seen.

There are many other types of lake formations which are not included here, such as glacier lakes, naturally dammed lakes and so on. More specific information about lakes which might be encountered while touring Turkey is provided in the Places of Interest Section. The selection of lakes mentioned is related to their interest value to tourists as opposed to their size or formation.

Dams

These were mostly built within the last few decades to obtain energy, to provide irrigation for agriculture, and to provide drinking water to urban areas.

The major power plant dams are the Atatürk, Karakaya and Keban on the Euphrates; the Altınkaya and Hirfanlı on the Kızılırmak; the Gökçekaya and Sarıyar on the Sakarya; the Demirköprü on the Gediz; the Kemer on the Büyük Menderes and the Oymapınar and Manavgat on the Manavgat.

MOUNTAINS

Anatolia's highest peak is in the east: Ağrı Dağı (Mount Ararat) 5,165 m / 16,940 ft.

Turkey is a country of highlands with an average altitude of 1,130 m / 3,700 ft. 80% of Anatolia is above 500 m / 1,640 ft in height which is much higher when compared to other continents. The average height in Asia is 1050 m / 3,444 ft; in Europe 330 m / 1,082 ft and in Africa 650 m / 2,130 ft.

Except for a relatively small segment along the Syrian border, Anatolia is part of the great Alpine-Himalayan mountain belt.

Generally, most of the mountain lines in Anatolia lie in the

Harvest next to Mount Ararat [18]

east-west direction. There are two important ranges of mountains in Anatolia: The *North Anatolian Mountains*[28] along the Black Sea in the north and the *Taurus Mountains* in the south. Both of them run parallel to the coastline. The North Anatolian Mountains increase in height toward the east, where their highest peak, **Kaçkar Dağı** (3,937 m / 12,910 ft), is found. The Taurus Mountains rise to 3,734 m / 12,250 ft in the **Aladağ** Chain. Composed mainly of limestone, there are caves, underground streams and potholes.

RIVERS

Throughout history, water has always been a very important element for man in the development of his environment,

[28] Also called Pontic Mountains in the past

89

for agricultural and industrial production, and for transportation. Therefore people prefer to live close to or in areas served by rivers.

520 billion cubic m / 680 billion cubic yards of water (rain, snow, etc.) fall annually in Turkey and 32% of this amount forms rivers. Although this is a very large volume of water, not many of the rivers are very long. They are plentiful in number due to the existence of many hills, ranges of mountains, plateaus and plains in the country.

Generally, rivers originate from heights of 1,000-2,000 m / 3,280-6,560 ft and flow into the sea after 700-800 km / 435-500 miles which is a comparatively short distance. Consequently their speed is fast and they carry large amounts of alluviums. These alluviums have contributed to some of the geological formations over the centuries. The harbors of some ancient cities such as Ephesus, Priene or Troy, which once graced shorelines, are present day ruins located a few kilometers inland due to silting up of shores. The lakes of Bafa and Sapanca were once bays before their entrances became closed by alluvium deposits.

In spring, especially in April, the rivers carry the maximum amount of water which is muddy in color because it carries a lot of soil. The season in which the minimum water is carried is the autumn, especially September.

The majority of the rivers in Anatolia are not navigable, having irregular, shallow beds and seasonal depth changes.

Often many rivers are named according to their colors; Kızılırmak (red river), Aksu (white water), Bozçay (gray river), sometimes with the names of places or surrounding things; Değirmendere (mill river), Köprüçay (bridge river), or with some adjectives describing the nature of the river; Deliçay (crazy river), Cehennemdere (hell river), İkizdere (twin rivers).

Most Turkish rivers originate within the country's borders, a feature which gives Turkey a strategic power because there is no risk of water limitation by its neighbors.

Rivers of Anatolia

The Euphrates and Tigris join together in Iraq and flow into the Persian Gulf. Less than half of the Euphrates and one third of the Tigris are within Anatolia today.

Yeşilırmak and Sakarya are the longest rivers after the Kızılırmak, and flow into the Black Sea.

The Aras and Kuruçay flow beyond Turkey's borders into the Caspian Sea in western Asia.

The Susurluk, Biga and Gönen flow into the Marmara Sea.

The Gediz, Büyük Menderes, Küçük Menderes and Meriç flow into the Aegean Sea.

The Seyhan, Ceyhan and Göksu flow into the Mediterranean Sea.

> The Kızılırmak (Halys) is the longest river originating and flowing within the borders of Turkey; 1,355 km / 842 miles.

CLIMATE

Because of the geographical formation of the country with mountains that run parallel to the coast, Anatolia is a focal point of contrasting climates.

While in *coastal areas* winters are mild and summers are moderately hot, the *inland areas* experience extremes of temperature. The hot summers have high daytime temperatures with generally cool nights and the cold winters have limited precipitation with frost occurring on more than 100 days during the year.

Average Daytime Temperatures		
	Centigrade	Fahrenheit
January	9	48
February	9	48
March	11	52
April	16	62
May	21	70
June	26	78
July	29	84
August	29	84
September	25	76
October	21	70
November	15	60
December	11	52

In the Mediterranean, Aegean and Southern Marmara regions, the general **Mediterranean climate** is dominant; summers are hot and dry, winters are mild and rainy. Frosts are rare and snowfall is almost unknown.

On the **Northern coast of the Marmara Sea,** the temperatures are lower.

The Black Sea region, enjoys mild winters and a fair amount of rainfall throughout the year.

In **Central Anatolia,** a typical plateau climate prevails where the summers are hot with minimum precipitation, and winters are cold with heavy and lasting snows. Villages may be isolated by severe snowstorms.

Eastern Anatolia is rugged country with higher elevations, a more severe climate and greater precipitation than the central plateau. The climate of this region is most inhospitable. Summers are hot and extremely dry, winters are bitterly cold. Spring and autumn are both subject to sudden hot and cold spells.

RAINFALL

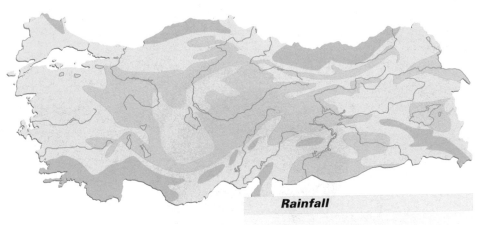

Rainfall

Annual average

- 150-200 cm or more (60-80 inches)
- 50-150 cm (20-60 in)
- 30-50 cm (12-20 in)
- 30 cm (12 in) or less

The rainfall is maximum in the middle and eastern coasts of the Black Sea and the western part of the Mediterranean. It is minimum around Lake Tuz and in Konya Plateau. Except for these areas and the Central Anatolia, the rainfall is average all over Turkey.

POPULATION

The first census after the foundation of the Republic was conducted in 1927, the second in 1935 and then every 5 years until the census of 1990. The general census of 1997 was conducted to find out the population distribution and social (educational, economic, etc.) levels of people after continuous migrations. The population in 1997 was 62.8 million.

Turkey is the 17th most densely populated country in the World.

Population projection over the years is as follows:

2001	66.6 million
2002	67.6 million
2003	68.5 million
2004	69.6 million

The majority of the population consists of young people, about 40% of whom are under the age of fifteen. 72% are below the age of 35. The average age in Turkey is 27. In more developed countries the average age is much higher.

Birth rate	2.7%
Death rate	0.8%
Population growth	1.47%

The rate of birth is different throughout the country. It is dependent on the education of people and socio-economic conditions. The rate is higher in the rural and eastern areas compared to urban and those of the West.

| Male population | 50.4% |
| Female population | 49.6% |

(opposite page)
A Baby Lamb [19]

Previously, because of World War I, the proportion of women was greater than men, but recently it has become almost equal.

The average life span is 69. This is shorter when compared to other developed countries.

Population Distribution and Settlement

The population distribution is closely related to topographic conditions, soil and rainfall. Settlements are most heavily concentrated in European Turkey and in the fertile valleys and lowlands of the Marmara, Aegean and Black Sea coasts. This area, accounting for about 25% of the country's territory, is inhabited by nearly half of the population.

population density	
General	73 / km^2 (190 / sq mile)
İstanbul	1,023 / km^2 (2,650 / sq mile)
İzmir	194 / km^2 (502 / sq mile)
Ankara	108 / km^2 (280 / sq mile)

23% of the population now live in three main cities which means that the population density in these cities is very high, as seen in the table above.

Compared to 1927, when 84% of the population lived in rural areas the percentage living in rural areas has now dropped to 54%.

The urban population started to increase after the 1950s because of the intensive migration from the rural areas to the urban centers.

Only 40% of the current population of İstanbul and 60% of Ankara or İzmir consist of people who were originally born in those cities. These figures also include the children of newly migrated people.

NON-MOSLEMS

From the religious point of view, although there is no official religion, 99% of the people living in Turkey are Moslems, the majority of whom are Sunnis[29]. The remaining 1% are of different religions or indeed irreligious.

Under the frames of the Lausanne Peace Treaty signed on July 24, 1923, the definition of the minorities was made as "**non-Moslems**" and their rights were granted as follows:

- The freedoms of living, religious beliefs and migration
- The rights of legal and political equality
- Using the mother tongue in the courts
- Opening their own schools or similar institutions
- The holding of religious ceremonies

Minorities enjoy equal legal rights under the Constitution, which describes Turkey as a secular state and guarantees "freedom of conscience, religious faith and opinion" to all citizens, each of whom is legally a Turkish citizen.

a) Armenians of Anatolia

Armenians have lived in İstanbul since 1197 AD. New settlements appeared in Kumkapı, Yenikapı and Samatya after Mehmet II's conquest of the city (1453).

The Armenians started to emigrate worldwide from 1896 onwards, however many returned after the inauguration of the first Turkish Parliament (1908) and took part in political life. Their population fell from around 240,000 in the 1850s to 150,000 at the turn of the century.

Today a total of 55,000 Armenians live within the boundaries of Turkey. They contribute to the country's culture, science and the arts by continuing their traditions, intermarriages and trades (particularly as printers, jewelers and coppersmiths).

[29] See Islam on page 146

b) Jews of Anatolia

The history of the Jews in Anatolia goes back to the 4C BC. Some ancient synagogue ruins have also been found in Sardis, dating from 220 BC.

When the Ottomans captured Bursa in 1324 and made it their capital, they found and welcomed a Jewish community which had been oppressed under Byzantine rule.

The Balkan Jews were aware of the Ottoman tolerance towards other religions and migrated to Murat I's territories. Later Ashkenazi Jews fled to Anatolia, followed by Byzantine Jews and received by Mehmet II. It was Bayezit II who offered safety for the refugees of the Spanish Inquisition in 1492.

Throughout history, Jews have not only found religious asylum in Turkey, but also become part of its society and assumed important roles in different fields.

Today 26,000 Jewish people live in Turkey. The vast majority live in İstanbul, with a community of about 2,500 in İzmir and other smaller groups are located mainly in Adana, Ankara, Bursa, Çanakkale, İskenderun and Kırklareli.

The Jewish minority is more complex than other minorities because it lacks homogeneity in language and history.

Most Jews are Sephardic whose ancestors fled from the Inquisition or were expelled from Spain and Portugal during and after 1492. In general they speak different mother tongues, such as Turkish, Ladino or French.

c) Rums (Greeks of Anatolia)

Rums in Turkey are of Byzantine origin. In the 1970s they formed the largest non-Moslem minority in the country. Their number, however, is decreasing and according to recent estimates there are less than 25,000 Rums most of which are Eastern Orthodox Christians. İstanbul Rums are successfully engaged in business and finance and some live on the two islands of Gökçeada and Bozcaada, off the entrance to the Dardanelles.

ANATOLIA, AN ETHNIC MOSAIC

As previously discussed, Anatolia has been a melting pot of racially and culturally distinct groups since early prehistoric times. Throughout history, because of its location and fertility of the land, it has always attracted the attention of various peoples. These people, with different origins, have always lived in peace providing a good example for other countries.

The policies of the National State, without taking into consideration the ethnical or historical differences, encourage people to unite under a "national identity". In other words, the ethnic-historical identity will not always be identical to the official-national identity.[30]

The number of the ethnic groups that take part in today's Turkey is about 50. The major ethnic groups are Turks, Kurds, Circassians, Laz people of the northern coast, Caucasians, Georgians, Bosnians and Albanians.

The majority of these ethnic groups have lost their ethnic identity within the unity of Anatolia. However, there are some who still continue to preserve and nurture their identities, traditions and language.

A Regional Problem

The largest of the ethnic groups after the Turks is the Kurds. An estimated 5-10 million people are ethnically Kurdish. The majority of these people speak Turkish and they do not live solely in the east or southeast but in all regions of Turkey.

[30] Güvenç Bozkurt, *Türk Kimliği*, Kültür Bakanlığı, 1993

However, the Kurdish terrorist organization, PKK which has been active in the southeast of Turkey, claims:

1. The majority of people living in the southeast of the country are originally Kurds and therefore the region should be granted autonomy.

2. Kurds in Turkey are treated as second class citizens.

3. Kurds cannot use their mother tongue.

4. Kurds in Turkey are deprived of their political rights.

Their mottoes are "Freedom for the Kurdish Nation" and "War on behalf of Identity and Freedom". Since the beginning of terrorism by the PKK in 1984, thousands of citizens and security staff have been killed or wounded. Thousands of terrorists have been caught.

This outlawed separatist terrorist organization, under the pretense of fighting for freedom, does not recognize any international laws and in particular the Universal Declaration of Human Rights by conducting attacks, killing infants, women, men, old and young. They have also set hospitals and schools on fire and have killed teachers and doctors. The Turkish Armed Forces try to prevent attacks and protect civilians.

The PKK managed to give a false impression both to some people in the region and to the world at large. However this impression is not accepted by many countries and the PKK has been declared internationally as a terrorist organization and all activities of the PKK have been banned in those countries today. It is generally thought that the PKK is a separatist group which should not be confused with the Kurdish people and it is not considered representative of the Kurds.

The 10th article of the Turkish Constitution states that "All citizens are equal before the law with no discrimination as to language, race, color, political leanings, philosophy, reli-

(preceding page)
FATHER AND SON [20]

gion and similar factors." All citizens have the right to vote and to be elected. As a result, there have been many Kurdish generals, professors, politicians and citizens of prominence. The eighth Turkish president, Turgut Özal, was of Kurdish origin.

Speaking Kurdish, publishing books, magazines and newspapers or the singing of Kurdish songs are not prohibited. But for the sake of unity and considering the richness of ethnic origins, the official language is Turkish.

TURKS AS CITIZENS OF OTHER COUNTRIES

Turks living in other countries can be summarized as follows:

- People who, from Central Asia, have not come to Anatolia with others.
- People who have stayed out of the borders after the Republic.
- People who have gone to other countries as workers.

When the borders of the Ottoman Empire became smaller after World War I and the foundation of the new Republic, many Turkish people chose to stay outside Turkey's borders. Since then, some of them have migrated to Turkey but there are still many ethnically Turkish people living in different countries such as Greece, Bulgaria, Syria and Iraq. Among these are Turkish Cypriots who form a problem on the island.

The Cyprus Problem

The island of Cyprus in the eastern Mediterranean is the homeland of two distinct peoples, one is Turkish the other is of Greek origin. The majority of these are Greek and they are the descendants of the people who came to the island in the year 1100 BC. The Turkish people on the island consist of those who came during the Ottoman Empire, 16C and those who migrated afterwards. These two peoples have different national, linguistic, cultural, social and religious characteristics.

In 1960, independence and sovereignty were transferred to a joint bi-communal State on the basis of a contractual constitution, which created an equal partnership between the two peoples.

This partnership came to a violent end three years later as a result of disagreements between the two peoples.

The intervention of Greece and Turkey took place in the following years. In 1974, the military junta in Athens instigated a coup in Cyprus in an attempt to unite the country with Greece. Turkey used military force on the island to protect the Turkish population and war between Greece and Turkey was narrowly averted.

In the present political situation, there are two independent governments and administrations belonging to Greek and Turkish Cypriots in each the north and south of the island.

The core of the problem in Cyprus is the relationship between the Turkish and Greek Cypriots, which is not one of majority or minority, but one of equal partnership.

The question to which an answer is sought today is this: "Can the Turkish and Greek Cypriots form a new political partnership in federal form through which they will peacefully share power on the basis of political equality?"

Emigration

Emigration reached its peak between the years 1960-1970. In the beginning it was in the direction of Western Europe but later also to some Arabic countries. The number of people who have emigrated from Turkey, including their families is around 2.5-3 million. 1.6 million of these people live in Germany today.

In order to contribute to the postwar reconstruction of Europe, the Turkish people were invited as "guest" workers. Those who were mostly from the so-called backward areas of Turkey did not always create a favorable image of Turkey in the countries to which they went.

Most immigrants in Western Europe are first generation and regard where they live as their home rather than as a temporary place of abode. For the second generation, the tendency to regard Europe as their home is understandably stronger.

Although they are increasingly becoming an important factor in the economies of those countries, in many instances they have not yet been given the right to stand or even vote in local elections.

STATE POLICIES

ADMINISTRATION

The legislative power of the Turkish Republic is the Turkish Grand National Assembly (TGNA), which performs its function on behalf of the Turkish Nation.

THE TURKISH GRAND NATIONAL ASSEMBLY

The TGNA was first empowered to exercise legislative power in Ankara on April 23, 1920, by Mustafa Kemal. The total number of the members in TGNA is 550. The duties of the TGNA include enacting and amending laws, monitoring the actions of the Cabinet and Ministers, debating the budget, ratifying international agreements and declaring a war.

Anybody above the age of 30, who has minimum primary school education and who has security clearance can be elected as a deputy. The deputies represent not only the regions in which they were elected but the whole Nation. Elections are held every 5 years. According to the Constitution, all Turkish citizens over 18 years of age have the right to vote in elections and to take part in referendums. One third of the Assembly is enough to hold a session. The decisions are taken by an absolute majority vote of those present.

PRESIDENT

The President is the Head of State and represents the unity of the Turkish Nation. He oversees the workings of the Constitution and ensures that the departments of the state function harmoniously. He is elected for a period of seven years.

(opposite page)
MAIN BUILDING OF
ANITKABİR
(MAUSOLEUM OF
ATATÜRK), *Ankara* [21]

His duties include calling the parliament to session, publishing laws, returning laws to parliament for reconsideration, deciding upon renewal of parliamentary elections, appointing the Prime Minister or accepting his resignation.

THE CABINET

The Cabinet which is politically responsible to the Legislature is composed of the Prime Minister and the ministers. After the general elections, the leader of the party winning the majority is appointed as the Prime minister by the President. The ministers are selected by the Prime Minister but again appointed by the President.

In addition to 15 state ministers, the government is formed of the following ministries; Justice, National Defense, Finance and Customs, National Education, Public Works and Housing, Health, Transport, Agriculture and Rural Affairs, Labor and Social Security, Industry and Commerce, Energy and Natural Resources, Culture, Tourism, Forestry, the Environment, Home and Foreign Affairs,

LOCAL ADMINISTRATION

The local administration system was established to meet the common needs of the people living in a specific region and is managed by bodies elected by those people.

The three types of local administration operating in Turkey are the municipalities, provincial local governments, and the villages.

a)The Municipalities

All municipalities are public corporate entities. Municipal organizations must be set up in all provincial and district centers. Besides carrying out duties related to health and social assistance, public works, education, agriculture, the economy and the well-being of its citizens, municipalities are required to take the necessary measures to meet all civic needs. These include municipal services including law enforcement, collection of municipal taxes, duties, fees, and domestic refuge. They also provide drinking water, gas, electricity and public transport facilities.

The Mayor is the chief executive and representative of the municipality and is elected for a term of five years.

b)Provincial Local Governments

The functions of the provincial local government organizations can be grouped as follows:
◆ Health and social insurance
◆ Public works
◆ Culture and Education
◆ Agriculture and animal husbandry
◆ Economic and Commercial functions.

The governor, the representative of the central administration, is also the head of the provincial local government and its chief executive. The governor usually acts in line with the decisions made by the provincial general assembly.

c)The Villages

A village is formed by people living in scattered or closely packed houses with their yards, gardens and land, together with their common property such as a mosque, school or pasture.

A village administration is formed in villages where at least 150 people live. This administration is a corporate entity.

The basic body in the village administration is the Village Assembly composed of villagers over the age of 21. This assembly elects the village headman for a term of five years. The headman represents the central administration and supervises the planning and operation of village projects and services.

ECONOMY

Since the Republic of Turkey was founded on the social and economic heritage of the Ottoman Empire, it inherited a heavy burden of debts and an economic structure that had been based completely on agriculture. Areas of economic value remained outside the border of the new Republic.

Economic policies were geared to spreading private ownership of land, appropriating land for landless farmers and migrants, protecting domestic production by customs policies and refraining from external borrowing.

New laws were also introduced and banks as well as financial institutions were founded.

Positive economic developments produced new policies including statism. Under the statist policies, the private sector was not excluded from the national economic scene but was supported.

Public corporations were also developed to handle general daily needs. These corporations were owned either partly or completely by the state and were called State Economic Enterprises (KİT in Turkish), and whilst being an autonomous body were for the public's benefit.

Another problem for Turkey was World War II. Although Turkey did not take an active part in the war, a major part of the country's natural resources were allocated to defense. This caused production to fall, external trade relations to be stopped and therefore new extraordinary measures had to be introduced.

After World War II, a new capitalist system, which derived from America, was dominant in the world. During this period, America was giving credit to Western European countries. This played an important part in the reconstruction of their economies. Under this framework Truman's Doctrine and the Marshal Plan (1947-1948) were developed to help the European countries against the Soviet threat. Turkey was one of the countries receiving aid and as a result became a member of the IMF (International Money Fund) and NATO (North Atlantic Treaty Organization).

During the years that followed, democratic improvements and radical changes made way for the introduction of a liberal economic system.

Demand for exported Turkish products, particularly agricultural, grew considerably during this period. The Korean War contributed to this demand.

During the second half of the 1950s the economy reached a stalemate.

According to the 1961 Constitution, economic planning became a legal requirement and as a result The State Planning Organization was established. Five-Year-Development Plans started to play an important role from 1963 onwards.

A package of economic stability measures which came to be known as the January 24 Decisions was introduced in 1980, when Süleyman Demirel was Prime Minister and Turgut Özal was holding an important and leading position in The State Planning Organization. The main aims of the package concentrated on foreign trade and economic liberalization.

After the military coup of 1980 the Armed Forces recognized the January 24 Decisions. This was the point at which Turgut Özal came onto the political scene as he had been responsible for designing the package. When Turgut Özal became Prime Minister, he used many novel ideas in order to integrate Turkey with the rest of the World on an economic basis. The main achievement was the introduction of a free market economy. He represented liberal tendencies and often said, "you can never make rivers flow in the opposite direction".

Following the same path from 1993 onwards, the Prime Minister Tansu Çiller tried to overcome the deficit in the budget by putting emphasis on the privatization of State Economic Enterprises in international markets, the prevention of inequality in the tax system and reducing the rate of inflation (70% a year).

In 1994 Turkey suddenly started to loose economic stability and the Çiller Government, through emergency measures, was forced to introduce another package of policies known as April 5 Decisions.

This new package required that extra taxes were collected from the rich, and non-profitable State Economic Enterprises were shut down.

In order to obtain international support, Turkey suggested that there are two types of Islamic countries. The first is traditional and fundamentalist while the second, of which Turkey is a leading member, is more modern in its outlook. If Turkey, for any reason, cannot succeed, it will mean victory for the fundamentalists which could be seen as an important threat for the Western world.

Turkey is an associate member of the European Union and has been applying for full membership since 1987. Numerous reasons and excuses have been used by the EU committees to postpone full membership, however, the first step towards the EU was taken with the Customs Union in January 1996.

[31] Figures represent people who are in work force.

(top) WOMEN SELLING THEIR CROPS IN THE MARKET PLACE [22]
(middle) MELON SELLERS [23]
(bottom) SHOESHINE MEN; *one of many ways of making ends meet in a country where the unemployment rate is high* [24]

ECONOMIC DAILY LIFE

Standard of Living

60% of the population earn between $100-$350 per month. The legal minimum salary is $100, but 6% of people receive less than the minimum salary.

Income Tax

25-55%

Unemployment Rate[31]

	Urban	Rural
Men	9.8%	6.2%
Women	20.5%	2.5%

AN OLD ANATOLIAN MAN
DRINKING HIS TEA IN
THE TRADITIONAL TINY
GLASS [25]

Institutions for Social Insurance

There are three big social security institutions established
by the state:

- ◆ The Retirement Trust (Emekli Sandığı)
- ◆ The Social Insurance Board (Sosyal Sigortalar Kurumu)
- ◆ The Social Insurance Board for small businessmen, crafts-
  men and others (Bağ-Kur)

There are also Private Institution Companies.

Retirement

Men can retire after working 25 years; women, after 20 years.
Pensions are based on 70-75 % of their last salaries.

Housing

Because the size of families has become smaller and urbanization problems have arisen, people have started to live in
apartment blocks in the urban areas and in smaller houses

in the rural areas. Generally apartments have 3 bedrooms with an average surface area of 100 m² / 120 yd². In larger cities apartments are more expensive to own with, the minimum price being about $30,000. The average citizen cannot easily afford such a price even with the help of a mortgage. Renting is a possibility, or good fortune may mean inheriting an apartment.

The housing problem increased in the 1960s and the Mass Housing Fund was established in 1980. The fund gave credit to construction cooperatives and many people became the owners of their own apartments by forming these cooperatives.

Nearly half of the people living in big cities rent their flats rather than own them. The average rent is $200 a month. In smaller cities, flats are less expensive and more people own their houses or apartments. The proportion of people who rent their houses nationwide is 25%. Some of these people, who work for the state, live in apartments which belong to the state and they pay a very small amount of rent. There is also a large group of people who live in their relatives' houses in which case they either do not pay rents or pay minimum amounts.

MAJOR INDUSTRIES

These include mining, the production of vehicles (cars, buses and trucks), cement, construction, lumber and petroleum products, iron and steel, cotton, textiles, leather goods, fertilizers, beer, wine and foodstuffs.

MAJOR IMPORTS

These include petroleum products, chemicals, pharmaceuticals, plastics, iron, steel, vehicles, and machinery.

Total imports to Turkey are valued at about 49.5 billion US Dollars (1998)

Total exports from Turkey are valued at about 27.5 billion US Dollars (1998)

MAJOR EXPORTS

These include iron and metals, machinery, buses, chemicals, cement, ceramics, glass, cotton, textiles, leather, agricultural goods, tobacco, fruits, and foodstuffs.

NATURAL RESOURCES

Turkey is one of about only 8 countries in the world which consistently produces surplus food and cattle for export.

Turkey is believed to be rich in a wide variety of mineral deposits which are mostly governed by the state sector. Relatively few of these have been exploited on a large scale. This is due to a lack of domestic capital for exploration and exploitation, political pressure that has discouraged wide-scale investment from abroad, and inadequate processing facilities.

Agriculture and Farming

Agriculture accounts for less than 20% of the GNP, although it employs well over half of the national labor force.

A WORKER IN A COTTON FIELD [26-B]

(preceding page)
A WOMAN SELLING FLOWERS [26]

Turkey's total land	
36%	agricultural land
30%	forests and brushwood
28%	grazing land
6%	swamps, river beds, rocks and water surfaces

Agricultural production is generally carried out by small family enterprises in Turkey. 5% of the farm land belongs to the large enterprises and 95% to smaller concerns.

HARVEST [27]

77% of the cultivated land produces grain with wheat ranking as the first. Wheat is common all over the country except in the Black Sea Region. Barley ranks as second, corn is third. Corn requires humid weather conditions during summer time, so the Black Sea Region is very suitable for its growth.

Vegetables account for 62% of agricultural production. Lentils, chickpeas and beans are common. Broad beans and peas also grow in Turkey but on a smaller basis. Chickpeas grow in Central Anatolia, broad beans in western parts and lentils especially in Southeastern Anatolia. The growing of potatoes has recently increased.

Industrial vegetables such as cotton, flax, sesame seeds and opium poppies have been grown for a long time in Turkey, but since the industrial developments after World War I new industrial vegetables such as sugar beet, sunflower seed and tea have also been produced.

Tobacco is grown in the Aegean, Marmara and Black Sea Regions. Soybeans are grown in the Mediterranean. Many kinds of fruit are grown in most parts of the country. Turkey ranks the first in the production of hazelnut, apricot, fig, raisin and eggplant.

Animal Husbandry

Animal husbandry has considerable potential for Turkey. In parts of the country where agriculture and farming are limited, people make their living with animals, especially in Central, Eastern and Southeastern Anatolia. Generally, traditional techniques are used, and the results are not as satisfactory when compared to modern countries.

Fishing

Because Turkey is surrounded by different seas on three sides, and has numerous lakes and rivers there is a big seafood potential. Unfortunately, because of the primitive techniques that are used, production and consumption of seafood per person is below the world average. The annual seafood catch per capita is around 12 kg/26.4 lb.

Anchovy, small mackerel and bonito are the most common fish in Turkey. The major freshwater fish are carp and trout. Besides fish, mussels and shrimps are also abundant.

Overfishing and water pollution are two problems for Turkey.

Seafood Catches	
87%	Black Sea
7%	Marmara Sea
4%	Aegean Sea
2%	Mediterranean Sea

Forestry and Plants

Large areas in the South, West and Northwest are covered by Mediterranean vegetation, consisting mainly of thick, scrubby underbrush in the lowlands and deciduous or coniferous forests at higher altitudes up to the timberline. The humid northern margins of the country are the most densely wooded regions of Turkey. On the eastern Black Sea coast there are subtropical forests. The Anatolian interior is a region of steppes. Forests of mostly oak and coniferous trees exist only on the elevated areas.

The forest areas comprise of 26% of the total area of Turkey.

POPLAR TREES [28]

Forests	
58%	Irregular and infertile
39%	Real forest areas for production
1.5%	Nature reserves
1.5%	National parks (21 in total)

99.8% of the forests belong to the state. Much of the wood harvest is burned and used for energy.

Forests in Turkey are very rich regarding plant types.

As a country with different climates and different ecosystems, Turkey has a tremendously rich flora and fauna.

The number of species of flowers in Turkey is approximately 9,000, out of which 3,000 are endemic, whereas in Europe there are 11,500 species.

Kardelen *(L Galanthus, Snowdrop)*

Out of 20 species in the world Kardelen is one of the 9 species found in Turkey. It raises its head from the snow with its green umbrella between January and April at an average altitude of 2,000 m / 6,560 ft. The export of Kardelen from Turkey without permission is not allowed. Even with permission there is an annual limit of 7 million bulbs of this flower. However, this figure is generally exceeded.

(opposite page) **DAĞ LALESİ**, *Anemone coronaria* [29]
(top inset) **ANKARA ÇİĞDEMİ**, *Crocus ancyrensis* [30]
(bottom inset) **NERGİS**, *Narcissus tazetta* [31]

KARDELEN, *Snowdrop, Galanthus elwesii* [32]

KELAYNAK, *Bald Ibis, Geronticus eremita* [33]

Animal Life

Increasing population, developing industries, larger residential areas and unregulated hunting have been causing the destruction of natural resources which has a negative effect on wildlife.

Throughout the country today there are 120 species of mammals, 439 birds, 130 reptiles and 345 fish. Many of these species are very rare.

Turkey is rich in wild animals, insects and game birds. Wolf, fox, wildcat, lynx, jackal, marten, hyena, bear, deer, gazelle, boar, mountain goat, snake, scorpion, spider, beaver are among the animals still found in secluded and wooded regions. Major game birds are partridge, wild goose, quail and bustard.

Indigenous animals found in Anatolia include shepherd dog from Kangal, White Cat of Van region, and Tiftik Keçisi (Angora goat) from Ankara (Angora). Bald Ibis (Geronticus eremita) from Birecik is extinct.

Sea Turtles

There are 7 species of the sea turtles in the seas of the world. Two of these species living in the Mediterranean basin are Caretta Caretta and the green turtle known as Chelonia Mydas.

Sea turtles nest on some of the sandy beaches of the countries neighboring the Mediterranean.

Sea turtles do not leave the sea except during the period they lay their eggs. At night, the female turtle comes onto the sandy beach to lay her eggs. She digs a hole of 40-50 cm / 16-20 inches deep in the sand, leaves around 100 eggs each as big as a table tennis ball, covers the hole and returns to sea. This whole process is accomplished in 1-1.5 hours and during this period there must be no sound, light or movement on the beach as this would frighten the female turtle and she would not come out to lay her eggs.

The nesting period is from May until the end of August. Baby turtles hatch after 55-65 days and, leaving their egg shells, go directly into the sea.

There is no precise information on their exact number or the behavior of sea turtles in the sea. It is estimated that they live for 30-50 years and the population is around 10,000 in the Mediterranean Sea.

Development and construction along beaches, sea pollution, the hunting of the turtles and the destruction of nests by animals and man have caused the population of sea turtles to continually decline.

Mines

Turkey is not so rich in mining. The mines are divided into three categories: Metals, industrial raw materials and energy raw materials.

The main metals are copper, lead, zinc, mercury, iron, chrome, aluminum, gold and silver. Industrial raw materials include asbestos and phosphate. Energy raw materials are coals, uranium, oil and geothermal sources.

Energy Sources

1998	
37%	oil
18.6%	lignite
12.5%	coal
7.0%	natural gas
8.8%	wood
4.0%	animal waste
12.1%	others

Electricity

Electricity consumption per capita: 1,900 kw / hour (1998)

(January-June 1995)	
37.8%	hydro electric
62.2%	fossile fuel

The Southeastern Anatolia (GAP) Project

GAP is the largest regional development project ever undertaken in Turkey. It is a multi-purpose and integrated development project comprising of 22 dams and 19 hydroelectric power plants on the Tigris and Euphrates rivers and their tributaries.

When completed, it is planned to irrigate over 1.7 million hectares / 4.2 million acres of land and produce 27 billion kilowatt / hours of electrical energy per year. The planned total irrigation area will cover 8.5 million hectares / 21 million acres of productive land.

GAP is not limited to energy production, irrigation and farming alone. It is obvious that the development in agriculture will affect all other sectors of the regional economy, industry, mining, transportation, education, health and communications. The population of the region is around 5 million today but it is growing day by day. With new investments a minimum of 2 million people will have new job opportunities in the area. The migration from the rural to urban districts will stop and it is hoped that people will start migrating back to this region again. With the opening of the Urfa tunnel in 1994, the construction of new factories in the private sector has already started.

The Atatürk Dam on the Euphrates is the biggest in Turkey and fourth in the world. It is at the core of the GAP project and is almost complete.

Crude Oil

82%	Import
18%	Domestic production.

76% of the domestic production is by the state (TPAO) and the 24% is by Turkish or foreign private companies like Shell, Mobil or Ersan.

Nearly all the domestic production is concentrated in Southeast Anatolia: Batman and Adıyaman.

Crude oil is processed at five major refineries: İzmit, Aliağa (İzmir), ATAŞ (Mersin), OAR (Kırıkkale) and Batman.

Tourism

Income from Turkish tourism is around 9 billion US Dollars.

The number of tourists coming to Turkey is between 8-10 million which has been increasing rapidly in the last few years. This figure means that Turkey has a share of 1.5% of the total number of tourists traveling throughout the world.

Most of the tourists coming to Turkey are from Germany, the Commonwealth of Independent States, Iran, Israel and the USA.

The number of Turkish tourists going abroad is about 5 million per year.

EDUCATIONAL SYSTEM

Many reforms in education were made immediately after the foundation of the Republic. The most important was its secularization.

Education has been made a top priority of national development. However, only 2.5 % of National Income is spent on Education.

The aim of the Turkish educational system is to nurture productive, happy individuals with broad views on world affairs who will unite in national consciousness and thinking to form an inseparable state, and will contribute to the prosperity of society through their skills. This is thought to be instrumental in making the Turkish nation a creative and distinguished member of the modern world.

CHILDREN PLAYING GAMES [34]

Nursery Schools

Apart from the general educational system, pre-school training is available only on a private basis or with public sector facilities. However, this level of education is not yet common and is limited to about 5-10 % of Turkish pre-school children.

Special Training Institutions

These include Special Education Schools for the mentally or physically handicapped or enhanced learning centers for exceptionally bright children.

The Turkish educational system in both state and private sector is divided into 3 levels:

1. PRIMARY EDUCATION

CHILDREN IN THEIR
SCHOOL UNIFORMS [35]

This level of education consists of *Primary School* which is compulsory for 8 years, starting generally at the age of 7, depending on the physical development of children, sometimes at 6.

The national attendance at primary schools is about 90%. In some rural areas parents cannot physically manage to get their children to school if there is not a school in the village.

A special feature of primary schools is that one teacher takes care of all the students in one class, from the first grade and continues with those children for five years. With the sixth year, the system of one teacher for each class changes to a specialist teacher for each subject. After the fourth grade, students can choose one foreign language from English, French or German. Religious Education lessons, depending on the present government's policy, is often optional, and is actually a comparative study of religions rather than only of Islam.

CIRCUMCISION BOY [36]

The school age population of Turkey is very large and often school buildings and teachers are insufficient to cope. This results in two sessions of school, one in the morning and one in the afternoon. This helps to explain why so many children are seen in the streets during weekdays.

The average number of students in each classroom is 25-40, but in some rural areas, where there are not enough teachers, even more students have to fit into the same classroom.

All over the country, in each classroom above the blackboard, a portrait of Atatürk is hung. On one side you will see his Speech to the Turkish Youth and on the other, the National Anthem.

There are no fees for education until college or university. Students attend school in uniforms which are usually blue or very occasionally black. Parents have to buy uniforms, pens, pencils and notebooks.

At the beginning of the week on Monday mornings and at the end of the week during Friday afternoons, flag ceremonies are held with all the teachers and students present in the courtyard or playground of each school.

Each morning, primary school students say the pledge of allegiance in chorus in which they pledge to be honest and studious, to protect the young and respect the old, to love their country more than themselves and to give their existence as a present to the Turkish Nation. The chorus is concluded by saying "So happy is the man who says he is a Turk".

2. SECONDARY EDUCATION

This consists of *High School* which normally takes 3 years.

The aims of these schools are to secure a level of general knowledge, develop an awareness of individual and community problems and to contribute to the economic, social and cultural growth of the country as well as preparing students for higher education.

Anatolian, Science, Fine Arts, Vocational, Technical, Islamic Theological and Private High Schools are different from the general *High Schools*, but are still a part of the Secondary Education system.

The Anatolian, Science and Private High Schools are the best and consequently most popular. In these schools there is an extra year (prep class) at the beginning to teach one foreign language and in the following years, all science lessons are taught in that foreign language.

High School students must wear uniforms. The education at this level is free of charge except at the private schools where an average fee is about 3,000 - 3,500 US Dollars per year.

Students show respect for their teachers by addressing them "sir" or "teacher", by standing up as a class when a teacher enters the classroom, or by standing up while speaking.

3. HIGHER EDUCATION

This consists of universities and schools of further education which are all affiliated to an autonomous Higher Education Council.

There are 53 state and 16 private universities with more than one million students in Turkey. Students are admitted to universities through a two-phase examination held once a year. The first phase is for selection and the second for placement. In order to obtain a good future, students want to study in good departments at good universities. This is why they start studying for the entrance exams as much as two years in advance, generally taking private courses as well.

Generally speaking, 1,450,000 students per year take entrance exams, out of this number approximately 350,000 students are actually placed in schools of further education.

Unlike the earlier educational levels, students have to pay a fee of approximately 100-350 US Dollars per year at higher education facilities.

HEALTH SERVICES

Examination, diagnosis, cure and rehabilitation of the general public are included in the responsibilities of the Ministry of Health and Social Welfare. However, other ministries, state economic enterprises (most of which are to be shut down or privatized) medical schools and some private sector agencies, also help to perform these services.

> The number of persons per bed is 411, per doctor 896 and per dentist 5,336.

General practitioner services, although planned, have not started in Turkey yet. Therefore when somebody becomes ill, first he must see a doctor in an infirmary or the health department at his work place if there is one. If necessary they are then sent to a hospital. Children and housewives of working people or retired people can only go to hospitals directly without any previous visits or referrals from an infirmary or a health department.

In order to obtain the medicine prescribed, retired people have to pay 10% and others 20% of the list price. The rest of the amount is covered by social insurance institutions.

HOSPITALS

In the first years of the Turkish Republic, there were 3 hospitals with a total bed capacity of 950. The number of state hospitals rose to 941 with a total bed capacity of 139,600 (1991).

More than half of the doctors in Turkey are specialists and 40% of them work in the public sector.

1. Public Hospitals

a) State Hospitals

Members of the Retirement Trust and Bağ-Kur and their families can utilize these hospitals.

b) Social Insurance Board Hospitals

Members of this board are employed contributors, who along with their families, benefit from this plan.

2. University Hospitals

These are possibly the hospitals of the highest standard in Turkey. The people who use these hospitals are members of the Retirement Trust, patients transferred by another hospital or any direct private patient provided that the services received are paid for.

3. Hospitals of State Economic Enterprises

These hospitals belong to state enterprises such as PTT (Post, Telephone & Telegram), DDY (State Railways) or are akin to various professions such as Military hospitals, Teachers' hospitals and Police hospitals. The facilities of these hospitals are used by members of the given professions and their families.

4. Private Hospitals

These vary widely in standard and are generally found in the major cities where the income levels of some people enable them to afford private medical care. Some of these private hospitals are internationally recognized for their high standards.

AIDS

The number of known people who have AIDS in Turkey is about 864 (December, 1998). Unofficially, it is estimated to be thousands. The recorded number of people who have died because of AIDS is around 100. However, it is also estimated that there are about 300 people in Turkey who are "carriers" of the AIDS virus.

NATIONAL DEFENSE AND THE ARMED FORCES

The primary, most important defender of Turkey's independence is the Turkish Armed Forces. The role of the Turkish Armed Forces is to defend and protect the land and the Republic against internal and external threats and to fulfill the NATO duties agreed by international treaties.

Because of the geopolitical importance of its location as a member of NATO, Turkey has the largest army of any of the NATO countries after the USA, with about 800,000 soldiers

(1996). With this size it is the 7th largest in the World. Approximately 10-13% of the national budget is allocated to the Ministry of Defense.

MILITARY SERVICE

Since the Ottoman period different systems of military service have been used at different periods. Today, under the Military Service Law, all male citizens who are physically eligible must perform military service between the ages of 20 and 46. The compulsory service period is 18 months including one month of holiday. Up until the age of 46 men might be recruited at different times for short periods as reserves in this so-called Reserve period.

The Turkish Armed Forces consist of The Army, The Air Force, The Navy and The Gendarme. The uniforms of the Air Force staff are blue; the Navy, white in summer and black in winter; and the others are various shades of khaki.

The Social Function of Military Service

Military service is a very important social event in men's lives. It has the distinct effect of dividing it into two phases: Life before and life after military service.

Generally men serve in places other than their home regions without returning except for their vacations. Before leaving, the family provides a big meal in their son's honor and invite relatives, friends and neighbors. A large group of friends escort the boy to the central bus or train station with musical instruments, usually drums and clarinets, the louder the better. They may even carry him on their shoulders.

Military service is a kind of school in which the young men of Turkey reach maturity through the experiences that they live. This is a place where they become acquainted with manners. For some, it is the first time they live away from home. Being away from family is also an opportunity to learn to stand responsibly on their own feet.

In some rural parts of Turkey, young men cannot get married before completing their military service, since this period is accepted as a major step in the transition to manhood. In these areas especially, if a young man is not recruited because of physical or mental reasons, he gets disappointed and tries his best to convince the authorities that he wants and can perform his duty. Young men who are not accepted into the military service often suffer insults or loss of status among their peers.

ANATOLIAN CULTURE

Language

THE LANGUAGES OF ANATOLIA [32]

Cuneiform Script

From the Latin cuneus, "wedge," and forma, "shape" is a system of writing used by a number of ancient Near Eastern languages from c.3000 BC to the 1C AD. Primarily a Mesopotamian system, cuneiform was inscribed on clay, stone, metal and other hard materials.
It was from 1950 BC that, cuneiform script was adopted by the Hittites, Hurrians, Mitanni, Urartians and Persians to write their own languages.

a) Hattic

A language of central Anatolia, Hattic, often called Hattian or proto-Hittite, is preserved largely in Hittite records, where both Hattic words and whole Hattic sentences are found. It became extinct in about 1400 BC and has no affinities with any other known language.

b) Hurrian

A language of southeastern Anatolia that was still alive at the beginning of the 1st millennium BC. Hurrian is preserved both in its own inscriptions and in Hittite texts. Hurrian is related to Urartian.

c) Urartian

Urartian was spoken in eastern Anatolia around Lake Van. Urartian is also known from an important Urartian / Assyrian bilingual text. Written records date from 900-600 BC. Urartian is closely related to Hurrian, though not derived from it.

(preceding page) **AFTER A LONG DAY'S WORK,** [37]

[32] Grolier *Electronic Publishing, Inc., 1993*

d) Phrygian

Phrygian, a language of western central Anatolia, had two

literary periods, Old Phrygian (730-430 BC) and New Phrygian (100-350 AD). The later stage used a Greek-like script; the earlier had an eclectic alphabet based on North-west Semitic models.

e) Thracian

Thracian was spoken along the west coast of the Black Sea and south of the Danube. Although no significant inscriptions exist, numerous words are known from Greek and Roman texts. In addition, a large number of personal and place names have been recorded. Thracian is of Indo-European origin.

f) Hittite

The most important language of the Hittite-Luwian group is Hittite. It was translated early in this century by the Czech scholar Bedrich Hrozny, who showed, to the surprise of most linguists, that the language was Indo-European, although it maintained certain features that had been lost in all the other Indo-European languages. Hittite used a form of Akkadian cuneiform writing.

g) Lydian

Lydian was spoken on the west coast of Anatolia and was written in the Greek script from 500 to 300 BC. An Aramaic / Lydian bilingual text has proved of great value in establishing an understanding of the language. In addition to inscriptions in Lydian, about 50 other words are found in the writings of various Greek authors.

h) Cuneiform Luwian

The most thoroughly understood language of the Luwian

subgroup, Cuneiform Luwian is known from 1400 BC in south central Anatolia. It is called "cuneiform" after the type of writing system in which it is preserved and to distinguish it from its very close relative, Hieroglyphic Luwian. It differs from Hittite both in vocabulary and in its phonological system.

i) Hieroglyphic Hittite

Also called Hieroglyphic Luwian, it is not yet well understood and its pictographic script has not been completely deciphered. The language is clearly related to Cuneiform Luwian, but it probably represents a later stage of development. The language is recorded from 1200 to 700 BC in what is now northern Syria and south central Turkey.

j) Lycian

Spoken in the southwest corner of Anatolia, Lycian is recorded from 500 to 200 BC in about 150 short inscriptions written with a West Greek alphabet.

k) Turkish

The official language in Turkey is Turkish and this is spoken by about 90-95% of the population. About 5-10% of the Turkish people who come from different ethnic origins, speak their mother tongues in daily life besides Turkish.

Evolution of the Turkish

Turkish is a branch of Ural-Altaic languages. These were originally spoken by the Altai people who lived in the steppe area around the Altai mountains which form part of the border between China, Mongolia and Russia. The Altai spread out over a vast geographical area reaching as far as the

Balkans and today 100-120 million people speak these languages, generally called the Turkic Languages.

As a version of these languages, Turkish came to Anatolia with these people from the 11C onward and it can be classified in 3 separate periods:

1) Turkish in the Pre-Islamic Period

This is the period until the 10C AD, before the Turks adopted Islam and came to Anatolia. The Turkish language was pure during this period because it was not influenced by any other languages. Göktürk and Uighur Alphabets were used.

2) Turkish in the Islamic Period

This is the period between the 10C and 20C. From the 11C onward the Turks started to settle in Anatolia in large numbers, first as Seljuks and then later as Ottomans. They had already adopted Islam, which meant they were influenced by Arabic since the Koran was written in that language. However, Persian remained the language of art, refined literature and diplomacy.

Common people spoke Turkish but used the Arabic alphabet to write it. This mixture was called Ottoman Turkish or the Ottoman language.

3) Modern Turkish in the 20C

In the beginning of the 20C, parallel to all the changes and reforms in the country, there was consciousness towards the language as well. In this period no one played a more important role in the development of modern Turkish than Atatürk, the founder of the Turkish Republic. His language reforms as a result of his Westernization philosophy—for instance the replacement of the Arabic alphabet with the Latin, or "purifying" it of the Arabic and Persian words and idioms that had invaded the literary language during the Ottoman Empire— have profoundly affected the course of Modern Turkish spoken today. This is a remarkable fact but not actually so difficult to achieve in an era when the literacy rate was less than 20%.

Language reform has closed the language gap that used to exist between the classes in Turkish society and a certain democratization of language and literature has occurred during the 20C.

Anatolia's Contribution to English

The Anatolian culture has contributed various words and expressions to the English language. Indeed, the names of cities, places and people of Anatolia have become part of the English language and are used as common expressions today.

Some examples with their definitions from English dictionaries[33] are as follows:

angora	(ancient name for modern capital, Ankara) the hair of the Angora goat
bergamot	(from Turkish "bey-armudu", prince's pear) a pear-shaped orange whose rind yields an essential oil used in perfumery
bulgur	parched crushed wheat prepared for human consumption
byzantine	complicated; labyrinthine; of or practiced by people who delight in inventing new and painful ways of making others suffer
caique	a light skiff used on the Bosphorus
divan	a council; a large couch or sofa usually without back or arms and often designed for use as a bed; an author's collection of poems

[33] *Webster's New Collegiate Dictionary* and *Longman Dictionary of Contemporary English*

Gordian knot	a knot tied by Gordius, King of Phrygia, held to be capable of being untied only by the future ruler of Asia and cut by Alexander the Great with his sword; an intricate problem
kiosk	an open summerhouse or pavilion
mausoleum	a large tomb, usually a stone building with places for the entombment of the dead above ground
meander	(ancient name of the Menderes River in Anatolia which has many curves) n. a turn or winding of a stream; v. to follow a winding or intricate course
parchment	the skin of a sheep or goat prepared for writing on (first discovered in Pergamum); any of various types of paper of good quality that look like this material
sherbet	a cold drink of sweetened and diluted fruit juice
turban	a headdress
turquoise	(*Turkish* in French) a mineral that is bluish-green or greenish-blue in color and regarded as precious
yoghurt or yogurt	a fermented slightly acid semisolid food made of whole and skimmed cow's milk and milk solids to which cultures of two bacteria have been added

Religi

MOTHER GODDESS OF ANATOLIA

The symbol and mythology regarding the mother goddess are found in many diverse cultures of the ancient world. She represents the creative power of all nature and the processes of fertility, along with the periodic renewal of life. Representations of the mother goddess date from Paleolithic times.

The Neolithic settlement of Çatalhöyük (c.7000 BC) in Anatolia provides archaeological evidence that the cult of the mother goddess has been continuous. The chief deity was a goddess who simultaneously incorporated the roles of young woman, mother in childbirth and old woman.

The worship of a great goddess was particularly dominant in Middle Eastern religions, especially in the cult of Cybele. We only learned her various names after the introduction of writing to Anatolia in 1950 BC: Kubaba, Kumpapa, Kybele, Cybele, etc. She was a fertility goddess involved with a young male consort who died but was continually reborn. This element of the dying male deity, representing vegetation, is a later development in the cult of the mother goddess and is regarded as a transition from her primal state of being an unmarried mother to having a son, a lover, or both.

Artemis of Ephesus is the extension of the mother goddess

STATUETTE OF MOTHER GODDESS OF ANATOLIA FROM HACILAR, *Neolithic period, Museum of Anatolian Civilizations, Ankara* [38] and the source of the Virgin Mary cult which parallels virginity and motherhood.

Further cultural integration occurred with the adoption of the Egyptian Isis cult by the Greco-Roman world. Isis became a universal goddess, incorporating local goddesses and identified with the mystery of fertility. The cult of Isis persisted during the first four centuries of the Christian era, until persecution finally halted cult activities.

In Christianity the figure of the Virgin Mary as theotokos, or the "Mother of God," has clear affinities with that of the ancient mother goddess. Her role, however, is diminished and that of the divine child is central.

RELIGION IN MODERN TURKEY

There are 935 million Moslems in 172 countries of the world today. This is nearly 18% of the world's population. 6% of Moslems live in Turkey. More than 33% of the world population are Christian.

Among the Islamic countries there are two different models: The first is fundamentalist, like Iran or other Arab countries and the second is modern like Turkey. Although 99% of the Turkish population are Moslem, Turkey is a secular state and people have freedom to choose their religion and beliefs. No one is forced to participate in any religious ceremonies or rites against his will and no one is viewed as being at fault because of his beliefs.

In secular Turkey all Islamic religious affairs are carried out by a central government organization affiliated to the Prime Ministry, namely the Department of Religious Affairs. The function of this organization is to carry out tasks related to the beliefs, divine services and moral principles of Islam and to enlighten citizens on religious matters.

NUDE FEMALE
REPRESENTING THE
MOTHER GODDESS,
*Early Bronze Age,
Museum of Anatolian
Civilizations, Ankara* [39]

ISLAM [34]

Islam is the name of the religion that arose in the Arabian Peninsula where its founder, the Prophet Mohammed, was born in 571 AD in the city of Mecca.

A pious, charismatic man, Mohammed was a merchant by trade, who in his youth searched for a purer and more meaningful religion than the polytheistic beliefs that surrounded him.

In his fortieth year he received his first revelation. He was called to be the Prophet of God to his people. He began to preach oneness of God and to preach the message entrusted to him—that there is but one God, to whom all humankind must commit themselves. The polytheistic Meccans resented Mohammed's attacks on their gods and finally he emigrated with a few followers to Medina. This migration, which is called the Hegira (Hicret), took place in 622 AD; Moslems adopted the beginning of that year as the first year of their lunar calendar.

In Medina, Mohammed won acceptance as a leader. Within a few years he had established control of the surrounding region and in 630 he finally conquered Mecca. The Kaaba, a shrine that had for some time housed the idols of the pagan Meccans, was rededicated to the worship of Allah and it became the object of pilgrimage for all Moslems.

The believers of Islam are called Moslems (Muslims). The Arabic word Islam means the act of committing oneself unreservedly to God and a Moslem is a person who makes this commitment.

The religion of Islam is the youngest of the three great monotheistic religions. According to Moslems, all the universe is Islam, all the religions that have ever existed are Islam and the prophets with their followers are Moslems. God sent

[34] All the contribution rates to the Islamic practices are the author's estimates.

Mohammed as a messenger from among the Arabs, bringing a revelation in "clear Arabic". Thus, as other peoples had received messengers, so the Arabs received theirs.

Islam is the last religion and Mohammed is the last prophet. Islam does not deny or ignore previous religions or their prophets. The Koran records that Mohammed was the Seal of the Prophets, the last of a line of God's messengers that began with Adam and included Abraham, Noah, Moses and Jesus. The Koran is said to be the perfection of all previous revelations.

The Five Conditions of Islam

1) To say and to believe *"I witness that there is no God but Allah and Mohammed is his prophet"*. When somebody believes in this, it means he believes and acknowledges everything declared by Mohammed.

2) To practice *namaz* 5 times a day; early in the morning, at noon, in the afternoon, in the early evening and at night.

Namaz

Each prayer is called namaz in the Persian language. The leader of the prayer is the **İmam** and his assistant during the prayer is the **müezzin**. The time to pray is announced to people by the müezzin. In former times this took place from the top of a minaret, but now it is announced over loudspeakers.

All Moslems in the world pray in the Kaaba direction and call it *"kıble"* which represents a spiritual unity. The word kıble derives from Kaaba which is associated with Kybele (the mother goddess of Anatolia) as there was previously a cult of Kybele in Kaaba.[35] For a Moslem the Kaaba is the sanctuary that Abraham and his son İsmail built for God.

[35] Tuncer Ömer, *İşte Anadolu*, Arkeoloji ve Sanat Yayınları, 1993

It is a symbol of God's uniqueness.

It is accepted as being more correct if people practice namaz in the mosque, although they are not obliged to do so. Women generally practice at home except the holy days. Each set of prayers is about 10-20 minutes long.

The average number of people practicing namaz in the mosque, regularly 5 times a day, is not more than 4-8% of the total male Moslem population in Turkey.

For a Moslem, Friday is the holy day as is Sunday for a Christian or Saturday (Shabbat) for a Jew. The İmam gives a sermon to the people in Turkish at the noon time prayers on Fridays. According to the law, they are not allowed to speak about politics in their sermons. For men, these noon time prayers on Friday have to be practiced in the mosque and the average number of people attending rises to 30-40% of the total male population. In many places you may notice that shops close so that workers may attend the Friday noon time namaz.

Early morning prayers on the first days of the two religious holidays (*Şeker* and *Kurban* Bayramı) are the two most important prayer times for men in a year. Attendance at these times can rise to 70-80% of the male population.

3) **Oruç:** To fast for 30 days during the holy month of Ramadan (*Ramazan* in Turkish). From sunrise to sunset eating, drinking, smoking and having sexual intercourse is forbidden for all except the sick, the weak, pregnant women, soldiers on duty, travelers on necessary journeys and young children.

The coming of Ramadan is a big social event throughout the country. To celebrate it minaret balconies are lit as hundreds of lights *(mahya)* are stretched between the minarets

of mosques with some figures, words and expressions to welcome or praise Ramadan. The figures are of flowers, boats, bridges or mosques. Papers, magazines and TV channels have special features and programs during Ramadan.

CHILDREN STUDYING KORAN *in one of the courses offered in mosques by imams during summer months* [40]

The process of fasting starts at about 3 o'clock in the morning with the street drummer's music. Each vicinity has its own drummer who makes music to wake people up each morning during the whole month. All his efforts are to make a living from the tips he collects at the end of the holy month from his neighborhood.

After being awakened by the drummer people have the opportunity to eat before sunrise as it is then which marks the beginning of fasting for the day. While fasting eating is not the only thing prohibited. Bad behavior, such as cursing,

lying, doing harm to others are also forbidden.

People who fast expect respect from others. This means, especially in smaller cities, that restaurants will be closed during the daytime and people will not eat, drink or smoke in public.

At sunset, the müezzin's call for the early evening prayer marks the end of the day's fasting. Olives, salt, dates and water are religiously accepted as being the best foods to break the day's fasting.

About 20-25% of Turkish people fast in Ramadan in urban areas and 60-70% in rural areas.

4) *Hac:* Visiting Mecca on a pilgrimage is only achievable for those who can financially afford it. Generally people prefer going to Mecca when they come to a certain age usually between 50-60 although there is no age restriction. The returning pilgrim is entitled to use the honorific **hacı** (pilgrim) before his name, a title that indicates his piety. He is then more careful to refrain from any sin for the rest of his life.

5) *Zekat:* To give alms to the poor as a part of one's wealth that being 1/40 each year. In practice lots of people give alms to the poor, but sometimes not at the established rate.

Attributes Of God

He is called *Allah*. He exists. There is no beginning or end to His being. He is unique. He does not look like any creature. The cause of His being has nothing to do with anything except Himself. He is omniscient and omnipotent. He hears, sees and speaks without using sounds or letters. God sent a messenger to each society and Mohammed was sent for all societies which means that he is actually the last prophet.

In Islam, the lives of individuals and of society are organized by the Holy Koran, which was revealed to Mohammed

(opposite page)
INTERIOR OF KOCATEPE MOSQUE, *20C,*
Ankara [41]

as vouchsafed through the angel Gabriel. According to the Koran, everybody is born as an innocent Moslem being regardless of his mother or father, but should practice the main beliefs of Islam as he grows up. No one can or should come between God and the worshipper.

Believing in the hereafter as well as God is also emphasized in the Koran. Man's life is not limited by his death. On the contrary, the gates of a higher world open with death. The position of the human being in the hereafter will be determined by his behavior on earth. The punishment is hell and the reward is heaven.

According to Islam, murder, cruelty, adultery, gambling, usury and the consumption of carrion, pork, blood and alcohol are strictly forbidden. Women should dress "decently" so that other people cannot see their hair, legs or arms. Boys have to be circumcised before the transition to manhood.

The language of Islam is Arabic because the Koran is God's words in Arabic. A translation into another language may give the meaning of the revelation, but its sacred character is lost. Turkish people do not speak Arabic, because in formal education Arabic is not taught except in İmam Vocational Schools. If families want their children to learn Arabic, they send them to Arabic courses given in the mosques by the imams or müezzins during the holidays. On these courses, due to the limited time, they can only learn how to read the Holy Koran.

Islamic countries are generally ruled by the **Şeriat,** Canonical Law (Islamic Law). Despite the absence of a formal church structure, religious functionaries played an important role in the Ottoman state. Islamic law regulated all aspects of life. The sultan, the supreme head of the empire, ruled as the shadow of Mohammad.

(opposite page)
ORTAKÖY (BÜYÜK MECİDİYE) CAMİSİ,
1853, İstanbul [42]

However, the Republic of Turkey is a secular state which means religious affairs are not combined with those of the state.

The Alevis

Today's Moslems are mainly divided into 2 types: **Sunni** and **Shia**. Sunnis acknowledge the first four Caliphs (**Ebubekir, Ömer, Osman, Ali**) as rightful successors of Mohammed, whereas Shias believe in Ali and the İmams as the right successors of Mohammed. More than two thirds of the Turkish population are Sunnis. The Shias of Anatolia are not the same as Shias of Iran. In Anatolia they are called **Alevis** which comes from the word Ali. It is a mixture of Anatolian cultures together with a deep belief in the incarnation of God in Ali. Compared to the Sunnis of Anatolia, the Alevis are more flexible. For example, they stopped going to mosques on the rationale that Ali, the son-in-law of the Prophet Mohammed and the founder of Alevism, was murdered in a mosque, thus violating the sanctity of the building; and they stopped formal prayers for safety's sake. A system of traveling holy elders (dede) replaced the more traditional Moslem structure of authority. The ban on wine and alcohol was relaxed, with wine actually used for religious ceremonial functions. The month of fasting was converted into eight days during the month of Muharrem.

MOSQUES

A mosque (from the Arabic *mescit*) is a place of public worship in Islam. The Turkish word for mosque is *cami* and it means "a place where people gather" in Arabic. Mosques must have an area for ritual ablutions and be positioned as such so that worshippers face Mecca during prayers. The

leader (imam), when opening services at prayer times, stands in or before the *mihrab*, prayer niche in the mosque which indicates the direction of Mecca. The preacher, generally the imam himself, speaks from the minber. An additional liturgical requirement is the *minare* (minaret), a high, generally pointed tower from which Moslems are called to prayer.

In the Koran, the term mescit refers either specifically to the Holy Sanctuary (the Kaaba Mosque) in Mecca or to religious buildings in general. Early Islam did not require a specially built space for the performance of the principal

A MAN IN THE ACT OF RITUAL ABLUTION BEFORE GOING TO PRAYER [43]

liturgical obligation of common prayer. The obligation could be met anywhere, provided the direction in which worshippers must face during prayer (kıble) was properly determined. Soon after the Prophet Mohammed's death (632), his house in Medina, which had often been used for gatherings of the faithful, became a model of the proper kind of meeting place in which to pray at formally appointed times as well as to perform a variety of social, political and administrative functions related to the Moslem faith.

Generally, but with notable exceptions, mosques have assumed the form of large enclosed spaces serving the collective needs of the Moslem community and decorated with quotations from the Koran and with ornaments intended to heighten the unique quality of the monument. Statuary or other images of living beings are uniformly absent from the mosque; geometric or floral motifs predominate in its carved-wood, plaster, tile, or mosaic decoration. The floors of mosques are generally covered with rugs; hanging lamps, candlesticks, stands for holy books and platforms for readers are often placed within the interior.

The Anatolian-type mosque was created under the influence of the local Anatolian architecture of the 13-14C, reaching its perfection with the growth of the Ottoman Dynasty in Bursa, Edirne and eventually İstanbul. It is characterized by the domination of a single dome covering the main prayer hall. Inside, brilliantly patterned supports extend gracefully from the top of the cupola and in the exterior courtyard tall minarets frame the soaring dome. The Anatolian-type mosque appeared in all the lands that came under Ottoman rule, but its masterpieces are the 16C creations of the great Turkish architect Sinan in Edirne (the Selimiye Mosque) and in İstanbul (the Süleymaniye Mosque).

SETTLEMENTS

Settlements are classified according to the number of in-habitants: Less than 2,000 inhabitants is a village (*köy*), be-tween 2,000 and 20,000 is a town *(kasaba)* and a population of more than 20,000 is a city *(şehir)*.

a) Cities

A few large cities dominate the nation. The principal eco-nomic, political and social forces converge on İstanbul, An-kara and, to a lesser extent, İzmir, Adana and Bursa.

City people, except for the elite, are organized into social groups, not necessarily exclusive and enduring, but interact-ing with each other at different levels.

Occupational groups are more stable and easily recogniz-able than others and are more significant in cities than in rural areas.

Urbanization

After the 1950s there has been continuous migration from the east to west Turkey, from rural areas to urban and from smaller cities to larger ones.

The process of migration takes place in nuclear families and usually starts with the younger members of the male population. After completing their education and military service, these young men go to larger cities in order to ob-

tain better living conditions through better jobs. They are convinced to migrate by friends or relatives who had migrated before them. This tends to result in people from the same place (village or neighborhood) living in the same quarter in metropolitan cities. When they have attained their level of expectations their families are taken to the city as well.

This continuous migration has not only increased the number of big cities, but also created serious socio-economic problems in large city centers such as İstanbul, İzmir and Ankara.

Uncontrolled and rapid urbanization has led to the mushrooming of *gecekondu* houses, slums or shantytowns; literally, "built or roofed overnight". They have been protected by former religious laws which did not allow authorities to demolish houses with roofs. People finish the roofs in one night and are guaranteed that their houses will not be demolished.

(opposite page)
ALWAYS HOPEFUL [44]

(bottom)
BARBERSHOP [45]

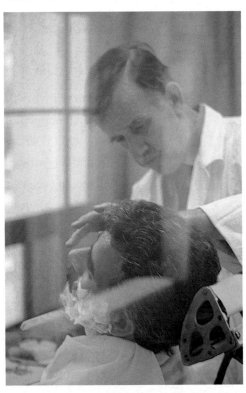

b) Towns

Towns range from simple settlements around marketplaces to large population centers offering a variety of goods, services and facilities as well as serving the basic economic and political functions. In general, the towns where the primary function is economic tend to be small, conservative and rural in character. In small towns, where occupational groups are few and weak, relations among residents tend to be more personal, non-

A VILLAGE BAKERY [46]

institutionalized and informal. The small-town merchant, trader or artisan identifies himself with the community. Whereas when the political function has joined or overridden the economic function, towns tend to be larger, progressive and urban. However rural a town may appear to the outsider, there is a distinct difference between a town and the surrounding villages.

c) Villages

Village Life

In rural Turkey the focus of life is agriculture. 54% of the national population is rural.

In a typical village, houses with their courtyards are built around a central place. Land for agriculture surrounds the village. In each village, there is usually a mosque, a school, a coffeehouse, guest rooms and some small shops.

Village life starts very early, usually before sunrise. After cleaning and tidying up the house, the animals are taken care of. Milking the sheep or cows and eating breakfast are early morning tasks before the serious work starts. Only after all this do children go to school and people to the fields to work.

The large majority of Anatolian villages are self sufficient. They produce their own food according to their production

VILLAGERS IN AN
OXCART [47]

range and for winter they prepare food grown in the summer or autumn months. Among the foods they prepare are
flour, bulgur (pounded wheat), oil, kavurma (preserved fried
meat), dried vegetables and fruit, yufka (dried thin layers of
pastry), macaroni, jam, pickles, tomato paste, molasses,
cheese, butter, etc. They obtain their other needs like clothing from bigger settlements in the vicinity.

The tools used in daily life are clearly very old in design.
The light wooden plow, or *saban* in Tr., is drawn easily by
one pair of oxen. It has an iron-tipped share but no mold

board so that it does not turn a furrow. Sowing is traditionally done by hand and reaping with a sickle or scythe. The crops are carried to the village for storage on four-wheeled horse-drawn carts or on the traditional two-wheeled oxcart, the *kağnı*. Threshing involves driving an ox-drawn sledge about five feet long over the crops, round and round, day after day. Flint teeth on the underside of the sledge break the grain from the ears and chop the straw into chaff. This mixture is winnowed by hand with wooden forks and put into woolen sacks.

In homes, people sit on rugs or mats spread on the floor. Houses have built-in divans running along the walls and very often a stone or wooden floor. Tables and chairs, once rare, are now becoming more common.

(top) **VILLAGERS PLAYING A GAME** *at a coffeehouse* [48]

(bottom) **SABAN,** *wooden plow drawn by a pair of oxen* [49]

Most peasants wear cloth caps and the famous Turkish baggy trousers which are exceedingly full in the seat. Shepherds, whose work may involve withstanding intense cold, wear a special large cloak, *kepenek*, made of felted wool and a hood with attached scarf that winds around the head and protects the ears. Village women still generally prefer traditional costume. They wear some locally customary combination of baggy trousers, skirts and aprons. In many areas it is

A VILLAGER ON THE WAY TO HIS FARM [50]

still possible to identify a woman's town or village and her marital status by her dress; village women in Turkey have never worn the veil, but they have traditionally covered their heads and mouths with a large scarf.

Most village areas contain weavers, masons, carpenters and smiths including tinsmiths. Some villagers go to town for craft services and a number of craftsmen travel around the villages—particularly specialists, such as sieve makers or sawyers.

Women are measured by rigid standards of purity; sex is a forbidden topic between close kin; and a young couple is forbidden to show any interest in each other if anyone else, even a member of the household, is present. A man leaving

A VILLAGER COOKING IN HER HOUSE [51]

for a trip does not say good-bye to his wife publicly, nor does he greet her publicly on his return.

Most Anatolian villages can be described as economically homogeneous, differences in wealth are small with many Turkish villagers owning their own land. The frequency with which large landowners once dominated the socioeconomic structure diminished significantly in the early republican period.

Where large landowners do exist, they dominate the political, economic and social life of the village by linking it with national life.

The criteria for social ranking are usually wealth, descent, occupation and social conformity, among which wealth is coming increasingly more important.

Although there are village headmen from an administrative point of view, they may not be the real leaders in places where wealthier people are eager to be dominant or in control.

The relationship between wealth and social rank is nowhere better seen than in the institution of the guest room. Perhaps only 10% of the houses have guest rooms, because only the wealthy can afford them. Most evenings men gather in these rooms and spend much of their time there, particularly during the winter months.

Village Types

Coastal Villages

Villages in European Turkey, along the Black and Aegean Seas and to a lesser degree along the Mediterranean Sea have long been in contact with urban and western influences. Coastal villages have almost always lacked the self-sufficient subsistence patterns of the Anatolian villages.

Economic rather than traditional kinship considerations tend to pattern social relations. Most coastal villagers have a broader social awareness than other Anatolian villagers and are more susceptible to national influences.

In these villages, large landowners, by providing employment and land for tenants and by serving as an economic link between the village and the outside

AN AEGEAN VILLAGE [52]

(top) **An Anatolian Farmer** [53]

(bottom) **Village Life** [54]

world, are the primary holders of power and prestige.

Mountain Villages

As a country of highlands, Turkey naturally has many mountain villages. In places higher than 1,800 m / 5,900 ft, you can find people living for the summer months with their herds of sheep, cattle or goats who return to their permanent houses in the winter. This is called *yaylacılık*.

Apart from these very high places, there are also permanent mountain villages whose geographical conditions mean that they are generally very small and perhaps without a school. Where there is no school students have to travel to a neighboring village.

Economically, as there is often no suitable land for agriculture, animal husbandry is dominant in these mountain villages.

Forest Villages

In forest villages, life is much more difficult than in normal villages, because of the daily living difficulties and transportation problems.

The villages also cause a certain amount of destruction in

the forests. That is why these villages are supported by the state and villagers are encouraged to use coal for heating instead of wood, and other animals instead of goats whose grazing habits are harmful to the trees.

Southern and Eastern Villages

Many of the farmers in the villages of the South and East are descendants of nomadic herders who have settled in the past 100 years. Groups of these people formed tribal units. Social and political relations were largely feudal and the measure of strength was the number of warriors at the command

A WATER WELL [55]

of each group. Weak tribes depended on the strong and gave them economic and military support in exchange for protection.

Because of the changes through government settlement programs and modernized farming, families are being detached from traditional structures in order to compete with others for jobs. Therefore these kinds of villages are losing their typical characteristics.

Economic Village Types

1. Cultivation Villages: Together with a little animal husbandry, agriculture is dominant. Vast agricultural lands produce mainly grains.

2. Garden Villages: Limited but very fertile land is used to grow fruit and vegetables.

3. Breeder Villages: Pastures are dominant and the number of animals is higher than the number of people. Animals may be taken to pasture on very high plateaus during summer months (yaylacılık). Agriculture is always secondary in these villages.

4. Forest Villages: Life is based on the utilization of forests and pasture animals.

5. Craft Villages: Because of very limited and insufficient land people have had to learn other crafts like bricklaying, masonry or painting. In the spring inhabitants go to other larger settlements to find jobs and return home in the winter.

6. Craft-agriculture Villages: Besides agriculture, people try to make their living with different crafts, such as weaving, silk processing, etc.

7. Fishing Villages: These are located by the sea or a lake. Together with agriculture, fishing is the dominant occupation.

The Old Anatolian House

The traditional Anatolian city developed in conformity with one of the basic principals of modern urban planning; that is, necessity for the location of the residential and commercial quarters separately.

From greater to smaller the traditional living units are as follows; city, district (*mahalle*), street (*sokak*), courtyard (*avlu*), paved entrance hall (*taşlık*), central reception room (*sofa*) and room (*oda*).

Regional differences in Anatolia led to the use of a great variety of building systems, materials and plans. Southeast-

A TRADITIONAL
BEDROOM [56]

ern Anatolia is characterized by the use of stone, Central Anatolia by the use of a combination of stone and adobe (originally Hittite style), while the Aegean and Mediterranean regions are characterized by their cubic stone structures. In the inner Aegean region, the upper floors are built on the timber frame principle with mud brick filling, while in the Eastern Black Sea region the houses are made entirely of wood.

This variety can be explained both as a result of climatic differences and of the very different cultures that have existed in Anatolia during the course of the centuries.

The Street

Traditional streets are narrow and filled with stones on the surface. Generally there is a sloping downward from both sides to meet in the middle, to keep the rain water away from the walls of the houses. The large eaves of the roofs serve the same purpose.

In the traditional streets, residents could fill their pitchers or passers-by could drink from the street fountains built into one of the walls and sometimes located in a *cul-de-sac* (blind alley).

The old miniatures and pictures show that the houses were painted white, indigo, pale pink, light yellow and green.

Courtyard-Garden-Entrance Area

Traditional houses always had a garden, quite irrespective of the size of the house itself. The Turks built the garden before proceeding to build the house. This attracted the attention of the French architect **Le Corbusier** who is regarded as one of the greatest of our age and he wrote: *"The Turk first of all lays out the garden and plants trees; the Frenchman cuts down the trees to build the house."*

The gardens were planted with climbing roses, honey-suckle, geraniums and fruit trees. Lanterns used to be hung at different places in the gardens.

As a result of the agricultural social basis, old houses had large garden gates, wide enough to allow the passage of the horse and carts. The handles performed the function of door-knockers; when the door opened, the bell suspended behind the door would ring and inform the residents that someone had arrived.

For practical reasons, the store-room, pantry, granary and stable were placed on the ground floor. The kitchen, bath, bakery, fountain (sometimes a well with a pump) and toilet were located outside in the garden.

The sofa

The *sofa* was the central space to which the other rooms opened out. Foodstuffs for winter use were prepared either in the sofa or in the garden; the carpets, kilims and other fabrics were woven in the sofa.

The room

The rooms were multi-functional. During the daytime they were used as living rooms with a hearth, during meal times as dining rooms and at night as bedrooms with bathrooms. One part of the cupboard served as the bathroom. and water was carried in buckets or just heated on a brazier.

The wall cupboards filled with mattresses, quilts and sheets

PEOPLE EATING AT A **SOFRA** *on the floor in a village* [57]

171

ÇAKIRAĞA KONAĞI (MANSION), *c. 1761, Birgi, Ödemiş* [58]

might well be regarded as prototypes of the "fold-out beds" to be found in some modern houses.

The windows were long and narrow. Balconies were not common. Instead, they had bay-windows which provided 3-sided vision of the street. According to Islamic belief women especially had to protect their privacy from potential onlookers, so they sat unseen behind the curtains.

The rooms were surrounded on 3 sides by *divan*s, with white lace covers or carpets upon which cushions would be laid. A favored pleasure of traditional life used to be fresh Turkish coffee in the traditional living room.

Turkish coffee

Coffee-beans used to be roasted on the hearth, left to cool in a wooden bowl, ground in a brass coffee mill and with the fresh aroma of coffee poured into the coffee jar. The process continued by making coffee in a little brass pot with a long handle on the brazier or a spirit stove, and finally drunk from a small porcelain cup.

As a Turkish proverb says "A cup of coffee guarantees 40 years of friendship" as you can never forget a sincere and hospitable offer of a cup of bitter Turkish coffee.

There is a very obvious resemblance in plan between the traditional Anatolian house and the "atrium-type" house which was developed in Anatolia centuries ago.

The factors that gave rise to Turkish architecture should be traced in the synthesis of the Anatolian arts and the Islamic culture.

Anatolian House Types

As a result of an old rule, the way to make houses depends upon the natural conditions of regions. According to the basic mentality, in forest areas houses will be made of wood, or in places where there are quantities of stones, houses will be built of stones.

a) Mud-brick houses

Bricks made of mud including high amounts of clay are commonly used in rural Anatolia, especially in regions where stone and wood are rare. Nearly one third of all village houses are made with mud-bricks in Anatolia.

The size of a brick is about 20-30 cm / 8-9 inches and is made stronger by adding pieces of straw or dried plants into its mud before drying.

When the walls are laid with bricks, the roof is covered with pieces of trunk and these are filled with tree branches or plants. The last stage involves covering the roof with clay and pressing it flat with a cylindrical instrument. These flat roofs provide many advantages for villagers, such as a place to sleep on during hot summer nights, to dry fruit and vegetables, and to preserve things like straw or dried dung.

b) Stone houses

Another common method of building houses is using suitable stones. Stone is the dominant building material in the Taurus Mountains, the Aegean region and parts of eastern Anatolia. Some stones are easy to shape, in which case, stones are placed on top of each other like bricks and it is even possible to build houses with more than one floor. Cappadocian stones are good examples for this kind of building. To prevent a house collapse, big wooden beams are used as supports inside the walls.

c) Wooden houses

Wooden houses are typical in the Black Sea area. In forest or mountain villages, houses are generally made of wood. Long pieces of trunk are joined by clamps or big nails and different materials such as pieces of stones, mud plaster, dried plants and such are filled in between. In humid areas, spaces between the trunks which act as rafters are left empty and not filled.

d) Brick houses

In some villages, but mostly in towns and cities, the most common material is bricks produced from special soil in factories. Bricks are attached to each other by cement. This is comparatively the strongest system and with this technique it is possible to build many floors.

In addition to these are houses made with new construction materials produced parallel to technological developments.

FAMILY

Families are divided into several types according to social, economic and local conditions. The *traditional extended* and *nuclear* families are the two common types of families in Turkey. The traditional extended family generally means that three generations live together: grandfather, adult sons and sons' sons, their wives and their unmarried daughters—a married daughter becomes a member of her husband's family and lives there. There is a unity of production and consumption together with common property. This type of family is becoming more and more rare today. The nuclear family, parallel to industrialization and urbanization, replaces traditional families. The nuclear family consists of a husband, wife and unmarried children and is more suitable to modern Turkish social life today.

There are some economic, traditional and emotional conditions that form the duties and responsibilities of the modern nuclear family member. As for the economic conditions, each individual is supposed to play a part in supporting the continuation of the family. The father is usually responsible for making the basic income, the mother may perhaps contribute by working and if not, will assume full-time take care of the home. Grandparents may also supply help with incomes from their pension or returns from owned property and rents. Younger children help with the housework (re-

AN ANATOLIAN MAN [59]

pairing, painting, cleaning) and when older contribute by usually covering at least their own expenses. Tradition places the father as the head of the family, but the mother has equal rights. The father is the representative and protector of the family whereas the mother takes care of all the day to day things.

Respect has a very important place in the Turkish family. Here are some examples in order to understand the concept of respect inside the family. Some of them however are diminishing in city family life.

- To stand up and give a seat when an older person comes in.
- To greet elders by kissing their right hand and bowing to touch the hand kissed with the kisser's forehead.
- To call one's elders, for example, "uncle" or "grandmother", not by first names.
- To understand the wishes of one's elders and to act upon them.

♦ Not to interrupt elders while they are talking.

♦ To ask advice when necessary from the older family members.

♦ To be careful with one's sitting position when sitting with the elders. For example, sitting cross-legged is considered as disrespectful.

♦ Not to smoke without asking permission from elders if in the same room.

♦ To use polite language.

Emotional conditions include giving and receiving affection and protection, instilling confidence and exercising compromise. These conditions are elements which help to bind the family in unity.

WOMEN

As Turkey is essentially an Islamic country, Islam plays an important role in the lives of women. Having begun in Arabic countries in 7C AD, Islam was influenced by the traditions and customs of these countries and the way in which women were treated. Men could marry or live with as many women as they liked, kill women and even bury new born girls alive. When Islam made marriage laws and put a limit on the number of wives allowed, it was accepted as the first system to give some economic rights to women by saving them from the sole sovereignty of their husbands.

In Turkey, following the declaration of the Republic in 1923, one of the most significant elements in the social revolution planned and advocated by Atatürk was the emancipation of Turkish women, based on the principle that the new Turkey was to be a secular state.

In 1926, a new code of Turkish civil law was adopted which suddenly changed the family structure. Polygamy was abol-

ANATOLIAN WOMEN WEAVING CLOTH [60]

ished along with religious marriages and divorce and child custody became the right of both women and men. A minimum age for marriage was fixed at 15 for girls and 17 for boys. Perhaps most importantly, the equality of inheritance was accepted as well as the equality of testimony before a court of law; previously, under Islamic law, the testimony of two women was equal to that of one man. With the secularization of the educational system, women gained equal rights with men in the field of education as well and no longer had to wear the veils and long garments required by the old religious beliefs. The right to vote for women was granted at the municipal level in 1930 and nationwide in 1934. Theoretically, Turkish women were far ahead of many of their western sisters at that time, for instance in France where women only gained the right to vote in 1944.

The charter of the International Labor Organization adopted in 1951, declaring equal wages for both sexes for equal work was ratified by Turkey in 1966.

Although all the new regulations brought the status of women to a very improved level, the actual status of women within the family institution did not provide for proper equality between men and women. Still today, the husband is the head of the family. A woman does the housework, and if a woman needs to work outside the home she has to get the approval of her husband. As a Turkish proverb says "a hus-

band should know how to bring food and the wife to make it suffice" confirming once again a woman's place in the home.

MEETING HELD FOR THE RIGHT TO VOTE FOR WOMEN, *1934*[61]

Anatolian Women Throughout Ages[36]

1. In Assyrian traders' colony, Kültepe (2000 BC), trade judges were women.
2. The judges of Priene were women .
3. Amazons, a race of women warriors, were Anatolian.
4. According to Herodotus, Lydian women chose their husbands themselves.
5. When Neleus, the legendary founder of Miletus, compelled the resident women to marry the newcomers, the women swore not to sit at the same table with their husbands and also not to call them by their names.
6. Alexander the Great, after conquering Miletus, allowed his soldiers to marry well trained woman soldiers.
7. The women of Xanthos bravely killed themselves before surrendering to the Persians (545 BC).

[36] Tuncer Ömer, *İşte Anadolu*, Arkeoloji ve Sanat Yayınları, 1993

Women today

Social life consists of two different places: Inside and outside the home. Women leave the outside world to the men, generally remaining in the home. Women get married at an earlier age than men and settle into their role of housewife and home maker. As the education level of women increases, the fertility rate decreases. Nearly every female university graduate has only one child.

9 million of the 21 million working population of Turkey are women. In the rural areas, the rate of working women, especially in agriculture, is very high. However, women work in this sector as an extension of their housework and not to make a living. In urban areas, women hold important posts in both public and private sectors, the arts and sciences. Today, Turkish women are bank employees (35%), doctors (16%), lawyers (20%), judges, journalists, pilots, diplomats, police officers, army officers or prime ministers.

Nearly two thirds of health personnel including doctors and pharmacists, one quarter of all lawyers and one third of banking personnel are women.

As for the politics, in the elections of 1937, the number of woman MP's was 18, which meant 4.5%. Today, unfortunately, this rate is much less than before. However, Turkey has also seen Tansu Çiller as the first woman Prime Minister.

Although men and women are equal before the law, men are tolerated in regard to adultery and women are more advantageous in terms of working conditions.

A new law proposition

A package called "Democratization of the family" is a new law preposition awaiting parliamentary discussion and enactment and it will include changes in the position of women, some of which are as follows:

- The cancellation of former obligatory permission from their husbands for women to work.
- Equality in the case of adultery.
- In the case of divorce, equality in the sharing of belongings which were acquired after marriage.

Feminism

An important stage of feminism in Turkey started in the 1980s and is different from the previous stages because it was initiated by women who spoke for themselves, rather than by men who had manipulated the female image for their own po-

CARICATURE BY ORHAN COPLU [62]

litical agenda. At this stage of feminism women spoke for themselves, beginning by arguing the reality of their bodies and their physical needs as opposed to the idealization and the symbolization of the female body as used for the national image.

Feminism strongly challenges the image of some Turkish women as covered, almost sexless beings and also as sacrificial mothers who would do and endure anything for their children and family.

To very briefly summarize the position of women in Turkey today, it can be said that unless you are a woman living in a metropolitan city and financially independent, life is still likely to be bound by the customs of traditional family life.

PROCEDURES AND ARRANGEMENTS
FROM ENGAGEMENT INTO MARRIAGE

In the traditional family, marriage is still a family rather than a personal affair. Marriages are not conducted by the imam anymore as they were before the republic. By law they have to be civil. Approximately 40% of marriages are only civil, 50% are both civil and religious, 10% are only religious which means they are not legal. Polygamy is very rare and only in some villages with a rate of 3%.

It is legally forbidden to marry before the age of 15 for women and 17 for men. The average age for girls to marry is around 17-18. Early marriages are more frequent in rural areas. For young men in big cities the problems of receiving an education, military service and acquiring a job are among the reasons that delay marriage.

Because respect for elders plays an important role in families, young people cannot always easily express their desire to marry as they feel shy about it. For instance, there are some regions in which boys at marriageable age express their wish to marry by thrusting a knife into a loaf of bread or spoon into a plate of rice before leaving a meal or speaking about going away for a long journey.

Although it is very difficult to make generalizations due to regional, traditional, economic, urban, rural effects, the procedures and arrangements from engagement into marriage might be classified as follows:

a) Decision to marry

Marriage is a very serious institution and people try to be very careful with their decisions. Parents want their children to marry the "right" people. There are several common methods of pairing couples which lead to marriages in Turkey.

1. *Görücü usulü (Traditional marriages):* The decision makers of marriages are family elders rather than the young prospective partners themselves. In this kind of marriage, matchmakers are elderly women and the young people do not even see each other. It is a kind of matching in which people always have their cancellation rights. Some time is given to both sides and, if the answer is positive at the end of this time, the decision to marry is taken. This is valid only in very traditional rural places. But inevitable changes of rural life, due to urbanization, are making this custom less common.

2. *Beşik kertmesi (Arranged marriages in babyhood):* This is a kind of engagement while yet in the cradle and is sometimes an intermarriage which might derive from the idea to prevent the division of a family's belongings. Upon hearing of the birth of a girl, members of another family send a full cradle as a present to the newborn child's family with whom they want to establish kinship bonds. This present-sending activity acts as a kind of engagement and continues for many years especially on special days until the children grow up. With these marriages it is thought that people at least know their partners. This system is hardly seen anymore.

3. Family elders choose the partners or suggest alternatives but the final decision belongs to the young couple concerned.

4. In instances where approval is not given by elders, usually because of economic reasons, the young couple may decide to elope *(kız kaçırma)* usually with the help of friends or possibly relatives. To the disapproval of parents, the customs of the first night after a wedding is broken as the couple spend it together unmarried. Later, reconciliation between the couple and the respective parents brings about permission and eventual marriage. This avoids potential court cases

and in time results in happiness for the couple, but sadly not always for parents.

5. A less common arrangement is that some couples live together without marrying. This can only be seen in major cities.

Regarding decisions to marry, the girls' side is always passive and has to wait for suitors. In the meantime they only might try to give clues publicly about their availability. For instance, in some regions, pitchers are put on top of their houses' roofs to signify the number of adult girls in the house.

b) *Söz kesme* (Marriage agreement)

In rural areas, where agriculture is dominant, if the daughter of a family gets married and leaves her house it causes loss of work which somehow has to be covered. The custom developed regarding to this loss is the so-called brideprice paid by the groom's family to the bride's, and is called "*başlık*". This custom is losing its popularity even in rural areas nowadays. When the custom of brideprice was active, it was a matter of pride for the girl's family. In cases of economic inadequacy on the part of the boy, the girl's father never objected to elopement in order to protect his pride. Saying to people that their daughter eloped with somebody was accepted as much better rather than willingly accept a brideprice below the public expectation.

After whatever kind of selection, when the boy's side decide to marry him with somebody, the step that has to be taken is a kind of agreement. Elders on the boy's side visit the girl's family with some presents usually during an evening. In the middle of this visit an authoritative person from the family opens the subject by saying "With the order of God and approval of the prophet, we thought of your daughter as

(preceding page) **A GIRL IN HER FOLKLORIC COSTUMES** [63]

an appropriate match for our son" and asks if there is agreement. The answer is always "let's think about it" because it is not polite to say "yes" immediately. In these cases another visit is necessary for the marriage agreement to be settled. Alternatively, if the intended couple know each other and the answer is apparent then the marriage agreement is made by exchanging rings at the time.

After this agreement and depending on opinions variable from region to region, a young couple can meet alone or with company several times. There had been times that couples did not see each other at all. However today, everyone understands that people need to get to know each other before marrying.

c) *Nişan* (The engagement ceremony)

This stage is the main ring exchanging and the expenses are the responsibility of the girl's family. The names of the young couple are written inside each other's ring. There may be a simple meeting of the family members in a house with limited guests or a big ceremony with lots of people from both sides in a hall with music and dancing. Two rings are tied together with red ribbon and brought in on a silver tray. When all visitors are present, the girl and the boy stand together and a respectable person from either family puts the rings on the couple, cuts the ribbon and offers some kind of congratulatory words. From this moment on, the couples are accepted as engaged.

d) Preparation for the wedding

Preparations for marriage come after the engagement ceremony. If the engagement period is long, preparations will be done slowly. All the expenses of the new house will be borne by the families or relatives. For instance the bedroom expenses belong to the girl's side and the living room and other parts belong to the boy's side. The relatives or friends will buy presents which will be useful for the new couple.

Girls, especially in rural places, start from an early age up until they get married preparing lace, needlework, embroidery, etc. to be used in their future married lives. These are the *çeyiz* (trousseau) of the girl.

During the engagement period last preparations for the trousseau are hurriedly finished by helpers. When everything is ready, the collection of the trousseau is taken to the new house in a convoy and the new house is decorated. People are invited to the new house for the display of the trousseau on a special day. The trousseau is very important for a traditional girl, forming the sign of her talent, her feelings and her whole personality. It includes her embroidery and scarves and on the display day they are hung on the walls or stretched on wires from one corner to another.

The first gifts sent to the new house by the girl's family are a copy of the Holy Book, a mirror, a candle, a small bag of rice and wheat and another small bag of sugar each of them symbolizing belief, amplitude, eternity, fertility and sweetness respectively.

e) *Kına gecesi* (The henna night)

A night before the first night, the bride and her friends and relatives gather to tinge the bride's fingers with henna which is sent as a present by the groom's family. This is the last night that is why, symbolically, it has to be sorrowful. Therefore they sing sad songs for a while. But later on the atmosphere becomes cheerful. In general, people eat good food and enjoy themselves in a festive atmosphere.

f) *Düğün* (The wedding)

This is the most serious stage of a marriage. All the expenses of the wedding are of the groom's family.

The wedding dress is generally white. The father of the bride puts a red ribbon on the bride's waist which symbolizes her virginity.

The wedding is performed by the mayor or somebody appointed by him, in the wedding hall of a municipality or in a ceremonial hall. The bride and groom, as individuals, swear vows before two witnesses in presence of the mayor. After they sign, everybody stands up and the mayor declares the couple as husband and wife.

Visitors congratulate the newly married couple and some of them give presents, jewels or cash money on the spot. Families who are not satisfied with civil weddings also hold religious ceremonies by calling the imam to their houses. Celebrations with music take place right after these steps till the new couple go to their room for the first night. Virginity is still important in Turkish society though it is slowly diminishing in big cities. In some rural parts of the country, there are people

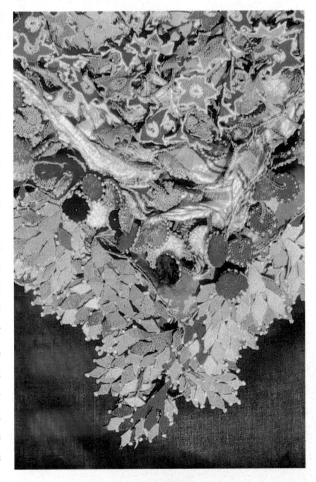

TURKISH HANDMADE OYA (LACE) [64]

189

who expect to see the sheet of the bridal bed with blood proving virginity.

In cases of elopement or the weddings of widows, *düğüns* (wedding ceremonies) are generally not held.

g) After the wedding

Because a honeymoon is completely a matter of time, finance and personal choice, it is not necessarily something which all couples give importance to.

Each of the partners after the wedding has two fathers and two mothers and every effort is made to find ways to sustain this relationship in peace.

In a traditional family, the new bride joins her husband's relatives and lives under the critical surveillance of her new mother-in-law. She is regarded as the lowest-standing member of her husband's family. Unless the bride establishes a close personal relationship with her mother-in-law, friction and tension might occur. In such cases the husband will always be expected to side with his mother against his wife. A woman only begins to gain status and security in her husband's home when she gives birth to sons.

"I had a rose when I bore a son; he became a stranger when he married" is a proverb which sheds light on families' attitude towards their sons.

Women compensate for the lack of emotional warmth in their marriage through the closeness of their relationships with their sons, who often remain in or close to the parents' household. As the traditional family structure disintegrates and as the extended family is fragmented into nuclear family units, the relationships within the family change considerably. A young wife no longer has to cope with her mother-in-law.

(opposite page) **BRIDE AND GROOM IN RURAL LIFE** [65]

BIRTH

The continuity of a family is provided by children. With the development of people's educational levels, the belief in the continuity only being provided by sons is losing its effect.

At the pregnancy of a new bride, an excitement among family members grows. Upon hearing the good news, a golden bracelet comes immediately as a present from the mother-in-law. In rural areas a pregnant woman declares it with some symbols mostly on her clothing; her scarf, motifs on it and suchlike.

For the births, in rural places midwives are present, whereas in big cities hospitals are common. After the birth, the new mother receives presents of gold and the child gets all manner of gifts. The mother is not supposed to go out from her house for 40 days. If she works, she has a holiday of 40 days automatically. Relatives, friends and neighbors are all helpful. In the first three days only close relatives come to visit, but in the following days the others also come to visit with lots of presents. Breast-feeding continues normally until the age of two or even later and then weaning is sudden.

In Anatolia there is a custom of planting trees in the names of newly born children. Chestnut, mulberry and apple trees are planted for girls, poplar or pine trees for boys. Planting trees for boys is a kind of investment for him to be used in his marriage when he grows up.

Naming a child

Turkish names always have meanings. Some of the children's names may derive from the time in which he was born; Bayram (Feast), Şafak (Dawn), Bahar (Spring), Ramazan (the holy month, Ramadan), or the events during the birth; Yağmur (Rain), Tufan (Storm), or express the parents' feeling about the child, if they want him to be the last one; Yeter (Enough), Söngül (Last rose) and sometimes names of elder people in families are chosen as displays of respect.

When a name is selected, it is given by an imam or an elder person in the family by holding the child in the direction of Mecca (*Kıble*) and chanting holy words into his left ear and repeating his name three times into his right ear.

SÜNNET (CIRCUMCISION)

Circumcision is an operation in which the foreskin of the penis is removed. It is a practice of great religious significance among certain religious groups, notably the Jews and the Moslems. Circumcision is known to have been practiced in ancient Egypt even before it was introduced to the Jews as part of God's covenant with Abraham. In Islam, however,

A BOY IN HIS SPECIAL COSTUME BEFORE CIRCUMCISION [66]

the authority for circumcision came not from the Koran but from the example of the Prophet Mohammed. In Islam, whatever the prophet does or says is called **sünnet;** therefore this word stands for circumcision in modern Turkish.

Urologists claim that circumcised males have far fewer urinary tract infections and are less at risk for catching sexually transmitted diseases than are uncircumcised males. On the other side, pediatricians say that the medical risks attendant upon the surgery far outweigh the possible future consequences of foregoing the operation.

As an Islamic country, in Turkey all Moslem boys are circumcised between the ages 2-14 by licensed circumcising surgeons. From the social point of view, the most prominent feature of circumcision is the introduction of a child to his religious society as a new member. This explains the reason for circumcision of people who convert into Moslems as a first step. It is impressed on a boy at a very early age that circumcision is a step for transition to manhood. As long as they are accepted as very important events in people's lives, circumcisions are generally made with big ceremonies in festive atmosphere.

If a family has more than one boy, they wait for an appropriate time to perform it altogether. In this case the younger child might be less than 4. In some rural areas, villagers sometimes share expenses of a circumcision feast like they do with the work. Wealthy people may take poor boys or orphans together with their children for circumcision. Charity organizations make collective ceremonies for poor boys and orphans. Considering school periods of children, circumcisions are held in summer months while the children are on vacation, from June through September at weekends.

Circumcision Ceremony

When a family determines a date for their feast, they invite relatives, friends and neighbors by sending invitation cards in advance. Depending on the economic position of families, feasts might take place in a ceremonial hall or a hotel instead of a house. They prepare a highly decorated room for the boy with a nice bed and many colorful decorative things. Boys should also wear special costumes for this feast; a suit, a cape, a scepter and a special hat with *"Maşallah"*, meaning "God preserve him", written on it.

In the morning of the feast, the children of guests are all taken for a tour around in a big convoy with the boy either on horseback, horse carts, or automobiles. This convoy is also followed by musicians playing the drums and the clarinet.

After they come back, the boy wears a loose long white dress and, is circumcised by the surgeon while somebody holds him. This person who holds is called *kirve,* and has to be somebody close to the boy. In the eastern parts of Anatolia, this is the first contact of a big relationship which will continue for lifetime. He will play an active role in the boy's lifetime and have nearly equal rights with the father in decisions. This is similar to a godfather in Christianity. Although there is no blood relation to his kirve, the boy will not even be allowed to marry his kirve's daughter in order not to have incest because he is considered to have become somebody from the family.

A BOY AFTER CIRCUMCISION *with his presents of gold* [67]

After the circumcision, the boy is in pain and has to be kept busy with music, lots of jokes or some other animation. Presents also are given at this time to help him forget his pains. In the meantime words from the Koran are recited and guests are taken to tables for the feast meal which is a special one laid with different food changing from region to region. After a few days the boy recovers and festivities end.

Today, there is a small group of people who prefer their children to be circumcised in hospitals while they are in hospital after birth, whereby ignoring the traditional side.

DIVORCE

Divorce is not very common. Although many women are not satisfied with their marriages, they do not have the courage to divorce. Therefore they continue their lives for their children's sake or not to suffer from the social pressure it may evoke.

The other reason is economic. If a woman does not work, she does not have many alternatives when divorced. After a certain age, in a country where employment is a problem, it is really a risk to survive.

From the legal point of view, when couples divorce, each of them gets his own belongings without taking the things obtained together into consideration. A new law proposal is waiting to be enacted in parliament. The change will allow the sharing of everything equally.

BAYRAM (HOLIDAYS)

a) Official public holidays

"New Year's Day" (January 1) is a holiday to celebrate the end of the year which has passed and the beginning of a new year. It has nothing to do with Christmas with which it is sometimes confused. This holiday starts in the afternoon of December 31 and continues until the end of January 1. People start sending greeting cards for the coming of the new year from a few weeks before. Some people send greetings by telephone only. Buying small gifts for family and friends is also becoming common. Preparing a variety of foods, social gatherings and having fun by playing the most common New Year's game *tombala* (bingo), listening to music and watching television, as TV channels broadcast their best programs, are among the things enjoyed over this holiday.

Some people prefer traveling, going to resorts to ski or to places of entertainment on   New Year's Eve.

There is another group of people who, under the influence of the Christian Western world, enjoy themselves with Christmas celebrations (Christmas trees and Father Christmas costumes, etc.).

National holidays

From the nationalistic point of view, these are important days because they give people the opportunity to feel and exhibit national unity. On these days all ceremonial activities are carried out by official institutions like schools, state organizations or military forces,

A FESTIVAL IN RURAL TURKEY[68]

and people join these activities. Preparations in schools or military places start from a few weeks before with rehearsals for performances. Students and others who take part in the parades or shows are smartly and colorfully dressed. Ceremonies follow the parades in halls, stadiums or school courtyards. Poems are recited, and speeches are given, followed by fireworks or cannon shots.

April 23 is "**National Independence and Children's Day**". On this date in 1920 the Turkish Grand National Assembly was established in Ankara by Mustafa Kemal. As this was the written record of the transition from a religious community to a nation, this date was accepted as a national holiday. From 1929 onward it was declared as the first Children's Day in the World by Kemal Atatürk, as he acknowledged the importance of children for the futures of nations.

May 19 is "**Atatürk Commemoration, Youth and Sports Day**". On this date in 1919, Mustafa Kemal set foot on Anatolia at the Black Sea port of Samsun which marks the beginning of his organizing the nationalist forces before the Independence War.

August 30 is "**Victory Day**". On this date in 1922, the fifth day of the big attack against the Greeks, the Dumlupınar Battle under the command of Mustafa Kemal was won and determined the result of the Independence War. This big attack ended in İzmir with the defeat of the Greeks on September 9.

October 29 is "**Republic Day**". The Republic of Turkey was proclaimed by the Turkish Grand National Assembly in 1923.

b) Religious holidays

There are two religious holidays or feasts, the first is **Şeker Bayramı** (3 days) which comes immediately after 30 days of fasting in the Ramadan and the second is **Kurban Bayramı** (4 days) which follows 70 days after Şeker Bayramı. In Turkish, **Bayram** is "feast" or "holiday", şeker is "sweets" and **kurban** is a "sacrifice".

The dates of religious holidays come 10 days earlier each year because of the difference between the Lunar Year (354 days) and the Solar Year (365 days). Although not all the people in Anatolia are religious, these religious feasts are very traditional and have become essential. They are taken as seriously as Christmas is in the Christian world. People make lots of preparations in celebration of these feasts like cleaning houses, shopping, buying feast gifts, new clothes, sending greeting cards and so forth.

On the first day of the feast, very early in the morning,

people get up, wash themselves, wear fragrance or cologne and put on their new clothes. The majority of the male population go to mosques for the early morning prayer which is extremely important. School aged children are also taken to mosques by their fathers or older relatives in order to make them acquire the habit of going to prayers. So many people go to mosques that they do not fit inside or even in the courtyard. When this is the case, they take small carpets from home to mosques, put them in the streets near the mosque and join in with the service. The İmams give sermons as this is an opportunity to preach to so many people together. The dominant subject these days is peace, and they always try to encourage brotherhood and general goodwill among all. After prayers in the mosque everybody gives feast greeting to each other by shaking hands. The next stage is at home where feast greetings continue. In the traditional extended fami-

A DRUMMER [69]

lies these greetings do not take too much time as all members are at the same place. But in nuclear families it might take a much longer time. Couples with their children visit their parents or grandparents, give gifts, kiss their hands, and they eat candies or chocolates. Children are pleased as they are given some pocket money in addition to candies.

Another place which should not be missed is a visit to the cemetery where the deceased members of the family are buried and need to be remembered. Flowers are taken and the soil of the grave is watered. Meanwhile family members read from the Koran in the name of the deceased.

The main visiting is over and now it is the time for some shopkeepers to open shops. Children are eager to spend their pocket money in grocery shops or amusement parks. In the following days visits among friends, neighbors and other relatives will continue in festive spirit. For people living far away from their families, feasts are a good reason to come together so lots of people travel distances in order to make this possible.

Kurban Bayramı is the same as Şeker Bayramı except the additional sacrifice as the name of the feast bears.

The sacrificial animal, a ram, a goat or any of the cattle will be made ready to sacrifice and from the first morning onward, at anytime, will be sacrificed by one of the members of the family or somebody who represents him. The meat from the sacrificed animal is divided into three parts; one for the poor, one for the neighbors and relatives and the last is for the family. The sacrificing is generally done in courtyards of houses or if these do not exist then it is conducted in specially arranged public places. People can also make a donation to the same value of a sacrifice to a charity instead of doing it themselves.

DEATH AND BURIAL

Throughout the ages in Anatolia, many different rituals regarding death and burial have been applied. Types of graves have differed. Graves under the floors of houses, wooden rooms, tumuli, chamber-like graves, rock-tombs, sarcophagi, domed or conical tombs (*türbe, kümbet*) and mausoleums are some places where the dead have been laid.

Tumulus

Tumuli are a kind of grave formed by making a very large pile of soil and stones on the chamber of a grave. *Kurgan* in the eastern Turkish language is used for the same kind of graves.

According to the belief of people who used tumuli, the more important the deceased the bigger the tumulus. In Anatolia the tumulus was common among the Phrygians and Lydians. Gordion, the capital of the Phrygians, housed approximately eighty Phrygian graves including the **Midas Tomb** notable as the largest burial tumulus in Anatolia, 53 m / 174 ft in height. In Bintepeler near Sardis, there are hundreds of Lydian royal tumuli.

Rock-Tomb

Rock-tombs are the graves formed by carving rooms in rocks. This type was only seen as early as in the bronze and iron ages because the rocks could only be carved by bronze or iron materials. The living rock is a convenient and freely available material for tomb excavation. Large rock-cut tombs were often made to resemble houses, with doors and details to imitate wooden originals. Many of them have several rooms, just like a house. The work involved in such tomb construction, depending on the rock, would not necessarily be great;

ROCK-CUT TOMBS,
Caunus [70]

structural problems would be small and, if more space were needed, another chamber would be excavated. In the more sumptuous tombs, the facade would be decorated to resemble a house for the living.

In Anatolia, the earliest examples of this kind date back to the Urartian period. The more important the person the higher the tomb was carved and the more ornate the decorations. After the Urartians the rock-tomb was common among the Phrygians, Lydians and Lycians.

In many rock-tombs, the facade is similar to a temple's architecture with pediments and sometimes columns. Pediments of the Hellenistic temples might have come from the triangular decorations of Phrygian rock-carved tombs.

Mausoleum

Among the most magnificent tombs of ancient times was the structure built (c.350 BC) at Halicarnassus (Bodrum) for Mausolus, the ruler of Caria and his spouse, Artemisia. The colonnaded edifice, now almost totally destroyed, was about 50 m / 165 ft high and was surmounted by a truncated pyramid supporting a four-horse chariot. Considered one of the Seven Wonders of the World, the Mausoleum of Halicarnassus is the origin of the word "*mausoleum*", which may be applied to any above ground architectural funerary monument. The Mausoleum of Atatürk in Ankara therefore derives from the Mausoleum of Halicarnassus.

Sarcophagus

A sarcophagus is an ancient coffin (chest and lid) made of wood, terra-cotta, marble, alabaster, or metal and generally ornamented with painting, sculpture, or both. Sarcophagi were usually adorned with vividly colored, elaborately carved reliefs, or friezes, of either continuous scenes or rows of single figures in architectural settings. Sarcophagi are an invaluable record of sculptural style, technique and subject matter, especially with regard to funerary sculpture. The term sarcophagus derives from two ancient Greek words meaning "flesh-eating." This stemmed from the use of coffins lined with a type of stone with caustic properties that was believed to consume a corpse in 40 days during prehistoric ages.

Found in Hellenistic kingdoms, it dates from the 4C BC

SARCOPHAGUS,
Termessus [71]

and remained in use during Roman times. A fine example is the brightly painted Alexander Sarcophagus (4C BC; Museum of Archeology, İstanbul).

Romans preferred cremation to burial until c. 2C AD. The "Roman type" of sarcophagus was carved in high relief, often with representations of garlands, battles and mythological subjects.

On Christian sarcophagi, biblical themes replaced mythological and historical subjects. The continuous narrative of the Roman sarcophagi was supplanted by crowded, superimposed scenes, or niches, separated by small columns and enclosing figures.

Anatolia retains a large number of sarcophagi, because the best material for the construction of sarcophagi was finely grained marble of which several varieties were available locally.

Vessels were ordered direct from the quarry to be finished on site, because many sites still have unfinished sarcophagi. The marble or limestone block would be hollowed out inside at the quarry so as to reduce weight and facilitate transport. But all over Anatolia there are so many unfinished vessels in existence, why? Lack of local craftsmen, a change in personal fortune, or even an actual preference for unfinished designs are all possibilities.

Türbe

A monumental tomb in Islam, in general, is called a *türbe*. It normally has a dome at the top. When there is a conical top it is called a *kümbet*. This came to Anatolia with Seljuk Turks. Ottomans followed the tradition. They are highly decorated from outside like statues. Inside there is only one room, also called symbolic sarcophagus room, which is changeable in plan; round, rectangular, hexagon or octagon. In cases where they are not round, transition from angular main room to either dome or conical top leaves space in the corners. To fill these spaces, pendentives, stalactites or the Turkish triangles are used. Walls are mostly covered with tiles and the coffins are symbolic, empty. People are buried downstairs in the crypt.

Today

Although it is difficult, death is considered to be as a natural part or aspect of life. There are many people who prepare themselves for death by putting necessary amount of money for funerals in their bank accounts, keeping winding sheets ready, or buying land in a cemetery in advance. Dying as martyrs is an honorable thing. In Islam, it is believed that martyrs go directly to heaven.

PEOPLE IN FRONT OF A COFFIN *taking part in a funeral service in the courtyard of a mosque* [72]

When somebody dies, the corpse is laid on a bed in a separate room, the head facing the direction of Mecca, eyelids closed, the big toes are tied to each other and the two arms rest on both sides next to the body. Burial has to take place as soon as possible during the daytime. If somebody dies in the late afternoon, he is buried the next day. The corpse might rest for a period of time in a cool place or a mortuary but only if there are close relatives coming from a far away place.

According to religious belief, if somebody is buried without an ablution, he is not allowed to enter heaven. Therefore, dead people have to be washed by authorized people, and always women by a woman, men by a man. Meanwhile the death is declared from a mosque minaret by a müezzin with some words from the Koran together with his name, funeral time and place. After the ablution the corpse is dressed in a white shroud, put in a wooden coffin covered with a green piece of cloth. A martyr's coffin is covered with the Turkish flag. The coffin is carried to the table outside in the courtyard of a mosque on people's shoulders before prayers. Nobody stands in front of the funeral procession and people in the street stand up and salute the funeral motionless and in silence.

While the coffin rests guarded on the table outside, people perform their regular prayers. From within the mosque, following the prayers, they all come out and line up in front of the coffin to take part in the funeral service under the leadership of the İmam. Women are not allowed to join this service. At the end of the service, the İmam asks people what they thought of the deceased and answers are always positive: "He was good. May God bless him. Mercy be upon his soul, etc." Funeral services are not held for parricides or the stillborn.

Interment

The coffin is carried to the cemetery by a hearse followed by a long convoy. Graves are rectangular in shape and designed to accommodate only one person. The deceased is buried in only the shroud not the coffin. The body is laid on its right shoulder facing the direction of Mecca. The tombstone is on the head's side.

The İmam's prayers signify the end of the burial. The deceased is commemorated on the seventh and fifty-second days of his death with Islamic readings; *mevlit*. Sometimes big funerary meals or halvah are offered to the poor and surrounding people.

OTHER CUSTOMS AND BEHAVIOR

- Bread is the most respected food. It is not thrown away or stepped on. When somebody sees a piece of bread in the street he may pick it up and put it in a corner where it will not be stepped on. If people have spare bread at home it cannot be thrown into the garbage. Bread is sacred and many oaths are taken on bread.

- Turkish people like guests and are very hospitable. In Turkey you are never just another tourist but a guest, who deserves great consideration and will be welcomed in the best possible manner even in the smallest village. They are even ready to offer food which they cannot afford for themselves.

- Before entering a Turkish house it is customary for people to take off their shoes and leave them by the door. Inside houses, the floors are covered with carpets. Slippers for the guests are kept somewhere by the door and offered to the guests before their entrance to houses. Presents received by visitors are usually not opened in the presence of people who gave them.

- There is a good deal of formality which developed during the Ottoman period. For example, when people go to visit others at their home they have a fixed conversation although it serves no purpose. Each of the older and respected people is asked the same questions by the younger and the host: "How are you?, How are things going?, How about the children?, How is business going?"

- As an extension of hospitality, guests are often offered a splash of cologne to refresh their faces and hands in homes, shops, or public buses on long journeys.

- Men might kiss each other on the cheeks together with

shaking hands when they meet. They may walk arm in arm or they may even put their hands on each other's shoulders while walking in the street. This should not be mistaken as signs of homosexuality, particularly by Western visitors.

♦ Pointing your fingers at somebody, pointing at something with a foot, blowing your nose or cutting nails in public especially in restaurants, kissing or embracing the opposite sex in public are regarded as bad manners.

♦ While accompanying somebody from the family on the start of a journey, the moment the person leaves, it is customary to pour water on the ground from something like a bucket. This is based on the belief that his journey is going to be as swift as the water's.

♦ Before visiting a mosque shoes should be left at the door. In religious places like mosques, tombs or cemeteries, it is always better to dress "decently". Scarves for women and trousers instead of shorts for men are necessary. Walking in front of or taking photographs of worshippers is not considered polite or correct.

A FEW PROVERBS

Oral tradition continues with proverbs. When considering daily life, proverbs embody the deepest feelings and beliefs of the Turkish people. They reveal a nation's character in its finest details.

Following is a selection of some proverbs from among thousands:

♦ If God wants to make a poor man happy he first makes him lose his donkey and then allows him to find it again.

♦ He who handles honey has the chance to lick his fingers.

♦ When a bald man dies, everybody remembers "what golden

hair he had"; when a blind man dies, they say "what beautiful eyes he had".

◆ Two tightrope walkers cannot perform on the same tightrope.

◆ A vinegar seller with a smiling face makes more money than a honey seller with a sour face.

◆ The hunter is sometimes hunted.

◆ Stretch your legs to the length of your blanket. (Know your limits)

◆ Water priority to the youngsters, talking priority to the elders.

◆ You reap whatever you sow.

◆ A pen is sharper than a sword.

◆ A tree is bent while yet it is young.

◆ There is nothing more expensive than what is bought cheaply and there is nothing cheaper than what is bought expensively.

NEIGHBORLY DUTIES

In many places except neighborhoods of big apartment blocks, people live with good neighborly relations. Some selections from these unwritten duties of neighbors are as follows:

◆ Visiting a new neighbor to welcome them and ask if they need anything.

◆ Introducing them to other neighbors and shopkeepers in the neighborhood.

◆ Helping them in extraordinary instances and situations.

◆ Offering them samples from specially prepared food. In these cases the plates are never returned empty. They are kept till the gesture is returned with a portion of the new neighbor's specially prepared food.

MERCANTILE HABITS

There are still some habits which are common among the small businessmen and craftsmen such as:

- Opening new shops on Fridays,
- Sacrificing an animal, usually a ram, at the opening and delivering its meat to the poor,
- Throwing the first money that comes from the first sale in the morning

(siftah) on the floor and then touching it on the beard with an expectation that it will multiply as plentifully as the number of hairs in the beard,

- No sale on credit is done before the first sale,
- Having the belief that the customer is always right.

(top) MEN SMOKING WATERPIPE IN A TRADITIONAL COFFEE HOUSE, *18C, İstanbul* [73]

(bottom) MARKET PLACE [74]

TRADITIONAL COMMUNICATION
IN RURAL PLACES

In rural areas, communication is original and fitting to the social system. All the rules of the communication system of urban life also exist in rural life. The main feature of communication in villages is oral and it is done face to face.

In cities, invitation to ceremonies or feasts (wedding, circumcision, etc.) is done by cards. In villages, invitations are oral and carried by messengers. All the elements except the means are the same: There is to be a ceremony and people are to be invited. A messenger goes to the households of the invited and offers them a small package of a few candies. Meanwhile they are orally invited to the ceremony. The receiver accepts the candies if, conditions willing, they agree to be present. However, if the invited person refuses then they do not get the candies. As it is seen everything is obvious and clear in the process. By counting the remaining candy packages it is easy to know the number of the participants.

Because communication is mostly by word of mouth, there are sometimes difficulties of proof within such processes of communication. For example, a rich man may send a courier to his house in order to fetch some belongings. The problem is how can people in the house be sure that the courier is telling the truth. To cover this hesitation the rich man gives the courier one of his typical personal belongings (prayer beads, scarf, lighter, handkerchief, etc.) as proof. When this rich man's wife recognizes the proof, she immediately sends whatever her husband has requested with the courier. If no proof is shown, communication will be disconnected and the errand is not completed.

In village life, although many people are literate, writing is not frequently used. There must be a special reason for villagers to write, otherwise it is not used. For instance, writing letters to their sons in the army or in a foreign country, is one of these special reasons. Letters written by sons from far away places are addressed to all the members of the whole community, being relatively small and closed places. When a letter arrives, it is read in public and people of the community get the sections which are related to them. One consequence of this is that senders might not be able to address their wives directly, therefore they use indirect and somewhat hidden methods when addressing their private contacts. Somebody who is married to the daughter of the headman will send his regards to his wife like so: "..regards to the daughter of the headman."

In places where loudspeakers do not exist, announcements are made through imams in mosques or by town criers.

Naturally, people tend to create their own rules and practical systems, where modern means of communication do not exist.

SOME SUPERSTITIOUS BELIEFS AND BEHAVIOR

• If somebody's clothes need repairing with stitches, this should not be done while they are being worn, because this will bring bad luck.

• Kissing people in the eyes brings separation. When a child is kissed in the nape, he is believed to become a liar. When he is kissed on the lips, he starts speaking late.

• When somebody jumps over a child, he is destined to remain short. Should anybody do so, he has to jump back again in the opposite direction to "undo" the superstition.

• If two people's heads butt each other, they have to repeat the butt, otherwise they will become bald.

- People cutting their nails at night-time will have shorter lives.
- Doing housework during the Friday noon time prayers brings bad luck.
- When somebody hears ringing in his ears, it means that he is being thought of by someone.
- A baby's crawling predicts visitors.
- He who sees a standing stork for the first time in the new season is believed to travel a lot.
- The howling of a dog is a kind of announcement of somebody's death.
- The handing of scissors or a knife brings argument between two people.
- Having an itching palm is the sign of some amount of money to come.
- It is generally believed that children or beautiful people are vulnerable to evil eyes either because of jealousy or over affection. Therefore people, when they fondle children, prefer using negative adjectives for them. Sprinkling or taking salt as a present provides protection against the so-called evil eye. Another protection system is attaching an eye with Maşallah (God preserve him) written on it on children's clothes or things to be protected against any kind of evil eyes. This eye, (*nazar boncuğu*) is made of a blue bead as blue has a very effective impact, and acts as a charm to ward off evil influences from others.

Yağmur Duası (Public prayer for rain)

In the traditional agriculture communities, natural powers play very important roles on agriculturists because fertility depends on climatic conditions. From a villager's point of view, God is the owner of nature and gives rain whenever

He wants while sometimes He creates aridity to punish people. Therefore, not having the facilities of modern technology, people have to somehow ask for water from God. When this demand is formalized by a group through religious leaders as a ritual, it is called a public prayer for rain.

Upon continuous and severe aridity, people unite and decide to pray to God on a determined date for rain. The decision is declared to the public in the mosque by the imam. The next step is the collecting of seven thousand pebbles and saying prayers on each of them which takes a few days. Each household makes a financial contribution of a certain amount according to their income levels for the purchase of animals to be sacrificed. No bargaining should be done.

NAZAR BONCUKLARI, *Evil Eyes* [75]

The day of the prayer starts early in the morning with the participation of all villagers on a long walk after the morning prayer. People who do not participate are looked down on. The destination of the walk is to a high hill to be closer to God and the imam leads the group. Together with the sacrificial animals, necessary things are carried to cook rice and pounded wheat in big pots. On the way prayers are said and the first children of families with pebbles are drenched in the river. Before noon, at an appropriate place, animals are sacrificed and the preparation of the food starts.

In the meantime the group continues the long walk. When they arrive at the highest place, they pray together loudly in a begging tone. Then they come back palms facing the ground as if miming the rain and eat their meal. Suddenly, right after the meal, they start to give the impression that rain is about to come and they have to hurry to go back. This is the end of the prayer.

Prayers for rain show that people look for solutions in praying to God when they are beaten by nature and they are the result of strong needs.

Small things like pebbles or drenching the children are similar to imitation principles in primitive life magic.

The İmam is the leader and he adds a religious element to the activity. The headman and the teacher are also leaders, but they just contribute to the size of the group. Children are taken to be culturally trained. The most important role of the public prayer from the social and cultural point of view is the solidarity shown against any kind of danger.

As Turkey develops, belief in these rituals is almost extinct today.

FOLK HEROES

Nasreddin Hoca (1208-1285 AD)

He is a folk hero of the Seljuk period who was born in Sivrihisar and lived in Akşehir. He received religious education first from his father who was an imam and later at a theological school. He also worked as an imam for a period of time.

Hoca's view of the world and his opinions on the essential or even metaphysical questions of life are frank, natural and often disarmingly candid. Straightforward common sense is one of the secrets of his oriental wisdom and solace.

As a philosophic humorist he became the symbol of people's creativity and sense of humor of his time. His witticisms have become popular sayings and are quoted in everyday conversations. These can be regarded as anonymous folk jokes. Here are some examples:

Who are you going to believe?

One day a friend wants to borrow Hoca's donkey. Hoca does not want to lend it and tells him that his donkey is not there.

In the meantime the donkey starts to bray. The man says: "But Hoca, I can hear the donkey! It's in the stable." Hoca stays cool and answers with dignity: "Who are you going to believe, me or the donkey?"

In the shop

Hoca goes to the market to buy some trousers. After trying on a few pairs he chooses some trousers and tells the salesman to wrap them. Right after they are wrapped he changes his mind and wants the salesman to give him a shirt instead. He takes the packaged shirt and walks off. The salesman calls him:

"-Sir, you haven't paid for the shirt yet." To which Hoca replies,

"-But I left you the trousers."

"-You didn't pay for the trousers either!", exclaims the salesman.

"-Of course not! Why should I pay for trousers that I didn't get." concludes Hoca.

NASREDDİN HOCA [76]

None of your business

A man gossips to Hoca:

"-Hoca, I saw them taking a big plate of stuffed turkey."

"-It's none of my business, replies Hoca."

"-But I think they were taking it to your house."

"-Then, it's none of your business!" says Hoca.

Question

A neighbor asks Hoca: "Why do you always answer a question with another question?" He replies: "Do I?"

Karagöz and Hacivat

KARAGÖZ
AND HACİVAT [77]

These are the two folk heroes of Karagöz shadow-puppet theater. The language they use, the way they look at life and the class they represent are never the same. With these clashes and also a wide range of folk characters, they play out a rich social and political satire.

Legend has it that these two types were construction laborers who worked on the building of the Ulucami in Bursa. They spent most of their time clowning around and stirring up trouble by keeping the other workers from working. The sultan, who was upset with the delay of the construction of Ulucami, had them executed. People felt sorry for them and have continued to remember their jokes. It is from these that the Karagöz theater derives.

For the production of Karagöz figures, dried camel and calf skin are used because of their translucent quality. Hides are treated, shaped and painted. The puppets are colorful and semitransparent with jointed limbs. The performances are back projections of shadows on curtains.

The Karagöz shadow-puppet plays have enjoyed great popularity for many years. With the emergence of technologically advanced visual entertainment means such as cinema, television and video, Karagöz has become a museum exhibit today.

Yunus Emre (c.1238-1320 AD)

This is an Anatolian folk poet and mystic who transcended his period. He played an important role in the shaping of Anatolian poetry, the Turkish language and above all, the Turkish language as a poetic medium.

He introduced mystical philosophy originating in Neo-Platonism into the Turkish intellectual environment.

He established a bridge connecting earlier Anatolian cultures with the present. The concepts of "earth", "fire", "wind" and "water" which appeared in his poetry are integral elements of "Being" to be found in earlier Anatolian philosophy. The same concepts were put forward by philosophers of Anatolia centuries ago; water, for example, by Thales, wind by Anaximenes and fire by Heraclitus.

Yunus Emre was a poet whose thought was based on love, whose faith on longing and whose actions on knowledge.

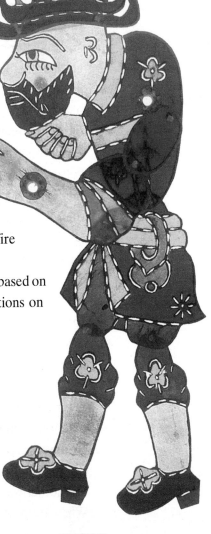

Mythology

Anatolian mythology is a rich mixture from different cultures and histories. There were always many civilizations in Anatolia throughout prehistoric and historic ages. With migrations, battles and commercial transactions, Anatolia has influenced and been influenced by other civilizations. Most of the 12 major deities came from Anatolian origins. Zeus is the most prominent deity in mythology. He is clearly of Indo-European origin and is a celestial deity related to and symbolized by the sky and is a phenomena of the sky. He is the thunderbolt, a god of lightning, a god of rain. He is a father ruler, a sovereign figure and controller.

In Homer, Zeus is a reigning god who sits on a throne at the top of Mount Olympus. He is attended by his council of deities: Hera, Apollo, Poseidon, Artemis and Athena. Each of these has his or her own dwelling on Olympus. The palace and walls were built by Hephaestus.

Poseidon is the creator of thunder but more often the wild horse. In the time of Homer he was called earth-shaker and this name may be related to the sound of horses' hooves. Several stories tell of Poseidon's mating with goddesses in the form of mares.

Dionysus is probably Phrygian in origin as the god and his cult were widely spread. The myth of his birth suggests that his mother was Semele and that he was fathered by Zeus. When Hera, Zeus's wife, learned of Zeus's infidelity and the approaching birth, she disguised herself as Semele's nurse and convinced Semele to demand that Zeus reveal himself in the totality of his godliness to her. Zeus appeared to Semele in the fullness of his thunder and lightning. The appearance struck Semele dead, but just before her death Zeus snatched Dionysus from her womb, cut open his thigh and placed the child therein. Nine months later Dionysus was born from the thigh of Zeus. Dionysus was the so-called "twice-born" from the womb of Semele and the thigh of Zeus.

Dionysus's appearances always seemed to be accompanied by some violent activity that presented a threat to conventional order. As the center of an orgiastic mystical cult, he tended to break the bonds of social life.

Apollo stands in contrast to Dionysus. Whereas Dionysus oriented his devotees to wild orgiastic rites, Apollo was the god of moderation and represented the legal or statutory meaning of religion. Apollo was foremost a god of law in being the source of law. In his role as provider of law, Apollo is to be referred to as the precedents for the gods and laws of the city.

Apollo, like Dionysus, was related to the oracle of Delphi and his devotees there were enthusiastic and ecstatically possessed. W. K. C. Guthrie, in The Greeks and Their Gods, suggests that Apollo originated in Siberia and that the ecstatic powers attached to his cult were derived from the tribal shamanism of that area rather than from the Dionysian cult at Delphi.

Aphrodite (Venus)

She was the beautiful and voluptuous goddess of love.

Aphrodite is variously described as being the daughter of Zeus and Dione and as having been born from the foam of

APHRODITE,
*Museum of Archeology,
Antalya* [77-A]

the sea. She had many lovers, among them Adonis and the war-god Ares, but she was the wife of the smith-god Hephaestus, who was both ugly and lame.

One important myth in which Aphrodite plays a major role is the so-called beauty contest under the judgment of Paris.

Apollo

APOLLO,
Museum of Archeology, Istanbul [77-B]

Apollo and his twin sister, Artemis, were the children of Zeus and Leto. He was also identified closely with Delphi where he killed the serpent Python and founded the most renowned center for prophecy in the ancient world, the shrine of the Delphic Oracle. Areas of special concern to Apollo were prophecy, medicine, the fine arts, archery, beauty, flocks and herds, law, courage and wisdom. Associated with him were the tripod, omphalos, lyre, bow and arrows, laurel wreath, palm tree, wolf, hawk, crow and fawn.

Of Apollo's many loves, one of the best known was Daphne, who fled his embraces and was turned into his tree, the laurel. From that time on, Apollo wore a laurel wreath. Laurel wreaths became the prize awarded in athletic and musical competitions.

In Roman mythology, Apollo represented the literary and fine arts, culture and the law. The walls of his temple at Delphi bore two maxims in Greek, "Know Thyself" and "Nothing in Excess."

Ares (Mars)

Ares, the son of Zeus and brother of Eris, was the god of war. Although he was not greatly admired among the Olympian gods, he was loved by Aphrodite, by whom he became the father of several children. In Homer's Iliad, Ares is depicted as a warrior god who exults in bloodshed and violence. Called variously the avenger, the slayer and the curse, Ares used a spear as his emblem. The vulture and the dog were sacred to him.

In the Trojan War, he favored the Trojans.

Artemis (Diana)

Artemis was goddess of the hunt, the mistress of wild things and the protectress of youth and women. In contrast to the voluptuous Aphrodite, Artemis was associated with chaste love; she is usually depicted as lean and athletic and is frequently accompanied by a deer. She was the twin sister of Apollo and the daughter of Zeus and Leto.

In her role as protectress of women, Artemis was often called upon to ensure a painless and swift death and women who died in such a manner were said to have been slain by one of her silver arrows.

ARTEMIS, *Museum of Archeology, İstanbul* 77-C

Athena (Minerva)

She was born fully armed and from the forehead of the chief god, Zeus. Athena was her father's favorite child. He entrusted her both with the Aegis, his breastplate and with his terrible thunderbolt.

Athena's role as a goddess was varied. On the one hand, she was a major warrior figure and most images depict her dressed in armor and holding a spear. In the Iliad, Homer describes her as a fierce battle goddess. On the other hand she took an interest in handicrafts and agriculture and the olive tree, which she is said to have created, was sacred to her.

She was also noted for her wisdom and good sense; this explains her close association with the owl, an ancient symbol of wisdom and reason.

ATHENA, *Museum of Archeology, Antalya* 77-D

DIONYSUS,
Museum of Archeology,
İstanbul 77-E

Dionysus (Bacchus)

He was the god of fertility, ritual dance and mysticism. He also supposedly invented wine making and was considered the patron of poetry, song and drama.

Among the 12 gods on Mount Olympus, he was depicted as a handsome young man often carried in a leopard-drawn chariot. Dressed in fawn skin shirt and holding drinking cup and *thyrsus* (staff), he was typically accompanied by deer and attended by Pan, Satyrs and Maenads.

The Dionysian festivities were often orgiastic; worshippers were sometimes overcome with ecstasy and enthusiasm or religious fervor. The central feature of his worship was called *sparagmos*: the tearing apart of a live animal, the eating of its flesh and the drinking of its blood; participants believed they were in fact partaking of the god's body and blood. Plays were also staged at these festivals.

Hera (Juno)

She was the queen of the Olympian gods. She was worshipped as the goddess of marriage, women and childbirth; her sacred emblems were the apple, pomegranate and peacock. Hera's marriage to Zeus, King of the gods, was troubled by his many infidelities.

In the Trojan War, Hera favored the Achaeans because the Trojan Prince Paris slighted her by naming Aphrodite the most beautiful of the goddesses.

Heracles (Hercules)

He was famous for his courage and strength. The many feats of Heracles are customarily divided into the 12 labors and other exploits. Some of the 12 labors, which were performed for the King Eurystheus as a result of Hera's enmity, were:

killing the Nemean lion; capturing the Cretan bull; capturing the man-eating mares of Diomedes and obtaining the girdle of Hippolyte, Queen of the Amazons.

His other exploits included erecting the Pillars of Hercules with the aid of his father, Zeus and tricking Atlas into holding the world on his shoulders again. He also inaugurated the Olympian Games, in honor of Zeus and won every event in the first Olympics.

Hermes (Mercury)

Hermes was the god of merchants and commerce, of science and astronomy, of thieves, travelers and vagabonds and of cleverness and eloquence. The messenger of the gods, he was represented in art as a young man with winged hat, sandals, herald's staff, a ram, a lyre and a shepherd's staff.

Because his interests were broad and always changing, Hermes was one of the most loved of the Olympian gods.

HERACLES RELIEF, *the Hercules Gate, 2C AD, Ephesus* [78]

Hestia (Vesta)

Hestia was the goddess of the hearth. Her name meant hearth. She remained forever a virgin, refusing marriage both with Poseidon and with Apollo. Of all the gods, Hestia alone never took sides in disputes of any sort and never participated in wars. She was the protector of suppliants, representing the security and hospitality of the home. She was the patroness of the family. In Rome, where she was identified with Vesta, her priestesses were called vestal virgins.

HERMES RELIEF,
Domitian Square,
Ephesus [79]

MARSYAS,
Museum of Archeology,
Antalya [79-A]

Marsyas

He was a Phrygian Satyr. When Athena abandoned the double flute because playing it distorted her face, Marsyas took it up and became famous for his beautiful music. He challenged Apollo to a musical contest, on the terms that the winner could do what he wished with the loser. At first both played equally well, but Apollo then challenged Marsyas to play his instrument upside down; this could be done on Apollo's instrument, the lyre, but not on the flute, so the Muses, who were judges, awarded the contest to Apollo. He hanged Marsyas from a pine tree and flayed him. Marsyas's blood, or the tears of his friends, is said to have formed the River Marsyas. In another version, the judge was Midas, who declared Marsyas the winner; Apollo punished Midas by giving him the ears of an ass. Marsyas was a popular subject of Roman art; his statue stood in the Forum.

Medusa

Medusa was the only mortal of the three Gorgons, daughters of the sea god and his sister-wife Ceto. Originally very beautiful women, they were transformed into ugly monsters, with serpents for hair, claws of bronze and staring eyes capable of turning anyone who looked at them into stone. The hero Perseus killed Medusa by cutting off her head and the winged horse Pegasus sprang from the blood that spurted from her neck. Perseus used Medusa's head to petrify Atlas (hence the Atlas mountains) and a few personal enemies, but he later gave the head to Athena, who put it in the center of her shield.

Nemesis

Nemesis is personification of divine justice and the vengeance of the gods, sometimes called the daughter of the Night goddess. She represented the righteous anger of the gods against the proud and haughty and against breakers of the law; she distributed good or bad fortune to all mortals. No one could escape her power.

NIKE,
Museum of Archeology,
İstanbul 79-B

Nike (Victoria)

Nike was the goddess of victory, who presided over all military and athletic contests. She was primarily an abstraction rather than a mythological figure but achieved great popularity. She was represented in art as winged and standing on a globe, holding laurel and a palm branch.

Poseidon (Neptune)

Poseidon was the god of the sea and of earthquakes. He has been portrayed as a violent and powerful god who was involved in many battles. His chief weapon was the trident, a three-pronged spear and he was closely associated with bulls, horses and dolphins.

Priapus

Priapus was the son of Aphrodite and Dionysus. Portrayed as a grotesque little man with a huge phallus, he was associated particularly with fertility rites and also protected crops and gardens from animals, birds and thieves.

POSEIDON,
Museum of Archeology,
İstanbul 79-C

PRIAPUS,
Ephesus Museum,
Selçuk 79-D

Prometheus

Prometheus "Forethought" was the Titan who stole fire from the gods and gave it to humans, along with all human arts and civilization.

Zeus had Prometheus chained to a rock on Mount Caucasus, where an eagle ate away at his liver, starting afresh each day after the liver had grown back during the night. One source has Prometheus eventually freed by Hercules and brought to Olympus to join the gods he had defied.

Satyrs

Satyrs were immortal creatures of the forest and hills and symbols of nature's wealth. The satyrs were attendants of Dionysus. They had the head, arms and torso of a man and the horns, ears and hind legs of a goat.

Satyrs loved to frolic, drink, chase nymphs and play reed instruments.

TYCHE,
Museum of Archeology,
İstanbul 79-E

Sirens

The Sirens sang melodies so beautiful that sailors passing their rocky island were lured to shipwreck and death.

Triton

Triton was a gigantic sea god, part man and part fish who raised rocks from the sea and created islands with his trident and he blew on a trumpet made from a conch shell.

Tyche (Fortuna)

The goddess of luck, fortune and chance, had the power to lift up lowly mortals and cast down the mighty. Her Roman counterpart was Fortuna and her symbols in art were a ship's rudder and a cornucopia.

Architecture

ANCIENT CITIES

Cities did not become possible until people were able to produce more than they consumed and had found ways of storing the surplus. It was necessary to learn how to store and preserve food for large numbers of people living close together and away from the fields.

The earliest cities were inhabited by officials and priests, who administered empires and invoked the gods. The lower classes of draftsmen, artisans and laborers lived around them in the city. The inhabitants were supported by the labors of those living outside the city who worked on the land.

In Anatolia, people built walls around their towns when they wanted to defend themselves against outside dangers. Hittites, for instance, built 6 km-long walls around their capital, Boğazköy.

There was the extra demand for kings' security which resulted in separate inner defense walls for kings. Defense walls of palaces continued in Anatolia for thousands of years. In the Aegean civilizations especially in Ionia, an "acropolis" served the same purpose. In Roman, Byzantine and Ottoman periods palaces were defended separately with extra defense systems.

In the Hellenistic period, the typical city-state was built on an elevated place called an acropolis and surrounded by fortifications. Since it depended on the hinterland for supplies, the city had to be strong enough to dominate and defend this area against enemies. Therefore, from its walled safety the city sent out soldiers, who kept order in the hinterland and defended it from roving marauders and incursions by other city-states. In this period each city belonged to a certain god. The god saved the city and it was his sanctuary.

In former years people built their houses randomly according to their requirements. However as cities became bigger, new priorities and considerations emerged. A consciousness of functional urbanism started with Anatolian city planner Hippodamus[37] in the 6C BC. The first reaction to Anatolian functional urbanism of Hippodamus came from Pergamum in the form of ornamental urbanism. This reaction appreciated that functionalism was necessary, but that aesthetics were not to be neglected.

The trading function has been important for cities throughout history. Cities grew at the intersections of land trade routes and at harbors or at the mouths of rivers with easy access to the sea.

Slavery[38]

Slaves were, in fact, almost always of a different ethnic group, race, religion, or political unit than their owners; early custom frowned on enslaving members of an individual's own tribe or kind. The earliest slaves were probably war captives, although debt slaves also existed in ancient Egypt, where a person could sell himself or his wife and children into bondage to liquidate debts.

In one important respect the code of the Hittites, in effect in Anatolia from 1800-1400 BC, was more humane; it conceded that a slave was a human being, although of an inferior order.

[37] See Hippodamus on page 394

[38] Grolier *Electronic Publishing, Inc., 1992*

In ancient Persia slave breeding became a major source of supply in addition to slave acquisition through conquest. Persian victories in the Aegean islands of Chios and Lesbos resulted in the enslavement of entire populations.

The poems of Homer supply evidence that slavery was an integral part of ancient society, possibly as early as 1200 BC. Philosophers questioned slavery as an institution but did not condemn enslavement. Aristotle considered slaves as mere tools, lucky to have the guidance of their masters. Wars, piracy and debt were the main sources of slavery. In slave markets of ancient cities, a thousand slaves might change hands in an afternoon. After a major battle as many as 20,000 captives might go on the block.

Agricultural slaves and state-owned slaves serving in road gangs were sometimes inhumanly treated, but mine slaves were even worse off. Bound in chains, they were forced to work in appalling underground conditions and were brutally flogged. Household slaves, artisan-slaves, slaves in minor official positions and public slaves who served the temples seem to have been treated with greater tolerance. Laws protected them from excessive abuse, but they were nonetheless chattels, without rights in courts of law.

The semi-legendary Aesop, teller of fables, is alleged to have been a freed slave of the 6C BC.

In Roman times, wars yielded enormous numbers of slaves and produced a slave population eclipsing any in earlier history. By the 1C BC a kind of agricultural slavery known as estate slavery had developed. Under this system great gangs of slaves labored on wealthy estates, having no contact at all with their owners. Plutarch notes that on a single day in the year 167 BC, 150,000 slaves were sold in a single market. Syria, Galatia, North Africa and Gaul were the most productive regions in satisfying the needs of the vast slave system. Owners had virtually unrestricted power and treatment was truly barbaric. Such conditions, combined with the numerical superiority of slaves over free men, inevitably led to large-scale revolts, such as that fomented by the Thracian slave Spartacus, who in 73 BC escaped to Sicily and formed an army of 40,000. More-merciful treatment of slaves prevailed during the reign of Claudius, at the beginning of the Christian era. Slaves of that period often fared better than poverty-stricken free Romans and some slaves rose to occupy fairly important positions in government. Their great numerical preponderance, which diluted the mass strength of the free population, is presumed to have contributed eventually to the downfall of the Roman Empire.

City walls

If walls were primarily to defend, in the Hellenistic and Roman worlds, they clearly had a secondary function. This was to impress the visitor as much as the monuments contained within them. This suggestion is supported when one observes the extreme care with which many of the walls in Turkey have been constructed. Building beautiful walls was therefore a fashion and one especially noticeable in the Hellenistic period. This is not to say that overt decoration - friezes, reliefs, statues or even inscriptions - were common, but simply that some walls (especially from the Hellenistic period) are in themselves works of art, because their stones had been precisely and beautifully cut.[39]

[39] Greenhalgh Michael, *Turkey: Classical Architecture & Sculpture*, Australian National University

Acropolis

The word acropolis which in ancient Greek means "uppermost city" refers to the highest and most defensible part of an ancient city. Every important settlement had an acropolis, on which were placed temples, treasuries and other important civic buildings. In times of attack the acropolis became the last bastion of defense. As democracy became more dominant the prominence of an acropolis made way for the use of an agora.

Agora

In ancient cities, an agora was a public area where people gathered for political, commercial and social reasons. They were usually located in the middle of the city or near a harbor. Generally square in shape, they were always surrounded by a colonnade of single or double ranges of columns. In early times public assemblies were held in the agora. Later it functioned primarily as the center of commercial life in the city; markets were held there and it was the site of all kinds of transactions. In later times the agora also became a religious center and contained temples, altars, commemorative statues and sometimes even the tombs of important personages. The porticoes were often decorated with murals. The Roman forum in the following period was essentially an adaptation of the agora.

Forum

The word forum, a Latin word meaning "open space" or "market place," refers to the open space in any Roman town or city where business, judicial, municipal affairs and even, at times, religious activities were conducted. In many ways a forum was like an agora, except that in a forum the space was more clearly defined, with buildings set closely together, often aligned on predetermined axes.

A typical forum was surrounded by market buildings,

temples and basilicas (spacious, roofed structures for conducting business or legal proceedings). In planned towns that had begun as military camps, the forum lay often at the meeting point of the principal north-south street, the *cardo* and the principal east-west street, the *decumanus*. The Roman architect Vitruvius (46-30 BC) suggested in his architectural treatise that a forum should be large enough to contain a crowd but not so large as to dwarf it and that its proportions be 3:2 (length to width).

Stoa

In the public areas of ancient cities, as in the agora, there often stood a portico (a sheltered walkway) along the walls of the more important buildings. This type of promenade, which probably evolved from extended eaves supported on posts, was called a stoa. It also became the symbol of the agora. Eventually, stoas became quite elaborate, with interior colonnades and sometimes even a second story.

A stoa would form a shelter against hot sun, wind and rain. Stoas were also used for different purposes; a place for commerce, courts, philosophical arguments or as entertainment places.

Stoas and Streets

There are differences between a stoa and a street. The stoa was occasionally used in multiples to form a kind of basilica. Although it could be and frequently was used on its own, it tended to be employed on one or more sides of a square. The colonnaded street, on the other hand, could curve sharply or smoothly from side to side, or elegantly descend a hill, as does the Curetes Street at Ephesus. A colonnade could be interrupted by cross-roads or fountains, could employ ornamental motifs and appear much more festive than anything seen in the staid stoa, while still serving as a shady walkway in front of shops similarly to the stoa. With increased preference for the colonnaded street the stoa form itself became outdated. The Romans replaced it with the **basilica**, again a more flexible format offering far broader possibilities for extravagant decoration, including statues in niches and on pedestals as well as the use of fountains.

Sculptural decoration

An effective addition to street "appeal" was provided by the increased prominence given in the Roman period to sculptural decoration, sometimes in bas-relief, but often in three dimensions and in life-size or greater. Statues might decorate a colonnade, as mentioned above or they would be set within an even more impressive architectural framework, which could be extensive and multi-storied. The figures depicted might be gods or goddesses, mythological figures, kings, emperors, or prominent local heroes or citizens.

Terracing

If the colonnade was one way of articulating streets, terracing was another. On many sites this could not be avoided in order to profit from the natural contours of the land.

Bouleterion

This was one of the important major buildings in an ancient city. It was the Senate House which was used by the *boule,* the advisory council of the city. It has always been very difficult to identify bouleterion buildings as they did not have typical characteristics.

COLUMN PIECE WITH A
RELIEF DEPICTING A
BOWL AND SNAKES,
Asclepieum, Pergamum [80]

Prytaneion

What characterized a Prytaneion building as different from a Bouleterion was an eternal flame or the sacred hearth of Hestia in the Prytaneion which is kept burning eternally. From an architectural standpoint it was like a private house. It contained administrative rooms, the state archives and a large dining hall in which officials, foreign visitors, and for example winners of races were welcomed.

Aqueduct

An aqueduct is a structure built to carry water from a source to a distant destination. Its name comes from the Latin *aqua* "water" and *ducere* "to lead". The aqueducts of ancient times usually only required the force of gravity to move the water.

The earliest known aqueducts are from the 7C BC belonging to Assyrians. The most extensive ancient aqueduct system was that built by the city of Rome. Pipes made of stone, clay, lead, or wood channeled the water underground and many of them employed the siphon principle used in modern conduits.

Fountain

Fountains, which are channels or spouts through which water is directed under pressure for decorative or cooling effects, have been an important feature of cities, gardens and private houses throughout history. The earliest fountains were natural springs. The ancient Hellenistic custom of regarding springs as sacred sources of life was perpetuated by the Romans, who devised the nymphaeum, a structure enclosing a pool. Fountains decorated the villas and gardens of wealthy Romans, but also served a practical function in cities as sources of public water supply.

Bath

The custom of bathing dates from prehistoric ages. In early times, bathing was important not only for cleanliness but also as a social activity and a religious ritual. Public baths achieved their most elaborate form during the Roman Empire.

Bathrooms were incorporated into the palaces and urban houses of many ancient civilizations. In the Hittite capital of Hattusha (c.1400 BC), houses contained paved washroom areas with clay tubs, some with built-in seats.

OMPHALOS BOWL, *8C BC, Phrygian period, Museum of Anatolian Civilizations, Ankara* [81]

From the 3 BC on, wealthy Romans included elaborate baths in their town houses and country villas. These usually consisted of a dressing room, separate rooms for damp and dry heat and warm and cold tubs: Frigidarium, Tepidarium and Caldarium. The whole building was heated by a hypocaust-a furnace with flues that channeled hot air through the walls and under the floors. The furnace also heated the boiler that supplied hot water. Reservoirs were supplied by aqueducts.

During the Roman Empire, in order to prevent the consumption of forests to heat baths, there were some written laws stating, "whoever cuts down a tree for the purpose of a bath has to plant another".

According to Roman architect Vitruvius, it was necessary to build the entrances of the baths facing south towards the sun to prevent loss of heat.

The public baths (hamam) was of special importance in the Ottoman Empire. The Moslem bathhouse, as an extension of the Roman baths, included a dressing room, cold bath and warm bath clustered around a domed, central steam chamber. All areas were heated by a furnace with a system of flues, similar to the Roman hypocaust. The hamam survived and has developed into the Turkish bath of today.

The *hamam tası* (bowl) used in the Turkish hamam is not something new. The same style of bowl was met in the relief with snakes on the column at the entrance to the Asclepieum, Pergamum or as *phyales* in the Phrygian civilization. In some ancient texts, it was also called *omphalos* which meant navel. In Anatolia, navel has been the symbol of the mother goddess.

The Turkish Hamam Experience

In a Turkish hamam there are either two separate sections for each of the sexes or different days and hours allocated to men and women.

When you enter the first section or the changing area of a hamam you begin by taking off your clothes and putting on a peştemal, which is a piece of striped cotton cloth. This is wrapped around the midriff and tucked into place. Some people choose to wear their bathing suits underneath. A kind of wooden clog called nalın are worn on the feet.

Dressed with peştemal and clogs, you go to the next room where a göbek taşı (navel stone), a marble heated table, is situated in the middle surrounded by marble sinks and taps. Here, you sit next to one of these sinks and start pouring lukewarm water over yourself with a hamam tası (bowl). You keep pouring water until your skin softens, meanwhile increasing the temperature of the water as your body gets used to it.

CAĞALOĞLU HAMAMI,
İstanbul [82]

The hamam attendant, tellak, will take you to the göbek taşı when your skin is ready and start rubbing your body with a special glove, kese. Tiny black pieces will get rubbed off your body which most people think is dirt. This is in fact the top layer of dead skin. At this stage a massage is optional. Next, the tellak will give you a soapy rub down and wash you with water in decreasing temperature in order to make your pores close.

Now it is time to go back to the changing area to lie down and drink tea in the traditional tiny glasses.

Gymnasium

The word derives from the Gr. word *gymnos* meaning "naked". Gymnasium literally means a place where exercises are practiced by naked athletes. In Hellenistic and Roman times the imposing structures of gymnasiums were found in every important city. In addition to apparatus designed for physical exercise, the ancient gymnasium usually included baths, porticoes and dressing chambers. They were often adorned with works of art and became meeting places for philosophers, lectures and social events.

The **Palaestra** was an important section of a gymnasium in which wrestling was practiced and taught. It derives from the Gr. word *palaistra* and means "to wrestle" hence, school or place of wrestling (in a gymnasium). Gods of gymnasiums were generally Hermes and Heracles.

Theater

Theater originated in the cultures of primitive societies, whose members used imitative dances to ease the supernatural powers that were believed to control events crucial to their survival. A shaman, priest, or medicine man taught complicated dance steps and led these ritual dance-dramas

to persuade or compel supernatural forces to regulate the seasons and elements, to ensure the Earth's fertility and to grant the tribe success in hunting and warfare. Other ritual dances were believed to expel evil spirits that caused disease and to force the souls of the newly dead to depart from the world of the living. The priests and performers in these dance-dramas wore *masks*, which sometimes represented the spirits invoked and costumes made of skins, rushes and bark.

A later development, more relevant to the evolution of the theater and drama of today, was the enactment of legends of gods and tribal heroes. Similar dramas were also performed in early civilized societies.

The Hellenistic Theater

It is generally assumed that the ancient Hellenistic theater grew out of religious rituals that were probably performed in a roughly circular space.

The first Theater of Dionysus was built by constructing a dancing circle, or orchestra, at the base of a hillside, thus forming a natural theater. The seating area, which surrounded the orchestra on three sides held the audience.

At first the main performers were the chorus, but the increasing prominence of the individual actor led to modifications in the performing area that took place over a period of several hundred years. With tragedies a stage house or *skene* was required and these were placed at the rear of the orchestra, opposite the audience. In addition to its functions as dressing room, storage area and architectural background, it concealed the actors, who entered the stage through its three doors. A raised stage called the proskene was added to the front of the skene and gradually encroached on the orchestra until, by the 2C BC, the orchestra was little more than a semicircle.

The Roman Theater

Roman theater dates back to as early as the 2C BC. The *auditorium*, or *cavea*, of a typical Roman theater was a semicircle around a smaller semicircular *orchestra*. It does not necessarily rest on a hillside. In cases where it is built without any hillside, it is usually built over barrel-vaulted substructures. The orchestra was often used for additional seating or sometimes flooded for aquatic spectacles. The stage, between 6-12 m / 20-40 ft deep and as much as 60 m / 200 ft long, was backed by an elaborate facade often three stories high. The scene facade had between three and five doors and numerous niches, statues, frescoes and pediments. The stage was often roofed and an awning could be stretched across the cavea to shelter the audience.

Ancient Drama[40]

The history of theater begins with annual festivals held in honor of the god Dionysus. It appears that the poet Thespis developed a new musical form in which he impersonated a

[40] Grolier *Electronic publishing, Inc., 1993*

single character and engaged a chorus of singer-dancers in dialogue. As the first composer and soloist in this new form, which came to be known as tragedy, Thespis can be considered both the first dramatist and the first actor. He soon had imitators and in 534 BC a contest in tragedy was instituted at a festival held in honor of Dionysus, the god of wine, fertility and revelry. This soon became an annual event at festivals throughout the Hellenic world.

All of the roles were played by men, as women were not allowed to perform in Hellenistic theater. The early playwrights not only wrote and frequently acted in their plays but also served as directors, choreographers and some may also have composed their own music. By the 4C BC the playwright no longer controlled all aspects of production.

Roman drama consciously imitated Hellenistic forms. The religious motivation for the drama, however, had long ago diminished and Roman drama entered further into the realm of commercial entertainment. The foremost writer of Roman comedy, is Plautus.

The Romans staged their productions on a raised stage before an elaborately decorated stage building and reduced the orchestra, as well as the auditorium, to a semicircle. They rarely set their theaters into hillsides but built freestanding structures that could be covered by huge awnings and are reputed to have seated as many as 40,000 spectators.

Roman tragedy, which very early veered toward bombast, spectacle and violence to please the masses, was an art that began to rot before it bloomed.

As Christianity took root in Rome, opposition to the theater grew, but the church never succeeded in killing off the Roman theater. This was accomplished later by invaders in the 6C AD.

Odeon

Small theater buildings of the Roman period for musical performances, lectures or small shows were called odeons. They were usually covered with roofs or awnings and generally had the same plan as the Roman theaters.

Stadium

A stadium is a structure specifically designed for sporting contests and other spectacular events. The history of the stadium is directly connected to the history of the Olympic Games, perhaps the oldest organized sports event. The name comes from the Latinized ancient Greek word *stade*, a unit of measurement equivalent to about 185 m / 606.95 ft, which was the length of the footrace in the ancient Olympics and the overall length of the ancient *stadia*.

Hippodrome

Gr. *hipp-* horse + *dromos*, racecourse. Hippodromes were places built for chariot races. These were wider than the horseshoe-shaped stadia used for athletic contests and could accommodate several chariots pulled by four-horse teams. Chariot races appear to have become part of many athletic competitions as early as the 7C BC.

The Romans built another type of stadium, called an *amphitheater*. It is made of two words, *amphi*, "around, both sides" and *theatron*, "theater" hence, a kind of elliptical or circular stadium used for gladiator fights, uneven encounters between Christians and hungry beasts and the various other savageries the Romans called games. The size of the arena or the playing area, was not standardized in the amphitheaters and was less important than providing an unobstructed view from each of the seats. It is important to note that theaters and amphitheaters were never the same.

Gladiators

In the Roman period, gladiators were chosen from among prisoners of war, criminals, slaves, or volunteer freed men as professional combatants for public entertainment at festival games.

Although some gladiators fought against wild animals, the combats generally featured a pair of human contenders. The gladiators fought in various styles, depending on their background and training. Unless the audience or emperor indicated that he should be spared, a defeated gladiator usually lost his life. Increasingly elaborate, the imperial games sometimes exhibited thousands of pairs of gladiators in a series lasting several months; some private individuals sponsored fights with as many as 100 pairs. Despite their condemnation by many observers, the gladiatorial contests survived until the early 5C AD.

Camel wrestling

As a possible extension of the Roman period animal fights, today there are many annual camel wrestling festivals especially in the Aegean region. These festivals are held in winter, from December through March. A few weeks in advance they are announced to the public and hundreds of wrestler camels are brought to the place from great distances. On the day of the fight and particularly in the morning, they are dressed in very beautiful and colorful decorative cloths.

Wrestler camels belong to a special breed called tülü. They are only bred to wrestle and never used for other purposes. Camels are put in pairs. In order to excite the camels, an attractive female camel is paraded out of reach of the suitors. Two excited camels meet and within a few minutes start wrestling with each other. They start foaming at their mouths. Kneeling, rolling to the ground or running away from the arena are causes of defeat. There is a team of referees with different responsibilities during wrestling. There is also a team of ropers who are supposed to separate tangled camels when necessary.

The wrestling continues all day long and the owners of winners collect cash prizes.

House

The houses in the early towns of the world like Çatalhöyük, Hacılar or Çayönü, were all made of mud bricks. Their plans were simple and they consisted of small rooms with hearths and sitting benches. In 3000 BC, especially in Western Anatolia, houses were long and rectangular in shape. This type of a house was called a *"megaron"* consisting of two small rooms with a hearth in one room. The megaron was dominant in Anatolia for many centuries. Surprisingly, the architecture of temples was influenced by megaron houses.

Temple

Temple architecture in general can be divided into three categories: the open-air sanctuary; the cave or rock-cut temple (a secret place of worship); and the house for the deity or cult object, also called the freestanding temple. Synagogues, churches and mosques are not considered to be temples.

The oldest (c.6000-5650 BC) artificial temples extant are those discovered at Çatalhöyük. Constructed of mud brick on a timber framework, these cave-like enclosures have plas-

tered walls covered with paintings and molded sculpture dedicated to a Mother Goddess cult.

Hittite temples have central courtyards open to the sky, entrances on the axis, pillared halls on at least one side and
subsidiary rooms. The cult chamber is usually located off-
axis. Typical examples (c.1400-1250 BC) can be found at
Boğazköy. Doric and Ionic temples of the archaic period
(600-480 BC) display tendencies toward larger scale, more
harmonious proportions and greater use of marble and decorative sculpture. A Hellenistic temple was something like a
house of god. This was a conclusion of a mentality that imagined gods in human form. A temple was not a mass worship-

CAMEL WRESTLING, [84]
(bottom left) [85]
(bottom right) [86]

ping place. They took place in open-air sanctuaries. The architectural form of temples derived from Anatolian megaron type houses. The revolutionary development was the surrounding columns.

During the Hellenistic period the Ionic order prospered, the Corinthian order became more popular and the Doric order declined. Among the huge Ionic temples that were erected during the 4C BC in Anatolia, particularly striking examples are the Temple of Artemis (rebuilt 4C BC) at Ephesus, the Temple of Apollo (4C BC) at Didyma and the Temple of Artemis (4C BC) at Sardis. All of these buildings are noteworthy for their complicated interiors. Sardis has a double *cella* and Didyma a temple within a temple.

The altar was much more accommodating to decoration and a fine place for display because it was the focal point of ceremonies. Every temple possessed at least one. It was located outside in the open air, usually completely separate from the temple and therefore entirely visible. Since a temple was the house of the deity and not a gathering place for a congregation, any yearnings for theatricality might therefore have best been satisfied by concentrating on the altar.

It was common to have cult statues and altars without a temple to house them. At Ephesus, for example, an altar and statue base were found in situ in the East Baths, suggesting that the emperor cult was practiced there.

Basilica

Originally in Roman architecture, a basilica was a large, oblong building used particularly as a court of law and a place of public assembly.

In Early Christian times, the function of the basilica became exclusively religious and the plan was often varied by transepts, or side wings, frequently with domes over the resultant crossing. Main entrances were at one end of the rectangle, but it also had a doorway in the center of each long wall. An inner, rectangular colonnade supported the roof, but the center may have been open to the sky (in later basilicas these colonnades were reorganized to form aisles). At the end, opposite the main doors was a rectangular tribunal, two stories high, with a subsidiary room on either side. Although the ends of basilicas could be rectangular or semicircular (forming an apse) and could include the side rooms or not, the scheme remained basically constant in Roman practice.

The form of the basilica lent itself to public assembly for religious rites and was widely used for synagogues as in Sardis, 2C AD. When early Christian congregations grew too large to meet in houses, they adopted the basilican form for their own use. Although variations were many, the hall remained long and rectangular. If it was extremely wide, it might be divided by colonnades or arches into three or more aisles, the center aisle, or nave, remaining the most important. In many basilicas the ceiling of the nave was raised by placing a wall pierced with windows. The hall might be beam-roofed, vaulted, or domed. An altar took the place of the Roman tribunal. The rooms on either side could be used for the sacraments, books and vestments in the Byzantine church.

BASILICA
(1)narthex, (2)nave, (3)aisles, (4)altar, (5)apse, (6)transept [87]

ICONOGRAPHY

Iconography (from Gr. eikon, "image" and graphia, "writing") is the study of the subject matter, or content, of works of art, as opposed to their style. The content of a painting or a sculpture can convey the artist's meaning in several ways. In general, works depicting only real persons, places and objects—that is, portraits, landscapes and the like—may be said to have only one level of meaning, the surface or primary level. A secondary level of meaning is added when a work contains an imagined person or a fictional or mythological scene or when the artist attempts to render some abstract concept in concrete terms. Because these secondary levels of meaning cannot be explained in words in a painting or a sculpture, the artist must use a type of sign language—a visual shorthand, drawing on conventions and formulas that the observer will recognize.

The function of iconography is to recognize and explain images of this kind and to search for the origins of personages and scenes.

A symbol, however, is an object or figure that by itself represents something else, often an abstract idea.

The earliest recorded images were those associated with the rites of ancient religions, especially those in which the deity had a human form. To propitiate or petition the gods, worshippers offered sacrifices to statues in temples; the statue was thought to contain the actual presence of the deity and the temple was considered to be his "house." This was developed significantly by the great poet Homer who organized the ancient gods into a kind of family or pantheon and gave each one an individual personality and specific physical characteristics. Following Homer's lead, the classical artists endowed each god with recognizable attributes: Zeus was sometimes accompanied by an eagle, the bird sacred to him; Poseidon, who ruled the sea, carried a trident; Artemis, the huntress, had a bow and a quiver; and so on.

Arches, columns, altars and public buildings were decorated with sculpture commemorating the triumphs of Roman generals and patrician families basked in the reflected glory of the images of the ancient gods and heroes from whom they claimed descent. Statues of the later emperors, who regarded themselves as gods, often depicted the rulers with the appropriate divine attributes. Along with symbols and attributes, allegory was well understood by the Romans.

> The Romans used art to magnify the glory of their own accomplishments.

Early Christian Iconography

The symbols and attributes used by the Romans contrasted sharply to the few, simple images used by the early Christians, who had to be circumspect in the face of religious persecution. On sacramental cups, seals and lamps the Holy Spirit was symbolized by a dove and Christ by a fish (perhaps because at the time fish was one of the elements of the sacred meal)[41] or by a shepherd carrying a sheep on his shoulders. The Savior was also represented by a monogram formed by combining the ancient Greek letters chi and rho (XP), the first two letters of the Greek word for Christ.

Byzantine Iconography

When Christianity became the official religion of the Ro-

[41] See the comment for fish in Geyikli Kilise on page 489

man Empire, its imagery began to reflect borrowings from the emperor's court at Constantinople. Christ was no longer depicted as a youthful shepherd, but as an enthroned emperor and judge with a dignified beard. The Virgin Mary appeared crowned and robed like the empress and saints dressed like courtiers approached the throne of God with veiled hands, as was the custom in the courts of Eastern monarchs.

The repertoire of symbolic subjects included scenes from the New Testament reflecting the annual cycle of the principal festivals of the Church. Subjects from the Old Testament, which earlier had served as examples of God's power to save—the Hebrews in the fiery furnace, Noah and the Flood—now reflected the belief that, as part of God's plan, certain episodes in the Old Testament prefigured events in the New Testament. Jonah, who formerly symbolized the idea of salvation, now became the type—the original model—of Christ, whose death and resurrection was seemingly foreshadowed by Jonah's miraculous encounter with the great fish.

PAINTING

Roman Painting

The Romans decorated their villas with mosaic floors and exquisite wall frescoes portraying rituals, myths, landscapes, still-life and scenes of daily activities. Using the technique known as aerial perspective, in which colors and outlines of more distant objects are softened and blurred to achieve spatial effects, Roman artists created the illusion of reality.

Early Christian and Byzantine Painting

Surviving Early Christian painting dates from the 3-4C and

consists of fresco paintings and mosaics on the walls of churches. Certain stylization and artistic conventions are characteristic of these representations of the New Testament events. For example, Christ was shown as the Good Shepherd, a figural type adopted from representations of god Hermes; the resurrection was symbolized by depiction of the Old Testament story of Jonah, who was delivered from the fish.

The otherworldly presentation became characteristic of Byzantine art and the style came to be associated with the imperial Christian court of Constantinople, which survived from 330 AD until 1453. The Byzantine style is also seen on icons, conventionalized paintings on wooden panels of Christ, the Virgin, or the saints, made for veneration.

A BYZANTINE ICON OF THE ANNUNCIATION, *Antalya Museum* [88]

FRESCO PAINTING

Fresco (an Italian word meaning "fresh") is a technique of durable wall painting used extensively for murals. Fresco, a fresh wet layer of plaster is applied to a prepared wall surface and painted with pigments mixed with water. The pigments soak into the plaster, which, when dry, forms a permanent chemical bond fusing paint and wall surface. Another type of fresco, painting on a dry surface with adhesive binder flakes, is not permanent. Because all fresco is susceptible to humidity and weathering, its use is limited.

SCULPTURE

Two ancient sculpture techniques are carving and modeling. Carving is a direct subtractive process and carved sculptures were fashioned from such durable materials as stone, ivory and wood. Modeling is a direct additive process in which a pliable material is built up around an armature or skeletal framework.

Sculpture may be created in two or three dimensions; relief sculpture and the round. Depending on how far the figures emerge from the background plane, relief may be of varying degrees; low (bas-relief), middle, or high.

Small fertility figures or mother goddesses modeled in terracotta found in Çatalhöyük (5500 BC) and Hacılar are among the earliest examples of sculpture in Anatolia.

Archaic Period (7-6C BC)

Monumental sculpture in limestone and marble appeared during the archaic period. The first statues were influenced by Egyptian sculpture, which in the 7C BC already had a long tradition. Egyptian sculpture, however, showed little stylistic change over the centuries. Sculptors used the prototype of a standing figure with one foot advanced and the hands clenched to the sides and developed it so that within a hundred years the same general type was no longer stylized but had become a naturalistic rendering with subtle modeling. This type of figure is usually called a kouros (Gr. "boy") and is pictured in the nude. The female equivalent, or kore, is always dressed in rich drapery enhanced by incision and color. Color was also used for the hair and facial features of both male and female statues. The figures do not seem to represent a divinity, nor are they usually portraits, but they are images of the ideal masculine or feminine form instead.

Classical Period (5-4C BC)

Especially in the earliest phase, sculpture was carved in a severe (or formal) classical style. The male body became a broad-shouldered, trim-hipped athlete, often shown in arrested motion. The female figures were still severely draped; the earlier archaic smiles were sometimes softened in expression.

Hellenistic Period (4-2C BC)

After the death of Alexander the Great, his extensive empire was dissolved into many different kingdoms. This fragmentation was symbolic of the diversity and multiplicity of artistic tendencies in the Hellenistic period. The great centers of art were in the islands and in the cities of the eastern Mediterranean—Alexandria, Antioch and Pergamum.

The Hellenistic period was a period of eclecticism. Art still served a religious function or to glorify athletes, but sculpture and painting were also used to decorate the homes of the rich. There was an interest in heroic portraits and in colossal groups, but also in humbler subjects. The human being was portrayed in every stage and walk of life; there was even an interest in caricature.

The awareness of space that characterized architecture also began to emerge in sculpture and painting. As a result landscapes and interiors appeared for the first time in both reliefs and painted panels. The great Altar of Zeus from Pergamum (c.180 BC), created by artists for King Eumenes II, was enclosed by a high podium decorated with a monumental frieze of the battle between the gods and giants. Many Hellenistic tendencies were realized in this work. The basis for its iconography was firmly rooted in classical tradition. The baroque style of the sculpture was characteristic of the time in its exaggeration of movement, physical pain and emotion, all set against a background of swirling draperies.

Early Christian and Byzantine Sculpture

After the shift of the empire's administrative center (AD 330) from Rome to Constantinople, official interest in monumental sculpture declined. Large sculptures in the round were viewed as idolatrous by the early Christians.

High relief work continued to be carved on the sides of sarcophagi, modified so that figures from pagan mythology either disappeared or were adapted as Christian images and symbols.

MOSAICS

Mosaic is the art of embedding small pieces of cut stone or pigmented glass in a plaster bed to serve as floor or wall decoration. Mosaic reached its greatest heights in Early Christian and Byzantine art and architecture. The earliest mosaics found in Anatolia date back to Phrygian period; palace ruins in Gordion.

Solidity, resistance to moisture, durability and color-fastness made mosaic a practical form of architectural decoration. The process of constructing a mosaic begins with cubes of cut stone, pigmented glass, or gold or silver leaf sandwiched by glass. These cubes are known as *tesserae*.

The sophisticated mosaics evolved from the practice of gathering pebbles from the beach and setting them in a cement bed to provide durable flooring in homes and temples. At first randomly scattered and set, the pebbles later were arranged in simple ornamental patterns.

Although pebble mosaics continued to be used as simple and inexpensive floor covering, they were largely displaced in the Hellenistic era by tessellated mosaics of cut stone, colored glass paste and occasionally of mother-of-pearl, shells and terra-cotta. Once freed from dependency on the random shapes, sizes and colors of beach pebbles, Hellenistic mosaicists executed works of great splendor, intricacy and scale.

Mosaic pavements became (3C BC) the fashion in the homes and villas of the wealthy throughout the Mediterranean area. Hellenistic examples served as models for Roman mosaics until the 1C AD, when changing aesthetic tastes and economic factors brought about the temporary displacement of polychrome pictorial mosaics by a black-and-white mosaic style. Beginning on a small scale in private homes, where black figures and decorative motifs were silhouetted against a field of white marble or limestone, this style soon carpeted the floors of public baths, marketplaces and other areas of public assembly. Because it withstood the effects of humidity and moisture and because the tesserae were color-fast, mosaic was often used to decorate garden walls, fountains and baths in the ancient world.

Mosaic as a form of wall decoration achieved its greatest expression in Early Christian and Byzantine art.

In Constantinople, the center of Byzantine civilization, relatively few schemes of mosaic decoration are preserved be-

cause of natural loss and the destruction wrought by icono-
clasts and the Crusaders.

ISLAMIC ART

The Islamic style is distinguished by the novelty and extraordinary quality of techniques used in the making of utili-
tarian objects. These techniques include the application of
lustrous glazes and rich colors in ceramics and glassware;
intricate silver inlays that transform the surfaces of bronze
metalwork; lavish molded stucco and carved wood wall panels; and endlessly varied motifs woven into textiles and rugs.
In nearly all instances the objects decorated—whether ew-
ers, cooking cauldrons, candlesticks, or pen cases—served
fundamentally practical purposes; their aesthetic effect was
aimed above all at making the daily activities or architectural setting more pleasurable.

In the Moslem world a concrete message is transmitted
through its abstract forms. The Moslems tended to reject
the representation of the visible in their art to emphasize
that visible reality is but an illusion and that Allah alone is
true. Abstraction thus became a way to make a very specific
theological point.

Another characteristic of Islamic art is its rejection of the
representation of religious images and other living beings.
Islamic art modified the art of previous centuries by tending
to avoid the representation of humans and animals.

A strong, centralized state, the Ottoman Empire concentrated its creative energies on the development of a uniquely
logical mosque architecture. As early as the 14C and 15C, in
Bursa and İznik, the Ottomans chose to use the single dome
as the focal compositional element of their monuments. This
fascination with the cupola was in large part inspired by the

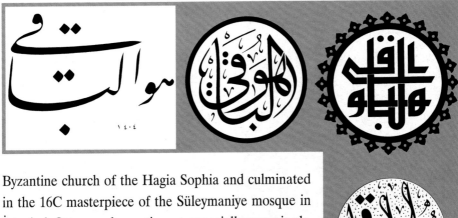

Byzantine church of the Hagia Sophia and culminated in the 16C masterpiece of the Süleymaniye mosque in İstanbul. Ottoman decorative art, especially ceramic objects and tiles and miniature painting are largely derivative of other traditions, although many examples are noteworthy for the exceptional precision of their execution.

CALLIGRAPHY

Calligraphy (from Gr. meaning "beautiful writing") is the art of fine handwriting. The term may refer to letters, words, pages, or even whole documents to which aesthetic principles and skilled penmanship have been applied.

In Islamic culture, calligraphic writing is accomplished by using a broad-edged reed, quill, or nib pen held at a slant.

In a country where Islam is practiced, calligraphy is of great importance since depictions of humans and animals are not allowed. The copying of the Koran is considered a religious act and Islamic calligraphy is much esteemed because of its religious associations. Major styles of script are *Kufi*, a formal style with an angular character, *Sülüs*, a cursive flowing script written with rounded letters, *Divani*, generally used for writing the decrees, and *Talik*. These scripts are also classified in themselves according to the places that they are used or their sizes.

(from top left to bottom)

TALİK SCRIPT *written in Arabic meaning "Only He is everlasting" by Muhittin Serin* [89]

SÜLÜS SCRIPT *written in Arabic meaning "Only He is everlasting" by Mehmet Aziz* [90]

KUFİ SCRIPT *written in Arabic meaning "Only He is everlasting" by Emin Barın* [91]

DİVANİ SCRIPT *written in Arabic meaning "Only He is everlasting" by Ali Alparslan* [92]

ÇİNİ (CERAMIC TILES)
of İznik [93]

MINIATURE PAINTING

Painting of pictures on a small scale. The word miniature is derived from minium, the name of a red oxide of lead used for the decoration of sacred texts. The techniques developed in this art of illuminating manuscripts were later applied to the creation of many small portraits, known as miniatures. Miniature painters generally work in a microscopically minute technique, using thin, pointed brushes on such varied surfaces as the backs of playing cards, stretched chicken skin, vellum, metal and ivory.

Miniature painting was highly developed among Ottoman Turks who produced delicate, stylized examples.

(ÇİNİ) CERAMIC TILES OF İZNİK

İznik (Nicaea) was the largest tile production center during the Ottoman period. The İznik tiles were different to Seljuk tiles in color and quality.

According to the records of 17C traveler Evliya Çelebi, there were 340 ateliers of tiles in İznik when he visited there. When an Ottoman sultan wanted to build a new building, he sent a message to the governor of İznik. All the work was distributed to the ateliers. Tiles used for interior decorations were 24x24 cm / 9.45x9.45 in and 2-3 cm / 0.7x1.2 in thick. In the beginning of the 16C, motifs on tiles had blue, dark blue and yellow colors on white background. In the second half of the century more motifs were used and color combination becomes more complex. The certain shade of coral which was first seen in the middle of 16C suddenly disappeared in 17C which can only be explained with the death of its master.

EBRU (PAPER MARBLING)

Ebru is a traditional Turkish art. Although the origins are unknown, it is likely that it came to Anatolia from Central Asia. Natural dyes mixed with ox gall are sprinkled with brushes made of horse tails on the surface of water in a deep ebru tray. The oily dyes are designed on the surface of water. After the design is ready, tray-size papers are left on the tray to absorb all the dyes as they are, with their formed shape.

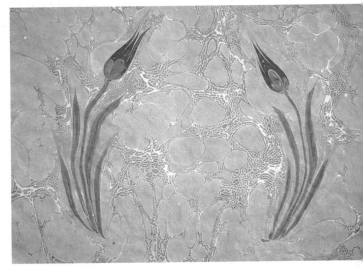

EBRU *by Sabri Mandıracı, 1995* [94]

Ebru is an abstract art in which a considerable amount of randomness is involved. The artist's control is decidedly limited as he cannot determine the precise shape, size or position of each droplet of color. What he does is to try to apply his colors according to the "mood" of the ebru tray as he perceives it. The colors then float and expand depending on the condition of the liquid and the tray, the ambient temperature, the humidity and the amount of dust in the air. The ebru tray has just as much to say as the artist, or more, in the kind of ebru that is going to emerge.

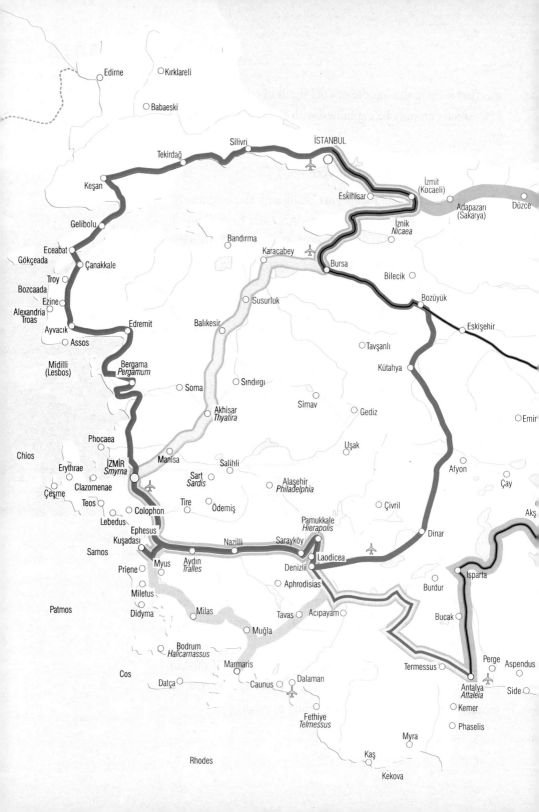

Sinop

İnebolu

Boyabat

Safranbolu
Kastamonu

ak
Karabük

Merzifon

Ilgaz

Mengen
Yeniçağa
Gerede

Çankırı
Çorum

Kırıkkale
Delice
Hattusha

eypazarı

ANKARA

Yozgat

ion Polatlı

isar

Boğazlıyan

Kırşehir

Kulu

Hacıbektaş

Avanos
Venessa

Cihanbeyli
Kayseri

Nevşehir
Göreme

Sultanhan
Aksaray
Derinkuyu

Ilgın

Niğde

Konya
Karapınar

Beyşehir
Çatalhöyük
Ulukışla

Ereğli

Karaman

Adana

Mersin
(İçel)
Tarsus

Alanya
Mut

Karataş

Silifke

Anamur

Most common routes in Western and Central Anatolia

A

İstanbul **2-3** Çanakkale, Ayvalık **1** İzmir **1** Kuşadası **1-2** Pamukkale **1** Antalya **2-3** Konya **1** Cappadocia **2** Ankara **1** Bursa **1** İstanbul **1**

B

İstanbul **2-3** Çanakkale, Ayvalık **1** İzmir **1** Kuşadası **1-2** Pamukkale **1** Bursa **1-2** İstanbul **1**

C

İstanbul **2-3** Bursa **1-2** İzmir **1** Kuşadası **1** Pamukkale **1** Antalya **2-3**

D

İstanbul **2-3** Bursa **1-2** Ankara **1** Cappadocia **2** Antalya **2-3**

E

İstanbul **2-3** Bursa **1-2** İzmir **1** Kuşadası **1** Marmaris **1-2** Pamukkale **1** Antalya **2-3**

F

İstanbul **2-3** Bursa **1-2** İzmir **1** Kuşadası **1** Pamukkale **1** Antalya **2-3** Cappadocia **2** Ankara **1** Abant **1** İstanbul **1**

● Possible numbers of overnights

Bulgaria

Black Sea

Edirne ○   ○ Kırklareli

○ Babaeski

Ergene N.

Greece

Silivri ○   İSTANBUL

Tekirdağ ○

Metis N.   Keşan ○   *Marmara Sea*

İzmit (Kocaeli)

Eskihisar ○   ○ Topçular   *Sapanca G.*   Adapazarı (Sakarya)   Düzce ○

Gelibolu ○

İznik *Nicaea*
İznik G.

Bandırma ○   Karacabey   Bursa

Eceabat ○   *Biga Ç.*   *Gönen Ç.*   Uluabat G.   Bilecik ○   *Sakarya N.*

Gökçeada

Çanakkale ○   Uludağ (Olympus)   Bozüyük ○

Bozcaada   Troy
○ Ezine   *Susurluk Ç.*   Susurluk ○

Alexandria Troas   Ayvacık ○   *Kaz Dağı (Mount Ida)*   Edremit ○   Balıkesir ○   Eskişehir ○   *Porsuk Ç.*

○ Assos   *Simav Ç.*

Midilli (Lesbos)   Bergama *Pergamum* ○   Tavşanlı ○

Bakırçay   Soma ○   Kütahya ○

Sındırgı ○   Simav ○   Gediz ○   Emir ○

Aegean Sea   Akhisar *Thyatira* ○

Phocaea ○   *Gediz N.*   Uşak ○

Chios   Erythrae ○   İZMİR *Smyrna*   Manisa ○   Salihli ○   Afyon ○

Çeşme ○   Clazomenae ○   Sart *Sardis* ○   Alaşehir *Philadelphia* ○   Çay ○

Teos ○   Tire ○   Ödemiş ○   Çivril ○   Akş
Lebedus ○   Colophon ○

THE MARMARA REGION

İSTANBUL

Although it is not the capital, İstanbul is the largest city in Turkey as the leading industrial, commercial and cultural center. Population of the city is estimated to be more than 10 million.

The city is situated on both sides of the Bosphorus, the strait that separates Europe from Asia. İstanbul Province is bounded in the north by the Black Sea, in the east by Kocaeli (İzmit) Province, in the south and southwest by the Marmara Sea and in the west by Tekirdağ Province. Located in a large agricultural region, İstanbul Province produces cotton, fruit, olive oil, silk and tobacco. The city is the chief seaport and commercial and financial center of Turkey. A large share of the trade of Turkey passes through İstanbul. Industries in İstanbul include shipbuilding, liquor distilling and the manufacture of cement, cigarettes, foodstuffs, glass, leather products and pottery. The city is an important rail center, with several international lines terminating on the European side and a railroad beginning on the Asian side.

The oldest institution of higher education in the city is İstanbul University (1453); other major universities are İstanbul Technical University (1773), Marmara University

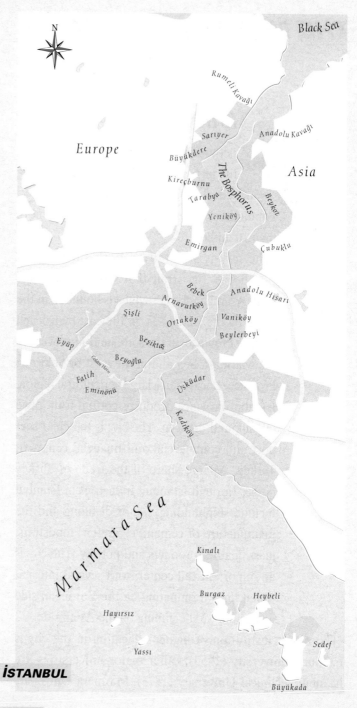

Black Sea

N

Europe

Rumeli Kavağı

Sarıyer   Anadolu Kavağı

Büyükdere

Kireçburnu   The Bosphorus   Asia

Tarabya   Beykoz

Yeniköy

Emirgan   Çubuklu

Bebek   Anadolu Hisarı

Arnavutköy

Şişli   Ortaköy   Vaniköy

Beşiktaş   Beylerbeyi

Eyüp   Beyoğlu

Golden Horn

Fatih   Üsküdar

Eminönü

Kadıköy

Marmara Sea

Kınalı

Burgaz   Heybeli

Hayırsız

Sedef

Yassı

Büyükada

İSTANBUL

OLD CITY, *İstanbul*[95]

(1883), Yıldız University (1911) and the Bosphorus University, formerly the American College in İstanbul (1863), in which English is still the language of instruction.

İstanbul is the headquarters of the Ecumenical Patriarch of the Greek Orthodox church and the archdiocese of the Patriarch of the Armenians in Turkey; the city has 157 Christian churches. İstanbul also hosts 2,000 mosques, 17 synagogues and 10 monasteries.[42]

History

According to Strabo, İstanbul is thought to have been founded by the colonists from Megara led by Byzas in the 7C BC. The popular legend has it that Megarians, before coming here, went to the oracle in Delphi and asked his instruction about the place to found their settlement. The answer was "opposite the city of the blind". When they came to the peninsula of the old city, after seeing an earlier settlement in the Asian side, they concluded that these people must be blind not to see such a beautiful place here on this side. And remembering the words of the Delphic oracle, they

[42] *Hürriyet*, March 17, 1995

founded their city "Byzantium" which derived from their leader's name "Byzas".

Over the next thousand years, Byzantium became a trade and commerce center. But despite great prosperity, Byzantium never distinguished itself culturally, as did so many contemporary cities in Anatolia.

In 324 AD, Constantine I defeated Licinius and became sole ruler of the Roman Empire. He also began to build a new capital at Byzantium, later named Constantinople (Constantine's polis or city).

In 330 AD, Christianity was declared the official religion of the Roman Empire and Constantinople was dedicated as capital of the Byzantine Empire and splendidly rebuilt by Constantine I.

Constantinople itself was not only the new capital of the Empire but also the symbol of the Christian triumph.

İstanbul is famous as one of the most often besieged cities in the world. Before it was conquered by the Turks, its assailants included the Persian Darius (513 BC), the Athenian Alcibiades (408 BC), the Macedonian Philip II (339 BC), the Arabs (673-78, 717-18 AD), the Bulgarians (813, 913 AD) and the armies of the Fourth Crusade, which twice succeeded in taking the city (1203, 1204 AD). After Constantinople was taken by the Turks in 1453, the city became the capital of the Ottoman Empire until 1923, when the newly founded Turkish Republic declared Ankara (then Angora) the capital. From 1918 until 1923 Great Britain, France and Italy occupied the city.

Under the Ottomans, the city went through several name changes, among them *Konstantiniyye, Polis, Stimpol, Estanbul, İstambol* and *İstanbul*. The name was officially changed to İstanbul in 1930.

Conquest of Constantinople

Turks had already tried to conquer Constantinople four times until Mehmet II. After becoming sultan, Mehmet II immediately built the Rumeli Fortress and restored the Anadolu Fortress in order to prevent the passage of any reinforcements through the Bosphorus.

Preparations, which took two years, included enhancing the fleet and manufacturing cannons.

In April 1453, an army of 200,000 soldiers and a fleet of 400 ships were ready in front of Constantinople. In the meantime, the Byzantines blocked the entrance of the Golden Horn by stretching chains across it. The walls of Constantinople were supported with more soldiers. The main intention of the emperor was, in case of attack, to gain time with an expectation of help from the western world.

The siege started on April 6 and continued unexpectedly. Mehmet II, to the surprise of the Byzantines, took his ships to the Golden Horn over a hill near Tophane by pulling them with animal and human power on oily wood pieces. A siege of 53 days ended on May 29, 1453. Mehmet II ceremoniously entered the city and this considerable victory gave him the title Fatih "conqueror" in the Islamic world.

THE CONQUEST OF CONSTANTINOPLE, *a painting by Zonaro, 19C, AD, Dolmabahçe Palace* [96]

The tolerance of the Ottoman Turks has meant that a majority of religious buildings from the Byzantine period still exist, if only as churches converted to mosques. Compared to many other countries where these kinds of buildings were generally destroyed, it should be noted that religious tolerance was not a new tradition in Anatolian civilizations.

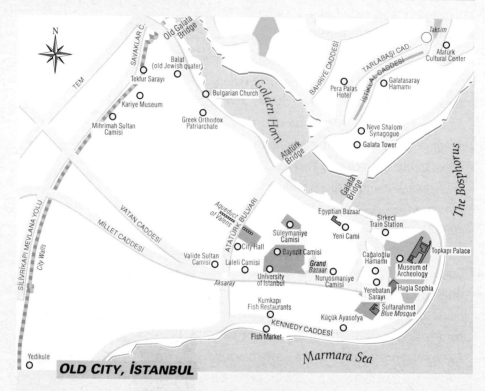

OLD CITY, İSTANBUL

WALLS OF İSTANBUL

İstanbul has been surrounded by walls four times since the day it was founded.

1- Walls built by Byzas in the 7 BC.

2- Walls built by Septimus Severus in 196 AD.

3- Walls constructed by Constantine I in the 4C AD.

4- Walls of Theodosius II, the 5C AD.

Final walls of İstanbul are among the longest walls in Europe with a length of 21 km / 13 miles:

a) Inland walls between the Marmara Sea and the Golden Horn: 7 km / 5 miles

b) Walls facing the Golden Horn: 5 km / 3 miles

c) Walls facing the Marmara Sea: 8 km / 5 miles

Among these, the inland walls are the strongest which consist of inner walls and also outer walls with moats in front of them. The walls facing the sea simply consist of inner walls. In the walls of İstanbul there are more than 50 gates and 300 bastions.

HIPPODROME[43]

The original building of the Hippodrome was built by the Roman Emperor Septimus Severus in 203 AD when he rebuilt Byzantium. Constantine the Great reconstructed, enlarged and adorned it with beautiful works which were brought from different places of the Roman Empire when he chose Byzantium as his new capital.

Although there is not much left from the original building except the Egyptian Obelisk, Serpentine and Constantine Columns, according to the excavations carried out, the hippodrome was 117 m / 384 ft wide and 480 m / 1575 ft long with a capacity of 100,000 spectators. It is said that one quarter of the population could fit into the hippodrome at one time.

During the Byzantine period, the Hagia Sophia was the religious center, a place which belonged to God; the palace belonged to the emperor; and the hippodrome was the civil center for the people.

Chariots drawn by either 2 or 4 horses raced here representing one of the four factions divided among the people. Each faction was represented by a color. Later on these four colors were united in two colors; the Blues and the Greens. The Blues were the upper and middle classes, orthodox in religion and conservative in politics. The Greens were the lower class and radical both in religion and politics. One of these political divisions ended with a revolt which caused the death of 30,000 people. This revolt was named after

[43] See *Hippodrome* on page 244

271

people's cries of "nika" which meant "win" and this Nika Revolt took place in 531 AD.

The central axis of the hippodrome was called *spina* and the races took place around the spina. The races used to start by the order of the emperor and the contestants had to complete seven laps around the spina. The winner was awarded a wreath and some gold by the emperor.

The hippodrome was destroyed and plundered in 1204 by the Crusaders. After the Turks it lost its popularity and especially with the construction of the Blue Mosque, the ancient hippodrome changed its name and became *At Meydanı* (Horse Square) a place where Ottomans trained their horses. The only three remaining monuments from the original building are the Egyptian Obelisk, the Serpentine Column and the Constantine Column.

DİKİLİTAŞ (THE EGYPTIAN OBELISK), *15C BC, İstanbul* [97]

Dikilitaş (The Egyptian Obelisk)

It was originally one of the two obelisks which were erected in the name of Thutmose III in front of Amon-Ra Temple in Karnak in the 15C BC. It is a monolith made of granite and the words on it are in Egyptian hieroglyphs which praise Thutmose III. The original piece was longer than today's measurement of 19.60 m / 64.30 ft which is thought to be two thirds of the original. [44] It was broken either during shipment or intentionally to make it lighter to transport.

The Roman governor of Alexandria sent it to Theodosius I in 390 AD.

The obelisk is situated on a Byzantine marble base with bas-reliefs. These reliefs give some details about the emperor from the *Kathisma* and races of the time. The Emperor Theodosius I, on four sides of the obelisk, is watching the erection of it, or a chariot race, receiving homage from slaves or preparing a wreath for the winner of the race.

Burma Sütun (The Serpentine Column)

After defeating the Persians at the battles of Salamis (480 BC) and Plataea (479 BC), the 31 Greek cities, by melting all the spoils that they obtained, made a huge bronze incense burner with three entwined serpents to be erected in front of the Apollo Temple in Delphi. Originally it was 8 m / 26.3 ft high, but today it is only 5.30 m / 17.4 ft.

This column was brought here from Delphi by Constantine I in 4C AD. By looking at the records, it is possible to understand that it was standing at its place until the 16C. However it is not known what happened to the serpent heads after the 16C.

Örme Sütun (The Constantine Column)

Unlike the Egyptian Obelisk, this is not a monolith but a column built of stones. Who erected it and when it was built are not known. According to the inscriptions, it was renovated and restored to have a more beautiful appearance by Constantine VII Porphyrogenitus and his son Romanus II in the 10C AD. The original column should have been from the 4C or 5C AD.

It is 32 m / 105 ft high and after three steps comes the marble base at the bottom. It is also thought that all the surfaces of the column were covered with bronze relief pieces which probably were plundered during the 4th Crusade in 1204, and today it is possible to find some of these pieces used in the decoration of St. Mark Square in Venice.

[44] In some sources it is given as "one third"

SULTAN AHMET CAMİSİ (BLUE MOSQUE)

SULTAN AHMET CAMİSİ (BLUE MOSQUE), *17C, İstanbul* [98]

An interesting fact about Sultan Ahmet is that he ascended to the throne at the age of 14 as the 14th ruler and died only 14 years later. [45]

SULTAN AHMET CAMİSİ (BLUE MOSQUE), *17C, İstanbul* [99]

Built by Sultan Ahmet I as a part of a large complex, among the Turkish people it is called Sultan Ahmet Mosque. However, tourists fascinated with the beautiful blue tiles always remember it as the Blue Mosque. The complex consisted of a mosque, tombs, medreses, fountains, a health center, kitchens, shops, a bath, rooms, houses and storehouses.

A 19-year-old Sultan started digging ceremoniously in the presence of high officials until he was tired. Thus began the construction in 1609 which continued until it was finished in 1616. Being close to the Topkapı Palace, Sultan Ahmet Mosque was regarded as the Supreme Imperial Mosque in İstanbul. Even though the palace was left and the sultan moved to the Dolmabahçe Palace, Sultan Ahmet Mosque shared this pride with the Süleymaniye Mosque.

The architect was one of the apprentices of Sinan, Sedefkar Mehmet Ağa. He designed one of the last examples of the classical period's architectural style.

The mosque is situated in a wide courtyard which has five gates. There is an inner courtyard next to the mosque with three entrances. The inner courtyard is surrounded by porticos consisting of 26 columns and 30 domes. The şadırvan in the middle is sym-

bolic, because the actual ones are outside on the walls of the inner courtyard. There are three entrances to the main building, one from the inner courtyard and two from both sides of the building. There are four minarets at the corners of the mosque hav-

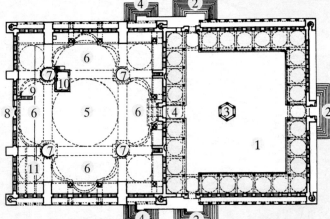

SULTAN AHMET CAMİSİ (BLUE MOSQUE);
(1) inner courtyard,
(2) entrances to inner courtyard,
(3) şadırvan,
(4) entrances to the main building,
(5) main dome,
(6) four semi-domes,
(7) elephant legs,
(8) mihrab,
(9) minber,
(10) müezzin's section, and (11) sultan's private chamber [100]

ing three *şerefes* each. The two minarets at the far corners of the courtyard have two şerefes each. There are six minarets in all, each of which is fluted.

The interior of the mosque is a square with a width of 51.65 m / 170 ft and a length of 53.40 m / 175 ft covered by a dome. The main dome rests on four semi-arches and four pendentives. The diameter of the dome is 22.40 m / 73.5 ft and the height is 43 m / 141 ft. The four piers carrying the dome are called elephant legs as each has a diameter of 5 m / 16.4 ft.

There are 260 windows which do not have original stained glasses any longer. The walls all along the galleries are covered with 21 thousand 17C İznik tiles having many flower motifs in a dominant blue color.

Sound-and-light show

On summer evenings, generally beginning at 8:00 pm, a sound-and-light show, which is worth seeing, is presented between the Blue Mosque and the Hagia Sophia. The languages of the show Turkish, English, French and German rotate daily with one each night.

[45] Belge Murat, *İstanbul Gezi Rehberi*, Tarih Vakfı Yurt Yayınları, 1993

AYASOFYA (THE HAGIA SOPHIA), *6C AD, Byzantine period, İstanbul* [101]

AYASOFYA (HAGIA SOPHIA)

The Hagia Sophia was probably the largest building on the world's surface, barring the Egyptian Pyramids, or the Great Wall of China. For many centuries it was the largest church and today is the fourth largest in the world after St. Paul's in London, St. Peter's in Rome and the Duomo in Florence. The great Ottoman architect Sinan, in his autobiography, says that he devoted his lifetime in the attempt to surpass its technical achievements.

It was dedicated to the Hagia Sophia which means the Divine Wisdom, an attribute of Christ.

Today's Hagia Sophia is the third building built at the same

place. The first one was a basilica with a wooden roof and was built in 390 AD. This original church Megale Ecclesia (Great Church) was burned down in a rumpus in 404. Theodosius replaced it with a massive basilica which was burned down in the Nika Revolt against Justinian in 532. Justinian began rebuilding the Hagia Sophia in the same year. The architects were two Anatolian geniuses, Anthemius of Tralles[46], an engineer and a mathematician and Isidorus of Miletus[47], an architect. They started collecting materials from all over the empire. In the construction ten thousand workers worked under the supervision of one hundred master builders.

Justinian reopened it in 537 entering the Hagia Sophia with the words "Solomon, I have surpassed you!".

Because the building is near a fault line in an earthquake zone and the city passed through many riots and fires, the Hagia Sophia was destroyed and underwent restorations several times.

Another major event during the Byzantine period was the removal of all religious images from the church in the iconoclastic period. During the Fourth Crusade in 1204, the church was pillaged and some disgusting events took place in the Hagia Sophia. After conquering Constantinople in 1453, Sultan Mehmet immediately went to the Hagia Sophia and ordered that it be converted into a mosque. This was done

> Throughout Byzantine history, the Hagia Sophia played an important role as emperors were crowned and various victories were celebrated in this remarkable building. The Hagia Sophia even gave refuge to criminals.

[46] See *Anthemius* on page 389

[47] See *Isidorus* on page 394

HAGIA SOPHIA, *6C AD,*
İstanbul [102]

by adding the Islamic elements such as minarets, the mihrab and the minber all of which were appropriately positioned to face toward Mecca, 10 degrees south of the main axis of the building. The architect Sinan was also assigned to make some restorations and add Islamic elements to the building. Buttresses were added in the Ottoman period. Two huge marble jars were brought from Pergamum in the 16C and probably used to keep oil for candles. The eight round wooden plaques at gallery level are fine examples for Islamic calligraphy. The names painted on these plaques are Allah, Prophet Mohammed, the first four Caliphs Ebubekir, Ömer, Osman and Ali, and the two grandsons of Mohammed, Hasan and Hüseyin.

In time Ayasofya became a complex consisting of tombs, a

fountain, libraries, etc. It has been thought that when Turks converted the church into a mosque, all the pictures were covered which is not correct. According to the narration of travelers, pictures were still standing but figures' faces were covered.

Ayasofya was used as a church for 916 years and as a mosque for 481 years. In 1934, by the order of Mustafa Kemal Atatürk, it was made a museum and has since been open to visitors.

Architecture

The Hagia Sophia has a classical basilica plan and the main ground plan of the building is a rectangle, 70 m / 230 ft in width and 75 m / 246 ft in length. The central space of the Hagia Sophia is divided on both sides from the side aisles by four big piers and 107 columns (40 downstairs, 67 upstairs) between them. The space is covered with a huge dome which is 55.60 m / 182 ft high. The dome, due to earthquakes and restorations, is slightly elliptical with a diameter of 31.20 m / 102 ft on one axis and 32.80 m / 107.60 ft on the other.

HAGIA SOPHIA, *6C AD, İstanbul* [103]

Mosaics

Most of the mosaics are from periods after the iconoclastic period. Whitewash or plasters either of the iconoclastic or the Is-

MOSAIC IN HAGIA SOPHIA, 10C AD, the Virgin Mary and infant Jesus Christ in the center, Constantine offering the model of the city on the right, Justinian offering the model of the Hagia Sophia on the left [104]

lamic period helped to protect the mosaics. Mosaics of major importance are as follows:

In the **inner narthex** above the main entrance, also called the Imperial Gate, there is a 10C mosaic depicting Jesus as pantocrator seated upon a jeweled throne, dressed like an empire, and making a gesture of blessing with his right hand. In his left hand he is holding a book with an inscription of these words: "Peace with you, I am the light of the world." On both sides of Jesus Christ are two medallions. The Virgin Mary on the left and an angel with a staff on the right. Emperor Leo VI is depicted kneeling in front of Jesus.

On the **pendentives** are depicted winged angels with covered faces. The ones in west pendentives are imitations in paint from Fossati's restoration.

Above the **main apse** is the mosaic depicting the Virgin Mary with the infant Jesus. She is sitting on a bench with her feet resting on a stool. Her right hand is on her son's shoulder and her left upon his knee. Jesus is raising his right hand in blessing and holding a scroll in his left hand.

The **galleries;** the 13C mosaic of the *Deesis* scene, Jesus as the pantocrator flanked by the Virgin Mary and Saint John the Baptist who are shown interceding with him on behalf of mankind.

At the far end of the last bay in the south gallery is a mosaic showing Christ enthroned with his right hand in the gesture of benediction and the book of Gospels in his left hand. On the left is the figure of the 11C Byzantine Emperor Constantine IX Monomachus offering a money bag and Empress Zoë holding a scroll on the right. The emperor's face in the mosaic was changed each time Zoë changed her husband. Constantine IX was Zoë's third husband.

To the right of the mosaic of Zoë there is a 12C mosaic showing the Virgin Mary with the infant Jesus flanked by Emperor John II Comnenus offering a bag of gold and red-haired Empress Eirene holding a scroll. At the extension of the mosaic on the side wall is the figure of Prince Alexius.

At the **end of the inner narthex**, before going out to the courtyard (today's exit) stands the 10C beautiful mosaic: The Virgin Mary with the infant Jesus in her lap, on one side Emperor Constantine offering a small model of the city as he is accepted as the founder, on the other side Emperor Justinian offering the model of the Hagia Sophia as the emperor who had it built.

Iconoclasm (726-843 AD)

Iconoclasm, an ancient Greek word that means "image-breaking," refers to the religious doctrine that forbade the veneration of images (icons) of Christ and the saints in Christian churches.

In 726 AD, Emperor Leo III ordered the image of Christ at the Chalke Palace in Constantinople to be destroyed. In the following years, other measures were taken to suppress the veneration of images.

Empress Theodora, however, presided over the restoration of icon veneration in 843 AD, an event still celebrated by the Orthodox Church as the Triumph of Orthodoxy.

The iconoclastic movement was motivated by a variety of factors that possibly included Moslem influences, as well as the concern that the cult of icons was a form of idolatry. The Council of Nicaea also specified that images should be venerated but not worshipped, since worship belongs to God alone and the worship of icons would mean idolatry.

YEREBATAN SARAYI
(BASILICA CISTERN OR UNDERGROUND PALACE)

İstanbul was one of the most often besieged cities in the world and has always needed permanent water supplies. And as a result many underground cisterns were built during the Byzantine Empire. Water was brought to these big reservoirs from far away sources through aqueducts. It is still possible to see remains of a large aqueduct in Unkapanı. This is called Bozdoğan Kemeri (Aqueduct of Valens) and was built in 375 AD by the Emperor Valens. Because Turks have always preferred running water, after capturing the city from the Byzantines, they did not use cisterns properly. Most of them were usually converted into either small bazaars or storehouses. The largest and most ornate of these cisterns is Yerebatan Sarayı. In its construction, columns and capitals of earlier temples were used and this provides a very decorative appearance. This is why it is called *saray* which means "palace" in Turkish.

Yerebatan Sarayı was dug and built probably after 542 by Emperor Justinian I. There are 336 columns most of which are topped with Byzantine Corinthian capitals. The cistern is 70 m / 230 ft wide and 140 m / 460 ft long.

Between 1985-1988, the Municipality of İstanbul cleaned and restored it thoroughly and built a walkway between the columns. In addition to that there are special effects presented by a light and sound show. By looking at the water level marks on the plaster walls which reach the height of the capitals, it is possible to understand that the cistern was very full in times gone by.

YEREBATAN SARAYI (BASILICA CISTERN), 6C AD, İstanbul [105]

Two Medusa heads were used to form bases for two columns in a far corner of the cistern. The position in which they were placed suggests that the people who put them there were Christians and did not want to revere a god of a pagan period. The water inside the underground cistern is collected rain water. The carp in the water are decorative and an incidental protection against pollution. Some people even think that the Byzantines originally also raised fish in the cistern.

TOPKAPI SARAYI (TOPKAPI PALACE)

The Topkapı Sarayı was the second palace in İstanbul after the conquest. The first was in the Bayezit area and it was called the Old Palace after the construction of Topkapı. Called the New Palace initially it was named as the Topkapı Palace after a summer palace near the sea at Sarayburnu in the 19C.

The construction of the Topkapı Palace, including the walls, was completed between 1465 and 1478. However, different sultans having ascended to the throne added parts to the palace which now gives the appearance of a lack of unity and style. The changes were made for reasons of practicality, to commemorate victorious campaigns or to repair damage caused by earthquakes and fire.

The Topkapı Palace had never been static but was always in the process of organic development with the influences of the time. The first of these influences was the parallelism between the palace and the empire. As the empire became larger, the palace was likewise enlarged. The second is that as the sultans felt insecure and withdrew themselves behind the walls removed from nature, there was an attempt to bring nature inside the walls in the form of miniatures, tiles and suchlike.[48]

If late Ottoman period palaces are excluded, only the Topkapı Palace survived from the glory days of the great Ottoman Empire, which implies that palaces for the Ottomans were something different than the ones we know today. There is a kind of humble simplicity and practicality in the Ottoman palaces.

The Topkapı Sarayı was a city-palace with a population of approximately 4,000 people. It covered an area of 70 hectares / 173 acres. It housed all the Ottoman sultans from Sultan

[48] Belge Murat, *İstanbul Gezi Rehberi*, Tarih Vakfı Yurt Yayınları, 1993

Mehmet II to Abdülmecit, nearly 400 years and 25 sultans. In 1924 it was made into a museum.

The palace was mainly divided into two sections, *Birun* and *Enderun*. Birun was the outer palace and Enderun the inner. Out of four consecutive courtyards of the palace the first two are Birun. Enderun, the inner palace, consisted of the third and fourth courtyards with the harem.

The first courtyard which was open to the public started after the *Bab-ı Hümayun* (Imperial Gate). This was the service area of the palace consisting of a hospital (with a capacity of 120 beds), a bakery, an arsenal, the mint, storage places for various things and some dormitories. This courtyard acted something like a city center.

Topkapı Palace, as well as being the imperial residence of the sultan, his court and harem, was also the seat of govern-

FUNERAL OF SULTAN ABDÜLAZİZ *in front of the Topkapı Palace (1830-1876)*[106]

THE MARMARA

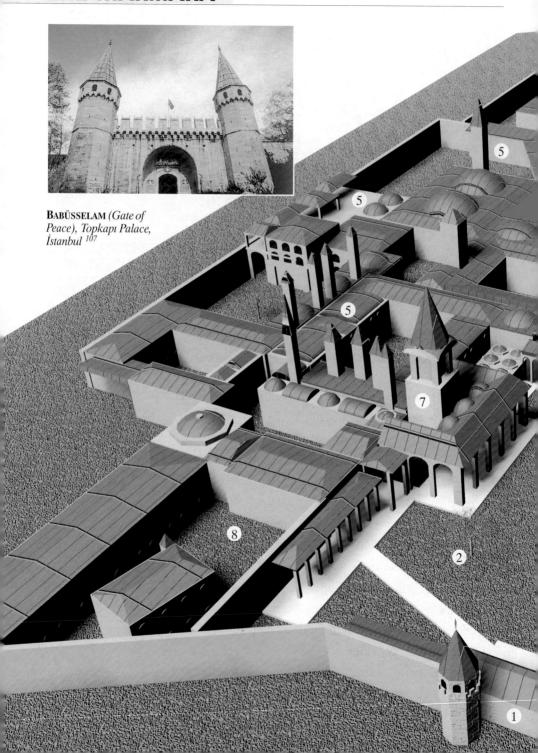

BABÜSSELAM (*Gate of Peace*), *Topkapı Palace, İstanbul* [107]

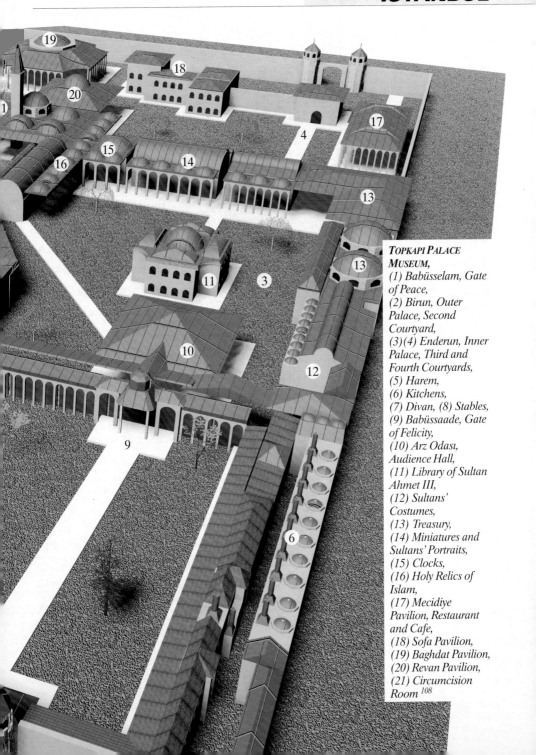

TOPKAPI PALACE MUSEUM,
(1) Babüsselam, Gate of Peace,
(2) Birun, Outer Palace, Second Courtyard,
(3)(4) Enderun, Inner Palace, Third and Fourth Courtyards,
(5) Harem,
(6) Kitchens,
(7) Divan, (8) Stables,
(9) Babüssaade, Gate of Felicity,
(10) Arz Odası, Audience Hall,
(11) Library of Sultan Ahmet III,
(12) Sultans' Costumes,
(13) Treasury,
(14) Miniatures and Sultans' Portraits,
(15) Clocks,
(16) Holy Relics of Islam,
(17) Mecidiye Pavilion, Restaurant and Cafe,
(18) Sofa Pavilion,
(19) Baghdat Pavilion,
(20) Revan Pavilion,
(21) Circumcision Room

MINIATURE SHOWING A SULTAN'S ASCENSION TO THE THRONE in front of the Gate of Felicity [109]

ment for the Ottoman Empire, Divan[49]. The second courtyard, also called *Alay Meydanı* (Procession Square), which started after the *Babüsselam* (Gate of Peace), was the seat of the Divan and open to anyone who had business with the Divan. This was the administration center. The Divan met four times a week. In the earlier years the sultan would be present at these council meetings, but later on, he would sit behind a latticed grille placed in the wall and listen to the proceedings from there. The Council never knew whether or not the sultan was actually present and listening to them unless he decided to speak himself. The Divan consisted of two rooms: the Office of the Grand Vizier and the Public Records Office, the Tower of Justice.

In addition to the Divan there were also the privy stables and kitchens. The kitchens consist of a series of ten large rooms with domes and dome-like chimneys. In these kitchens in those times they cooked for about 4,000 people. The kitchens were used separately for different people, because different dishes for different classes had to be prepared.

In the kitchens today, a collection of Chinese Porcelain which are accepted as the third most valuable in the world, are on display together with authentic kitchen utensils as

[49] See Administration on page 72

well as both Turkish and Japanese Porcelain.

Just before entering the third courtyard, in front of the third gate, *the Babüssaade* (Gate of Felicity) or *the Akağalar* (White Eunuchs) Gate is the place where the throne was placed for all kinds of occasions, such as religious holidays, welcoming foreign ambassadors and funerals. Payment of the *Yeniçeri* salaries took place there too as well as the handing over of the *sancak*, the standard or the flag of the Caliph by the sultan.

The Enderun, inner palace, started after the Babüssaade and was surrounded by the quarters of the inner palace boys who were in

service to the sultan and the palace. The first building after entering into the third courtyard is *Arz Odası*, the Audience Hall. Many important ceremonies also took place there. Foreign ambassadors and results of Divan meetings were presented to the sultan in this chamber.

MINIATURE DEPICTING THE SULTAN EATING HIS MEAL *110*

KITCHENS, *15C, Topkapı Palace, İstanbul* *111*

In the middle of the courtyard is the library of Sultan Ahmet III. On the right is a section in which sultans' costumes are shown. Next to this is the treasury section where many precious objects are displayed. Among these the *Kaşıkçı Diamond* (the Spoonmaker's Diamond) and the *Topkapı Hançeri* (the Topkapı Dagger) are the most precious. The Kaşıkçı Diamond is 86 carats, "drop-shaped", faceted and surrounded by 49 large diamonds. The Topkapı Dagger, a

THE TOPKAPI DAGGER,
1747, Topkapı Palace Museum [112]

beautiful dagger ornamented with valuable emerald pieces was planned to be sent to Nadir Shah of Iran as a present, but when it was on the way it was heard that Nadir had been assassinated and so it was taken back to the palace treasury. Relics including a hand, arm and skull bones belonging to John the Baptist are also on display in the treasury section.

From the right-hand corner to the left in this courtyard are the sections of miniatures, calligraphy, portraits of sultans, clocks and holy relics of Islam. The holy relics are personal belongings of the Prophet Mohammed (a mantle, sword, seal, tooth, beard and footprints) and Caliphs, Koran scripts, religious books and framed inscriptions.

In the fourth courtyard there are pavilions some facing the Marmara Sea and others facing the Golden Horn.

Life at the Court

The focal point of the court was the sultan, of course. The sultan's daily life was very simple. In addition to daily regular activities, sultans, in order to broaden their perspectives, gathered scholars, poets, artists and historians at the palace.

In daily life at the palace, silence was dominant. Hundreds of people tried not to meet the sultan unless they needed to and in keeping voices down, it was even said that, people of the court sometimes developed a body language system among themselves.

Most of the sultans in the Ottoman Empire united many skills in themselves. They commissioned new works, manuscripts and bindings, were ardent readers, competent calligraphers, poets, archers, riders, *cirit* (javelin) players, hunters, composers, etc.

The Harem

The concept of the *harem* has provoked much speculation. Curiosity about the unknown and inaccessible inspired highly imaginative literature among the people of the western world. People always basically thought that in a harem there were hundreds of beautiful girls and a sultan who had fun with all of them. This is generally not correct as the sultan could not, perhaps unfortunately for him, just leap into a roomful of beauties and have his way. There were certain rules with life in the Harem.

The word *harem* which in Arabic means "forbidden" refers to the private sector of a Moslem household in which women live and work; the term is also used for women dwelling there. In traditional Moslem society the privacy of the household was universally observed and respectable women did not socialize with men to whom they were not married or related. Because the establishment of a formal harem was an expense beyond the means of the poor, the practice was limited to elite groups, usually in urban settings. Since Islamic law allowed Moslems to have a maximum of four wives, in a harem there would be up to four wives and numerous concubines and servants. Having a harem, in general, was traditionally a mark of wealth and power. Though the women of the harems might never leave its confines, their influence was frequently of key importance to political and economic affairs of the household, with each woman seeking to promote the interests of her own children.

MINIATURE DEPICTING WOMEN IN A HAMAM, *1789* [113]

ROYAL WOMEN ON AN
OUTING *114*

The most famous harems were those of the sultans of the Ottoman Empire. The harems of the Ottoman Turkish rulers were elaborate structures concealed behind palace walls, in which lived hundreds of women who were married, related to, or owned by the head of the household.

The Harem of the Sultan

The idea of the harem came to the Ottoman sultans from the Byzantines. Before coming to Anatolia, Turks did not have harems. After the conquest of İstanbul, sultans built the Topkapı Palace step by step. Parallel to it, a harem was also begun. Eventually it became a big complex consisting of a few hundred rooms. The harem was not just a prison full of women kept for the sultan's pleasure. It was his family quarters. Security in the harem was provided by black eunuchs. *Valide Sultan* (Queen Mother) was the head of the harem. She had enormous influence on everything that took place there and frequently on her son too.

Young and beautiful girls of the harem were either purchased by the palace or presented to the sultan as gifts from dignitaries or sultan's family. When these girls entered the harem, they were thoroughly assessed.

Among the girls there were mainly four different classes: *Odalık* (servant), *Gedikli* (sultan's personal servants; there were only twelve of them), *İkbal* or *Gözde* (those were Favorites who are said to have had affairs with the sultan), *Kadın* or *Haseki Sultan* (wives giving children to the sultan). When the Haseki Sultan's son ascended to the throne, she

MINIATURE DEPICTING MUSICIANS IN THE HAREM [115]

was promoted to Valide Sultan. She was the most important woman. After her, in order of importance came the sultan's daughters. Then came the first four wives of the sultan who gave birth to children. Their degree of importance was in the order in which their sons were born. They had conjugal rights and if the sultan did not sleep with them on two consecutive Friday nights, they could consider themselves divorced. They had their own apartments. The Favorites also had their own apartments. But others slept in dormitories.

Girls were trained according to their talents in playing a

musical instrument, singing, dancing, writing, embroidery and sewing. Many parents longed for their daughters to be chosen for the Harem.

It should not be thought that women never went out. They could visit their families or just go for drives in covered carriages from which they could see out behind the veils and curtained windows. They could also organize parties up on the Bosphorus or along the Golden Horn.

Kızlar Ağası (Chief Black Eunuch) had the biggest responsibility and was the only one who knew all the secret desires of the sultan. Eunuchs, owing to different methods used for castration, were checked regularly by doctors to make sure they remained eunuchs.

YENİÇERİ SOLDIER [116]

When a sultan died, the new sultan would bring his new harem which meant that the former harem was dispersed. Some were sent to the old palace, some stayed as teachers or some older ones were pensioned off.

Yeniçeriler (Janissaries)

Janissaries (Turkish *yeni* is new and *çeri* is a soldier), standing Ottoman Turkish army, were organized by Murat I. Ottoman armies had previously been composed of Turkoman tribal levies, who were loyal to their clan leaders, but as the Ottoman polity acquired the characteristics of a state, it became necessary to have paid troops loyal only to the sultan. Therefore, the system of impressing Christian youths (devşirme) was instituted and having been converted to Islam and given the finest training, they became the elite of the army. Special laws regulated their daily life cutting them off from civil society such as being forbidden to marry. Devotion to such discipline made the Janissaries the scourge of Europe. These standards, however, changed with time; recruitment became lax (Moslems were admitted, too) and because of the privileges Janissaries enjoyed, their numbers swelled from about 20,000 in 1574 to some 135,000 in 1826. To supplement their salaries, the Janissaries began to pursue various trades and established strong links with civil society, thus undermining their loyalty to the ruler. In time they became kingmakers and the allies of conservative forces, opposing all reform and refusing to allow the army to be modernized. When they revolted in 1826, Sultan Mahmut II dissolved the corps by proclamation, putting all opposition down by force. Thousands were killed and others banished, but most were simply absorbed into the general population.[50]

Tuğra (Monogram of a sultan)

Each sultan had a personal emblem called a tuğra, a calligraphic arrangement of the letters of his name and titles. They were used at the top of imperial decrees or in the inscriptions of buildings (gates, mosques, palaces, fountains etc.).

Sultans and the Caliphate

The Caliphate is the office and realm of the caliph as supreme leader of the Moslem community as successor of the Prophet Mohammed. Under Mohammed the Moslem state was a theocracy, with the Şeriat, the religious and moral principles of Islam, as the law of the land. The Caliphs, Mohammed's successors, were both secular and religious leaders. They were not empowered, however, to promulgate dogma, because it was considered that the revelation of the faith had been completed by Mohammed.

THE ILLUMINATED TUĞRA OF SÜLEYMAN THE MAGNIFICENT *(1520-1566), Topkapı Palace Museum* [117]

[50] Microsoft *Encarta*, 1994

In 1517, when Sultan Selim I captured Cairo, he also added the title of caliph to that of sultan. After that, all Ottoman sultans automatically became caliphs when they ascended to the throne.

The title held little significance for the Ottoman sultans until their empire began to decline. In the 19C, with the advent of Christian powers in the Near East, the sultan began to emphasize his role as caliph in an effort to gain the support of Moslems living outside his realm. The Ottoman Empire collapsed during World War I. After the war, Turkish nationalists deposed the sultan and the Caliphate was finally abolished in 1924 by the Turkish Grand National Assembly.

KAPALI ÇARŞI (GRAND BAZAAR)

During the Byzantine period the area of the Grand Bazaar was a trade center. After the Turks came to İstanbul, two bedestens which formed the essence of today's Grand Bazaar were built between 1455-1461 by Sultan Mehmet the Conqueror in an attempt to enrich the economic life in the city. Later on as people needed more places for their trade, they also added parts outside these bedestens. In time the Grand Bazaar was formed.

Throughout the Ottoman period, the bazaar underwent earthquakes and fires and was restored several times.

Today, shops selling the same kind of merchandise tend to be congregated in their own streets or in *hans* as this was originally the Ottoman system. In addition to two bedestens there are also 13 hans in the Grand Bazaar.

With 18 entrances and more than four thousand shops it is one of the greatest bazaars in the World.

The atmosphere of the Grand Bazaar is very interesting for tourists and has consequently become a very popular place for foreign visitors.

GRAND BAZAAR,
İstanbul [118]

(inset) **BELLY DANCER
OUTFITS**, *the Grand
Bazaar, İstanbul* [119]

It is open during working hours on weekdays, closing earlier on Saturdays, while on Sundays and religious holidays it is closed.

SÜLEYMANİYE MOSQUE

Süleymaniye, rather than a mosque, is an important historical symbol for the Turks.

Like other works of the time, Süleymaniye is not only a mosque but a huge complex. It is a work which typifies the Ottoman Empire at its peak. Its name, Süleymaniye, derives from the builder's name, Kanuni Sultan Süleyman (Lawgiver), Sultan Süleyman I the Magnificent. The architect was the greatest of Ottoman architects, the incomparable Sinan.

The Süleymaniye mosque was built between 1550-1557. A spacious courtyard surrounds the mosque. Similar to the

SÜLEYMANİYE CAMİSİ (MOSQUE), *16C*
Ottoman period,
İstanbul [120]

The Süleymaniye unites Sinan with Süleyman, one representing the best of the arts and the other most powerful of political strength.

Sultan Ahmet Mosque, there is another inner courtyard surrounded by porticos with 28 domes supported by 24 columns. This courtyard is a little smaller than the main building. In the middle is located a şadırvan. In the four corners of the inner courtyard stand four minarets having a total of ten şerefes.

The interior of the mosque is rectangular in plan, 61 m / 200 ft in width and 70 m / 230 ft in length. The main section is covered by a huge dome with a diameter of 27.5 m / 90 ft and a height of 47 m / 154 ft. The dome is held by four piers and supported by two semi-domes in the E and W. The transition to the main dome is provided by pendentives.

The acoustics were one of the distinctive features of the building which were achieved by placing 64 pots in different places in the walls and the floor. Except for those above the mihrab, the stained glass is not original. When the mosque was built there were 4,000 oil candles, the smoke from which could have endangered the paintings on the walls. The architect avoided this, however by creating a system for the circulation of air inside the building. Sultan Süleyman and Sinan are buried in their tombs in the Süleymaniye complex.

Sinan (c.1491-1588)

He was born in the village of Ağırnas in Kayseri probably in a Christian family. At the age of about twenty, he was levied for the service of the sultan. After being educated in the palace school, he joined some of Sultan Süleyman's campaigns. His promotion in the Ottoman army was parallel to his success in architecture and carpentry. At the age of 48, he was appointed *Mimarbaşı*, Chief of the Imperial Architects, a post he held for half a century during the reign of three different sultans; Süleyman I, Selim II and Murat III.

He was not just an architect but an equally accomplished engineer, urban planner and administrator. In his time, İstanbul was one of the world's largest cities with all the complex problems of a large urban population. When Sinan built, he took into consideration each structure's relationship with its environment and also estimated conceivable future difficulties that might arise.

What were his visual sources? Seljuk architecture, churches carved in solid rock in Cappadocia, domed churches of Byzantium and being well-traveled, his accumulated observations. He was constantly driven by the desire to learn to renew himself, to establish links between the past, present and future and to formulate reliable principles. Sinan retained this characteristic to the end of his life.

The total number of his works was 477 consisting of mosques, mescits, medreses, tombs, public kitchens, hospitals, aqueducts, palaces, storehouses, hamams and bridges.

> Sinan's creativity was born of sensitivity to the cultural heritage and his power of identifying its dynamic points and taking them to their ultimate conclusion.

As an architect who built so many works, Sinan never repeated himself, an important feature and for him a remarkable achievement. A major aspect of his talent was the ability to transfer any possible architectural problems into esthetic accomplishments.

KARİYE MÜZESİ (CHORA MUSEUM)

Kariye Museum originally formed the center of a Byzantine monastery complex. Only the church section, which was dedicated to Jesus Christ the Savior, has survived. After the arrival of the Turks in İstanbul, this building, like the Hagia Sophia, was converted into a mosque. In 1948 it was made a museum leaving no Islamic element in the building except the 19C minaret outside in the corner.

"Kariye" is the Turkish adaptation of an ancient Greek word "Chora" which refers to countryside. Considering the perimeter of the walls of Constantine (4C AD) the building was located out of the city. If this theory is correct, Chora Monastery should have been from the 4C. But unfortunately according to sources, the existence of Chora Monastery before the 8C is not certain.

Chora went through many restorations the last most significant instigated by Theodorus Metochitus, prime minister and first lord of the treasury, in the beginning of the 14C. The three most important features of the church, mosaics, frescoes and the funerary chapel (Paracclesion) are from that period. Theodorus Metochitus built the Paracclesion for himself and he was buried in the entrance of the church; his grave bears a marble stone. The art of painting in frescoes and mosaics were the indications of a new Byzantine art movement which was parallel to Italian Renaissance started by Giotto (1266-1337).

The building consists of the nave, the inner narthex, outer narthex and the paracclesion. The domes of the inner narthex and the paracclesion are lower than the main dome and are only seen from the rear of the church. The dome is supported on four huge pilasters in the corners and four great arches spring from these. The transition is supplied by pendentives. The drum has 16 flutes, each pierced by a window. Entrance to the nave is through both outer and inner narthexes. The niches in the paracclesion were built to keep sarcophagi, as this section was the funerary chapel.

In the mosaics, the lives of Jesus Christ and the Virgin Mary

MOSAIC OF JESUS CHRIST, *Kariye, Chora Museum, İstanbul* [121]

are depicted. Background elements and architectural motifs are highlighted to give depth. The scenes are realistic as if they were taken from daily life with figures correctly proportioned. Jesus has a humanitarian look upon his face.

Mosaics can be divided into 7 cycles: the nave panels; the six large dedicatory panels in the inner and outer narthexes; the ancestry of Jesus in the two domes of the inner narthex; life of the Virgin Mary in the first three bays of the inner narthex; the infancy of Jesus in the lunettes of the outer narthex; the ministry of Jesus on the vaults of the outer narthex and the fourth bay in the inner narthex; and finally the portraits of the saints on the arches and pilasters of the inner narthex.

Mosaics of major importance are as follows:

Nave; (1) *Koimesis,* the Dormition of the Virgin. Before ascending to Heaven, her last sleep. Jesus is holding an infant, symbol of Mary's soul; (2) Jesus Christ; (3) The Virgin Mary.

Inner Narthex; (4) The Enthroned Christ with the Donor, Theodorus Metochitus offering a model of his church; (5) St. Peter; (6) St. Paul; (7) Deesis, Christ and the Virgin Mary (without St. John the Baptist) with two donors below; (8) Genealogy of Christ; (9) Religious and noble ancestors of Christ.

The mosaics in the first three bays of the inner narthex give an account of the Virgin's birth and life. Some of them are as follows: (10) Rejection of Joachim's offerings; (11) Annunciation of St. Anne, the angel of the Lord announcing to Anne that her prayer for a child has been heard; (12) Meeting of Joachim and Anne; (13) Birth of the Blessed the Virgin; (14) First seven steps of the Virgin; (15) The Virgin caressed by her parents; (16) The Virgin blessed by the priests; (17) Presentation of the Virgin in the Temple; (18) The Virgin receiving bread from an Angel; (19) The Virgin receiving the

KARİYE MÜZESİ,
(Chora Museum),
İstanbul [122]

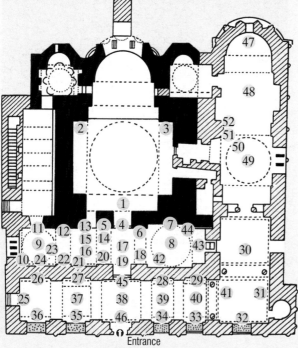

Entrance

skein of purple wool, as the priests decided to have the attendant maidens weave a veil for the Temple; (20) Zacharias praying, when it was   time to marry for the Virgin, High Priest Zacharias called all the widowers together and placed their rods on the altar, praying for a sign showing to whom she should be given; (21) The Virgin entrusted to Joseph; (22) Joseph taking the Virgin to his house; (23) Annunciation to the Virgin at the well; (24) Joseph leaving the Virgin, Joseph had to leave for six months on business and when he returned the Virgin was pregnant and he became angry.

Here it continues not chronologically: (42-44) Miracles.

Outer Narthex; (25) Joseph's dream and Journey to Bethlehem; (26) Enrollment for taxation; (27) Nativity, birth of Christ; (28) Journey of the Magi; (29) Inquiry of Herod; (30) Flight into Egypt; (31-32) Massacres ordered by Herod; (33) Mothers mourning for their children; (34) Flight of Elizabeth, mother of St. John the Baptist; (35) Joseph dreaming, Return of the holy family from Egypt to Nazareth; (36) Christ taken to Jerusalem for the Passover; (37) St. John the Baptist bearing witness to Christ; (38) Miracle; (39-41) Miracles.

(45) Jesus Christ; (46) The Virgin and Angels praying.

Paracclesion; The pictures here are frescoes. This chapel was designed to be a burial place. Among the major frescoes in the paracclesion are as follows: (47) Anastasis, the Resurrection. Christ, who had just broken down the gates of Hell, is standing in the middle and trying to pull Adam and Eve out of their tombs. Behind Adam stand St. John the Baptist, David and Solomon. Others are righteous kings; (48) The Second coming of Christ, the last judgment. Jesus is enthroned and on both sides the Virgin Mary and St. John the Baptist (this trio is also called the Deesis); (49) The Virgin and Child; (50) Heavenly Court of Angels; (51-52) Moses.

DOLMABAHÇE PALACE,
19C, İstanbul [123]

DOLMABAHÇE SARAYI (PALACE)

Towards the end of the Ottoman Empire, in the 19C, the Westernization movement was dominant. For the Ottomans who lived in İstanbul, "West" was in the "north" beyond the Golden Horn. In mid-nineteenth century they moved a few kilometers to the north for (Dolmabahçe Palace) and this change took the Empire to an entirely different dimension.[51]

"Dolma" is filled or stuffed and "bahçe" is garden in Turkish. The site of the Dolmabahçe Palace was obtained by filling the small bay on the Bosphorus giving the palace its name.

The architect Garabet Balyan managed to combine the Oriental and Western styles. The lifestyle and needs were Oriental but the plan was taken from European palaces. He also combined various architectural styles forming the eclectic style.

It covers an area of 25 hectares / 62 acres. The palace was

[51] Belge Murat, *İstanbul Gezi Rehberi*, Tarih Vakfı Yurt Yayınları, 1993

built by Sultan Abdülmecit as the outcome of his Westernization influences between the years 1844 and 1853. The official opening of the palace was after the Crimean War, 1856. Abdülmecit lived in his new palace for only 15 years. The palace was used by different sultans until the republic. During the republic the palace was used for foreign statesmen and democratic cultural activities. Mustafa Kemal Atatürk occupied a room at the palace on his visits to İstanbul and died there in 1938.

> The building was constructed to be seen from the sea and it is this feature which is new and unique in Ottoman architecture.

The construction of the palace was at a time when the economy of the Ottoman Empire was not at all good. This difficult situation was not taken into consideration and all the materials used at the palace were very expensive, of top quality and brought from different countries. Among the valuable items were **vases from Sévres, Lyon silk, Baccarat crystals, English candelabra, Venetian glasses, German and Czech Bohemian chandeliers and furniture in the rococo style**.

The palace consists of 285 rooms and 46 halls. There are approximately 600 paintings and very beautiful huge Hereke carpets specially woven for Dolmabahçe.

The Dolmabahçe Palace is an impressive building facing the sea with very high walls on the side facing inland. The main building is surrounded by magnificent palace gardens. There are nine gates on the inland side, two of which are monumental. On the front facing the sea there are five gates.

The palace was intended to be symmetrical in plan and decoration which was not something new. However with this palace the focal point is the sea.

The **reception hall** with its five and a half-ton[52] **English chandelier**, the **hamam** and the **crystal banisters** are of outstanding importance in the palace.

[52] In some sources it is given as "four and a half tons"

MISIR ÇARŞISI (EGYPTIAN BAZAAR)

It was built in 1664 as a part of the Yeni Cami complex which is located next to it. Mısır in Turkish means Egypt and it is called the Egyptian Bazaar because the shopkeepers used to sell spices and herbs which were brought from or through Egypt. During the Ottoman period it was known as a place where shops sold only spices. Today there are only a few spice and herb specialists. The rest sell dried fruit, börek, basket work, jewelry, haberdashery, drapery and suchlike.

The bazaar has an "L" shape with six gates. Similar to the Grand Bazaar, it is open on weekdays and only half a day on Saturdays.

İSTANBUL BOĞAZI OR BOĞAZİÇİ (BOSPHORUS)

The Bosphorus is a narrow, navigable strait between Europe and Asia connecting the Black Sea (Pontus Euxinus) to the Marmara Sea (Propontis).

It is about 31 km / 20 mi long and varies between 1 and 2.5 km / 0.5 and 1.5 mi wide. The narrowest point is 700 m / 2,300 ft between the fortresses of Rumeli and Anadolu. Swift currents make navigation difficult. The average depth is 50 m / 164 ft. In the Bosphorus there are two currents; one on the surface from the Black Sea towards the Marmara Sea and one below the surface in the opposite direction. The Black Sea is 24 cm / 9.5 in higher than the Marmara and this causes the current on the surface. The other current is because of the changes of salt rates in the two seas.

KULELİ, *a Military High School, İstanbul* [124]

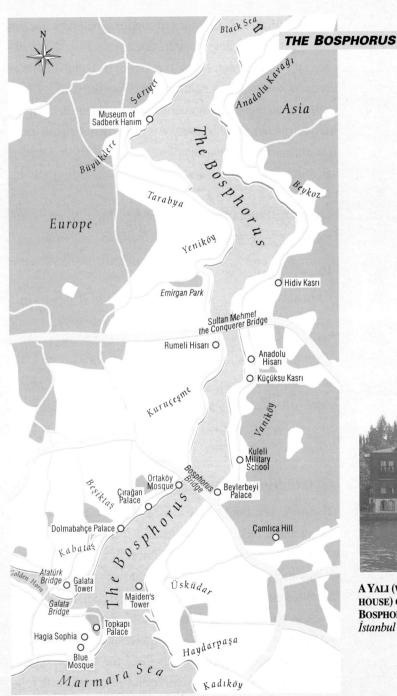

Black Sea

Asia

Europe

Anadolu Kavağı

Sarıyer

Museum of
Sadberk Hanım

Büyükdere

The Bosphorus

Tarabya

Yeniköy

Beykoz

Emirgan Park

Hidiv Kasrı

Sultan Mehmet
the Conquerer Bridge

Rumeli Hisarı

Anadolu
Hisarı

Küçüksu Kasrı

Kuruçeşme

Vaniköy

Kuleli
Military
School

Ortaköy
Mosque

Beşiktaş

Çırağan
Palace

Bosphorus
Bridge

Beylerbeyi
Palace

Dolmabahçe Palace

Çamlıca Hill

Kabataş

The Bosphorus

Golden Horn

Atatürk
Bridge

Galata
Tower

Üsküdar

Galata
Bridge

Maiden's
Tower

Topkapı
Palace

Hagia Sophia

Blue
Mosque

Haydarpaşa

Marmara Sea

Kadıköy

A Yalı (Wooden House) on the Bosphorus, *İstanbul* [125]

Along both shores are many attractions including ancient ruins, picturesque villages and forested areas. Near the southern end is the Golden Horn, the harbor of İstanbul, one of the most commodious natural harbors in the world. In ancient and medieval times almost all commerce between the Mediterranean and Black seas was routed through the strait. It is still an important artery of international trade. An average number of 38,000 ships pass through the Bosphorus annually.

The name Bosphorus means "ford of the calf" in ancient Greek and is derived from the myth of the maiden Io.

Io

In mythology, Io was seduced by Zeus and changed into a milk-white heifer to protect her from the jealousy of Hera. When Hera asked Zeus for the heifer, Zeus complied and Hera employed the hundred-eyed Argus to guard Io. After Argus was slain by Hermes at the behest of Zeus, Hera tormented Io with a gadfly, driving her from land to land crossing the strait between Asia and Europe and giving its name, Bosphorus.

Galata Kulesi (Tower)

The tower was built by the Genoese colony as part of their town defense fortifications in the 14C. In Genoese sources it was named as *Christea Turris* (Tower of Christ).

It was altered considerably, particularly by upper parts being added under the Ottomans during the course of the centuries. It was used at different times as a prison and a firewatch tower. In 1967, the tower was restored and an elevator was added. The present height of the tower is 63 m / 206 ft. Today two top floors serve as a restaurant with folkloric shows. During the daytime it is open to visitors for panoramic views of the region.

Flying Turk

Mankind has always longed to fly like a bird and the first human to try it successfully was an Ottoman Turk.

In the 17C, during the reign of the Ottoman Sultan Murat IV, Hezarfen Ahmet Çelebi, a scholar whose first name means "a thousand sciences", managed to fly by wearing rush-work wings, from the top of the Galata Tower to Üsküdar, an Asian settlement opposite and across the Bosphorus. An excited crowd including the sultan watched him achieve this feat.

Sultan Murat admired Hezarfen but he was also afraid that his unusual ability would win him excessive power. The sultan gave him a purse of gold and declared: "This man is one to be feared. He can do anything he wishes. The presence of such men is not auspicious." Hezarfen was then exiled to Algeria where he died broken hearted far away from home.

GALATA KULESİ (TOWER), 14C AD, İstanbul [126]

Kız Kulesi (Maiden's Tower)

One of the most distinctive landmarks in İstanbul. The Kız Kulesi was originally a 12C Byzantine fortress built on a natural rock. The present structure dates from the 18C and is used as an inspection station by the Navy. There are plans to restore it to become a cafe and restaurant.

Çırağan Sarayı (Çırağan Palace)

This palace was built by Abdülaziz I between 1863 and 1867. This was a period in which all Ottoman sultans used to build their own palaces rather than using those of previous sultans. Unfortunately because of a fire in 1910 this beautiful palace was just a ruin until very recently when it became one of the most exclusive hotels in İstanbul.

ÇIRAĞAN SARAYI
(ÇIRAĞAN PALACE),
1867, İstanbul [127]

Ortaköy Camisi (Ortaköy Mosque)

This mosque is also known as *Büyük Mecidiye Camisi* and was built by Abdülmecit in 1853. The architect is Nikoğos Balyan.

Beylerbeyi Sarayı (Beylerbeyi Palace)

The Architect Sarkis Balyan constructed the Beylerbeyi Palace between 1861 and 1865 for Abdülaziz. The exterior decoration was adopted from European Neo-Classicism but the interior was completed in the traditional Ottoman style.

This palace was used both as a summer lodge and as a residence for visiting royalty.

Boğaz Köprüsü (Bosphorus Bridge)

In 1973, on the 50th anniversary of the Turkish Republic, a suspension bridge similar to the British River Severn Bridge was opened at İstanbul linking the Asian and European shores of the strait.

It is 64 m / 210 ft high with 6 lanes. The total length is

1,560 m / 5,117 ft and the distance between two legs is only 1,074 m / 3,523 ft. The construction took 3 years and the cost was 22 million US Dollars.

During its first years pedestrians could walk across the bridge and the elevators inside the legs were open to the public. However, after many suicides it is no longer open to pedestrians.

BOSPHORUS BRIDGE, *1973, İstanbul* [128]

KÜÇÜKSU KASRI (KÜÇÜKSU SUMMER PALACE), *1856, İstanbul* [129]

Küçüksu Kasrı (Küçüksu Summer Palace)

A summer palace built by Sultan Abdülmecit in 1856 upon the ruins of an earlier building. The style is Western and the architect is Nikoğos Balyan.

Anadolu Hisarı (Anatolian Fortress)

This fortress was constructed on the Asian shore by Bayezit I in the late 14C, one century before Turks conquered Constantinople.

Rumeli Hisarı (Rumeli Fortress)

RUMELİ HİSARI
(RUMELİ FORTRESS),
1452, İstanbul [130]

Sultan Mehmet II made preparations for the siege of Constantinople. He decided to build a fortress on the Bosphorus opposite the Anadolu Hisarı in order to cut off the city from its sources of grain on the shores of the Black Sea. The construction was completed in 1452 in less than four months and it served its purposes well. After the conquest, it lost its military importance.

Fatih Sultan Mehmet Köprüsü
(Sultan Mehmet the Conqueror Bridge)

Due to the heavy traffic in İstanbul, another bridge at the narrowest point on the Bosphorus was constructed between the years 1985 and 1988.

This bridge is also 64 m / 210 ft high, but it has 8 lanes. The total length is 1,510 m / 4,953 ft and the distance between the two legs is only 1,090 m / 3,575 ft. The construction was completed by a Japanese company and the cost was 125 million US Dollars.

ADALAR (PRINCES' ISLANDS)

An archipelago that consists of nine islands just a few miles from Asian İstanbul in the Marmara Sea. It is less than an hour by ferry from the center of the city. Walks or tours with horse-carriages through the streets of the islands, restaurants or cafes in this peaceful atmosphere are among the simple joys to be found on these islands.

During the Byzantine period, the islands were collectively a religious center with many monasteries. The name "Princes' Islands" derives from the princes sent there in exile. Those were the ones regarded as pretenders to the throne. During the Ottoman period, the islands were a neglected backwater of little interest. Non-Moslem groups were attracted to the islands. The settlement of a steady Turkish population on the islands came about as late as the end of the 19C.

All nine islands together form a municipality, the mayor being in *Büyükada*, the largest of all. *Büyükada* and other large ones *Heybeli, Burgaz, Kınalı* have permanent settlements. *Sedef* is also recently becoming subject to new settlement. Currently the number of permanent residents on the islands is about 15,000. However this number increases more than tenfold during the summer, especially after the school year ends, when summer homes are inhabited.

Büyükada was called *Megalo* in the Byzantine period, both names having the same meaning; big. The majority of the population there at present are Jewish. Because Kınalı is closest to İstanbul it was called *Proti* which meant first. Kınalı in Turkish means "dyed with henna". Today, predominantly Armenians live there. Burgaz was called *Panormos* in the Byzantine period and is famous as the home of a Rum minority and a well known writer of short stories, Sait Faik Abasıyanık. Heybeli was called *Khalkitis* because of its copper mines. Heybeli is a Turkish name meaning "saddle-bag" and the shape of the island is similar to a saddle-bag. The other four islands are of minor importance with no inhabitants. Their names are *Kaşık, Yassı, Sivri* and *Hayırsız (Tavşan)*.

> The islands which are free of cars and have many beautiful wooden houses, have a resort atmosphere and offer peace and quiet in a natural environment.

OTHER PLACES OF INTEREST IN İSTANBUL

(top) **HALİÇ (GOLDEN HORN)** *from Cafe Pierre Loti, İstanbul* [131]

(middle) **MEHTER BAND** *GIVING A CONCERT at the Military Museum in Harbiye, İstanbul* [132]

(bottom) **ÇİÇEK PASAJI (FLOWER PASSAGE)**, *İstiklal street, İstanbul* [133]

With more time in İstanbul the following places are worth visiting or experiencing:

♦ Archeological Museum of İstanbul in the old city, near the Topkapı Palace,

♦ Turkish and Islamic Arts Museum in the old city, opposite the Blue Mosque,

♦ Mihrimah Sultan Camisi (Mosque), in Edirnekapı,

♦ Nostalgia at French writer Pierre Loti's (1850-1923) favorite cafe in Eyüp; Cafe Pierre Loti,

♦ Pera Palas Hotel, a place where Agatha Christie and many other celebrities have stayed,

♦ Walk from Taksim Square into İstiklal street (Beyoğlu), a pedestrian street with an old tram line, old buildings, modern shops and cinemas,

♦ A typical local dinner in one of the restaurants in Çiçek Pasajı (Flower Passage), also on the İstiklal street,

♦ A typical local fish dinner in one of many restaurants in Kumkapı; gypsies make music too,

♦ Mehter (Military) Band Concert at the Military Museum in Harbiye,

♦ Ortaköy at the base of the Bosphorus Bridge on the European side. An array of cafe-bars in the old narrow lanes. Open air craft market stalls on Sundays.

♦ Experience a Turkish hamam; Galatasaray Hamamı (İstiklal St.), Cağaloğlu Hamamı (Yerebatan St.)

♦ Sadberk Hanım Museum, Sarıyer.

KÜÇÜK ÇEKMECE LAKE

Location	On the way out, 15 km / 9 miles to the west of İstanbul, the first lake is Küçük Çekmece
Surface area	16 km² / 6.2 sq miles
Depth	Maximum 20 m / 65 ft
Altitude	Sea level
Formation	It was a small bay in the sea but in time it was transformed into a lagoon with the sand brought by the waves created by the South Wind
Water	Because it is still connected to the sea the water is half fresh-half saltwater

BÜYÜK ÇEKMECE LAKE

Location	It is located 12 km / 7.5 miles after Küçük Çekmece lake on the way out from İstanbul
Surface area	11 km² / 4.2 sq mile
Depth	Maximum 4 m / 13 ft.
Altitude	Sea level
Formation	The formation is similar to Küçük Çekmece's

There are two bridges on the lake one of which was built by the architect Sinan.

TEKİRDAĞ

Size	46th largest city in Turkey
Altitude	Sea level
Industry	Wine, Rakı and oil factories,
Agriculture	Grains, onion, sunflower, sugar beet, grapes
Animal husbandry	Sheep
History	Roman, Byzantine, Ottoman and Turkish Republic

The name of the city derives from a mountain nearby, *Tekfurdağ* which was later changed to Tekirdağ. *Tekfur* was the name given to provincial rulers in the Byzantine Empire. *Dağ* is a mountain.

Hungarian Independence Movement leader Rákóczy Ferenc asked for refuge from the Ottomans in 1717 and was granted a house in Tekirdağ where he spent the rest of his life until his death in 1735.

ÇANAKKALE BOĞAZI (THE DARDANELLES)

The Dardanelles is the 61-km-long (38-mi) strait between the Aegean Sea and the Marmara Sea. It is the westernmost section of the waterway that divides Europe from Asia and connects the Mediterranean and Black seas. The width is 1-6 km / 0.75-4 mi and the average depth is 100 m / 328 ft.

The name Dardanelles comes from Dardanus, mythical ancestor of nearby Troy. It was also called the Hellespont in ancient times. According to ancient writers, in mythology, the name derives from Helle who fell from the back of the golden-fleeced ram while passing through the strait on the way to Colchis in the Black Sea.

Despite unpredictable weather and swift surface currents the Dardanelles have been a strategic water route—and an object of conquest—throughout history.

Unlike the Bosphòrus in İstanbul, there is no bridge today on the Dardanelles. In the 5C BC the Persian King Xerxes built a pontoon bridge which stretched from Abydus to Sestus on his expedition against the Greeks.

Hero and Leander

(preceding page)
SUNFLOWERS[134]

In mythology Hero and Leander were lovers. Hero, a priestess of Aphrodite, lived in Sestus; Leander lived in Abydus, on the other side of the Hellespont (Dardanelles). Each night, guided by a lamp placed by Hero, Leander swam across the strait to be with her. One night a tempest arose, the lamp was extinguished and Leander drowned; when Hero saw her dead lover she threw herself into the water in despair and lost her life too.

The story is the subject of Christopher Marrow's unfinished poem "Hero and Leander" and Lord Byron's "The Bride of Abydus".

> The winds are high on Helle's wave
> As on that night of stormy weather
> When love, who sent, forgot to save
> The young—the beautiful—the brave
> The lonely hope of Sestus' daughter

Actually this legend inspired Lord Byron to swim the Hellespont in 1810. To commemorate this crossing he wrote a poem, "Written After Swimming from Sestus to Abydus".

Çanakkale Battles (The Gallipoli Campaign)

1915	
Feb. to March	Naval attempts to force the Straits
April 25	Allied landings at Helles and Anzac Cove
May to July	Attempts to expand beachheads in Helles and Anzac; arrival of reinforcement
Sept. to Nov.	Static trench warfare with no major attacks by either side
December	Evacuation of Anzac and Suvla Bay positions
January 1916	Evacuation of Helles, end of campaign

> "Damn the Dardanelles!
> They will be our grave."

(Admiral Fisher in letter to Churchill-April 5, 1915)

The Turkish Straits have possessed an enormous strategic importance as a result of the policies adopted by powers in their attempt to reach the high seas and warmer climates or to establish sovereignty over the Middle East.

The Gallipoli campaign of 1915 was an Allied attempt to knock Ottoman Turkey out of World War I and reopen a supply route to Russia. The initial plan, proposed by British Lord of the Admiralty Winston Churchill, called for an Allied fleet—mostly British—to force the Dardanelles Strait and then to steam to Constantinople to dictate peace terms. They began the campaign convinced that the Dardanelles would fall in one month.

The Allied fleet began bombarding the Turkish batteries at the entrance to the strait on November 3, 1914. This bombardment continued intermittently until March 12, 1916.

To be able to pass through the strait, it was understood that the lands of Çanakkale had to be captured as well. Within this perspective, preparations started on February 16. The principal fortifications were attacked on March 18. Sixteen battleships provided the principal firepower. Three battleships were sunk by an undetected minefield and three others were disabled. The Turks had nearly expended their ammunition, many of their batteries had been destroyed and their fire-control communications were out of action. The Allies, however, did not know this. The attack was called off and ships were withdrawn from the strait.

In the meantime, the Allies had hastily assembled a force of 78,000 men and dispatched it from England and Egypt to Gallipoli. As his flotilla gathered near the peninsula, however, the commanding general, Ian Hamilton, discovered that guns and ammunition had been loaded on separate ships. The transports had to steam to Egypt to be properly loaded for combat. The Turks, now alerted to the Allied plan, used the resulting month's delay to improve their defenses. Some 60,000 Turkish troops, under the German general Otto Liman von Sanders, awaited the Allies.

On April 25, British troops landed at Seddülbahir. ANZAC (Australian and New Zealand Army Corps) troops (at Arıburnu) waded ashore at what they thought was Kabatepe, but it was not. Their boats had drifted a mile north during the night and they landed instead at the bottom of the treacherous ridge. Many soldiers were killed or drowned. A few groups managed to scale the ridge up to Conkbayırı where Mustafa Kemal successfully commanded.

> "I do not order you to attack,
> I order you to die."

"...It was the last gasp of the battle. On both sides the men had been fighting for three days without sleep and with very little water and food. The trenches behind them were choked with the dead and wounded. The end of the nightmare became more important than the idea of victory. Kemal called out a few words of encouragement to his men as he crawled along.

> 'Don't hurry. Let me go first. Wait until you see me raise my whip and then all rush forward together.'

He stood up between the opposing trenches. A bullet smashed his pocket watch but he raised his whip and walked towards the British line. Four hours later not an Allied soldier remained on Sarı Bayır...."

Simultaneously, on the Asiatic side of the strait at Kumkale, one French division made a diversionary landing and on the neck of the peninsula, a naval force attempted to distract the Turks.

HEROIC VERSES INSCRIBED ON A HILLSIDE IN THE DARDANELLES, *Çanakkale* [135]

The Allied troops were soon pinned down in several unconnected beachheads, stopped by a combination of Turkish defenses and British mismanagement. Losses were high. The Turks ringed the tiny beachheads with entrenchments and the British and Anzac troops soon found themselves involved in trench warfare.

After three months of bitter fighting, Hamilton attempted a second assault—on the western side of the peninsula. This assault lacked adequate naval gunfire support; it failed to take any of its major objectives and resulted in heavy casualties. Hamilton was relieved on October 15 and by December 10 his replacement had evacuated the bulk of the troops and supplies. The remaining 35,000 men were withdrawn without the Turks realizing it on January 8-9, 1916. By contrast with the operation as a whole, the withdrawal was a masterpiece of planning and organization, with no loss of life. Estimates of Allied casualties for the entire campaign are about 252,000, with the Turks suffering almost as many casualties—an estimated 251,000.

> "Those heroes that shed their blood and lost their lives. You are now lying in the soil of a friendly country. Therefore rest in peace. There is no difference between the Johnnies and the Mehmets to us where they lie side by side here in this country of ours.
> You, the mothers, who sent their sons from far away countries, wipe away your tears; your sons are now lying in our bosom and are in peace. After having lost their lives on this land they have become our sons as well."[53]

[53] Mustafa Kemal Atatürk

Above is the letter Atatürk wrote to the Australian people

in 1934 which forms proof of his famous motto: *"Peace at home, peace abroad"*.

ÇANAKKALE

Size	59th largest city in Turkey
Altitude	Sea level
Industry	Canned food, cement, seafood
Agriculture	Grains, sugar beet, tobacco, sunflowers, grapes
Animal husbandry	Sheep
History	It was founded in the Ottoman Period and continues through the Turkish Republic

The name of the city comes from the shape of the fortress which was built by Sultan Mehmet II in 1452. It has a bowl shape and *çanak* in Turkish is "bowl" and *kale* is "fort".

Although it is a new city it played an important role during the Çanakkale Battles. From the ferryboat on the way to Çanakkale, it is possible to see a big inscription on the hillside N of Kilitbahir:

"*Dur yolcu!* (Stop passerby!)
This soil you thus tread unawares
Is where an age sank.
Bow and listen,
This quiet mound is where the heart of a nation throbs."

TROY

The name Troy refers both to the remains of a Bronze Age fortress and city at Hisarlık, near the entrance to the Dardanelles and to the legendary city of King Priam that was destroyed by the Achaeans in the Trojan War. There are reasons to believe that the physical remains in Troy today correspond to the city in mythology. Troy was also once known as Ilios or Ilion; this is reflected in the name of Homer's epic poem the Iliad, a work that claims to relate the story of Troy's fall.[54]

Mythological Story

According to sources in mythology the King of Troy was Priam and his wife was Hecuba. As a result of the gods and goddesses' plot against Troy, Hecuba dreamed of fire coming out of her stomach and of smoke covering the city walls. A soothsayer interpreted that the queen was pregnant and that the child would bring problems to the city. The interpretation found acceptance and, in order to avoid problems, the baby was left in the forest on Mount Ida where he would be looked after by a shepherd. The baby's name was Paris.

Many years later, Thetis, a sea goddess attended by the Nereids and beloved by both Zeus and Poseidon, married King Peleus. Eris, the goddess of discord and sister of Ares, was not invited to the wedding. She became angry and tossed an apple marked "for the fairest" among the gods causing trouble as they did not know to whom the apple was to be given. Three women were nominated: Athena, Aphrodite and Hera. They consulted Zeus but he recommended them the judgment of Paris who lived on Mount Ida. Each nominee promised something to Paris in order to get the apple. Athena promised victory, Hera, kingship of the world, and Aphrodite, the most beautiful woman. Eventually Paris gave the apple to Aphrodite.

Aphrodite's most beautiful woman was Helen who was married to Menelaus, King of Sparta. Paris fell in love with Helen and abducted her to Troy. This was the reason for the ten-year Trojan War between the Trojans and the Achaeans from the mythological point of view.

[54] See Homer on page 360

Agamemnon was the commander in chief of the Achaeans in the Trojan War. He was the King of Mycenae and a brother of Menelaus. Before coming to Troy, Agamemnon agreed to sacrifice his daughter Iphigenia in order to ensure a fair wind for his ships.

According to Iliad, in the tenth year of the Trojan War, Achilles withdrew from the fighting after Agamemnon seized his favorite slave girl. He sulked in his tent until the death of his close friend Patroclus stirred him to return to battle. The smith-god Hephaestus forged him a fine set of arms, including a famous shield on which was depicted the whole range of the human condition. Thus equipped, he avenged Patroclus's death in a

WOODEN HORSE, *an adaptation to mythological Trojan Horse, Troy* [136]

celebrated duel with the great Trojan hero Hector. After dragging Hector's body seven times around the walls of Troy behind his chariot, Achilles was persuaded to allow the slain Trojan hero a proper funeral. Later Paris killed Achilles. When the Achaeans understood that they would not be able to capture the city by war, they decided to prepare a trick. The Achaean fleet sailed out of sight, leaving the Trojan Horse behind as a "gift". Inside the large wooden horse was concealed a squad of soldiers who, after the horse had been dragged into the unsuspecting city and under the cover of darkness, emerged and opened the gates. After the fleet quietly returned, the soldiers entered Troy and great slaughter followed. Many Trojan women, including members of the royal family, were carried off into captivity.

Archeological Evidence

Troy was rediscovered and excavated by Heinrich Schliemann (1870-90). Many excavations have been carried out by different archeologists from different countries. From the evidence recovered by archeologists, there had been settlement in Troy from 3000 BC until 400 AD in nine different layers, each established on the previous layer.

Troy I (3000-2500 BC) The earliest settlement was a small fortress enclosed by a strong wall. Houses were built with foundations of stone and walls of clay brick. The settlers knew of copper but normally used bone and stone for tools and weapons. Most of their surviving possessions were of earthenware pottery. Troy I, like many other ancient settlements, came to its end in a devastating fire.

Troy II (2500-2200 BC) Although only 122 m / 400 ft across, was slightly larger than the preceding settlement and had more massive walls and larger buildings. It was one of the earliest cities in Anatolia to show evidence of town planning. It was wealthier than Troy I; it possessed more gold and silver and made much more use of copper. Its artisans were more advanced; the potter's wheel, for example, appeared at Troy during phase II, when the Trojans were in contact with both the Aegean world to the west and central Anatolia to the east. Troy's power and wealth were probably derived from its strategic position, controlling important trade routes between Asia and Europe. The ruler, his family and their most trusted retainers probably lived in the fortress, whereas the majority of the Trojan people lived in the surrounding countryside, grew grain and other crops, tended livestock and provided troops when required. Troy II, like Troy I, suffered catastrophic devastation by fire.

Troy III, IV, V (2200-1800 BC) Although the character of the fortress was preserved throughout these three periods, this era was undistinguished and of minor importance.

Troy VI (1800-1275 BC) A city established by newcomers with well-constructed walls. This phase was the high point of Troy's history. The area enclosed by the citadel was then about 230 m / 750 ft across, with finely crafted stone walls and stoutly fortified gates. Once again, the rulers of Troy occupied a position of power and importance in relation to the neighboring Aegean and Anatolian peoples. It was destroyed by earthquake.

Troy VIIa (1275-1240 BC) Resettled by the survivors of Troy VI, depended on the same fortifications. Its houses were crowded together; many had large storage jars sunk beneath the floors. Sewage system pipes dating from this period can be seen in the main street that goes to the southern gate. Just to give an idea to compare with Athens, at that time there was no Athens and even in the golden years of Athens (4-3C BC) there was no sewage system.[55]

The impression is that of a community under stress, possibly like Priam's citadel, the siege of which features in the Iliad and other stories of the Trojan War. According to tradition, Troy fell in 1184 BC. The archaeological evidence supports a date of about 1200 BC for the destruction of Troy VIIa.

Troy VIIb (1200-1100 BC) Resettlement followed on a small scale.

Troy VIII (700-350 BC) Troy in this period appeared to be a small market town.

[55] Tuncer Ömer, *İşte Anadolu*, Arkeoloji ve Sanat Yayınları, 1993

Troy IX (350 BC-400 AD) During this phase Troy was a Hellenistic and Roman city.

Heinrich Schliemann (1822-1890)

A pioneer in field archaeology, the German archaeologist Heinrich Schliemann is best known for his excavations at ancient Troy and Mycenae. Schliemann was largely self-educated. Because his family was poor, he had to leave school at the age of 14 to earn a living. He continued studying on his own, however, showing an exceptional ability in mastering foreign languages. He soon began to exploit his remarkable aptitude for business dealings, which enabled him to amass a large fortune early in life and to retire at the age of 41. From then on, he devoted himself to archaeology. He began to dig at Troy, his most famous excavation, in 1870.

Schliemann has been criticized for using methods that seem crude by comparison with the techniques of today. He also has been criticized for being a treasure hunter rather than an archeologist. The moment he found the so-called treasures of King Priam, he left the excavation with the treasures.

According to some he deserves great credit, however, for creating methods where none had existed previously and for demonstrating that excavation can be more than a mere treasure hunt—that it can, in fact, restore a knowledge of lost civilizations.

BEHRAMKALE (ASSOS)

Assos was an ancient harbor city which was also famed due to the stay of the philosopher Aristotle for three years as the head of a philosophy school. The Stoic philosopher Cleanthes was from Assos too. Lesbos Island in the Aegean Sea can be seen from here on clear days. Though it is not visited by many foreigners Assos is well known and has many of its archeological finds exhibited in the Boston Museum of Fine Arts, the Louvre in Paris and the Museum of Archeology in İstanbul. With its natural appearance and exotic atmosphere rather than its historical background, Assos has recently become very popular among Turkish people.

History of Assos

Mythologically, Assos was the capital of the Lelegians before the arrival of Aeolians who colonized Assos and made it their harbor in c. 1000 BC. As with all other cities in western Anatolia, Assos went through the Lydian, Persian, Alexander the Great, Pergamene, Roman, Byzantine and Ottoman periods. Notably in the 4C BC Assos was ruled by Hermias, one of Plato's students and a despot, who came to be known as the Tyrant of Atarneus. In order to establish a Platonic state there, Hermias invited a number of scholars among which was Aristotle, who married the Tyrant's niece. During the Persian conquest Hermias was executed and Aristotle had to leave Assos for Lesbos.

On his missionary journeys, Paul sailed from Assos. His visit to the harbor city of Assos strengthened the early Christian colony there.

Cleanthes (c. 331-232 BC)

He was a Stoic philosopher who proposed a form of materialistic Pantheism. He was one of the first philosophers to maintain that the sun was the central body in the cosmos. This concept was revived in the 16C by Copernicus. Cleanthes

TEMPLE OF ATHENA,
6C BC, Assos [137]

The Temple of
Athena is the only
surviving example of
Doric architecture in
Anatolia.

OTTOMAN HARPUŞTA
BRIDGE, *14C AD,*
Assos [138]

proclaimed that the universe and God, or the vivifying ether of the universe, are ultimately one and the same.

The Site

It consists of an acropolis with an inner defensive wall, a lower town with an outer wall, a harbor below the lower town and a necropolis outside. At the center of the acropolis in the inner walls was a 6C BC Doric **Temple of Athena** with Ionic influences. It is an andesite temple *in antis* with 13 by 6 columns. Five of its Doric columns are standing today. With some materials from the temple and other buildings an **Ottoman mosque** was built in the 14C. The cross in relief and an inscription in Greek show that either the stones were taken from a nearby Byzantine church or the building was converted into a mosque from a church. The dome has a diameter of 11 m / 36 ft.

The other remains are from the Hellenistic period and scattered below the acropolis facing the sea, among which are **an agora**, **a gymnasium**, **a small temple, a theater** and **a bouleterion**. **The necropolis** was outside the city and contained many sarcophagi made of local Assos stone. This stone was very appropriate as it accelerated the decomposition of the flesh. The word sarcophagus derives from the local stone of Assos.

Below the acropolis to the north a 14C AD **Ottoman Harpuşta Bridge** can be seen which crosses the Tuzla stream.

KAZ DAĞI (MOUNT IDA)

Kaz Dağı is located near the Edremit Bay between Ayvacık and Edremit. Kaz Dağı, also named Karataş Tepesi is 1774 m / 5,820 ft. It is a mountain nearly as popular as Olympus in mythology. Its fame is due to the first mythological beauty contest in the world which was held there under the judgment of Paris. In mythology, the Gods also watched the Trojan War from the top of Mount Ida.

MİDİLLİ (LESBOS) ISLAND

Lesbos, a modern Greek island in the Aegean Sea which can be seen from Assos or Ayvalık regions within less than 25 km / 15 mi from the coast, covers 1,630 sq km / 630 sq mi and has a population of more than 100 thousand people. *Mytilene* is the largest city on the island. By the 7C BC the island was a notable cultural center and home of the poet Sappho.

Sappho

A famous poet who became popular between 610-580 BC. In most of her poems she wrote about her love for other women so she was regarded as a homosexual. As she was from Lesbos island she was called "Lesbian" and when this word was associated with her so-called homosexuality, it started to stand for female homosexuality.

In the ancient world, sentimental poems were read with the music of lyres and since those times, poems of this kind have been called *lyrical poems*.

SAPPHO,
Museum of Archeology,
İstanbul 138-A

LYRE, *the musical instrument* [444]

"That man seems to me on a par with the gods who sits in your company and listens to you so close to him speaking sweetly and laughing sexily, such a thing makes my heart flutter in my breast, for when I see you even for a moment, then power to speak another word fails me, instead my tongue freezes into silence and at once a gentle fire has caught throughout my flesh and I see nothing with my eyes, and there is a drumming in my ears and sweat pours down me and trembling seizes all of me and I become paler than grass and I seem to fail almost to the point of death in my very self."[56]

İZNİK LAKE

Location	It is located near Orhangazi, 20 km / 12.5 miles from Yalova on the way to Bursa
Surface area	298 km² / 115 sq miles. The biggest lake in the Marmara region
Width	Elliptical in shape. 12 km / 7.5 miles
Length	32 km / 20 miles
Depth	30 m / 100 ft. One of the deepest lakes. The deepest part is 65 m / 210 ft
Altitude	85 m / 280 ft
Formation	Tectonic
Water	Freshwater

It is surrounded by olive trees, grapes and fruit gardens. The excess of water is carried to the Gemlik Bay.

More than 20 kinds of fish including mainly carp, pike and crawfish live in the lake.

İZNİK (NICAEA)

Nicaea, an important city of the Hellenistic-Roman Kingdom of Bithynia, was founded in the 4C BC by the Macedonian King Antigonus I and was later expanded by

[56] D. L. Page (ed.) *Lyrica Graeca Selecta* (1968) no. 199

King Lysimachus. Lying astride busy trade routes to Galatia and Phrygia, Nicaea flourished as a commercial and cultural center.

The city achieved fame as the site of two ecumenical councils in the Byzantine period and later for its tiles during the Ottoman Empire.

Councils of Nicaea

The two councils of Nicaea were ecumenical councils of the Christian church held in 325 and 787, respectively. The First Council of Nicaea, the first ecumenical council held by the church, is best known for its formulation of the Nicene Creed, the earliest dogmatic statement of Christian orthodoxy. The council also made explicit the relationship between the emperor and the Church: he was head of the Church as well as head of the state. The council was convened in 325 by the Roman Emperor Constantine I.

The Second Council of Nicaea, the seventh ecumenical council of the Christian church, was convoked by the Byzantine Empress Irene in 787 to rule on the use of saints' images and icons in religious devotion. At that time a strong movement known as Iconoclasm, which opposed the pictorial representation of saints or of the Trinity, existed in the Greek church. Prompted by Irene, the council declared that whereas the veneration of images was legitimate and the intercession of saints efficacious, their veneration must be carefully distinguished from the worshipping of God alone.

GEMLİK

A small town with a private port on the way to Bursa. It is both an agricultural and industrial place with some resort areas nearby.

Ports of Turkey

Ports gain their importance not only from their formations, but also from their hinterlands. For instance the port of Sinop is a very good natural port, but it has never developed because it is deficient in its inland areas. The largest port in Turkey is in İstanbul. It is also among the biggest ports in the world. Two more supporting ports in the Marmara Sea are in İzmit and Bandırma. The port of Bandırma has the longest docks. Another port in the Marmara Sea is the port of Gemlik which is private. The biggest export port is in İzmir. The port of Mersin is large and modern. The ports of Zonguldak and Ereğli are mainly used for coals. Other ports are Trabzon and Samsun on the Black Sea coast, with İskenderun and Antalya on the Mediterranean coast.

BURSA

Size	4th largest city in Turkey
Altitude	100 m / 328 ft
Industry	Textiles, automobiles and glacé chestnuts
Agriculture	Wheat, barley, corn, rice, sugar beet, tobacco, sunflowers, olives, peaches, strawberries, artichokes and peas
Animal husbandry	Sheep, chickens and sericulture
History	Bithynian, Pontus, Byzantine, Seljuk, Ottoman, Turkish Republic

The ancient city called Prusa was founded in the 3C BC and named after the Bithynian King Prusias I. Today's "Bursa" derives from Prusa. Bursa was the first capital of the Ottomans between 1326-1364. The city is also known as Yeşil (green) Bursa because many of its 15C buildings are painted in this color. Bursa is very rich in thermal springs, most of which are in the Çekirge area. Bursa today is the center of the Turkish silk industry , producing silk not only for fabrics but for the world-famous Hereke silk carpets.

Yeşil Külliyesi (Green Complex)

This complex, which consists of a mosque, a medrese, a türbe and an imaret, was built by Sultan Mehmet I between the years 1419-1424. The medrese today is a museum of Turkish and Islamic arts.

Yeşil Cami (Green Mosque)

Yeşil Cami is a mosque of the *Zaviye* plan. Zaviye is a kind of multi-functional mosque having the inverted "T" plan with additional rooms for traveling dervishes. This style was mostly seen during the first years of the Ottoman Empire. In addition to the normal mosque chamber, there are two more chambers forming wings of the inverted "T" on both sides with rooms for dervishes. In the middle of the building there is a pool which provides drinking water and şadırvan. Above the entrance is the sultan's lodge flanked by two balconies for the imperial family members.

By looking at the incomplete *son cemaat yeri* and missing inscriptions around the windows outside, it is possible to understand that it is an unfinished mosque. Two minarets are not original but from the 19C.

The name of the mosque comes from green tiles which at one time covered the dome and the tops of the minarets.

Yeşil Türbe (Green Tomb)

It is the tomb of Sultan Mehmet I. It has a single octagonal chamber surmounted by a dome. Walls were covered with

YEŞİL TÜRBE (GREEN TOMB), *15C AD, Bursa* [139]

turquoise tiles and the entrance is through a monumental gate. Inside the building there are nine sarcophagi, the biggest belonging to Mehmet I and others to members of his family and court. Actually these are empty and symbolic as people were buried downstairs.

The mihrab of the tomb is so beautiful that it can be compared to the one in the Green Mosque.

Ulucami

> Ulucami was the first congregational mosque built by the Ottomans.

Ulucami was the Great Mosque of Bursa which was built by Sultan Bayezit I between the years 1396-1400.

Unlike many other mosques, this one does not have one big central dome. The area of the building is covered with 20 equally-sized domes which are carried by 12 pillars inside. Transitions from the legs to the domes are through pendentives.

Mihrab, the prayer niche, is a fine example of the Ottoman stone work and dates from 1571. The 15C minber, the pulpit is made of walnut with representations of heavenly bodies. It does not have a typical courtyard. The şadırvan is in the shape of a pool inside the mosque. Like many other buildings in Bursa, Ulucami also underwent many restorations due to earthquakes and fires. The features which give the mosque the quality of a calligraphy museum are the beautiful hand writings dating from the 19C.

Koza Han

It is silk cocoon han which was built in 1451. After passing through many restorations, the Koza Han still survives today and continues to be the center of the silk industry. The courtyard in the middle is surrounded by two stories of shops. Each year in June or early July, silkworm farmers who have nurtured the silkworms for 6 weeks bring sacks of white cocoons which are ready for spinning. At this time of the year the atmosphere in the Koza Han is vividly hectic.

(top) **KOZA HAN**, *1451, Bursa* [140]

(bottom) **SILK MARKET IN KOZA HAN**, *June or July, Bursa* [141]

Sericulture

Silkworms were domesticated in China 5,000 years ago. The Chinese kept the secret of it in their monopoly till two monks,

during the reign of Justinian II in the 6C AD, smuggled silkworm eggs inside a hollow cane from China and cultivation of silk was begun in Constantinople.

The Byzantines were interested in this industry and the cultivation of silk became a state industry. The Ottoman Turks also encouraged the industry in two bases, one for production and the other for trade. The two major centers were Bursa and Edirne; two capitals of the early Ottoman Empire.

The process of sericulture

Silkworm eggs are very small; the weight of 2,000 eggs is not more than one gram / 15 grains. 20,000 eggs which are also called seeds, are put in standard boxes and left in the appropriate temperature. In 11-14 days, the worms emerge and start eating mulberry leaves. The continuous consumption of mulberry leaves for one box of silkworms weighs more than 500 kg / 1,100 pounds. The mulberry tree is the main factor in this process because without mulberry leaves sericulture is impossible. When the first eggs were smuggled to Europe, mulberry trees did not grow there. Therefore it was also necessary to bring the seeds of the tree to Europe.

(top) WORMS SPINNING COCOONS WITH GOSSAMER THREADS [142]

(bottom) SILK COCOONS ARE BOILED TO KILL THE BUTTERFLIES BEFORE THEY BREAK THROUGH THE COCOONS [143]

Worms complete their development in 24-28 days and start spinning cocoons for themselves with gossamer threads coming from their mouths in 48-72 hours. Each cocoon weighs about 1.5 g / 23 grains. The length of the thread coming from each cocoon is between 1,000-2,000 m / 3,280-6,560 ft. Nearly 80% of this can be obtained in the process. If development is allowed to continue normally, in about 2 weeks the chrysalis will break through the cocoon filament and emerge as a moth and live only a few days. Females lay 300-500 eggs before they die. Eggs lie in wait for the following spring.

OBTAINING OF SILK YARNS FROM COCOONS [144]

In order to obtain silk, the cocoons are passed through hot steam to kill the butterflies before they break through the cocoons. The next stage is to put silk threads onto cones by machine in factories. The production of raw silk can take place only where the climate is warm and mulberry leaves are abundant.

China produces most of the world's silk with Turkey being eleventh. Until the 1980s most of the production in Turkey was exported. However, after the development of the silk carpet production in the country, exports nearly stopped. The cultivation of silkworms is diminishing because it is chancy and troublesome and villagers prefer to deal with sure-profit crops.

Properties of silk

Silk is the strongest of all natural fibers, ranked in strength with the synthetic fiber nylon. Woven into material, silk is lightweight but retains warmth and is valued as an insulating liner in gloves and footwear. Nevertheless, it is the coolest of hot-weather fabrics and it can absorb up to 30% of its weight in moisture without feeling wet. The fiber is remarkably resistant to heat and will burn for only as long as a flame is directly applied to its surface. Its low conductivity makes it an excellent material for electric-wire insulation. Until the introduction of nylon, silk was the only fiber light and strong enough to be used for parachutes, sheer hosiery and surgical sutures.

ULUDAĞ (OLYMPUS)

Karatepe (peak)	2,543 m / 8,340 ft
Sarıalan; last stop of cable	1,621 m / 5,315 ft
Kadıyayla; first stop of cable	1,235 m / 4,050 ft

Also named Keşiş (monk) Dağı in the Ottoman period till 1925. The location is between the Marmara and Aegean regions. Bursa is located on the foothill of Uludağ.

Vegetation

Up to 500 m / 1,640 ft	chestnut and pine trees
600-1,600 m / 1,970-5,250 ft	beech-trees
1,600 m / 5,250 ft and above	fir trees and junipers

There are also Wolfram (Tungsten) mines on top of the mountain.

Uludağ is Turkey's most popular skiing center where there are 11 state and 14 private sector complexes with a 3,000 bed capacity.

Other Skiing Centers

Kartalkaya (Bolu), Erciyas (Kayseri), Palandöken

(Erzurum), Sarıkamış (Kars), Saklıkent (Antalya), Ilgaz (Kastamonu).

ULUABAT (APOLYONT) LAKE AND RIVER

Location	40 km / 25 miles west of Bursa in the direction of Balıkesir
Surface area	134 km² / 52 sq miles
Width	12 km / 7.5 miles
Length	24 km / 15 miles. Triangular in shape
Depth	A shallow lake; 1-2 m / 3-6 ft. The deepest part is not more than 10 m / 33 ft
Altitude	5 m / 16 ft
Formation	Tectonic
Water	Freshwater

After rains the water level rises and the excess water is dispersed via the Simav river. During normal conditions the receding water provides areas of fertile land for growing vegetables. The livelihoods of some villagers are dependent on fishing for crawfish and freshwater fish.

SUSURLUK (MAKESTOS) RIVER

With a length of 321 km / 200 miles the Susurluk is the longest river which flows into the Marmara Sea at a place opposite the İmralı island. The first section is also called Simav Çayı.

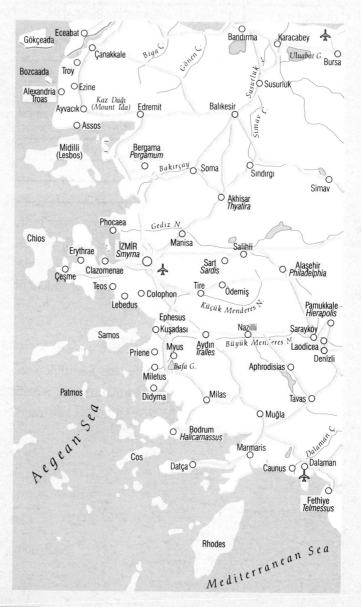

THE AEGEAN

THE AEGEAN SEA

The Aegean Sea extends from the Mediterranean northward between Greece and Turkey. It covers an area of about 214,000 km² / 82,625 sq mi and surrounds many islands. Its southern entrance is partially blocked by the islands of Crete (Girit) and Rhodes (Rodos). The Aegean extends about 640 km / 400 mi from Crete northward to the coast of Thrace and its width ranges from 195-400 km / 120-250 mi.

The coast of the Aegean is mountainous and only in Macedonia and Thrace in the north are there extensive coastal plains. The narrow waterway known as the Dardanelles enters the Aegean from the northeast and carries the discharge from the Black Sea. It gives access through the Marmara Sea and the Bosphorus to the Black Sea. A major feature of the Aegean is that no ship can be out of sight of land for long. In classical times, this encouraged navigation and facilitated movement between its shores. Today most of the islands in the Aegean Sea are Greek.

Tobacco

Depending on weather conditions, the size of the annual harvest varies greatly. On average 200 thousand tons of tobacco are grown annually. 65% is produced in the Aegean region, 20% in the Eastern Provinces near the Syrian border, 15% along the Black Sea coast and small quan-

TOBACCO GRADED AND PACKED IN BALES *awaiting merchant buyers* [145]

tities in the Marmara region.

Tobacco cultivation is still a family operation. A farmer will plant land of one hectare which will only be handled by members of his family.

At home with their morning's pickings, families sit in a sociable half circle to continue the hugely labor-intensive production process. Every leaf is strung on a flat needle and pushed onto a string to form a garland that measures 120-140 cm / 47-55 in. Each garland will contain between 500 and 1,500 leaves, depending on the tobacco type.

The garlands are then looped on curing racks. First they are left in the shade for a day to wilt, then they are gradually exposed to full sunshine for further treatment. The leaves dry out and change their color to a yellowish brown or red in about ten days. Against every wall and outside every barn stand the rainbow racks of leaves. The later processes are visible to the passer-by. After the curing is finished, the garlands are stored in barns until the autumn rains when the tobacco can be handled without crumbling. Each family's harvest is roughly graded and packed in bales and awaits the merchant buyers.

Excitement comes when the market opens and for a few hectic days there is intensive bargaining.

GEDİZ (HERMOS) RIVER

With a length of 401 km / 250 miles, the Gediz is 2nd longest river in the Aegean region. It originates from western central Anatolia and flows into the Gulf of İzmir near Foça. In the 19C there was a danger of the port of İzmir being blocked by its alluviums which is why another channel was dug in the northern part.

BERGAMA (PERGAMUM)

Pergamum was an ancient city founded by colonists on the Aegean coast of Anatolia at the site of the present-day city of Bergama. It was on a tributary of the Bakırçay (Caicus River), enclosed by high mountains. Fertile, self-contained and easily defended, it provided the perfect setting for the maintenance of a city state.

History of Pergamum

In the era following the death of Alexander the Great (323 BC), Lysimachus, one of Alexander's generals, chose Pergamum as the depository for his vast wealth, placing here 9,000 talents of gold under the guardianship of his lieutenant, Philetaerus. Upon Lysimachus's death, Philetaerus used this fortune and founded the independent dynasty of the Attalid Kings. Pergamum later became the capital of a flourishing Hellenistic kingdom and one of the principal centers of Hellenistic civilization. Under Kings Attalus I and Eumenes II, Pergamum reached the height of its independent powers. At the same time, however, it began to look to Rome for alliance against the warring Hellenistic rulers. After signalizing himself as a friend of Rome, Attalus I was awarded the Seleucid dominions, making Pergamum a powerful kingdom, comprising of Mysia, Lydia, Caria, Pamphylia and Phrygia. In addition to extending the kingdom, Attalus I adorned his capital with architectural splendors. Eumenes II also brought the city to the climax of its cultural prominence. During the reigns of these two prominent kings, the city so flourished that it could only be compared to Antioch and Alexandria.

King Attalus III bequeathed (133 BC) his domains to the Romans, under whom the city retained its position as the preeminent artistic and intellectual center of Anatolia but declined in political and economic importance.

The city went through the Arab, Byzantine and finally the Turkish period in the 14C.

Pergamum attained a high culture in the Hellenistic era, boasting an outstanding library that rivaled in importance that of Alexandria, a famous school of sculpture and excellent public buildings and monuments of which the Zeus Altar is the best example.

In the Roman period, Pergamum played an important role in the early history of Christianity. It was also numbered among the Seven Churches of Revelation.

Pergamum, One of the Seven Churches of Revelation

(Revelation 2:12-17)

(12) "Write this letter to the leader of the church in Pergamos:

"This message is from him who wields the sharp and double-bladed sword. (13) I am fully aware that you live in the city where Satan's throne is, at the center of satanic worship; and yet you have remained loyal to me and refused to deny me, even when Antipas, my faithful witness, was martyred among you by Satan's devotees.

(14) "And yet I have a few things against you. You tolerate some among you who do as Balaam did when he taught Balak how to ruin the people of Israel by involving them in sexual sin and encouraging them to go to idol feasts. (15) Yes, you have some of these very same followers of Balaam among you!

(16) "Change your mind and attitude, or else I will come to you suddenly and fight against them with the sword of my mouth.

(17) "Let everyone who can hear, listen to what the Spirit is saying to the churches: Every one who is victorious shall eat of the hidden manna, the secret nourishment from heaven; and I will give to each a white stone and on the stone will be engraved a new name that no one else knows except the one receiving it.[57]

[57] *The One Year Bible,* Tyndale House Publishers, Inc., 1985

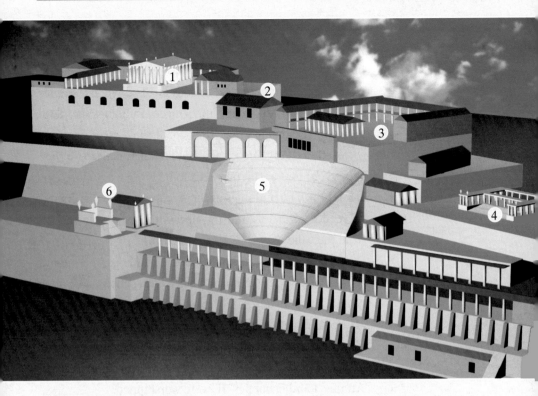

ACROPOLIS,
(1) Temple of Trajan,
(2) Library of
Pergamum,
(3) Sanctuary of
Athena, (4) Zeus Altar,
(5) Hellenistic Theater,
(6) Dionysus Temple [146]

Archeological Evidence

A young German engineer Carl Humann, who was engaged in building a road in Bergama in 1875 was told that a great quantity of loose stone was available among the ruins at the top of the hill behind the city. That which started as the need for road construction resulted in Humann's archeological studies and the uncovering of many beautiful pieces including the Zeus Altar and Gateway to the Sanctuary of Athena which were subsequently taken to the Pergamum Museum in Berlin.

Acropolis

The function of the acropolis in Pergamum was never the same as the function of the acropolis in Athens. In Athens everything was focused on religion, whereas in Pergamum it was on social and cultural activities, or in other words, daily life. As a result of this contrast, major buildings in Pergamum were reserved for public use in daily life. Even in the temples, religion was of secondary importance. Buildings had large areas for the public where they could walk, meet or join in social affairs. Pergamenes agreed that functionalism was necessary, but that aesthetics were to be given even more consideration. The buildings of the Acropolis were designed to be seen from below and to impress those viewing the city from the valley.

> Pergamum was the first city to react against functional urbanism of Hippodamus preferring ornamental urbanism.

Except for the Trajan Temple all the buildings were built in the Hellenistic period during which constructions were made of andesite and very rarely in marble.

Heroon, in general, is a shrine dedicated to a deified hero. The Heroon in the Acropolis of Pergamum was the imperial cult or the shrine in which kings of Pergamum, especially Attalus I and Eumenes II, were worshipped.

It was a peristyle building made of andesite from the Hellenistic period.

The Sanctuary of Athena was entered through a propylon which was built by Eumenes II. As written in its inscription, it was dedicated to victory-bringing Athena by King Eumenes. The entrance opens into a courtyard surrounded by three stoas of the Doric order. This also dates from the same period. At the corner near the theater was the Athena Temple in Doric order which was built earlier, in the 3C BC. It was built of andesite and stood on a crepidoma with two steps.

The Library of Pergamum, built by Eumenes II, was the second of the three famous ancient libraries[58]. It contained 200,000 volumes. A century later Mark Antony gave them to Cleopatra as a wedding present to be added to the collec-

[58] See libraries of the ancient world on page 377

tion of the library in Alexandria. The library building was next to the north stoa of the Athena Sanctuary. Most probably, the second floor of the stoa was at the same level with the first floor of the library. It had a large reading hall with many shelves all around, leaving an empty space between walls and shelves for the circulation of air to prevent humidity. Manuscripts were written on parchment then rolled or folded and put on shelves.

When the Egyptians prohibited the export of papyrus, the King of Pergamum ordered that a new material be found.

TEMPLE OF TRAJAN, *2C AD, Acropolis, Pergamum* [147]

The new discovery was "parchment", a fine material from sheep or goat skin, highly polished with pumice stone and slit into sheets. Therefore the name of Pergamum has been perpetuated and seen as synonymous with the word "parchment".

The Temple of Trajan was a 2C AD temple in Corinthian order, dedicated to Trajan, built by his successor Hadrian. Both emperors were worshipped there. The temple was built of marble, probably on the site of a previous Hellenistic building. Before the construction, the area was leveled off by using a suc-

TEMPLE OF TRAJAN,
*2C AD, Acropolis,
Pergamum* [148]

It is said that the
Theater in the
acropolis of
Pergamum is the
steepest raked
Hellenistic theater in
the world.

cessful arched and vaulted substructure. The temple is flanked by stoas on three sides, the one at the back being higher than the others. It was in Corinthian order to have a peripteros plan, with 9 by 6 columns.

The cavea of the **theater** which consists of 80 rows of seats is divided into three sections by two diazomas. The capacity was 10,000 people. The construction material is andesite. Because it was originally a Hellenistic theater, there was not a permanent stage building and people sitting on the cavea could see outside and beyond the playing area. In the Hellenistic period, performances were held in a festive atmosphere and took a long time. People spent a lot of time in the theater, usually the minimum of a full day. Therefore, they never wanted to block their view of outside and the stage building, being made of wood, was portable. Square holes at the back of the orchestra were for the portable stage building. The theater was also used during the Roman period with some alterations.

The finest altar ever built can be accepted as the **Zeus Altar** at Pergamum, of about 180 BC, which stands in its

HELLENISTIC THEATER, *Acropolis, Pergamum* [149]

own precinct but, most unusually, without a temple. The altar, a marble offering-table, stood on an enormous stone plinth, which also supported the double colonnade of Ionic columns enclosing it on three sides. On the fourth side it was approached by a fine stairway, nearly 20 m / 65 ft wide.

Much of the structure and almost all of the friezes are now in Berlin. Decorated with vigorous friezes of life-size figures depicting a battle between gods and giants, its contemporary context is probably King Eumenes II's celebration of his recent victories over the Gauls in Pontus and Bithynia. If this is so, then the context incorporates within its apparently straightforward mythology the King's assertion of his own triumphant role as the defender of traditions against barbarianism.

Kızıl Avlu (The Red Court)

This building was a 2C AD temple dedicated to Egyptian gods and goddesses from the time of the Emperor Hadrian. In the Byzantine period it was converted into a basilica. Because of the red bricks used in the construction and its court-like area, it was named the Red Court.

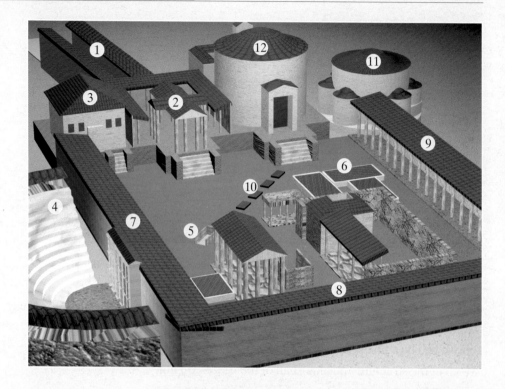

ASCLEPIEUM,
(1) Colonnaded Road,
(2) Propylon,
(3) Library, (4) Theater,
(5) Sacred Fountain,
(6) Pools, (7,8,9) Stoas,
(10) Tunnel,
(11) Treatment Center,
(12) Temple of
Asclepius [150]

Asclepieum

Asclepieum was a sanctuary and a healing center built in the name of the god of healing, Asclepius. It was similar to the one in Epidauros in Greece. Although this place was set up in the 4C BC, it had its peak in the Roman period.

Asclepius, son of Apollo, the god of healing, was a famous physician. His mother, Coronis, a princess of Thessaly, died when he was an infant. Apollo entrusted the child's education to Chiron, a centaur, who taught Asclepius the healing arts. Asclepius, when grown, became so skilled in surgery and the use of medicinal plants that he could even restore the dead back to life. Hades, ruler of the dead, became alarmed at this and complained to Zeus, who killed Asclepius with a thunderbolt.

The healing center, Asclepieum, had been something very similar to a modern natural healing clinic. Patients were given exercises, drugs, herbal remedies, or could take the honey cure, drink the waters of the spring or be treated by suggestion. They could walk among the trees and be calmed by the scent of pine. Over the gate had been inscribed the words: *"In the name of the Gods, Death is forbidden to enter"*. Snakes were sacred to Asclepius because of their power to renew themselves. That is why there was a relief of snakes at the entrance to the sacred area of the medical center symbolizing health. Among the famous physicians of the Asclepieum was Galen.

Galen (c.129-199 AD)[59]

Galen was the most outstanding physician of antiquity after Hippocrates. His anatomical studies on animals and observations of how the human body functions dominated medical theory and practice for 1400 years. Galen was born in Pergamum. A shrine to the healing god Asclepius was located in Pergamum and there young Galen observed how the medical techniques of the time were used to treat the ill or wounded. He received his formal medical training in nearby Smyrna and then traveled widely, gaining more medical knowledge.

GALEN
(c.129-199 AD) [151]

Galen dissected many animals, particularly goats, pigs and monkeys, to demonstrate how different muscles are controlled at different levels of the spinal cord. He also showed that the brain controls the voice. Galen showed that arteries carry blood, disproving the 400-year-old belief that arteries carry air. Galen was also highly praised in his time as a philosopher. He closely followed the view of the philosopher Aristotle that nothing in nature is superfluous. Galen's prin-

[59] Microsoft *Encarta*, 1994

NORTH STOA, *2C AD,*
Asclepieum,
Pergamum [152]

cipal contribution to philosophic thought was the concept
that God's purposes can be understood by examining nature. Galen's observations in anatomy remained his most
enduring contribution. His medical writings were translated
by 9C Arab scholars.

The Site

The Colonnaded Road connected Asclepieum to the city.
Originally it was 820 m / 2,700 ft. Today only a small part of
this road is visible. **The Propylon** was located at the end of

the colonnaded road and dates from 2C AD. It had 12 steps and opened into a large courtyard which was surrounded by stoas on three sides. It had beautiful acroteriums one of which can be seen in the Bergama museum. **Stoas** originally had Ionic capitals but after an earthquake in the 2C AD, some Corinthian capitals were also used. **The Library** was for both educational and entertainment purposes with many medical books for the physicians and other books for use by the patients. **The Theater** is a small building in Roman style with a capacity of 3,500 people. It was mainly used for performances to entertain the patients when not receiving treatment. **The**

TUNNEL IN THE HEALING CENTER,
Asclepieum,
Pergamum [153]

Sacred Fountain provided water believed to have had healing power. **Sleeping rooms** were used to make the patients sleep and analyze their dreams. **The Tunnel** is a vaulted subterranean passageway. It is 80 m / 262 ft long. Under the floor ran water which provided relaxing sounds. On the ceiling there are 12 windows to provide sunlight inside the tunnel. **The Round Treatment Center** was a two-storied building with six apsidal sections. Today only the lower floor remains. The walls and the floor were covered with marble and the roof was made of wood. Water coming through the tunnel, recesses for washing and the sun-terrace show that this

room was also used for the treatment of patients. **The Temple of Asclepius** was erected by the Consul of the time in the 2C AD. The main part of the temple was cylindrical and covered by a dome. The floor and the walls were decorated with marble mosaics. There were many statues of gods and deities related to health including those of Asclepius himself. This build-

AKHİSAR (THYATIRA) [154]

ing can be accepted as one of the earliest structures with a dome in Anatolia.

BAKIRÇAY (CAICUS) RIVER

It is a 129 km / 80 miles long river originating from mount Ömer which is in the south of Balıkesir. It pours into the sea at the Gulf of Çandarlı. Three main tributaries unite on Bakırçay plateau to form the river.

AKHİSAR (THYATIRA)

The ancient city of Thyatira is occupied by the modern town of Akhisar meaning in Turkish "white castle" named from the ruins of an old castle. Because of modern occupation, not much from its ancient archeological remains is seen.

Thyatira was an insignificant town until it was refounded by Seleucus Nicator in the beginning of the 3C BC. It was originally a military fort but lost this purpose with the *Pax*

Romana and became a wealthy commercial city. The city had a number of trade guilds. Every skilled worker was a member of a union some of which could be listed as tailors, woolworkers, tanners, potters, bakers, etc.

Commercial guilds in Thyatira were connected with the pagan religions of the city and involved participation in pagan ritual, feasts and celebrations.

Thyatira, *One of the Seven Churches of Revelation*

(Revelation 2:18-29)

(18) "Write this letter to the leader of the church in Thyatira:

" This is a message from the Son of God, whose eyes penetrate like flames of fire, whose feet are like glowing brass.

(19) "I am aware of all your good deeds—your kindness to the poor, your gifts and service to them; also I know your love and faith and patience and I can see your constant improvement in all these things.

(20) "Yet I have this against you: You are permitting that woman Jezebel, who calls herself a prophetess, to teach my servants that sex sin is not a serious matter; she urges them to practice immortality and to eat meat that has been sacrificed to idols. (21) I gave her time to change her mind and attitude, but she refused. (22) Pay attention now to what I am saying: I will lay her upon a sickbed of intense affliction, along with all her immoral flowers, unless they turn again to me, repenting of their sin with her; (23) and I will strike her children dead. And all the churches shall know that I am he who searches deep within men's hearts and minds; I will give to each of you whatever you deserve.

(24, 25) "As for the rest of you in Thyatira who have not followed this false teaching ("deeper truths," as they call them—depths of Satan, really), I will ask nothing further of you; only hold tightly to what you have until I come.

(26) "To every one who overcomes—who to the very end keeps on doing things that please me— I will give power over the nations. (27) "You will rule them with a rod of iron just as my Father gave me the authority to rule them; they will be shattered like a pot of clay that is broken into tiny pieces. (28) And I will give you the Morning Star!

(29) "Let all who can hear, listen to what the Spirit says to the churches.[60]

[60] *The One Year Bible*, Tyndale House Publishers, Inc., 1985

İZMİR (SMYRNA)

Size	Third largest city in Turkey
Altitude	Sea level
Industry	Textiles, cigarettes, soap and food processing plants
Agriculture	Wheat, barley, potatoes, cotton, tobacco, olives, grapes, figs
Animal husbandry	Not very common
History	Aeolian, Ionian, Lydian, Persian, Alexander the Great, Lysimachus, Roman, Arab, Seljuk, Ottoman and Turkish Republic

GENERAL VIEW,
İzmir [155]

İzmir (formerly Smyrna) is a city in west central Turkey on the Aegean Sea at the eastern end of the Gulf of İzmir. The ancient name Smyrna was

İZMİR

Port of İzmir

AEGEAN SEA
Bay of İzmir

Kordon

LİMAN CADDESİ

○ Train Station

Museum of Atatürk ○

☩

○ Soccer Stadium

TALAT PAŞA BULVARI

S. EŞREF BLV.

Lozan Sq.

Cumhuriyet Sq.
Büyük Efes
○ Hotel ☩
○ Hilton
Post Hotel Montrö Sq.
Office ☩

Kordon

Kültür Park

9 Eylül Sq.

MÜRSEL PAŞA BLV.

GAZİ BULVARI

○ Train Station

GAZİLER CADDESİ

FEVZİPAŞA BLV.

ATATÜRK CADDESİ

CUMHURİYET BULVARI

Ferry ⛴

○ City Hall

○ Clock Tower

Agora

YEŞİLDERE CADDESİ

N

○ Opera House

○ Museum of Archeology

Kadifekale

believed to be the name of an Amazon woman warrior.

The excellent port facilities and the introduction of the railroad contributed to early industrialization.

Agricultural products and carpets are major exports. The city is the home of the Aegean University (1955) and an archaeological museum. There are not many archeological remains to see except an **agora**, the **ancient aqueducts** and the exhibits in the **Museum of Archeology**. The splendid beaches in the İzmir area attract lots of tourists to the city.

At the end of World War I, İzmir was occupied by Greek forces and the Treaty of Sèvres (1920) awarded the city and its surroundings to Greece. Turkish nationalist forces captured the city in September 1922 and its large Rum population fled. The Treaty of Lausanne (1923) gave İzmir to the new Turkish Republic.

CLOCK-TOWER, *Late Ottoman period, İzmir* [156]

Smyrna, One of the Seven Churches of Revelation

(Revelation 2:8-11)

(8) "To the leader of the church in Smyrna write this letter:
"This message is from him who is the First and Last, who was dead and then came back to life.

(9) "I know how much you suffer for the Lord and I know all about your poverty (but you have heavenly riches!). I know the slander of those opposing you, who say that they are Jews —the children of God—but they aren't, for they support the cause of Satan. (10) Stop being afraid of what you are about to suffer—for the devil will soon throw some of you into prison to test you. You will be persecuted for "ten days." Remain faithful even when facing death and I will give you the crown of life—an unend-

ing, glorious future. (11) Let everyone who can hear, listen to what the Spirit is saying to the churches: He who is victorious shall not be hurt by the Second Death.[61]

Homer

Homer was the author of the earliest and finest epic poems, the *Iliad* and the *Odyssey*. Although modern scholars hold conflicting theories on the authorship of these poems, the ancient world believed that a blind poet named Homer had composed them. Tradition has it that he lived in the 12C BC, around the time of the Trojan War, in an Ionic settlement, Smyrna, where he made his living as a court singer and storyteller.

Modern archaeological research has uncovered artifacts similar to those described in the poems, providing evidence that Homer wrote at a later date. Because the poems display a considerable knowledge of the East or Ionia and are written in the dialect of that region, most scholars now think that Homer was Ionian of the 9-8C BC. Homer wrote nothing of himself in his poems.

The question of how the poems were composed remains a matter for debate. It is likely that Homer and his audience were members of a preliterate, oral culture and that his poems were written down long after their original composition. 19C scholars argued that one person could not memorize so long a text and that the poems must have been compiled by an editor, who merged several independent works into a consistent whole. This view is supported by scholars' opinions concerning the occasional inconsistencies of narrative and awkward transitions from subject to subject.

The 20C studies of preliterate societies have shown, however, that lengthy works can be composed orally by poets

[61] *The One Year Bible*, Tyndale House Publishers, Inc., 1985

whose recitations belong to a long tradition of storytelling. Homer was probably a practitioner of an inherited art, re-telling a story that his audience had heard many times before. Differences of language and style between the Iliad and the Odyssey have led some critics to argue that each is the work of a different poet.

A literary critic suggested, however, that the Iliad was the work of Homer's youth and the Odyssey of his maturity.

The Iliad portrays a universe marred by moral disorder, but the Odyssey shows gods punishing men for their sins and granting a good man his just reward. His influence on later literature may be traced from Hesiod to the present day.

Anaxagoras (c.500-428 BC)

The philosopher Anaxagoras was born in Urla (Clazomenae) near İzmir and went to Athens to teach at the invitation of Pericles, taking with him new ideas in science and philosophy from Anatolia. He described the cosmos as a continuous field in which different qualities flow and mix together. He maintained, however, that the motion of the world originated with the Mind, which interpreted and ordered the natural world but was not actually a part of it. Anaxagoras thought that other worlds exist besides our own and that, "they have men on them and these have houses and canals just as we do."

The Athenian public considered it against their religion to say that the Sun and Moon were not gods but rather hot stones revolving around the Earth; and that the divine mind in this system did not have human form. They accused Anaxagoras of impiety and he left Athens. He later died in Lapseki (Lampsacus). Socrates knew his writing and studied with a student of his but apparently they never met.

SART (SARDIS)

Sardis was an ancient political and cultural center of Anatolia, and the capital of the Kingdom of Lydia. The King of Lydia was Croesus and he was very rich. He is even referred to in the saying "as rich as Croesus". Much of the wealth of Sardis is thought to have come from a gold-bearing stream that ran through the city called the Pactolos River (Sartçay).

History of Sardis

Sardis was the capital of the Kingdom of Lydia. After prosperous days of Lydian period, Sardis fell to Cyrus the Great of Persia in 546 BC. The city continued to flourish through the periods of Alexander the Great, Romans and Byzantines until it was inhabited by the Turks and then deserted. It was here at Sardis that one of the "Seven Churches" had been founded. Investigations begun in 1910 by an American expedition exposed a well-preserved temple of Artemis along with a series of Lydian tombs dating from the 7C BC and later. Since 1958 ongoing archaeological research at the site has uncovered, in addition to important Lydian-period finds, several later monuments, notably a gymnasium and synagogue of the 2-3C AD and several Byzantine shops. Sardis also became the westernmost terminus of the **Royal Road** from Susa.

Ancient Roads

Royal Road

In the 6C BC, the Persians built the Royal Road that ran from Sardis, western Anatolia, to the eastern terminus Susa, southwest Iran. It was 2,575 km / 1,600 miles long.

Silk Road

The Silk Road which was an ancient trade route that linked China with the West in the eastern Mediterranean existed as early as the 3C BC. The Silk Road served both as a commercial bridge between East and West (Chinese and Roman Civilizations) and as a conveyer of heterogeneous political, social, artistic and religious customs and convictions, including Buddhism. Wool, gold and silver were sent to the East while silk made its way to the West. This 6,400 km / 4,000 mi long caravan road began in China and continued through Taklamaran Desert, Pamir Mountains and Afghanistan to reach the eastern Mediterranean. In those regions the goods were loaded onto ships and sent to the western world. Dominated sporadically by nomadic tribes and the Chinese, the Silk Road came under Islamic Turkish rule in the 10C AD and then under Mongol domination in the 13C. After the opening of a sea passage between Europe and India in the 15C, the Silk Road gradually declined in importance. Nowadays, studies to revive the historic Silk Road as a new tourist attraction have commenced in Turkey.

Sardis, One of the Seven Churches of Revelation

(Revelation 3:1-6)

(1) "To the leader of the church in Sardis write this letter:

"This message is sent to you by the one who has the seven-fold Spirit of God and the seven stars.

"I know your reputation as a live and active church, but you are dead. (2) Now wake up! Strengthen what little remains—for even what is left is at the point of death. Your deeds are far from right in the sight of God. (3) Go back to what you heard and believed at first; hold to it firmly and turn to me again. Unless you do, I will come suddenly upon you, unexpected as a thief and punish you.

(4) "Yet even there is Sardis some haven't soiled their garments with the world's filth; they shall walk with me in white, for they are worthy. (5) Everyone who conquers will be clothed in white and I will not erase his name from the Book of Life, but I will announce before my Father and his angels that he is mine.

(6) "Let all who can hear, listen to what the Spirit is saying to the churches.[62]

The Site

Sardis has the largest known ancient synagogue.

The ruins of Sardis can be divided into four areas: the Acropolis on Bozdağ (Mount Tmolos), the Pactolos Valley where the Artemis Temple was built, the city located on both sides of the modern highway between Ankara and İzmir and finally **Bintepeler** (the Thousand Hills) consisting of hundreds of Lydian tombs.

The ruins to the north of the highway are what were then public toilets, gymnasium and a synagogue. To the south of the synagogue was the main road of the city which had various shops, including a hardware store and a paint shop. The road once formed the westernmost stretch of the Royal Road. These ruins are of Byzantine period and have been dated to the 4C AD.

The Synagogue is from the 3C AD and once was a part of the gymnasium and restored to be a synagogue. Its size and grandeur are a testimony to the prosperity of the Jews in Sardis during Roman times and to their eminent position in the city. It was probably not originally planned to be a synagogue as it has a very different layout. It faces the direction of Jerusalem and the entrance is also from the same side through three gates, which open

SYNAGOGUE, *3C AD, Sardis* [157]

GYMNASIUM, *Sardis* [158]

from the courtyard into the main assembly hall. After entering, one has to turn back to see the two shrines between the gates. At the opposite end of the hall there is a semicircular apse with three rows of marble seats which were thought to be for the elders. The floors were mostly covered with mosaics.

The Gymnasium is a large complex consisting of a palaestra next to the synagogue, colonnades on three sides and the main building with the recently-restored ornate facade. According to its inscription, it was dedicated by the people of Sardis to Geta and Caracalla, the sons of Septimus Severus and to their mother Julia Domna.

It was a complex of symmetrically arranged rooms.

The Artemis Temple is located in the Pactolos Valley and was one of the seven largest ancient temples with eight columns at each end and twenty along each side. It was be-

[62] *The One Year Bible*, Tyndale House Publishers, Inc., 1985

ARTEMIS TEMPLE,
4C BC, Sardis [159]

IONIC COLUMNS OF
ARTEMIS TEMPLE
viewed from the 4C AD
Church, Sardis [160]

lieved that an altar dedicated to Artemis had existed there as early as the 5C BC. The temple was built in stages, the first part being constructed in 300 BC. Later further construction took place in the 2C BC. Again only part of the project was completed. The third stage started in the 2C AD. At this stage the cella was divided into two halves by an internal cross-wall, the western half dedicated to Artemis and

the other half to the Empress Faustina, who was deified after her death.

The fact that many Artemis temples in the Aegean region face west is testimony to Ekrem Akurgal's conclusion that all these temples were connected to each other by an earlier Anatolian religious cult.[63]

Ruins of a small building at the southeastern corner of the temple belong to a 4C AD church. According to some sources, it is referred to as one of the Seven Churches of the Revelation. However, this cannot be correct as congregations, not the actual buildings, were meant by churches at that time.

ALAŞEHİR (PHILADELPHIA)

Philadelphia was founded by Attalus II of the Kingdom of Pergamum in 189 BC. It was a relatively young city when compared to similar cities of Anatolia. It was built upon an elevated terrace above the valley which lay on the Persian Royal Road.

REMAINS OF A
BYZANTINE BASILICA,
Philadelphia [161]

Because of its founder's love and loyalty for his brother Eumenes II, the city was called Philadelphia which meant "city of brotherly love".

There is not much to see from the early days of the city except some ruins of city walls composed of rough stone blocks of coarse workmanship and a basilica. The workmanship, the type of arches and materials used in the construction indicate that the building dates from the late Byzantine period.

Philadelphia achieved its fame as one of the Seven Churches of Revelation.

Philadelphia, *One of the Seven Churches of Revelation*

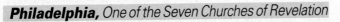

Philadelphia and Smyrna were the only two churches about which nothing negative was said by John.

(Revelation 3:7-13)

[63] Akurgal Ekrem,
Ancient Civilizations and Ruins of Turkey, Haşet, 1985

(7) "Write this letter to the leader of the church in Philadelphia:

"This message is sent to you by the one who is holy and true and has the key of David to open what no one can shut and to shut what no one can open.

(8) "I know you well; you aren't strong, but you have tried to obey and have not denied my Name. Therefore I have opened a door to you that no one can shut.

(9) "Note this: I will force those supporting the causes of Satan while claiming to be mine (but they aren't—they are lying) to fall at your feet and acknowledge that you are the ones I love.

(10) "Because you have patiently obeyed me despite the persecution, therefore I will protect you from the time of Great Tribulation and temptation, which will come upon the world to test everyone alive. (11) Look, I am coming soon! Hold tightly to the little strength you have—so that no one will take away your crown.

(12) "As for the one who conquers, I will make him a pillar in the temple of my God; he will be secure and will go out no more; and I will write my God's Name on him and he will be a citizen in the city of my God— the New Jerusalem, coming down from heaven from my God; and he will have my new Name inscribed upon him.

(13) "Let all who can hear, listen to what the Spirit is saying to the churches.[64]

EPHESUS

It can be said that Ephesus is one of the most beautiful ancient cities in the world. In ancient times its favorable location at the mouth of the Cayster River made it the foremost commercial city of a coastal region that also included the cities of Miletus, Smyrna and Pergamum, but the silting up of its harbor gradually resulted in the loss of this preeminence. The city has been excavated for more than one hundred years; the extensive remains are predominantly from the later Roman period.

Ephesus formed a focal point in the ancient world because of its protected harbor and as a starting point for the Royal

[64] *The One Year Bible*, Tyndale House Publishers, Inc., 1985

Road via Sardis to Susa. It was also a cult center attracting thousands of pilgrims for traditional worship of the female, first Cybele, then Artemis and finally the Virgin Mary in the Christian period.

Ephesus was also home for the early philosopher Heraclitus.

Heraclitus (c.540-470 BC)

Heraclitus of Ephesus was one of the most fascinating of the early philosophers. He introduced into philosophy a new self-consciousness about method and language and a self-critical interest in the faculties used to attain knowledge. He developed a theory of the human soul; he praised its creative resources and spoke of the importance of self-exploration. "The death of souls is to become water, the death of water to become earth; but from the earth water wins life, and from water the soul also wins life."

When he said that the universe is ruled by logos, he was probably speaking of the ordering of the shifting, changing world that is imposed by human beings in their discourse and thought. He always urged that close attention be given to the polarities and concealed structures embodied in language.

His famous claim that an individual can and cannot step into the same river twice reveals an interest in the criteria of unity and identity: even though all material constituents have undergone a change, it is still, in a sense, the same river. Preoccupied with change, he declared that fire is the central element of the universe and he postulated a world with no beginning and no end. Heraclitus's influence can be seen in Stoicism and, most recently, in the style and thought of Friedrich Wilhelm Nietzsche.

History of Ephesus

According to ancient historians the myth of the foundation of Ephesus goes back to the period before the Ionian colonization. As it was customary in ancient times to consult the oracle before any important event, Androclus, the son of Codrus, the legendary King of Athens did this about where to settle or found a settlement. The answer was simple: "at the place which will be indicated by a fish and a wild boar". After colonists landed in Anatolia, they were camping somewhere near Ephesus and were grilling fish. A burning fish set a bush on fire causing a boar to leap out of the bush and run away. Remembering the words of the oracle the colonists decided to found their settlement there.

Some sources say that the city was founded by the Amazons. The city was an Ionian colony formed sometime after 1000 BC. Some authorities have suggested that the history of the city goes back to the Hittite period, c. 1400 BC, and it was the city which the Hittites called Apasas. The earliest archeological evidence is the Mycenaean ceramics found on the Ayasuluk Tepesi (Hill). This does not imply that there had been a Mycenaean settlement in the region of Ephesus. Mycenaean ceramics were popular and found in many other places.

Ephesus has been located at different places in different times. *Ephesus I* was located on Ayasuluk Hill and inhabited by ancient Anatolians, Carians and Lelegians. At that time there was a cult of the Great Earth Mother which acted like a magnet attracting pilgrims and settlers even before the Ionian migration. *Ephesus II* was on the north slope of Panayır Dağı (Mount Pion). As with other cities of the Aegean coast of Anatolia, Ephesus came to be ruled by Croesus of Lydia in the mid-6C BC, before passing to the

Persians in 546 BC. It joined the Delian League after the Persian Wars. In 334 BC it fell to Alexander the Great and subsequently to his successors: Lysimachus and Seleucid rulers. In the 4C BC the harbor threatened to silt up the settlement and it was moved to a new location between Panayır Dağı and Bülbül Dağ (Mount Coressus) by Lysimachus to form *Ephesus III*. The remains of city walls from this period can still be seen on the slope of Bülbül Dağ (The Nightingale Mountain). Later it was controlled by Pergamum, eventually passing into Roman hands in 133 BC. During this period, Ephesus became the capital of a province of Asia Minor and the population reached a quarter of a million. After the 6C AD, due to the persistent silting up of the harbor and repeated raids by Arabs, the city changed its location back to Ayasuluk Hill forming *Ephesus IV*.

Ephesus and Christianity

Ephesus is vividly alluded to in Acts 19-20 in connection with St. Paul's extended ministry at Ephesus. Apostle Paul probably spent two and a half years in Ephesus during his third missionary journey, until a riot forced him to leave the city rapidly. Some authorities believe that St. Paul was imprisoned in the so-called **Prison of St. Paul** in Ephesus. Eventually the belief in Christ and the veneration of his Blessed Mother replaced the worship of Artemis and the other deities. Ephesus was the site of the third ecumenical council in 431 AD, at which the question of the Virgin Mary being the mother of God was debated. In this council it was decided that Christ had a double nature as God and man, and the Virgin Mary was *theotokos*, god-bearer.

Ephesus, One of the Seven Churches of Revelation

(Revelation 2:1-7)

(1) "Write a letter to the leader of the church in Ephesus and tell him this: "I write to inform you of a message from him who walks among the churches and holds their leaders in his right hand.

"He says to you: (2) I know how many good things you are doing. I have watched your hard work and your patience; I know you don't tolerate sin among your members and you have carefully examined the claims of those

BASILICA OF ST. JOHN, *6C AD, Ayasuluk Hill, Selçuk* [162]

who say they are apostles but aren't. You have found out how they lie. (3) You have patiently suffered for me without quitting.

(4) "Yet there is one thing wrong; you don't love me as at first! (5) Think about those times of your first love (how different now!) and turn back to me again and work as you did before; or else I will come and remove your candlestick from its place among the churches.

(6) "But there is this about you that is good: You hate the deeds of the licentious Nicolaitans, just as I do.

(7) " Let this message sink into the ears of anyone who listens to what the Spirit is saying to the churches: To everyone who is victorious, I will give fruit from the Tree of Life in the Paradise of God. [65]

ST. JOHN'S GRAVE, *Basilica of St. John, 6C AD, Ayasuluk Hill, Selçuk* [163]

Basilica of St. John

At his crucifixion Jesus asked his beloved disciple, John, to look after his mother. John and the Virgin went to Ephesus between 42 and 48 AD and lived there. John was martyred under the rule of the Em-

peror Trajan. There has been much discussion as to whether John the Apostle is confused with St. John the Theologian whose name, Hagia Theologos, gave the Turkish name first for the town and later only for the hill, *Ayasuluk*. A small church on the Ayasuluk Hill was dedicated to him in the 2C AD. This church was replaced in the 6C by a huge basilica built by the Emperor Justinian, the impressive ruins of which are still visible.

The basilica had a cruciform plan with four domes along its longitudinal axis and a pair flanking the central dome to form the arm of the cross. Under the central dome was the sacred grave of St. John. Pilgrims have believed that a fine dust from his grave has magical and curative powers. In the apse of the central nave, beyond the transept is the *synthronon*, semicircular rows of seats for the clergy. To the north transept was attached the treasury which was later converted into

BASILICA OF ST. JOHN,
*6C AD, Ayasuluk Hill,
Selçuk* [164]

[65] *The One Year Bible,*
Tyndale House
Publishers, Inc., 1985

İSA BEY CAMİSİ, *14C AD, Selçuk* [165]

a chapel. The baptistery is from an earlier period and now located to the north of the nave.

The **citadel** at the top of the Ayasuluk Hill is a 6C AD Byzantine construction which was later extended by the Seljuks. Lower down the slopes of Ayasuluk Hill is the **İsa Bey Camisi,** a 14C AD mosque of the Aydınoğlu Principality period. It was built by İsa Bey, a grandson of the founder of the Principality. This is the earliest known example in Anatolia of a mosque that has an arcaded courtyard and pool. It is also the earliest representative of an Anatolian mosque with columns and a transept.

The Artemis Temple or **Artemision** was one of the Seven Wonders of the World and located in Ephesus. Throughout the excavations in Ephesus, the actual location of the temple was presumed to be in different places. Its ancient cult dedicated to Artemis was famous in antiquity and made ancient Ephesus a much-visited pilgrimage place. Each year one month was considered a holiday and set aside for the religious ceremonious observations.

The first temple was built in the 6C BC and was Ionic dipteros with two rows of columns on both sides and three rows in the front and rear. There were totally 127 Ionic columns with a height of 19 m / 62 ft each. 36 of columns were bearing sculptures in relief. In 356 BC a madman known as Herostratus set fire to the temple in order to make his name immortal. On the same night in Macedonia Alexander the Great was born. Later when he came to Anatolia he offered to make an endowment for the temple on the condition that his name should be associated with it. However his offer was refused with a

(top) **ARTEMIS TEMPLE, 6C BC,** *Ephesus* [166]

(bottom) **THE ONE REMAINING COLUMN OF ARTEMIS TEMPLE, 4C BC,** *Ephesus* [167]

polite and tactful answer; "it was unseemly for one god to build a temple for another".

The second temple was built in the 4C BC on the same ground plan but this time being on a base with 13 steps. The fact that the temple faced West while Greek temples faced East as a rule is some proof of it being of Anatolian origin. This is the same in the temples of Sardis and Magnesia on Meander. The columns were shorter and more slender. The famous sculptor Scopas made the column reliefs while the relief on the altar was of Praxiteles. In the beginning of the 5C AD the temple was destroyed by a fanatical mob; this act was regarded as the final triumph of Christianity over paganism. Out of the magnificent temple only one of the 127 Ionic columns and foundation stones can be seen today. This was erected in 1972-3 out of different pieces of different columns without reaching its original height.

Meryemana
(The House of the Virgin Mary-Panaya Kapulu)

MERYEMANA *(The House of the Virgin Mary-Panaya Kapulu), Ephesus* [168]

The stigmatized German nun Anne Catherine Emmerich who had never been to Ephesus had a vision of the House of the Virgin Mary and described it in detail to the German writer Clemens Brentano who later published a book about it. Catherine Emmerich died in 1884. In 1891 Paul, Superior of the Lazarists from İzmir read about her vision and found a little building which corresponded with Emmerich's descriptions. Archeological evidence showed that the little house was from the 6C AD but that the foundations were from the 1C AD.

This place was officially declared a shrine of the Roman Catholic Church in 1896, and since then it has become a popular place of pilgrimage. Pope Paul VI visited the shrine in 1967.

Amazons

In mythology, the Amazons were a race of women warriors who lived in Anatolia and fought with the Trojans against the Achaeans in the Trojan War. At that time, their queen was killed by the Achaean hero Achilles.

According to legend the Amazons dealt with men for only two reasons, procreation and battle, and they reared only their female young. The Amazons were frequently depicted by artists as being in battle with men.

Libraries of the ancient world

The greatest library was established (3C BC) by Ptolemy I in Alexandria, Egypt. The library of Alexandria grew over several centuries and held about 500,000 papyrus scrolls. The second greatest library was at Pergamum[66] which is said to have kept 200,000 scrolls. The Celsus Library of 12,000 scrolls followed these in size and prominence.

The Site

There are two entrances to the site, one upper and one lower. As it is slightly downhill, it is a better idea to start from the upper gate. There are no shopping facilities nor toilets inside the site and that is why in summer months it is strongly recommended that the visitor bring drinking water and wear comfortable shoes as well as a hat. After entering

[66] See the Library of Pergamum on page 348

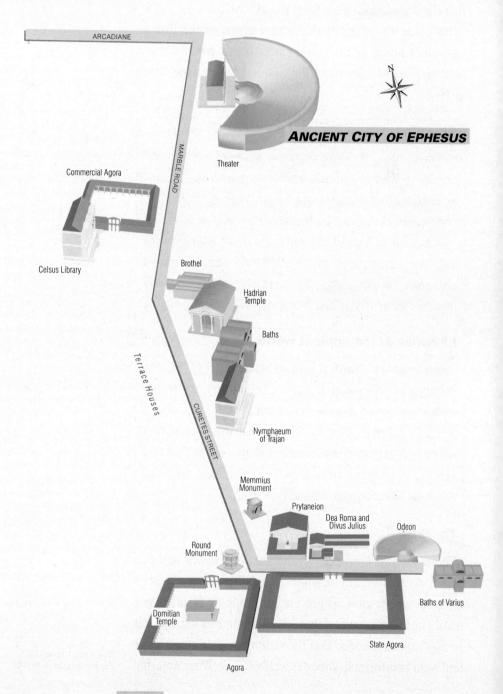

ARCADIANE

MARBLE ROAD

ANCIENT CITY OF EPHESUS

Theater

Commercial Agora

Celsus Library

Terrace Houses

CURETES STREET

Brothel

Hadrian
Temple

Baths

Nymphaeum
of Trajan

Memmius
Monument

Prytaneion

Dea Roma and
Divus Julius

Odeon

Round
Monument

Baths of Varius

Domitian
Temple

State Agora

Agora

the site from the upper gate, at the far right end there is the **Bath of Varius,** a 2C AD Roman baths complex. **The State Agora** was a vast public square laid out and remodeled during the reign of Augustus (27 BC-14 AD). The north stoa also had the function of a basilica, Ionic in style and divided into two aisles and a nave by two rows of columns. This three-aisled basilica replaced the single-aisled Hellenistic Hall. Meetings of the law courts were probably held there in the basilica. The construction of the basilica in the proximity of the prytaneion would not have been a coincidence. **The Odeon** in Ephesus was built in the 2C AD and had a double function. First it was a theater for theatrical performances as well as being the bouleterion for civic meetings. It was a two-storied building covered with a wooden roof with a seating capacity of 1,400 people. **The Temples of Dea Roma and Divus Julius** were Imperial Cult erected in the 1C AD with the permission of Augustus in honor of his adoptive father Julius Caesar, and of Rome. The Imperial Cult never became a true religion. Its aim was to create unity among people.

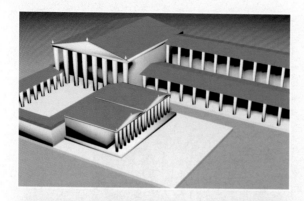

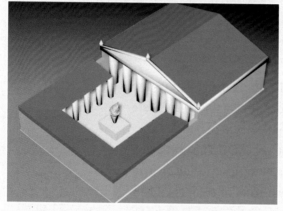

(top) **TEMPLES OF DEA ROMA AND DIVUS JULIUS,** *Ephesus* [170]

(bottom) **PRYTANEION (CITY HALL),** *Ephesus* [171]

The Prytaneion was the official administrative building or the city hall which housed the senior city officials. This was also the place of the Curetes, the six (later nine) priestesses of Hestia who were responsible for keeping the sacred flame burning eternally. It contained an assembly hall, administrative rooms, the state archives and a dining hall in which officials and foreign visitors were welcomed. In front of the assembly hall there was a Doric courtyard. Some of the stones of the prytaneion were used in the restoration of the Scholastica Baths. Three statues of Artemis "big", "beautiful" and "small" were found there. One life-size and the other double life-size Artemis statues are kept in the Ephesus Museum in Selçuk. **Memmius Monument** had an inscription which referred to dictator Sulla's capture of Ephesus in the 1C BC. The monument was a memorial which was dedicated to Memmius, son of Caius and grandson of Sulla. **The Polio Fountain** was a 2C AD building which was later restored in the 3C AD. Water brought by aqueducts is distributed from this fountain by a branching system of baked clay pipes. It was decorated with sculpture depicting Odysseus while he was blinding Polyphemus (cyclops) in order to escape from his cave.

During the Roman period, Ephesians erected many build-

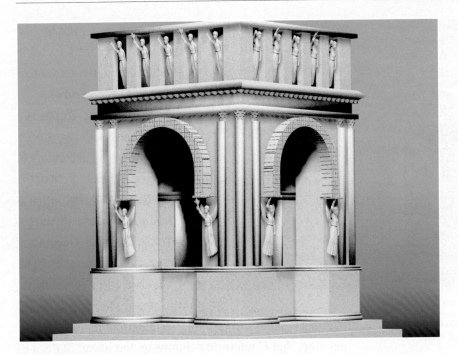

MEMMIUS MONUMENT,
Ephesus [172]

ings and temples, and dedicated them to emperors in order to secure good relations and the support of Rome. **The Domitian Temple** is one of them and is a 1C AD building. In the substructure of the building, parts of a huge statue which is four times larger than life were excavated and interpreted to be Emperor Domitian's. But according to more recent research the statue belongs to the Emperor Titus. Before this recent research it was believed to be the first temple erected in the name of a Roman emperor who referred to himself as "ruler and god".

The Hercules Gate can easily be identified by two reliefs of Hercules wearing lion's skin. The pillars date from the 2C AD but were taken there only in the 6C AD having originally stood elsewhere. The gate was made narrow to prevent wheeled vehicles which came from the Magnesian Gate going into the city. **The Curetes Street** lies between the Her-

HADRIAN TEMPLE, *2C AD, Ephesus* [173]

cules Gate and the Celsus library. It was named after the Curetes in the prytaneion. In literary sources the street was called **Embolos**.

The Nymphaeum of Trajan is a 2C AD building with two stories built by an Ephesian in memory of the Emperor Trajan. In front of the building there was a pool with water cascading from beneath the colossal statue of Trajan. One foot of his statue can still be seen. The pool was flanked by the building on three sides. The facade of the building is highly ornate with Corinthian columns on the upper story and Composite columns on the lower. Statues of other emperors, gods and heroes stood in niches. **The Terrace Houses** on the Curetes street belonged to the rich people of Ephesus. They date back to the 1C AD and some of them were used up to 7C AD. Many of them were three-storied and had open-air courtyards surrounded by rooms without windows but included frescoes and mosaics of mythological scenes. They were luxurious private houses with fountains and central heating. Between the street and houses was a portico with a mosaic floor, behind which were shops. A protective roof has been built to prevent valuable frescoes and mosaics decaying.

The Scholastica Baths, together with latrines and the public house, are part of a large complex which was built in the 2C AD and restored with stones brought from the prytaneion by a rich Christian lady named Scholastica in the beginning of the 5C AD.

The Hadrian Temple was built in the 2C AD and renovated in the 4C AD in the name of the Emperor Hadrian. It was originally in Corinthian style consisting of a cella and a porch (pronaos). The facade of the porch had a pediment supported by two piers and two columns including an arch in the middle. The columns and the arch remain but the pediment has not survived. The keystone of the arch has a relief of Tyche, the goddess of fortune. In the lunette over the entrance to the cella, there is another relief of a semi-nude girl, probably of Medusa, in acanthus leaves. Friezes were added there from different places in Ephesus during a restoration in the 4C AD. They are scenes relating to the legendary foundation of the city. From left to right: Androclus, the mythological founder of the city, killing a wild boar; Hercules rescuing Theseus, a mythological hero and the first true King of Athens, who was chained to a bench as a punishment by Hades for trying to kidnap Persephone from the underworld; Amazons, Dionysus and his entourage; Emperor Theodosius I, an enemy of paganism, and an assembly of gods including Athena and Artemis.

HADRIAN TEMPLE, *2C AD, Ephesus* [174]

The Latrines were part of the Scholastica Baths and built in the 1C AD. They were for public use. **The Private House (so-called brothel)** was also a part of the Scholastica complex. Though it has not been archeologically proven, some archeologists are of the opinion that this was a brothel with two floors, the upper floor being for ladies and the ground floor for visitors. In the main hall there are some remains of

LATRINES, *1C AD, Ephesus* [175]

CELSUS LIBRARY, *2C AD, and Gateway to Commercial Agora, Ephesus* [176]

mosaics depicting scenes of the four seasons. The statue of Priapus which is exhibited in the Ephesus Museum was found there.

The Celsus Library was built in the beginning of the 2C AD by Gaius Julius Aquila to be a memorial to his father Gaius Julius Celsus Polemaeanus, the proconsul of Province of Asia. In the Roman period all but the bodies of heroes were buried outside the borders of cities. Aquila was granted permission for his father to be buried in a marble grave in a burial chamber in the library. The columns at the sides of the facade are shorter than those at the center, giving the illusion of the building being greater in size. The three entrances are flanked by four niches with statues representing the virtues of Celsus, Sophia (Wisdom), Areté (Valor), Ennoia (Thought) and Epistémé (Knowledge). The semicircular niche on the main floor facing the central portal probably contained a statue of Athena. Although no traces have been found, it is thought that there was an auditorium for lectures or presentations between the library and the Marble Road. Between 1973 and 1977, an earthquake-proof reconstruction of the facade was completed.

The Commercial Agora was the center of the commercial world with a Doric stoa with two stories forming the eastern side behind which were shops and stores. The triple gateway next to the library opens into the agora forming its southeast gate. According

to the inscriptions in Latin and Greek on the gateway, it was built by two freed slaves Mazaeus and Mithridates in honor of Augustus and his wife Livia. In addition to the marketing of goods there was also a slave market of beautiful girls brought from different places by sea. A water-clock and a sundial stood in the middle of the agora.

The Marble Road is another main street between the library and the theater, but it was originally part of the **Processional Road** stretching to the Artemis Temple around Mount Pion through the Magnesian Gate. Traces of wheeled vehicles can be seen here. On the west side somewhere in the middle of the marble road, on the pavement is a piece of marble with graffiti showing a woman, a heart and a left foot. This is accepted as being the earliest advertisement in the world probably of a lady in the so-called brothel for sailors. It can be interpreted as "if you want to make love with this particular lady keep going in this direction and she is on the left-hand side of the street".

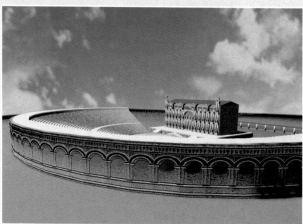

The Theater is one of the most impressive buildings in Ephesus. It was originally a 3C BC Hellenistic theater which was later restored, adapted and expanded in the 1C AD by the Romans until it reached its present seating capacity of 24,000 people. The cavea has a

HELLENISTIC THEATER,
3C BC, Ephesus
(top)[178] (bottom)[179]

horseshoe shape of 220 degrees and a diameter of 151 m / 495 ft. The uppermost row of the cavea is 30 m / 100 ft above the orchestra. The skene, the ruins of which are seen today, was a three-storied ornate building of the Roman period. The ground floor of the skene consisted of a long corridor

HELLENISTIC THEATER
viewed from Arcadiane,
3C BC, Ephesus [180]

with 8 rooms. This theater was the place where St. Paul preached. However, a goldsmith by the name of Demetrius provoked his fellow-craftsmen to a public outcry against Paul, with the cry "Great is Artemis of Ephesians". He did it because he thought this new religion could ruin their business. They made their living by selling statues of Artemis to pilgrims visiting there from far and wide.

The Arcadiane was a great colonnaded avenue which was renovated at the beginning of the 5C AD in honor of Emperor Arcadius. It was 530 m / 1740 ft long and 11 m / 36 ft wide leading from the harbor to the theater. It was paved in marble and had shops behind the colonnades. The two pedestrian walks in the colonnades were 5 m / 16 ft wide and paved with mosaics. At night the Arcadiane was lit by torches, making Ephesus, along with Rome and Antioch, one of the three ancient cities known to have had street lighting. Somewhere

STATUE OF ARTEMIS,
*with two animals
standing next to her, The
Ephesus Museum,
Selçuk* [181]

in the middle of the avenue stood a monument of four Corinthian columns probably erected in the 6C AD which supported the statues of the four apostles.

The Ephesus Museum is in the town of Selçuk at the eastern foothill of Ayasuluk Hill. The two best finds exhibited in the museum are the marble statues of Artemis. One is from the 1C AD and the other 2C AD. Rows of egg-shaped marble pieces on the goddess's chest have been interpreted differently as breasts, eggs, grapes or dates. In 1978 a new interpretation suggested that these pieces on the goddess's chest were bulls' testicles offered to her on feast days as symbols of fertility. Later excavations proved that the bull cult was really important. Similarly to Mother Goddess of Anatolia, she has two animals standing next to her.

Şirince Village

The charming mountain village of Şirince is situated in a remote spot among the mountain peaks 7 km / 4 mi from the town of Selçuk. The village is so beautiful that, contrary to the general tendency, migration to the village is from nearby towns or cities.

VILLAGE HOUSE,
Şirince [182]

Şirince was originally a *Rum* village. As part of the peace settlement after the Greeks were defeated in Turkey in 1922, a formal exchange of populations was agreed upon. As a result Turkey received about 500,000 Moslem Turks from Greece in exchange for nearly 2 million Rums who had been displaced since 1912.

The Rum population of the Şirince Village migrated to Greece as part of this exchange program. Their houses are the same old houses, though some have been restored and others converted into guest houses. Today the village is under conservation to retain its authentic appearance and offers visitors original views and nice experiences.

STATUETTE OF A SEATED WOMAN FROM ÇATALHÖYÜK, *with two animals, representing the Mother Goddess, Neolithic period, Museum of Anatolian Civilizations, Ankara* [183]

KÜÇÜK MENDERES (CAYSTER) RIVER

The river is 175 km / 109 miles long and originates from the east of Bozdağ and flows into the Aegean Sea after Selçuk. The harbor city of Ephesus which is today 8 km / 5 mi from the sea was built upon the abundant alluviums from the Küçük Menderes River.

AYDIN (TRALLES)

Size	34th largest city
Altitude	57 m / 187 ft
Industry	Olive oil, soap, textiles and cement
Agriculture	Olives, figs, oranges, tangerines, cotton, tobacco and sunflowers
Animal husbandry	Very little; sheep and goats
History	Ionian, Lydian, Persian, Alexander the Great, Roman, Byzantine, Seljuk, Aydın's Principality, Ottoman and Turkish Republic

The ancient name was Tralles. The modern name, Aydın was derived from the name of a leader of the Beyliks Period. It was the birthplace of Anthemius who was one of the two architects of the Hagia Sophia.

Anthemius of Tralles (c. 6C AD)

He was an architect, mathematician and engineer. Anthemius, with Isidorus of Miletus, built the great church of the Hagia Sophia in İstanbul for the Byzantine Emperor Justinian I in the remarkably brief span of five years (532-37 AD). Although Anthemius was not an architect or master mason by training, he wrote a treatise on the geometry of conical sections, had a knowledge of projective geometry and was familiar with the mechanical inventions of Archimedes.

The Church of the Hagia Sophia is still standing and still one of the most astonishing buildings in architectural history encapsulating a number of daring engineering and structural innovations.

BÜYÜK MENDERES (MEANDER) RIVER

The longest river in the Aegean region with a length of 584 km / 363 miles. The main tributaries are the Banaz, Çine, Akçay and Çürüksu. Due to the alluviums brought by the river, the bay where it flowed was filled and thus was formed Bafa Lake. For the same reason the harbor city Miletus is today 10 km / 6 miles further from the sea.

The river itself has so many turns and curves that its name contributed to international terminology; the word *"meander"* is now used to describe the winding, acute and frequent turns of streams and rivers, or zigzag movement.

PRIENE

The ancient harbor city of Priene probably changed its location when the silt of the Meander River threatened to bury it. Now it is nearly 16 km / 10 mi from the sea. The original place of the city has never been found but it was probably a peninsula with two harbors. Priene was laid out on a Hippodamian system of grid plan at the foot of a spectacular cliff on Mount Mycale and contained many famous examples of Hellenistic art and architecture. All the streets intersect at right angles. Remaining small with about 4 or 5 thousand inhabitants and never of great political significance it shared the same history as the other Ionian cities.

History of Priene

It was founded on the Ionian coast by the inhabitants of an abandoned Ionian city of the same name in c.350 BC. It participated in the Battle of Lade with 12 ships in 494 BC. Alexander the Great assigned the city to watch the unreliable city of Miletus. He also lived in the city and paid for the construction of the Athena Temple. After flourishing during the Hellenistic and passing through the Pergamene Kingdom periods the city declined under Roman rule and was later abandoned. Excavation began at the site in the early years of the 20C and the city has been partially restored.

BOULETERION,
Priene 183-A

The Site

The city is organized in four districts, the religious (Athena Temple), the political (bouleterion and prytaneion), the cultural (Theater) and the commercial (agora). In addition to the Athena Temple, the people of Priene built shrines dedicated to Zeus, Demeter and Egyptian gods.

The Theater is a 4 or 3C BC building and one of the finest extant theaters of the Hellenistic world. Although it was rebuilt in the Roman period it still remains as typically Hellenistic as the city of Priene itself. The theater was carved into the hillside and held a capacity of 5,000 people. Five marble seats with arms were provided for priests and dignitaries. In the middle of the *prohedria* there was an altar which was sacred to Dionysus. Performances used to start with sacrificial rites. The *proskene* is well-preserved and consists of a

TEMPLE OF ATHENA POLIAS, *4C BC, Priene* 183-B

colonnade supported with 12 Doric half-columns. The *skene* had an upper floor which no longer stands.

The Bouleterion is the most intact in Anatolia today. It was used for meetings of the town council. The bouleterion consisted of seats on three sides with a capacity of 640 people, and was covered with a wide wooden roof. The sacrificial altar was placed in the middle of the arc of seats.

The Prytaneion is located to the east of the bouleterion. It was the seat of the elected city administration and housed official receptions. Rooms were set around the courtyard. The shrine of Hestia was in an inner chamber where the eternal sacred flame was burned.

The Temple of Athena Polias was rebuilt in 334 BC as a gift from Alexander the Great and was a standard Ionic structure with eleven columns along its sides, six at the ends and two in antis. Athena Polias was the goddess of Priene and protectress of the city. The proportions of this temple were taken as a classical model or pattern by the Roman architect Vitruvius. The architect of the Athena Temple was Pytheos who also built the Mausoleum at Halicarnassus, one of the Seven Wonders of the ancient world.

MILETUS

Miletus, an ancient city located near the present Akköy at the mouth of the Büyük Menderes (Meander) River, owed its importance to its position on trade routes. It was one of the largest cities in Anatolia with a population of between 80,000 and 100,000. Highly prosperous, it founded many colonies and was the home of the 6C BC philosophers Anaximander, Anaximenes, and Thales, the town planner Hippodamus and architect Isidorus. Miletus seems to have produced geniuses the way Aphrodisias produced sculptors.

Thales (c.625-546 BC)

The philosopher Thales, who was considered as one of the Seven Sages, was born in Miletus. He is also said to have introduced geometry in the ancient world. According to Thales, the original principle of all things is water, from which everything originates and into which everything is again returned. Before Thales, explanations of the universe were mythological and his concentration on the basic physical substance of the world marks the birth of scientific thought. Thales left no writings and information about him is derived from an account in Aristotle's Metaphysics.

> Thales became famed for his knowledge of astronomy after predicting the eclipse of the sun that occurred on May 28, 585 BC.

Anaximander (c.610-545 BC)

Anaximander was born in Miletus and is seen as the earliest thinker about whom much is known. He wrote a comprehensive history of the universe. His bold use of nonmythological explanatory hypotheses radically distinguished his work from the earlier literary cosmologies.

Anaximander challenged Thales's view that a single element can be the origin of all. He argued that known elements are constantly opposing and changing into one another and that therefore something different from these elements must underlie and cause such changes. Anaximander believed that the universe is symmetrical, the Earth remaining stable at the center because it has no reason to move one way or another. He is sometimes referred to as the founder of astronomy.

Anaximenes (fl. c.545 BC)

The philosopher Anaximenes was the last of the Milesian School founded by Thales. Anaximenes's primary concern was the origin and structure of the universe. He maintained that the primary substance is air and that everything else in the world, including the gods, is no more than rarefied or condensed air. He believed that by rarefaction air became hot and turned into fire which formed the Sun and heavenly bodies. By condensation air became cold and formed wind, water and earth. Except for a few fragments, Anaximenes's writings have been lost.

Hippodamus (fl. c.500 BC)

Hippodamus is known to be the earliest town planner in the world.

The architect Hippodamus of Miletus is credited with having introduced geometric elements into urban planning. Many architects of the ancient world emulated the rectilinear grid system he used in planning the ancient cities, whereby buildings were constructed on streets which intersected each other at right angles. The public buildings were concentrated in the city center.

Isidorus of Miletus (6C AD)

Isidorus of Miletus was an Anatolian architect who, with Anthemius of Tralles, built the Church of the Hagia Sophia for the Emperor Justinian I in Constantinople. Similarly to his better-known partner Anthemius, Isidorus of Miletus was a theoretician or an academic rather than a professional architect. He taught stereometry and physics at the universities of Alexandria and Constantinople and wrote an annotated work on vaulting. When the original dome of the Hagia Sophia collapsed in 558 AD, either his son or nephew Isidorus the Younger built the new dome, this time with a steeper curvature.

History of Miletus

According to legend, the city was founded by Neleus, son of

King Codrus of Athens. Neleus came to settle with his men and killed the resident males compelling the women to marry the newcomers. After this took place the women swore not to sit at the same table with their husbands and also not to call them by their names.

In the 11C BC Ionians came to Miletus, and by the 7C BC Miletus was at its peak which was to last for more than two centuries. With other cities of Ionia in 499 BC, Miletus rebelled against the Persians, who had captured, burned it to the ground and enslaved its surviving population. This last battle was that of Lade in 494 BC, just outside the harbor of Miletus where the Persian fleet of 600 warships defeated the Ionian force. The destruction was so bad that when the play of Phrynichus, *The Capture of Miletus* was performed in Athens, as Herodotus reported, "the whole theater burst into tears, and the people sentenced the playwright to pay a fine". The role of Miletus was significant in the defeat of the Persians at the Mycale battle in 479 BC. Shortly after the battle, Miletus joined the Delian Confederacy with a contribution larger than that of Ephesus. Upon an agreement between the Persian Satrap and Athens, Miletus and other Ionian cities of Anatolia came under the rule of the Persians again. At the end of the 5C BC Miletus was ruled by the Carian satraps.

Captured by Alexander the Great after a siege in 334 BC and ruled by the Seleucid Dynasty in the following years, Miletus remained an important trade center into Roman times.

St. Paul stopped there in 57 AD on his way back to Jerusalem at the end of his third missionary journey. In Miletus Paul sent word to his friends in Ephesus to join him, and after speaking with them for the last time he bade them an

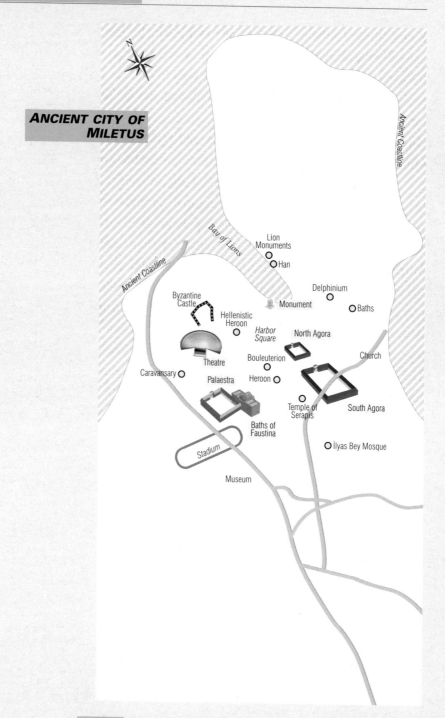

ANCIENT CITY OF
MILETUS

Ancient Coastline

Bay of Lions

Ancient Coastline

Lion
Monuments
Han

Delphinium

Monument

Baths

Byzantine
Castle

Hellenistic
Heroon

Harbor
Square

North Agora

Theatre

Bouleuterion

Church

Caravansary

Heroon

Palaestra

Temple of
Serapis

South Agora

Baths of
Faustina

İlyas Bey Mosque

Stadium

Museum

emotional farewell, boarded his ship in Miletus and sailed off via Cos and Rhodes to Patara.

THEATER, *2C AD, Miletus* [184]

The Roman period was followed by Byzantine and Turkish periods.

The Site

Miletus was a major port city located on a peninsula with four harbors. With the silting of the Büyük Menderes (Meander) River the ruins of the ancient city today are a few kilometers away from the sea.

The city had a grid plan which was developed by Hippodamus when it was rebuilt in the 5C BC after the Persians had sacked it.

The Theater was a small Hellenistic theater with a seating capacity of 5,300, but in the beginning of the 2C AD it was modified to a Roman theater and held about 15,000 people[67]. The lower section was built onto a natural hillside, and the

[67] In some sources the capacity is noted as 25,000 seats.

upper is supported by vaulted substructures up to a height of 40 m / 131 ft. The facade facing the harbor is 140 m / 460 ft long. During the Roman period the stage building had three stories and was 34 m / 111 ft wide. In front of the stage building it is still possible to see pieces depicting hunting scenes of Eros.

At the top of the theater hill was a **Byzantine fortress** which is thought to have been built mostly with the stones of the theater in the 7C AD but restored later by the Seljuks. **Harbor monuments** stood in front of the Lions' Harbor. There were two of them; different in size but similar in style. The large piece was 7.5 m / 25 ft high, mounted on a three-cornered base built on a round foundation with a diameter of 11 m / 36 ft. The smaller one was only 5.3 m / 17.5 ft.

(top) REMAINS OF ONE OF THE HARBOR MONUMENTS, *Miletus* [185]

(bottom) REMAINS OF HARBOR GATE AND 1C AD IONIC STOA, *Miletus* [186]

The Delphinium was a Hellenistic open air shrine surrounded by stoas on four sides with a 6C BC altar in the center. Together with Apollo, the dolphin was sacred for the Milesians as they believed that when the first settlers sailed they were guided by god in the form of a dolphin. The annual festival and celebrations of Didyma were started here. An **Ionic Stoa** lay parallel to the **processional road** on the south of the Delphinium. It is a 1C AD structure which had 35 Ionic columns and 19 shops behind the columns.

The Bouleterion was a 2C BC building which consisted of a propylon, a courtyard and an auditorium. The propylon had three Corinthian columns and friezes depicting war scenes. It opened into a courtyard with a monumental tomb in the middle. There were four gates that opened into the main hall. The auditorium seated 1,500 people and had a wooden roof.

The Nymphaeum was first built in the 2C AD and rebuilt in the following century. It faced the bouleterion across the processional road and had three stories with statues of gods placed in niches and water spouting from the mouths of bronze fish.

The South Agora lay behind the bouleterion. It was a Hellenistic structure which was later remodeled in the Roman period. Today **the North Gate** is unfortunately another of the gems from Anatolia currently housed in the Pergamum Museum in Berlin. The South Gate was 180 m by 150 m (196 yards by 164 yards) and destroyed during the construction of İlyas Bey mosque.

The Temple of Serapis lay between the south agora and the Faustina baths. It consisted of a pronaos and a naos with Corinthian columns and a relief of Serapis on the pediment. The temple was a 3C BC building which was rebuilt in the 3C AD with a donation by Emperor Julius Aurelius.

The Baths of Faustina were 2C AD Roman baths which were built by Faustina, Marcus Aurelius's wife who usually accompanied her husband on his journeys through the Empire. The frigidarium had a reclining statue of the river god probably personifying the Meander River.

İLYAS BEY CAMİSİ (MOSQUE), *15C AD, Miletus* [187]

İlyas Bey Camisi (The İlyas Bey Mosque) was part of a complex which consisted of a mosque, medrese, cemetery and an imaret. It was built in the early 15C by İlyas Bey, the regional Ottoman military commander. The dome of the mosque was made of bricks. At the entrance are three arched partitions separated by two columns. The entrance is through the center arch. The mosque was destroyed in 1955.

The Caravansary is a 15C building built by the Menteşe Principality which had a lower floor for animals and an upper for people.

DIDYMA

The word Didyma meant "twins" and was associated by some as being the meeting place of Zeus and Leto to have their twins Apollo and Artemis.

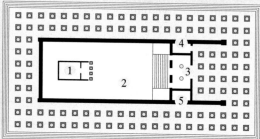

Didyma was famed as a prophecy center dedicated to Apollo which served a similar purpose as the Delphi of Anatolia. It was not a city but a sanctuary linked to Miletus by Milesians with a 19 km / 12 mi sacred road. However, this road may not have been constructed until the end of the 1C AD. In addition to pilgrimages made by sea, some festivals of drama, music and sports were held there every four years.

APOLLO TEMPLE,
4C BC, Didyma
(1) Ionic Shrine,
(2) Adyton,
(3) Antechamber
(Cresmographeion),
(4-5) Tunnels [187]

Apollo Temple

Even though it is thought that there was a shrine there before the Ionians came in the 10C BC, a temple at the same site was built in the 6C BC, and later destroyed by the Persians in 494 BC. In the 4C BC Milesians started to rebuild the temple but could not complete it because of financial problems. In the 1C and 4C AD Roman emperors tried but could not complete the construction either. Later in the Byzantine period Theodosius II had a church built in the open air courtyard which was destroyed by an earthquake in the 15C AD. Even in its unfinished state the Apollo Temple was regarded as one of the largest temples of the Hellenistic world, comparable to the Artemis Temple in Ephesus or the Heraion at Samos.

APOLLO TEMPLE,
4C BC, Didyma
(top) [188] *(bottom)* [189]

The temple was 110 m / 360 ft long and 51 m / 167 ft wide with a height of 24 m / 78 ft. It is a dipteros in Ionic order with 120 columns 108 of them surrounding the building by a double row and 12 in the pronaos. As George Bean points out in *Aegean Turkey*, the Apollo Temple "serves as a reminder that vastness in architecture was not purely a monopoly of the Romans". It was an unusual temple, not only because of its huge size but also for its antechamber with two Corinthian columns and two tunnels that led into the cella. The antechamber which was also termed as *Cresmographeion* probably served as an oracle office where prophecies were written out and delivered to people. In the middle of the temple there is an open air courtyard (adyton) with another Ionic shrine which housed the cult statue of Apollo. There were a few hot springs where the priestess of Didyma immersed her feet or inhaled the water's vapors for inspiration before prophesying.

The huge Medusa relief standing next

to the temple is a 2C AD piece which has fallen off the frieze. A little further stand the remains of an altar and a well. Before asking for a prophesy from the priests in the pronaos, people purified themselves with water from the well and gave votive offerings in the altar.

BAFA LAKE

Location	Midway between Selçuk and Milas, on the way to Marmaris or Bodrum
Surface area	65 km² / 25 sq miles. The largest lake in the Aegean region
Width	5 km / 3 miles
Length	16 km / 10 miles
Altitude	10 m / 33 ft
Formation	Originally the lake was a gulf (Latmos) in the sea, but because of the alluviums brought by the Büyük Menderes River it was blocked and formed into a lake
Water	In former times it was saltwater but during the course of time it has become a freshwater lake

BODRUM (HALICARNASSUS)

Founded possibly in the 11C BC, Halicarnassus came under Persian domination c.540 BC. The Persians ruled through native tyrants, one of whom, Artemisia, shared in the Persian defeat at Salamis (480). Later in the Persian Wars Halicarnassus joined the Delian League. The city enjoyed its greatest prosperity under Mausolus, a Persian satrap who achieved virtual independence in the 4C BC. The temple erected in his honor, the Mausoleum, became one of the Seven Wonders of the World. Captured by Alexander the Great in 334 BC, Halicarnassus soon declined. Early in the

(preceding page)
APOLLO TEMPLE, *4C BC, Didyma* [190]

15C AD, the Knights of Rhodes built a picturesque castle dedicated to St. Peter. Its walls were built largely of material derived from the ruins of the classical city. Remains of the Mausoleum, excavated in the 1850s, are in the British Museum in London.

Halicarnassus was also the hometown of the famous ancient historian Herodotus.

Herodotus (c. 5C BC)

Little is known with certainty about Herodotus's life. He was born in Halicarnassus in 484 BC. His work proves that he traveled widely throughout the Mediterranean.

Herodotus was a writer who wrote the first historical work in the conventional sense of the term history. He is therefore known as the father of history. Writers before him, such as Hecataeus (c.500 BC), wrote purely geographical treatises.

Herodotus tended to ignore the uncertain past. His theme, instead, was the enmity that developed between East and West from the time of Croesus of Lydia (c.550) to the Persian War of 480-79 BC.

Herodotus's History contains valuable and lively discussions of the customs, geography and history of Mediterranean peoples, particularly the Egyptians. In this respect he shows the influence of his great predecessor Hecataeus, but his work was written with wit and dramatic flair. Herodotus possessed a philosophical mind. Convinced that pride preceded a fall, he wrote history in part to show that evil deeds would be punished. He was also persuaded of the general instability of fortune for innocent and guilty alike: unchecked prosperity could not endure even for such well-meaning men as Croesus of Lydia.

MARMARİS *191*

MARMARİS

In winter it is a small fishing town. But in summer Marmaris is an attractively organized tourist resort. It is situated on the Aegean coast at the center of a scenically beautiful area of southern Turkey. The town lying at the head of a sparkling fjord is surrounded by pine covered hills with a backdrop of mountains.

Old Marmaris is clustered around an 11C AD Ottoman castle and many houses which have been restored to their original appearances.

The appeal of Marmaris is not the works of man but those of nature. Nature has endowed Marmaris with a wonderful harbor. There are regular ferry boat services to Rhodes from Marmaris. Marmaris is the best place to charter a Blue Cruise heading east along the Lycian coast.

DALYAN (FISH WEIR) AND CAUNUS

The modern town Dalyan is located on the east bank of the Dalyan Çayı (River) and the ancient Carian city of Caunus lies on the western bank. The Dalyan Çayı is the stream that meanders down to the sea from Köyceğiz Lake a short distance inland. The beach has been made a protected area as the breeding-ground of *Caretta Caretta*, the loggerhead turtle.

History of Caunus

The references about the past of Caunus has always been negative. According to Herodotus, people of Caunus were the natives of Caria and resisted to the Persians during their conquest of Caria in the 6C BC. Later it was sold to Rhodes by Egyptian generals in the 2C BC. In the 1C BC, they allied with Mithridates VI in Pontic king's wars and eventually lost. Malaria was endemic and many people contracted it.

ROCK-CUT TOMBS, *Caunus* [192]

Silting of the harbor was another major problem in the history of the city. As a result, Caunus had a bad reputation.

The Site

Hellenistic fortification remains with a tower and a gateway on the acropolis hill, rock-cut **Lycian tombs**, a **Hellenistic stoa**, a **fountain house**, a **palaestra**, a **theater**, a **Byzantine church** and the **terrace temple** are among the ruins of the ancient city of Caunus.

FETHİYE (TELMESSUS)

Fethiye has become popular for beach holidays and yacht cruises. The modern town of Fethiye covers the site of ancient Telmessus.

History of Telmessus

(preceding page)
Dalyan [193]

Ölüdeniz, *Fethiye* [194]

Although it was not then a Lycian city, Telmessus was first mentioned in the tribute lists of the Delian League in the 5C BC. It became Lycian in the 4C BC only after the siege of the city by Pericles, King of Limyra. Later, it was taken by one of the governors of Alexander the Great with a trick similar to the Trojan Horse. An orchestra consisting of women passed the guards and occupied the acropolis.

Telmessus became part of the Roman province of Asia in 133 BC. During the Byzantine period Telmessus was known as Anastasiopolis. Rum population lived in the area until 1922.

The Site

The hill behind Fethiye is encircled by a strong wall which is the only remain of a **medieval castle.**

ÖLÜDENİZ, *Fethiye*[195]

More than 20 **Lycian rock tombs** in the steep rock wall above the town are the rare surviving remains of the ancient times. Among these tombs the most prominent is the one which belongs to **Amyntas.** It dates from the 4C BC and is in the form of an Ionic temple with two Ionic columns. Most of the tombs are of the house-types imitating the Lycian wooden houses in their plans.

Kaya Köy (Rock Village)

A ghost village which is not to be missed is the Kaya Village. Until very recently there was a Rum population living in this village. After the great population exchange it was deserted and today it is a scenic ghost village.

Ölüdeniz (Dead Sea)

Dead is in the sense of calm. It is a sheltered lagoon of great beauty, almost totally cut off from the sea, at the northern end of a long cove. Stretching from the lagoon to the southern end of the cove is a long, sandy public beach.

GEYRE (APHRODISIAS)

"Imagine coming upon a city of antiquity so rich in archeological treasure that choice sculptures roll off the sides of ditches, tumble from old walls, and lie jam-packed amid colonnaded ruins." Those are the words of Turkish archeologist Professor Kenan Erim who directed the excavations at Aphrodisias under the auspices of the New York University. He is so

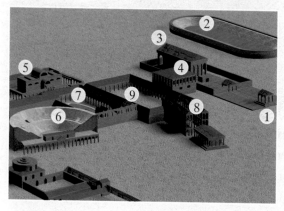

closely associated with the site that he can suitably be accepted as the father of Aphrodisias and therefore fully deserved to be buried near the Tetrapylon.

The name of the city has the same root as "aphrodisiac". Both words derive from the Greek name for the goddess of love, Aphrodite. Aphrodisias

ANCIENT CITY OF APHRODISIAS,
(1) Tetrapylon,
(2) Stadium,
(3) Temple of Aphrodite,
(4) Odeon, (5) Baths,
(6) Theater,
(7) Portico of Tiberius,
(8) Sebasteion,
(9) Agora [196]

was one of several ancient cities dedicated to the goddess of love. Within the borders of Caria, during the Roman period, Aphrodisias became an artistic center with a famous school of sculpture.

The site has been systematically excavated since 1961 by professor Kenan Erim and has yielded a wealth of art treasures to archaeologists.

Names of many sculptors from Aphrodisias have been seen in lots of works in Italy, Greece and elsewhere. Fame of Aphrodisias is not only limited to arts. It also had a number of renowned scholars and writers as well as philosophers, of whom the most notable was Xenocrates.

Xenocrates (c.395-314 BC)

The philosopher Xenocrates who had been a student of

Plato's and a friend and classmate of Aristotle's, lived in Aphrodisias. Deciding that the role of mathematics had been overemphasized, Xenocrates tried to return the Platonic forms to center stage. In doing this, he stressed their difference from the mathematical and natural things in a way open to misunderstanding if "difference" were taken to imply "irrelevance." Xenocrates seems to have introduced a kind of formal Atomism into physics and geometry.

School of Sculpture

Statues were carved from the local white, grayish blue Carian marble, mostly from Babadağ (Salbakos), 2,308 m / 7,572 ft high nearby mountain. Sculptors from other areas came to Aphrodisias for annual sculpture competitions. The eyes of the statues found here are full of expression and vitality and the bodies seem capable of moving. The public monuments in Aphrodisias were decorated with "peopled scrolls" which were one of the characteristics of stone carving produced by the school of sculpture in Aphrodisias.

History of Aphrodisias

Excavations in the 24-meter-high (78 ft) theater hill have revealed layers of settlement going back to the Bronze Age (c. 2800-2200 BC).

It was founded in the 5C BC and flourished under the Roman Empire (1C BC-5C AD). Mark Antony recognized the autonomy of Aphrodisias in the 1C BC. In the Byzantine period it was first the seat of an archbishopric, then of the metropolitan of Caria. In the 6C AD the name of Aphrodisias was changed to Stavropolis, the city of the Cross, to erase the pagan goddess of love from people's minds. As the capital of Caria Aphrodisias was finally called Caria which

GRAVE OF KENAN ERİM, *Aphrodisias* [197]

TETRAPYLON, 2C AD, Aphrodisias [198]

then became Geyre in Turkish. Later in the 13C it was abandoned.

The Site

The Tetrapylon is a monumental gateway which was probably built in the 2C AD during the reign of Hadrian. It had 4 rows of 4 columns. It is thought to have marked the intersection of a major street with a sacred way heading toward the sanctuary of Aphrodite.

The Stadium is one of the best preserved stadia in Anatolia. It is 262 m / 286 yards long, 59 m / 64 yards wide with 22 rows of seats with a 30,000 spectator capacity. Originally it had a blind arcade on top of the highest row surrounding all the seats. The stadium was used for sporting, musical and dramatic events. The eastern part of the arena was for gladiatorial fights.

The Temple of Aphrodite, a late Hellenistic building, was originally designed as an Ionic temple with 40 columns arranged in an 8 by 13 rectangle. It was converted into a church in the Byzantine period. The columns at each end were removed, an apse was built in the eastern section, and a baptistery and an atrium were added to the west.

The affinities between Aphrodite and Ishtar are generally well-recognized. In Mesopotamian mythology, Ishtar was the principal goddess of the Babylonians and Assyrians. She was both the compassionate mother of all life, who brought fertility and relief from sickness, and the lustful goddess of sexual love and war.

Life in the city was concentrated around the Temple

TEMPLE OF APHRODITE, *late Hellenistic period, Aphrodisias* [199]

STADIUM, *Roman period, Aphrodisias* [200]

(top) **ODEON,** *Aphrodisias* [201]

(bottom) **PORTICO OF TIBERIUS** *with a huge basin or pool, 1C AD, Aphrodisias* [202]

of Aphrodite. The cult of Aphrodite was so popular that it took some time before Christianity was fully accepted by Aphrodisians.

The Bishop's Residence consisted of halls and rooms, is thought to have been the residence of the bishop of Aphrodisias in early Byzantine times. Its large audience chamber was typical of a governor's residence in Roman provinces.

The Odeon is a semicircular building and has 12 tiered rows of seats with lions' feet. It actually had more rows of seats and was once roofed. The seating capacity was 1,700. A corridor at the back of the stage led to a porticoed area which was adorned with the statues of important Aphrodisians and was connected to the agora. The south-west corner of the portico of Tiberius is a long and narrow 1C AD **basilica,** an administrative and an official building of importance.

The Baths of Hadrian were built under Hadrian in the 2C AD. There were two pairs of large rooms on either side of a huge central hall called the caldarium.

Building of the **Portico of Tiberius,** whose Ionic colonnade has partially been restored, was started during the reign of Tiberius, 1C AD which explains why it was named after him. The central area of the portico is occupied by a huge basin or pool, 175 m / 574 ft long, 25 m / 82 ft wide and 1 m /

3.28 ft deep with two semicircular extremities at the north and east ends. The portico may well have been a gymnasium or a palaestra with an exercise area between the colonnade and the pool.

The Theater was built in the late Hellenistic period and later restored in the 1C BC, and according to its inscription it was dedicated to Aphrodite and the people of the city by Julius Zoilos, a former slave of Octavian. The seating capacity was 8,000. The stage building consisted of six vaulted dressing or storage rooms out of which four opened into the corridor behind the proskene. The stage building wall in the north parados had Greek inscriptions of important documents related to the history of the city such as letters of emperors to the city or senatorial decrees. The orchestra and the stage building were restored in the 2C AD in order to make the building more suitable for animal or gladiatorial fights. The theater was seriously damaged in the 7C, and the Byzantines built houses on top of the cavea and converted the hill into a fortress by circling it with walls and towers.

The Tetrastoon, originally surrounded by four (*tetra*) colonnades on all sides with a round fountain in the center, had several functions in the Roman and Byzantine city. First it was a meeting place for the citizens

(top) **THEATER,** *1C BC, Aphrodisias* [203]

(bottom) **SEBASTEION,** *1C AD, Aphrodisias* [204]

(top) SARCOPHAGUS from Necropolis, Aphrodisias [205]
(bottom) SCULPTURE REMAINS, Aphrodisias [206]

and also by having surrounding small shops served as a market place. Finally it gave access to the theater. To the south of the tetrastoon was the Imperial Hall with **Theater baths** which have not been completely excavated. Among very unusual discoveries of archeology is the **Sebasteion.** It was a 1C AD shrine in which the emperor was worshipped. Sebasteion derived from the Greek "Sebastos", which is the Greek equivalent of "Augustus". It consisted of a 14-meter-wide (46 ft) courtyard and two parallel three-storied porticoes with a length of 80 m / 263 ft, of half-columns on both sides. The south portico had three different column orders on each story, Doric, Ionic and Corinthian.

The Museum

The exhibits in the museum are not arranged in chronological order but thematically. There are galleries for busts, decorative sculpture and religious sculpture as well as ceramics and other objects. The museum should be visited in an anti-clockwise direction. The names of the halls in turn are as follows: The Imperial hall, corridor of Zoilos, hall of Melpomene, odeon hall, display cases gallery, hall of Penthesilea, hall of Aphrodite and courtyard.

DENİZLİ

STATUE OF APHRODITE,
The Museum of Aphrodisias [207]

Size	19th largest city
Altitude	428 m / 1,404 ft
Industry	Textiles, wine factories
Agriculture	Grain (all kinds), sugar beet, cotton, tobacco, grapes
Animal husbandry	Sheep, poultry, beekeeping
History	Seljuk, Ottoman, Turkish Republic

Although Denizli is surrounded by many ancient cities which date back to very early times, the city itself is not very old. It was founded by Seljuk Turks.

GONCALI (LAODICEA AD LYCUM)

Laodicea was once an important city in Anatolia, built on a natural trade route. In the Roman period it was the metropolis of Asia. It was a center of banking and exchange and a cloth weaving center, where the weavers used goats' wool. The wool was a distinctive jet black, the color being the result of the minerals in the water the sheep and goats drank.

The city was founded by the Seleucid Dynasty in the 3C BC. It was named after the wife of its founder. For a period

Laodicea belonged to the Kingdom of Pergamum. During the early Christian period it prospered and an important council was held there in the 4C AD in the name of Christianity. The city was abandoned after a severe earthquake in the 5C AD.

Today Laodicea houses remains of a **stadium**, a **water tower** (next to the stadium), a **gymnasium** and **baths** complex (east of the stadium), an **odeon** (further away from the stadium to the north), a **nymphaeum**, a few unidentified buildings (probably civic buildings), a large **Hellenistic theater**, a small **Roman theater** and some fragmentary remnants of the defense walls. Comprehensive excavations have not yet been done.

The water carried to Laodicea came from a hot spring, so that it was lukewarm by the time it reached the city. Evidently this was known by John for in Revelation he accuses the people of Laodicea of being only lukewarm Christians.

Laodicea, *One of the Seven Churches of Revelation*

(Revelation 3:14-22)

(14) "Write this letter to the leader of the church in Laodicea:

"This message is from the one who stands firm, the faithful and true Witness (of all that is or was or evermore shall be), the primeval source of God's creation:

(15) "I know you well—you are neither hot nor cold; I wish you were one or the other! (16) But since you are merely lukewarm, I will spit you out of my mouth!

(17) "You say, "I'm rich, with everything I want; I don't need a thing!" And you don't realize that spiritually you are wretched and miserable and poor and blind and naked.

(18) "My advice to you is to buy pure gold from me, gold purified by fire—only then will you truly be rich. And to purchase from me white garments, clean and pure, so you won't be naked and ashamed; and to get medicine from me to heal your eyes and to give you back your sight. (19) I continually discipline and punish everyone I love; so I must punish you,

STALACTITE FORMATIONS,
Pamukkale [208]

unless you turn from your indifference and become enthusiastic about the things of God.

(20) "Look! I have been standing at the door and I am constantly knocking. If anyone hears me calling him and opens the door, I will come in and fellowship with him and he with me. (21) I will let every one who conquers sit beside me on my throne, just as I took my place with my Father on his throne when I had conquered. (22) Let those who can hear, listen to what the Spirit is saying to the churches."[68]

PAMUKKALE (HIERAPOLIS)

Pamukkale has always been a very popular settlement where the hot springs were believed to have healing powers, so the city became the center of a pagan cult in antiquity and a spa resort today.

The city was on the borders of Caria, Lycia and Phrygia

[68] *The One Year Bible,*
Tyndale House
Publishers, Inc., 1985

and had a mixed population. Citizens were usually involved in the wool industry and little has changed as it is still a textile center.

The Natural Aspect

The terraces were formed by running warm spring water, at a temperature of 35 °C / 102 °F containing calcium bicarbonate. When the water loses its carbon dioxide it leaves limestone deposits. These are of different colors and shapes in the form of terraces with pools, overhanging surfaces and fascinating stalactite formations. Pamukkale which means "cotton castle" in Turkish takes its name from these formations. According to scientists, if the water had always flowed at this rate, the terraces must have begun forming 14,000 years ago.

NATURAL POOLS,
Pamukkale [209]
(opposite page) [210]

A little further away from Pamukkale, near Karahayıt village is another thermal spring, **Kırmızı Su** (the Red Water) with warmer water but less carbon dioxide gas where the running water creates a reddish effect different than the white cotton terraces of Pamukkale.

History of Hierapolis

The ancient city of Hierapolis was founded by Pergamum, probably Eumenes II, in the 2C BC. Hierapolis is believed to derive its name from Hiera, the wife of Telephus, both being legendary ancestors of kings of Pergamum.

Hierapolis was also interpreted by some as the "holy city". All the surviving ruins of the city except the foundations of the Apollo Temple date back to the Imperial Roman period.

In 133 BC the city was bequeathed to the Romans along with the Kingdom of Pergamum by the will of Attalus III. It is also thought that a large population of Jewish people lived there who contributed to the expansion of the Christian belief. Hierapolis suffered from frequent large earthquakes and was restored many times, one of them being a complete rebuilding by Nero in the 1C AD.

The Site

Hierapolis is among the cities of the ancient world in which the grid-plan was applied. **The Necropolis** is the largest ancient cemetery in Anatolia with approximately 1,200 graves. Although in the cemetery there are free-standing sarcophagi and some round tumuli, the main attraction is provided by large tomb-enclosures housing three or more vessels and often flanked outside by sarcophagi, presumably placed there after the interior was full.

Hierapolis gives the impression of a large cemetery which, although the tombs have been visited by robbers, very large numbers of the structures and also the vessels are still in place; only the tomb gates (presumably of bronze or iron) and decorations have disappeared. Many of the tombs here were Christian and there is at least one large Christian basilica, for the Apostle Philip was martyred here in 1C AD and the faithful wished to be buried as close as possible to the holy dead. The gardens of the tombs in the necropolis were maintained by specifically established guilds. It was these guilds' responsibility to put wreaths at the graves on special days.

The tomb of the Apostle Philip, **the Martyrium** was built in octagonal shape in the 5C, according to the legend on a spot where he was stoned to death. **The Roman Bath** after the necropolis was originally built in either the 2C or 3C AD. In the early Christian period, probably in the 5C it was converted into a **Basilica**. **The Triple Arch** is the northern gateway to the city and was built in the 1C AD by the proconsul of the Asian Province, Julius Frontinus in honor of the Roman Emperor Domitian. It was constructed out of the local travertine and flanked by two round towers. It also had an upper story which is no longer standing. **The Colonnaded Street** is 1,190 m / 1,300 yards long with 6-meter-long (20 ft) walks on either side separated from the street by columns.

The remains of a huge 2C AD **Roman Bath** serves today as a small archeological **museum** with local finds.

COLONNADED STREET WITH TRIPLE ARCH, *1C AD, Hierapolis* [211]

SACRED POOL, *Hierapolis*
(top) [212] *(bottom)* [213]

The Sacred Pool which coincidentally contains many ancient column pieces is located in the Pamukkale Motel and is not to be missed. This pool may well easily be the remains of the original pool of the antiquity near the Apollo Temple. As John Freely says, "There cannot be another hotel in the world that has a swimming pool like this." [69]

Somewhere under the surface of the high plateau on which the city was built there was a vent of poisonous gases, known to the people of those days as the **Plutonium.** It was a shrine of Pluto, the god of the dead and the under-world. Only a closed room and a paved courtyard survived

to modern day. Geographer Strabo describes it well: *"The Plutonium was a man-high, very deep opening under a gently sloping hill...the vapors were so thick that it was impossible to see the floor...but any living creature that enters will find death upon the instant. Bulls for example collapse and die. We let some little birds fly in, and they at once fell lifeless to the ground. The eunuchs of Cybele are resistant to the extent that they can approach close to the opening and indeed go in without having to hold their breath."*

ROMAN THEATER, *2C AD, Hierapolis*[214]

The Theater is a 2C AD building in Roman style with many reliefs depicting scenes representing the Emperor Septimus Severus and from the life of Dionysus. In the 3C AD it was thought to be restored during the reign of Septimus Severus. The seating capacity was 20,000. In the 4C the theater was restored again but this time with additional changes in the orchestra which offered the possibility of water displays.

[69] Freely John, *The Western Shores of Turkey*, John Murray, 1988

ACIGÖL (BITTER LAKE)

Location	In the midway (50 km / 31 miles) from Denizli to Dinar
Surface area	153 km² / 59 sq miles
Width	9 km / 5.6 miles
Length	27 km / 17 miles
Depth	A shallow lake
Altitude	836 m / 2,740 ft
Formation	Tectonic
Water	As its name bears in Turkish, it is a saltwater with bitter taste

There is little evidence of significant life in the lake and the water cannot be used for irrigation. As an enclosed lake with no outlets it is fed by small rivers and there are differences in the levels of water. Flamingos live around the lake.

The Opium poppy
(L *papaver somniferum* Tr. Haşhaş)

A narcotic drug, opium is obtained from the juice of the immature fruits of the oriental poppy. There are over 20 natural alkaloids of opium, including codeine and morphine. The latter and largest component, contributes most significantly to physiological effects. Heroin is the most important drug synthesized from these natural alkaloids.

The Opium poppy is an Anatolian plant with a length of 50-150 cm / 20-60 inches which has green leaves, bluish purple or white flowers and a capsule.

A good quality of opium (Tr. afyon) which contains morphine and codeine is obtained from the milk of this plant. Its seeds which do not have a narcotic effect contain an oil used in bread and soap production.

This plant grows once a year, generally at high elevations of 1,000 m / 3,280 ft. The milk which is the raw material for opium is obtained by making cuts into the capsules with special knives at night-time. The milk secreted from the scratches becomes thicker and darker until daytime when it can easily be collected.

Opium has been grown for many centuries for use in medical treatments. There are strict laws for growing opium poppies in Turkey. As a general rule, people need licenses to grow opium poppies and their lands should not be far away from official control posts. In 1986 more than 3,500 tons of opium poppy capsules were produced from 5,400 hectares / 13,340 acres of land. In the 1950s the annual production was around 20-30 thousand tons.

OPIUM POPPY
(L papaver somniferum) [215]

For medical purposes, in the 1980s the world's need for opium was more than 1,700 tons per year. Turkey and India are the two leading producers and exporters of opium.

More than half is grown around the city of Afyon, the name of which comes from opium. Other places include Konya, Denizli, Uşak, Isparta, Burdur and Kütahya.

The Mediterranean
is the world's
largest inland sea.

THE MEDITERRANEAN

AKDENİZ
(THE MEDITERRANEAN SEA)

(opposite page)
BLUE VOYAGES, [216]
(bottom)
IN THE BEACH, [217]

It lies between the continents of Europe and Africa. The name of the sea is derived from the Latin *medius* "middle" and *terra* "earth," or "land", indicating that the sea was once believed by certain civilizations to be at the center of the world.

The Mediterranean is linked to the Atlantic Ocean by the Strait of Gibraltar (Cebelitarık), to the Black Sea by the straits of Dardanelles and Bosphorus and to the Red Sea by the Suez Canal.

SALDA LAKE

Location	Near Yeşilova midway between Burdur and Denizli
Surface area	45 km² / 17 sq miles
Depth	Salda is one of the deepest lakes in Turkey; 184 m / 604 ft
Altitude	1,139 m / 3,736 ft
Formation	Crater lake
Water.	In general it is a saltwater lake except for areas in the south where rivers flow into the lake. The water includes soda and magnesium and the soil is clay.

There are no outlets for the water of the lake. Partridges, rabbits and foxes are common around the lake.

BURDUR (ASKANIA LIMNE) LAKE

Location	55 km / 34 miles to the south of Dinar, on the way to Antalya
Surface area	200 km² / 77 sq miles
Width	9 km / 5.6 miles
Length	34 km / 21 miles
Depth	The deepest part is 110 m / 360 ft
Altitude	854 m / 2,800 ft
Formation	Tectonic
Water	Saltwater

TURQUOISE COAST [218]
(inset top) [219]
(inset bottom) [220]

As it is a closed lake with no outlets, the water is salty with a ratio of 2.4% salt. Because the water contains arsenic there are no fish living in the lake.

TOROSLAR (TAURUS MOUNTAINS)

The Taurus (white bull) Mountains stretch for about 485 km / 300 mi along the southern rim of the Anatolian Plateau, parallel to the Mediterranean Sea, from Eğirdir Lake in the west to the Seyhan River in the east. Demirkazık (3,910 m / 12,829 ft), in the easternmost part, is the highest peak in the main range.

THE TURQUOISE COAST

The western Mediterranean coast is dominated by the Beydağlar range of the Taurus Mountains. The roads which cling to the mountainside wind and climb above the sea level.
Driving through the Turquoise Coast which stretches to the west of Antalya, one could think that the name of the semi-precious stone should have come from the color of the sea. Actually, the name of the turquoise stone (French for "Turkish") refers to the trade of the material from the famous, still-active mines at Neyshabur, Iran, through Turkey to Europe.

PHASELIS

Phaselis is an ancient city where only surface excavation has taken place. This is why it is still among pine trees and under green vegetation. The combination of ancient remains with a forest surrounded by sea on three sides makes it a beautiful national park.

History of Phaselis

Phaselis, located between the borders of Lycia and Pamphylia, was legendarily founded by colonists from Rhodes in 690 BC. Because the land was not suitable for agriculture, Phaselitans excelled as great traders. They are supposed

PHASELIS [221]

to have bought the land in exchange for dried fish which led the emergence of a proverb "Phaselitan sacrifice" to be used for cheap offerings.

Phaselis was overrun by the Persians in the 6C BC and freed in the 5C BC. They minted coins in the 5C BC which show the bow of a ship on one side and the stern on the other. Phaselis proved its independence from Lycia by siding with Mausolus, the satrap of Caria, in the 4C BC. When Alexander the Great came in 333 BC they offered him a golden crown. This attitude showed Phaselitans' reaction to authority. Phaselis was known as the most prominent port city to the west of the Gulf of Antalya, until the city of Attaleia

ROMAN BATH,
Phaselis [222]

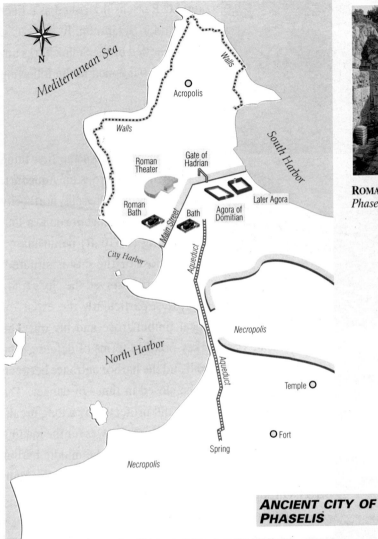

**ANCIENT CITY OF
PHASELIS**

was founded in the 2C BC. In the 2C BC Phaselis became
part of the Lycian Federation, but in the 1C BC was overrun and plundered by Cilician pirates.

Their obsequious behavior showed itself upon Hadrian's
visit to Phaselis in the 2C AD when they built numerous
buildings and erected statues dedicated to him. In the 7C

(top) **ROMAN AQUEDUCT**, *Phaselis* [223]

(bottom) **MAIN STREET**, *Phaselis* [224]

THEATER AND ROMAN BATHS, *Phaselis* [225]

and 8C Phaselis flourished as a fleet base under Byzantium. In the 12C it was inhabited by the Seljuk Turks until it was abandoned in the following century.

The Site

Near the parking lot the first thing that catches the eye is an **Aqueduct**. Three harbors of Phaselis, north, city and south, are arranged around a 400-meter-long (1,310 ft) peninsula on which most of the city is situated. These harbors served the city's trade activities, particularly the export of local timber, rose and lily oil. **The North Harbor** was the key point in terms of defense. **The City Harbor** had a sea wall and the harbor entrance between two towers which could be closed in times of danger. **The South Harbor** is the largest and protected by a long breakwater most of which is under water. This was for the loading and unloading of larger ships. Between the middle harbor and the monumental gate near the south harbor is the **Main Street**. On both sides of the 22-meter-wide (72 ft) main street are important Roman and Byzantine public buildings, baths complex, agora and suchlike. **The Monumental Gate**, built of gray-white marble blocks, was erected in the 2C AD in honor of Hadrian's visit and bears a dedication to him. **The Roman Theater** which probably had replaced an earlier Hellenistic theater, lies to the east of the main street on the hillside of **the Acropolis** and dates from the 2C AD.

MYRA

The ancient city of Myra, located a few kilometers out of Demre in the north, was one of the earliest Lycian cities. Myra was renowned throughout centuries as the city where St. Nicholas had lived in the 4C AD.

History of Myra

Although according to ancient sources the name of Myra only goes back as early as 1C BC, the inscriptions or coins found imply that it must have been from the 5C BC. Myra was always one of the most important cities in Lycia, and during the Hellenistic period was one of the six cities in the Lycian League that had the maximum quota of three votes at meetings of the federation.

When St. Paul was being taken as a prisoner to Rome in 60 AD, his ship called at Myra.

In the Byzantine period Myra was a prominent city not only

ROCK-CUT LYCIAN TOMBS, *4C BC, Myra* [227]

for religious reasons but also from an administrative point of view. During the reign of Theodosius II Myra became the capital of Lycia. However, in the Turkish period it was abandoned.

The Site

ROCK-CUT LYCIAN TOMBS, *4C BC, Myra* [228]

The ruins consist mainly of a theater and some of the best examples of Lycian rock-cut tombs. The rest of the city has not been excavated yet. The acropolis, as expected, is at the top of the hill.

The Roman Theater is well preserved. In the center of the two-meter-high wall (6.5 ft) backing the diazoma, near the stairs leading to the upper rows is a figure of Tyche, the Goddess of fortune, with an inscription *"Victory and good fortune to the city beneath"*. The stage building, like in all Roman theaters, is very ornate.

The 4C BC **Rock-cut Tombs,** some with temple facades and

beautifully carved reliefs representing the dead and their families or warriors, are among the most fascinating remains of Anatolia. Inscriptions are usually in Lycian. These house types are believed to have copied the dwellings of the early inhabitants of the region.

Climbing up the tombs is dangerous and not allowed.

St. Nicholas (c.300-350 AD)

STATUE OF SAINT NICHOLAS, *The Church of St. Nicholas, Demre* [229]

Saint Nicholas was born in Patara and became the bishop of the Christian church of Myra, in Lycia, about whom little is known with certainty. His reputation for generosity and compassion is best exemplified in the legend that relates how Nicholas saved a poor man from a life of prostituting his three daughters. On three separate occasions the bishop is said to have tossed a bag of gold through the family's window, thus providing a dowry to procure for each daughter an honorable marriage. The story provides the foundation for the custom, still practiced in many countries, of giving gifts in celebration of the saint's day, which was December 6. Saint Nicholas is the patron saint of children and sailors. Variations of his name range from Sant Nikolaas to Sante Klaas to Santa Claus; he is known as Father Christmas in England, Grandfather Frost in Russia, Pere Noel in France and Saint Nick in the United States.

Noel Baba Kilisesi (The Church of St. Nicholas)

St. Nicholas was buried in a tomb outside the city of Myra over which a chapel was subsequently erected. In the 6C it was replaced by a large church. This church is located in the town of Demre. The building was damaged by the Arab raids then repaired and surrounded with walls by Constantine IX and the Empress Zoë in the 11C. At the end of the 11C

Italians from Bari took the bones of St. Nicholas breaking his sarcophagus and built a famous pilgrimage church over his mortal remains in Bari. Several relics of St. Nicholas such as fragments of his jawbone and skull, are today kept in the Archeological Museum of Antalya. In the museum each year on December 6, the commemoration day of the saint, the Turkish government sponsors a St. Nicholas symposium attended by both scholars and clerics. On the same day a religious service is held in the church of St. Nicholas in Demre.

The church in Demre was restored a few times in the 19C and 20C. It has gained more popularity since 1950 because of its association with Santa Claus. The church is preceded by an atrium and a double narthex. The walls were covered with 11C and 12C frescoes fragments of which are still visible. The floor was decorated with mosaics of geometric designs. In the apse of the central nave is the *synthronon*, semicircular rows of seats for the clergy, with a special place for the bishop's throne and a walkway underneath. The central nave is separated from the side aisles by arcades. The roof was originally domed but covered with a vault during restorations.

The south aisle of the church, between two pillars and behind a broken marble screen, contains a damaged sarcophagus in which St. Nicholas is thought to have been buried. The lid does not belong to the sarcophagus. Where St. Nicholas was actually buried is still unknown. However, the processional way that led directly to the second south aisle was perhaps intended for pilgrims visiting the tomb.

In the niches of aisles are a number of 2C AD Roman marble sarcophagi taken there from Myra and reused for the entombment of church dignitaries. In the narthex there is a fresco depicting *Deesis*.

KEKOVA

Kekova is a name given to the most scenic area in Lycia along the Turquoise Coast. It covers a large area consisting of Kekova Island, **Kale** (Castle) village and **Üçağız** (the Three Mouths) village. Although there is a winding road that reaches this area, it is easier and more pleasant to go there by boat which takes about two hours either from Kaş or Demre. A **sunken city** was formed by the submergence of ancient cities probably due to earthquakes. The **Tersane** (shipyard) can still be seen on the shore of Kekova Island. Both the sunken city and the Tersane are thought to be from either the Lycian or Byzantine period, but neither of them has been excavated. On a narrow section of the western side of the island are the ruins of a **Byzantine Church** with its apse still visible.

The village of Kale has been identified as the Lycian town of **Simena** where there is still a settlement with stone cottages mixed in with Lycian and Roman remains. A **Lycian sarcophagus** standing in the shallows of the harbor of Simena is the most notable ruin. Other remains in the village are a 1C AD **Roman baths** complex, a **medieval castle** with its walls still standing to their full height, a small **theater** carved out of rock for approximately 300 people, **cisterns** and a **necropolis** with sarcophagi and rock-cut tombs out of the walls of the castle.

(top) A LYCIAN SARCOPHAGUS *in the shallows of Simena, Kekova* [230]

(middle) LYCIAN TOWN OF KALE (SIMENA), *Kekova* [231]

(bottom) KALE (SIMENA) *Kekova* [232]

PAMPHYLIA

Pamphylia which in ancient Gr. means "land of all tribes" is located on the Mediterranean coast of the Gulf of Antalya. By looking at the meaning of the word, it is understood that several tribes had been here at different times.

The northern and southern borders of Pamphylia were the Taurus mountains and the Mediterranean Sea. The western border with Lycia and the eastern border with Cilicia never stayed stable. Four major rivers traverse the Pamphylian plain, each associated with a city in ancient times. The Düden river was associated with Attaleia, The Aksu river with Perge, the Köprüçay river with Aspendus and finally the Manavgat river with Side.

The histories of the cities of Pamphylia are similar with the exception of Antalya, a later Hellenistic settlement.

ANTALYA (ATTALEIA)

Size	8th largest city
Altitude	Sea level
Industry	Ferrochrome, textile, food processing, fertilizer
Agriculture	Wheat, barley, rice, cotton, sugar beets, oranges, bananas, loquats,
Animal husbandry	Goats, beekeeping, sericulture
History	Pergamum, Roman, Byzantine, Seljuk, Ottoman, Turkish Republic

YİVLİ MİNARE (THE FLUTED MINARET), *13C Seljuk period, Antalya* [233]

Antalya, located in an area called Pamphylia, was founded by Attalus II, King of Pergamum, as a port city in the 2C BC. The name of the city, Antalya is derived from its founder's name.

Antalya had been a small city until very re-

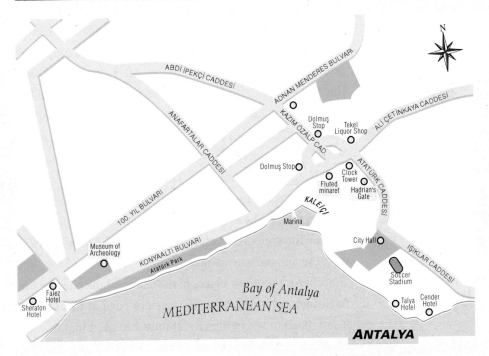

cently. Tourism has made Antalya one of the largest beautiful spots. Parallel to increasing tourism in the city, the population grows very fast these days.

Kaleiçi, which means "inner castle" in Turkish, has tourism to thank for its survival. Careful conversion of old houses into dwellings or pensions has subsequently maintained the original appearance of these fine buildings. Modern houses are not permitted. The walls of Antalya were built in the Hellenistic period but later restored and enlarged in the Roman and Byzantine periods. The impressive Roman structure of **Hadrian's Gate** was built by citizens of Antalya to commemorate the visit of the Emperor Hadrian in 130 AD. Located in Atatürk Street, it was made of marble and origi-

YAT LİMANI (MARINA),
Antalya 234

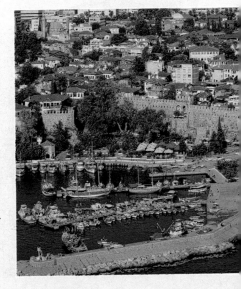

nally had two stories. It has three arched entranceways separated by piers with Corinthian columns in front of each. The gate is flanked by two 2C BC towers. After entering through Hadrian's Gate, a little further away in the old town center is the ruin of a mosque, **Kesik Minare** (Truncated Minaret). This building was originally a Roman temple which in the 5C AD was converted into a Byzantine church and finally in the 13C made into a mosque. **The Hıdırlık Kulesi**, a 2C AD round tower, is thought to have been the burial place of a local dignitary. **The Yivli Minare** (The Fluted Minaret) which became the symbol of Antalya, is part of a 13C Seljuk period medrese and mosque complex.

KESİK MİNARE
(TRUNCATED MINARET),
Antalya [235]

HADRIAN'S GATE, 2C
AD, Antalya [236]

Except for these few places in the center of the city and **the Archeological Museum** on the western edge of town, there is not much to see in the city. It must be noted that the Archeological Museum is one of the top five in the country, and not to be missed.

DÜDEN WATERFALL [237]

DÜDEN RIVER

 Although it is one of the major rivers of the southern Anatolia region, its length is not very long; 15 km / 9 miles. The water which forms the river travels underground from sources 40 km / 25 miles far away. In Düden park the water surfaces and continues till it reaches the sea. The water is used for irrigation of most of the parks in Antalya.

AKSU (CESTRUS RIVER)

 It is 162 km / 100 miles long and originates from Akdağ (2,276 m / 7,465 ft) near Isparta. Because of its sharp descent the water is not clear and deposits a great amount of alluviums. The river was navigable in the past.

PERGE

Perge is the best example of a complete Roman city in the Pamphylian plain. It developed from a Hellenistic hilltop settlement to a proper Roman city.

Apollonius of Perge (3C-2C BC)

Anatolian mathematician of the 3C and 2C BC, was known as the Great Geometer. In his Conics, an investigation of the mathematical properties of Conic Sections, Apollonius introduced the terms Ellipse, Hyperbola and Parabola. He was also an important founder of ancient mathematical astronomy, which applied geometric models to planetary theory.

History of Perge

According to ancient tradition the city, like Aspendus, was founded by Mopsus and Calchas in the 13C BC. Nevertheless, Perge did not appear in history until the 4C BC. Because the city was not fortified at the time of Alexander the Great, Perge willingly opened its doors to him. In the Hellenistic period Perge enjoyed rights of minting and considerable freedom under the Pergamene kings. The dominant motif used in art and on coins was Artemis of Perge. Artemis was associated with the Virgin Mary in the Christian period and worshipping her continued. Perge flourished and expanded in the Roman Imperial period during the first three centuries AD.

St. Paul and Barnabas visited Perge on their first journey on the way to and from Antioch. By looking at the existence of basilicas in Perge it could easily be concluded that Perge might have played an important role in the spreading of Christianity.

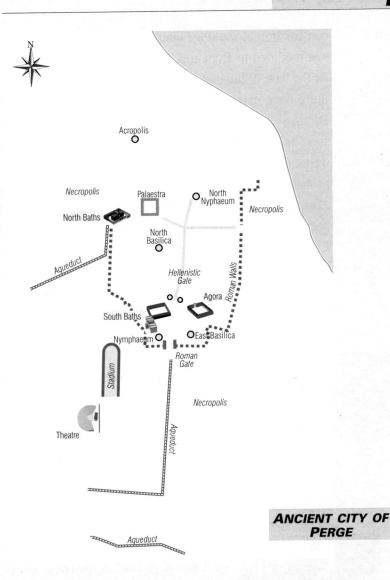

ANCIENT CITY OF PERGE

After the Roman period, Perge remained inhabited by the Byzantines until the Seljuks when it was gradually abandoned.

The Site

The Theater was originally a Hellenistic style theater with a horseshoe-shaped orchestra, but later, especially with the

[70] See Stadium on page 244

construction of the stage building in the 2C AD, the style was modified to Roman. The seating capacity was 14,000. At the base of the building, running around the stage area, there were many reliefs showing scenes from the life of Dionysus or river-god, Cestrus. By the outer facade of the stage building there was a 12-meter-high (40 ft) **nymphaeum** whose five fountain niches have survived. The theater was probably combined with the nymphaeum.

The Stadium[70] was built in the 2C AD, and is one of the best preserved in Anatolia. Others are in Aphrodisias and Laodicea. The 30 diagonally placed barrel-vaulted rooms under the rows of seats were used partly for access and partly as shops. The stadium seated approximately 12,000 spectators.

Access to the city was through the **Roman gate** which was located on the 4C AD outer wall. **The Baths Complex,** located to the west of the courtyard before the Hellenistic gateway, is preceded by a propylon. The typical succession of three rooms is notable, frigidarium, tepidarium and caldarium. Their basins, floors and walls were covered with marble. Statues which decorated the rooms are exhibited in the archeological museum in Antalya. Perge did not have marble quarries, all the marble was brought by sea mostly from Marmara Island in the Marmara Sea.

The Hellenistic gateway and walls are the only pre-Roman structures, 3C BC. The gateway consists of two round towers, which are a characteristic of the town

THE HELLENISTIC GATEWAY, 3C BC, Perge [238]

and a horseshoe-shaped courtyard. These imposing twin tow-ers were "updated" by Plancia Magna (the daughter of the Governor of Bithynia, chief priestess of Artemis and a bene-factress of the city) in the beginning of the 2C AD. She also commissioned a gateway with three doorways behind the courtyard in the direction of the colonnaded street. She was by no means the first to decoratively enhance the main gate of a city and its environs. What she accomplished there may have stood as a fine example of improvement to all the aris-tocrats and officials of the later Empire. To enter the city the visitor would pass from the large courtyard into the horse-shoe shape of the smaller one, decorated with statues of gods and of founders or legendary heroes of Perge.

The Colonnaded Street was a 20-meter-wide (65 ft) street lined on both sides with shops fronted by a wide, roofed col-

WATER CANAL
stretching through the Colonnaded Street to the Nymphaeum, Perge [239]

The statues in the courtyard were not simply decorative, but were used to express the heroic past of a city and to proudly salute its intellectual and physical achievements - scholars, gymnasts, heroes, lawyers, emperors and benefactors.

AGORA, *4C AD, Perge* [240]

ONE OF THE COLUMNS *with reliefs on the Colonnaded Street, Perge* [241]

onnade. It was flanked by statues of prominent citizens. An unusual feature of this city was the water canal lying in the middle of the street. It was not for drinking nor draining but to provide a delight to the senses by cooling the atmosphere during hot summers, giving a relaxing sound and reflecting sunlight on its moving water.

Its marble paving still shows the ruts of wagon-wheels. To the east of the street there are a few columns decorated with some reliefs on their tops. These reliefs are Apollo, Artemis with her bow and arrows, and a male figure in his *toga* pouring a libation. The colonnaded street stretches from the Hellenistic gate to the **Nymphaeum** and intersects with the other main street. **The Agora** of Perge is a small symmetrical rectangle surrounded by colonnades of shops. It was built when the city was enlarged in the 4C AD. There is a round structure in the middle of the agora either dedicated to Hermes, god of merchants or Tyche, goddess of fortune. There are still some signs of shops. Note a butcher's sign with a hook and a knife at the northeast corner of the agora.

KÖPRÜÇAY (EURYMEDON RIVER)

It is 184 km / 114 miles long and originates from the small rivers out of the southeast of Lake Eğirdir. It passes through the Köprülü Canyon (14 km / 8 miles) and flows into the Bay of Antalya. There are 2 Roman bridges on the river. In ancient times the Eurymedon was navigable as far as the city of Aspendus.

ASPENDUS

Aspendus was a major port city in the Roman period with the navigable river of Köprüçay. Visitors usually only see the theater on the hillside, however the aqueduct is also recommended.

History of Aspendus

According to ancient tradition the city was founded by Mopsus in the 13C BC. In the 6C BC the Lydian King Croesus took Aspendus. After Cyrus's victory over Croesus in the same century the city became Persian. In the 5C BC Aspendus minted its own silver coins. Alexander the Great

KÖPRÜÇAY (EURYMEDON) [242]

A WATER TOWER of Roman Aqueduct, Aspendus (top) [243] *(bottom)* [244]

took over from the Persians in the 4C BC. In the Roman period Aspendus entered into good relations with Rome.

The Site

Aspendus was founded on a hilltop near the Eurymedon river and it later spread down to the plain. The remains on the hilltop have not been systematically excavated. There are remains of an **agora**, a **basilica**, a **market hall** with shops and a **nymphaeum** on the hilltop. Water was brought to the city through a marvelous **aqueduct,** remains of which can be seen from the road further away from the theater. Remains of two water towers belonging to the aqueduct can still be seen. The aqueduct was the most impressive building after the theater.

Aspendus Theater is one of the largest ancient buildings in Anatolia and may well be accepted as the best preserved theater of antiquity. It was built by a local architect Xenon during the reign of Marcus Aurelius (2C AD). According to an inscription, it was a gift from the two brothers, Curtius Crispinus and Curtius Auspicatus, who dedicated this monument to the gods of the country and to the Imperial House.

ROMAN THEATER, *2C AD, Aspendus (top)* [245] *(bottom)* [246]

The theater's capacity is estimated to have been 20,000 people. The cavea has a diameter of 95 m / 313 ft and a height of 30 m / 98 ft. The stage building was three stories high. The uppermost facade was used to support an awning-like roof that projected out over the stage, erected more for its acoustical effect than for the shade it provided. The lower levels of the facade were decorated with a double colonnade, ten pairs of columns on each level, Ionic capitals below and Corinthian above. The central four columns on the upper level were surmounted by a pediment with a relief of Dionysus. Other panels were also decorated with many statues, portrait busts and reliefs. The doors under the stage building provided access to the orchestra for animals. The paradoi, unlike Hellenistic theaters, are roofed and parallel to the auditorium. The first row of the auditorium had special seats reserved for high officials.

SKENE OF THE ROMAN THEATER, *2C AD, Aspendus* [247]

The fact that the stage building is as high as the upper end of the colonnaded arcade surmounting the auditorium proves that it is a Roman theater. This is because the skene and auditorium is one complex and not separate constructions as in the Hellenistic style.

In the 13C during the Seljuk period the theater was restored to be a royal caravansary for the sultans who resided there on the way to their winter residences in Alanya. Red zigzag paintings are decorations from that period. There is a small museum to the left of the entrance exhibiting theater entrance tickets, coins and masks.

THEATER, *Side* [248]

Side is located on a peninsula penetrating into the Mediterranean. It was one of the important civilizations and has become one of Turkey's major holiday centers.

History of the City

Side was founded by **Aeolians** of the Aegean region. The history of the town extends back to the 7C BC. "Side" meant "pomegranate" in the local language. Until the Roman Imperial period, pomegranate was the symbol used on the coins of Side. In the two centuries following Alexander the Great, Side was dominated usually by the Seleucids of Syria and less often by the Ptolemy of Egypt.

The peak period of the city of Side started around 2C BC when it had established and maintained good relations with

APOLLO TEMPLE,
Side 249

the Roman Empire. This period continued until the 3C AD. The most impressive of the structures to be seen in town had been constructed during those times. Side lost its prominence during the 4C AD, however it prospered as a clerical center in the 5C AD. With earthquakes, Christian zealots and Arab raids, by the 10C AD, the site was completely abandoned, left to be buried.

The last massive settlement to Side has been in 1895 when Turkish immigrants from Crete were settled in the town. This settlement is the nucleus of the present town. But the old and the new are insolubly merged and intertwined in Side.

The Site

Entrance to the site is from among the well preserved **city walls** and through the **main gate** of the ancient city. But the gate itself has been damaged badly. After the main gate, starts the colonnaded street. The modern road follows exactly the course of the ancient avenue although the marble columns that were once used do not exist anymore. A few broken stubs can be seen near the old Roman baths.

The colonnaded street reaches first to the agora and to the theater. It was one arm of the two avenues of the **Corinthian** style. At the left side of the avenue are the remains of a **Byzantine Basilica**.

The remains of a public bath have been restored and now serve as the Museum. This building is situated before the **agora**, on the right side of the street. At the **Museum**, Roman period statues and sarcophagi are on display. The remains of the **agora** can be seen on the left side. This was also the place where pirates sold slaves.

After the agora comes the **theater** with remains of a **monumental gate** and a **fountain** at the entrance. The fountain has been restored. The present remains of the theater date from the 2C AD. The skene of the theater is in a bad state. The theater had a seating capacity of 15,000 people and was used in the late Roman period for gladiator fights as well. The theater was used as an open air church in the 5-6C AD. Near the theater was the Temple of **Dionysus** of the early Roman period.

The colonnaded avenue which starts at the gate and leads up to the theater used to extend on the other side, up to the harbor. This part of the avenue is now beneath the present town of Side. Near the harbor there are two temples side by side. One of these has been dedicated to **Apollo** and the other to **Artemis**. 6 columns of the **Apollo Temple** have been restored and re-erected. In front of the temples was a **Byzantine Basilica**.

MANAVGAT (MELAS) RIVER

It is 93 km / 58 miles long and originates from Şeytan Dağ (2,120 m / 6,954 ft). It has two dams; Oymapınar and Manavgat which has not been finished yet.

OYMAPINAR DAM

Location	It is 12 km / 7.5 miles to the north of Manavgat waterfalls
Surface area	4.7 km² / 1.8 sq miles
Depth	156 m / 512 ft
Altitude	185 m / 607 ft
Formation	Artificial dam
Water	Freshwater
Water capacity	300 million cubic meters / 392 million cubic yards

When it was built in 1984, it was the 3rd biggest dam in Turkey, but today it is in the 5th place. It has four turbines which are located underground and each of them has a capacity of 135 megawatts per hour. Total capacity is 540 megawatts. 45% of the electricity produced there is used in the Seydişehir Aluminum Complex.

KIZIL KULE, *Alanya* 250

ALANYA (CORACESION)

Alanya is the last major resort on the Turkish riviera and reached by a scenic road turning north toward the Taurus Mountains and Konya through banana plantations. Alanya's pride is its sandy beaches and the great fortress that crowns it.

Alanya has grown considerably in the past 20 years. New hotels and apartment blocks line the broad, elegant boulevards running along the sandy beaches stretching on either side of the town. During summer the population nearly doubles and the town turns into a lively colony of predominantly foreign tourists.

History of Alanya

The town did not play an important role in antiquity. At the end of the 2C BC, notorious pirate ruler Diodotus

ALANYA CASTLE [252]

Tryphon made it a base for his slaving activities. In 67 BC Pompey conducted a war on behalf of Rome against piracy on the Mediterranean coast of Anatolia. He completely destroyed the pirate fleet in a naval battle. Mark Antony presented Coracesion as a wedding gift to Cleopatra. A flight of brick stairs descending the cliffs is said to have been used by Cleopatra to go down for her morning swim. After the Romans and Byzantines Cilician kings ruled the city for about 150 years. Later the city was ruled by Seljuks. In the Seljuk period the town was renamed as Alaiye to honor the conqueror, and shortly after became the winter residence of the Seljuk sultans. Before the republic period the city was dominated by Ottomans.

The Site

The **fortress** is 117 m / 384 ft above the sea with medieval walls running 6 km / 3.7 miles around the summit. It was originally established as a smaller pirate fortress on the protected peninsula. It was conquered and destroyed by Pompey in 67 BC. Alaattin Keykubat captured the fort after a long siege and made Alanya an important naval base. Today's fine fortifications were built then. **Church of St. George** is a 6C AD Byzantine building. The platform pinned into the cliff at the edge of the citadel is said to have been the place from where condemned prisoners were hurled to their death.

The enormous **dockyards** (Tersane) and a **defense tower,**

Kızıl Kule (Red Tower) at the harbor contributed to the town's role as a naval base.

Among many caves the most famous is **Damlataş** (drop stone) on the western edge of the peninsula. It features an immense cavern with enormous stalactites and stalagmites that slowly continue to grow.

ISPARTA

Size	35th largest city
Altitude	997 m / 3,270 ft
Industry	Sulfur processing, carpet factories, rose products, wine, cement, fertilizer
Agriculture	Wheat, barley, sugar beets, opium poppies, roses
Animal husbandry	Sheep, goats
History	Lydian, Persian, Roman (Pisidia), Byzantine, Seljuk, Ottoman, Turkish Republic

EĞİRDİR LAKE [71]

Location	It is 35 km / 22 miles to the south of Isparta in the direction of Konya
Surface area	4th largest (2nd largest freshwater) lake in Turkey; 468 km² / 180 sq miles
Width	3-15 km / 2-10 miles
Length	50 km / 31 miles
Depth	6-7 m / 20 ft. In the south it reaches 13 m / 43 ft. The level of water rises in spring and decreases in autumn. The difference between the two levels is not more than 1 m / 3 ft. Because of cracks in the bed of the lake, the level decreases each year.
Altitude	916 m / 3,000 ft
Formation	Tectonic
Water	Freshwater

[71] Also called "Eğridir"

In the south, near Eğirdir there are 2 islands which are called Yeşilada and Canada. A part of the city's population live on Yeşilada. In the past, transportation used to be by boat but today the island is connected to the land. Water is supplied by small surrounding rivers. The excess water flows into lake Kovada which is 10 km / 6 miles to the south. Freshwater fish and crawfish can be caught in the lake.

BEYŞEHİR LAKE

Location	It is 90 km / 56 miles to the west of Konya on the way to Isparta, Antalya or Alanya
Surface area	3rd largest (the biggest freshwater) lake in Turkey; 656 km² / 253 sq miles
Width	20 km / 12.5 miles
Length	45 km / 28 miles
Depth	3-8 m / 10-26 ft. The deepest part is 70 m / 230 ft
Altitude	1,120 m / 3,675 ft
Formation	Tectonic
Water	Freshwater

MİHRAB OF EŞREFOĞLU CAMİSİ, *13C Seljuk Mosque, Beyşehir* [253]

There are 22 islands. On the islands and around the lake there are pelicans, cormorants, gulls and herons. To the west lie the Dede Mountains with a maximum height of 3,000 m / 9,840 ft.

BEYŞEHİR EŞREFOĞLU CAMİSİ (MOSQUE)

It is a very beautiful Seljuk mosque which was built at the end of the 13C AD by Eşrefoğlu Süleyman Bey, a local ruler. The walls are made of stone but the interior is wooden and is quite different from usual mosques. It has a minaret made of bricks. Next to the building there is an octagonal tomb with a conical stone roof.

42 octagonally-cut cedar columns divide the interior of the mosque into 7 *sahns*. Each of the columns has a diameter of 40 cm / 15.7 in and a height of 7.5 m / 25 ft. Columns are topped with wooden stalactite capitals. Inside the building, wooden stretchers encircle the walls below and above the windows. The *mihrab* is made of tiles with dominant colors of turquoise, purple and dark blue. The walnut minber is a very fine example of wood work.

EŞREFOĞLU CAMİSİ,
13C Seljuk Mosque,
Beyşehir [254]

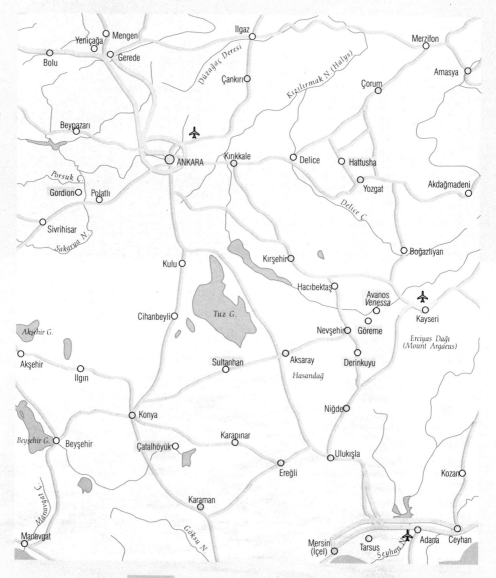

THE CENTRAL ANATOLIA

KONYA (ICONIUM)

The entire Konya basin was a lake 18 thousand years ago. Over 10 thousand years, it had drained to form a rich alluvial plain with fertile grazing land in the east and thick forest to the west and south.

PORTAL OF THE İNCE MİNARELİ (SLENDER MINARET) MEDRESE *by Emir Sahip Ata Fahrettin Ali, c. 1267, Konya* [255]

Size	7th largest city
Altitude	1,028 m / 3,372 ft
Industry	Aluminum, chrome, textiles, sugar, cement, animal foods, salt
Agriculture	Grain (90%), chickpeas, sugar beets, apples, grapes
Animal husbandry	Sheep
History	Chalcolithic, Hittite, Phrygian, Cimmerian, Lydian, Persian, Alexander the Great, Pergamum, Roman, Seljuk, Ottoman, Turkish Republic

In the days of the Roman Empire, Konya was called Iconium, "the city of icons". Konya has become a place of pilgrimage for Moslems because the leader of the Mevlevis, Mevlana Celaleddin Rumi was buried there.

The Mevlevis

The Mevlevi order of whirling dervishes is a mystic group whose members are followers of Mevlana Celaleddin Rumi, a great Turkish poet and mystic. The brotherhood is based in Konya, where its founder is buried.

Mevlana was never the head of an order, and the brotherhood was not established by himself but by his followers and devoted companions. The order derived its essence, rites, moral code and discipline from the mystical path first shown by Mevlana. It was a synthesis of spiritual love attained by a combination of music and dance which was considered to be the basic requirement for the spiritual ecstasy and devotion.

Mevlana Celaleddin Rumi (1207-1273)

Mevlana was born in 1207 in Balkh, Afghanistan. His father, Bahaeddin Veled, was a distinguished teacher who, because of his great learning, had been honored with the title of Lord of Scholars.

Possibly because of the threat imposed by the approaching Mongolian armies, Bahaeddin decided to take his family away from Balkh. They went to several places and after staying here and there, Bahaeddin felt drawn to Anatolia and came to Karaman in 1221. There they stayed for 7 years and Mevlana was married in 1225.

Alaattin Keykubat, the ruler of Konya, implored him to come to Konya. Bahaeddin finally acceded to the sultan's request in 1228 and he taught in Konya until his death in 1231. Mevlana took his father's place and quickly established a reputation for scholarship. He had an extensive understanding of all aspects of philosophy and was an avid reader of the works of classical authors.

One day in 1244, he met a ragged dervish who asked him a number of searching questions. This was the man known as Shams Tabrizi. Shams and Mevlana quickly became close friends and spent days and weeks closeted together in philosophical discussion. Mevlana left his teaching and appeared rarely in public. This caused jealousy and anger among his students and friends who believed that he had been bewitched by an evil sorcerer. In 1246 Shams disappeared as suddenly and as mysteriously as he had appeared. Mevlana became crazy and wrote poems about the separation of Shams. After long inquiries he finally learned that Shams was in Damascus. He wrote him letters begging him to return. Shams returned and their friendship and discussions resumed. In order to draw him more into his family, Mevlana offered his adopted daughter to Shams in marriage. However, one night in 1247, Shams disappeared for good. He was most probably murdered by his enemies.

A DERVISH *bowing to the sheik and kissing his hand, Sema Dance* [256]

Mevlana could not be comforted. He gave himself again to writing poetry about Shams. This time it was Hüsameddin Çelebi who helped him to continue his philosophical speculations. He inspired him to write his greatest work, the "Mesnevi". It was a collection of 25,600 poems in 6 volumes.

In 1273, Mevlana became sick and people around him knew that he was dying and they cried in sorrow. He told his friends that death was union with God and he was longing for this union. Finally he died on December 17, 1273, was buried in Konya, and a tomb was built upon his sarcophagus.

His views

Mevlana was not a man of reason, he was on the contrary a man of love and affection. His aim was unification with God.

According to him God could not fit into the universe but fit into the heart. Therefore we have to tend to the heart and not to reason.

SEMA DANCE *of Mevlevi Dervishes* [257]

TOMB OF MEVLANA *and his son Sultan Veled, Mevlana Museum, Konya* [258]

"Come, come again, whoever, whatever you may be, come: Heathen, fire-worshipper, sinful of idolatry, come.
Come even if you have broken your penitence a hundred times,
Ours is not the portal of despair and misery, come."

Instead of dealing with scholars of the time, Mevlana tended towards simple people like Hüsameddin Çelebi who was regarded as ignorant by others. According to Mevlana, a scholar was like a person carrying a big sack of bread on his shoulder. But, he asked, what was the maximum number of loaves they could eat?

The Sema

The Sema, rite of communal recitation practiced by the Mevlevis was traditionally performed in the semahane. It symbolized the attainment of the various levels of mystical union with God and of absolute perfection through spiritual fervor and controlled ecstasy.

The sheik is the representative of Mevlana on earth. From the sheik's animal skin garment extends an imaginary line across the floor of the chamber which is regarded as the cosmic guide to the ultimate truth.

The dervish wears a white coat over a long white skirt, which represents his burial garment. These are covered by a black cloak, which represents his tomb. The conical brown or white felt hat represents his tombstone. The only difference in the sheik's clothing is that his hat is encircled by a dark band. The ceremony starts with a communal recitation followed by a recital of the flute. Wailing of the flute expresses longing for the ultimate.

A FINE EXAMPLE OF CALLIGRAPHY, *Mevlana Museum, Konya* [259]

Before beginning their dance the dervishes bow to the sheik and kiss his hand. Then they let fall their black cloaks to symbolize their escape from the tomb and readiness to dance for God, they begin to turn slowly. Right arms are above the body palm facing upward whereas left hands face downward. This symbolizes that what they get from God's grace and blessing, they pass on to the world.

The dancers begin to move faster and faster. According to Mevlana, with the Sema, dervishes can reach out and touch the "ultimate".

MEVLANA MUSEUM, *Konya* [260]

Mevlana Museum

This place has been used as a museum since 1926. Inside the courtyard after the main por-

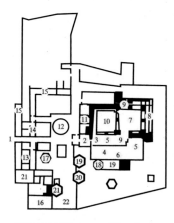

MEVLANA MUSEUM; (1)main entrance, (2)ante-room, (3)silver door, (4-5)graves of Mevlana's relatives and dignitaries, (6)green dome and sarcophagus of blue marble made for Mevlana and his son Sultan Veled, (7)semahane, (8)chambers for men and women, (9) partitions for musicians, (10)mescit, small mosque, (11) son cemaat yeri, (12)şadırvan, ablution fountain, (13-14-15)dervish cells, (16)kitchen, (17)the pool representing the Night of Union, (18-19-20-21)tombs, and (22)guest house [261]

CYLINDRICAL SPIRE consisting of 16 flutes on the Tomb of Mevlana, 14C AD, Konya [262]

tal, on both sides the cells of dervishes, kitchens and other buildings are located. The pool on the right is symbolically the Night of Union around which Sema took place each year on December 17. The anteroom before entering into the main tomb building was used as a place to read from the Koran by dervishes. Today fine examples of famous calligraphy artists are on display.

Inside the building on the right hand side of the hall, which is roofed by three domes, there are 55 graves belonging to Mevlana's relatives and dignitaries. Right under the center of the green dome lies a sarcophagus of blue marble made for Mevlana and his son Sultan Veled, made as a present by Süleyman the Magnificent. The blue marble sarcophagus is covered with a fine cloth with verses of the Koran embroidered in gold thread, a gift of Sultan Abdülhamit II in 1894.

The semahane is the hall where the Sema rituals took place. The lodges for men and women and partitions for musicians are also in this section. There is a selection of the instruments used to accompany the Sema -the ney, rebab, tef and tambur- and some of Mevlana's garments which have been preserved.

The small mosque section which is entered through a small door, was built during the reign of Süleyman the Magnificent. Valuable samples of calligraphy, illuminated manuscripts and book bindings as well as fine examples of Turkish carpets are on display.

There is one silk carpet in the collection with 144 knots per square centimeter (924 knots per square inch) which is considered to be the most expensive carpet in the world.

SULTANHAN CARAVANSARY

A caravansary on the way from Konya to Aksaray 40 km / 25 mi before the city. It was built by Sultan Alaattin Keykubat I during the Seljuk period, in 1229. It has two sections, one open with a courtyard and another covered. It is the largest of all Seljuk caravansaries in Anatolia with an area of 4,800 sq m / 1.2 acres.

Sultanhan is a monumental caravansary which looks like a fortress. The entrance is through a huge, geometrically decorated portal. The courtyard is surrounded by an arcade of rooms on the left and covered places on the right. In the middle is a small mosque. The entrance to the second part is through another portal which is located on the fourth wall. The center of this second part is barrel-vaulted, containing cathedral-like aisles covered with a dome and capped by an octagonal conical roof.

SULTANHAN CARAVANSARY, *13C AD, Seljuk period, Sultanhan* [263]

PORTAL OF SULTANHAN CARAVANSARY, *13C AD, Seljuk period, Sultanhan* [264]

Caravansaries

These are public buildings built on the caravan routes for trade in normal times and for military use in times of emergencies. Because they were made to be utilized by the caravans, the distances between them were arranged according to the usual distance a camel could walk. A caravan could walk for about a day, and would not want to continue at night time. This meant that caravansaries were needed every 25-40 km / 15-26 mi.

The Anatolian Seljuks particularly understood the importance of trade and did a lot to encourage it. In these buildings they provided the caravans with every possible service such as places to sleep, hamams, mosques, doctors and veterinarians, kitchens, coffeehouses, libraries, etc. There were times in which any service was free of charge for the sake of active trade. For example, they even gave animals without charge to people who may have lost them.

The rulers of caravansaries were responsible for security. As a general rule they closed the gates at sunset and did not open them until sunrise unless they were sure that no belongings of people had been lost. According to the weather conditions, people sometimes had to share the covered section with animals. In such cases the smell of animals was lessened by using a variety of incenses.

Today there are approximately 120 caravansaries still standing in Anatolia.

HASANDAĞ (MOUNT HASAN)

Besides Erciyas, another volcano which contributed to the formation of the Cappadocia region is Hasandağ. It is 30 km / 19 miles to the south of Aksaray. On a clear day it is even possible to see it from Cappadocia.

The height of Hasandağ is 3,268 m / 10,720 ft. It was formed in the same period as Erciyas however, Hasandağ looks younger.

HASANDAĞ [265]

MELENDİZ MOUNTAINS

The range of mountains between Erciyas and Hasandağ are the Melendiz Mountains and they are comparatively lower. The height is 2,898 m / 9,505 ft.

MOUNT ERCİYAS (ARGAEUS)

It is located to the south of Kayseri. On a clear day it is possible to see it from Cappadocia to the northeast. Erciyas is the highest mountain with a height of 3,917 m / 12,850 ft in Central Anatolia, and is one of the volcanoes that contributed to the formation of the Cappadocia region.

On some ancient coins it was shown as a bursting volcano. As it was always snow-covered the Hittites called it **"The White Mountain"**. According to the ancient geographer Strabo, one could see the Black Sea and the Mediterranean Sea from the top of Erciyas.

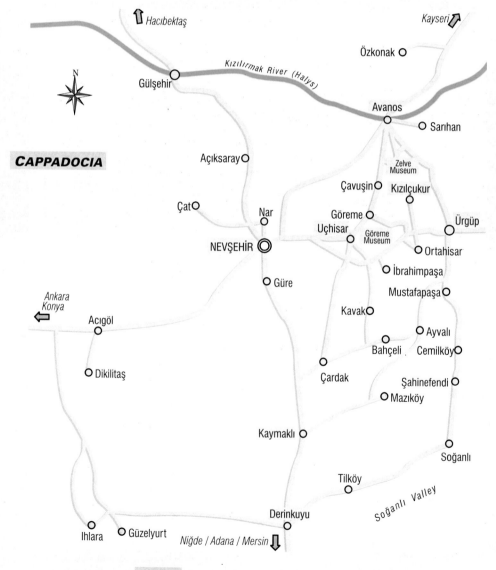

CAPPADOCIA

CAPPADOCIA [266]

Cappadocia (Kapadokya in Turkish) is the ancient and modern name of a remarkable region in Central Anatolia. It is a geological wonderland which is sometimes considered to have covered a triangular area between Kayseri, Niğde and Kırşehir, or more specifically, a smaller triangular area from Ürgüp to Avanos and to Nevşehir.

CAPPADOCIA [267]

Its harsh climate limits agricultural pursuits to growing grain and fruit. Its vast grassland was ideal for raising horses, sheep and other small stock. Silver, copper and salt have been mined.

Cappadocia can be viewed from three different aspects, natural, historical and religious.

VARYING FORMATIONS, *basalt is less affected by erosion and remains as a protective cover, Cappadocia* [268]

The Natural Aspect

The strange but beautiful formation of Cappadocia has had this appearance for millions of years. When the volcanoes in the region were active, the lava which poured out covered all previously formed hills and valleys forming a high plateau. This newly formed plateau consists mainly of tufa and some rare layers of basalt. This is the constructive stage of Cappadocia's formation. The destruction of the tufa and the basalt layers by erosion (heavy rains and melting snow in spring) and sharp temperature changes has continued for thousands of years and is still in process today. Wind in general has a circling effect while rivers have horizontal and rain vertical effects on the landscape.

The basalt is less affected by erosion when compared to the tufa and has served as a protective cover. This juxtaposition of different materials has produced capped columns, pyramids and conical formations with dark-colored caps known as *peribacaları*, fairy chimneys. A block of hard rock which resists erosion is left standing alone as the tufa around it is worn away, until it stands at the top of a large cone. A fairy chimney exists until the neck of the cone is eroded and the cap falls off.

History of Cappadocia

During the 19C BC, Old Assyrian traders were established among the numerous native city-states of Cappadocia. Between c.1750-1200 BC, Cappadocia formed the "Lower Land" of the Hittite Kingdom.

The Persians made Cappadocia a satrapy (province), through which passed the famous Persian Royal Road from Sardis to Susa.

CAPPADOCIA [269]

Cappadocia avoided submitting to Alexander the Great. After 190 BC Cappadocia was ruled by a native dynasty and the rulers became friendly to Rome. In 17 AD Cappadocia became a Roman province and was joined with the provinces of Galatia under Vespasian in 72 AD. Soon after, under Trajan, it was united with Pontus. The Roman period of Cappadocia continued from the 1C through the 4C AD followed by the Byzantine, Seljuk, Ottoman and Turkish periods.

CAPPADOCIA [270]

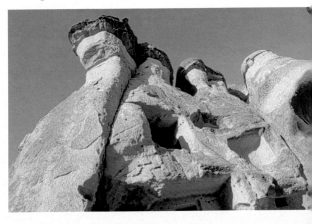

The monasteries of Cappadocia were abandoned after the arrival of the Turks and later occupied by the local people. Some of the Christian population continued to live here until the exchange of populations between Greece and Turkey in 1923.

PERİBACALARI (FAIRY CHIMNEYS), *Cappadocia* 271

The Religious Aspect

Christianity came early to Cappadocia. St. Paul passed through Caesarea (today Kayseri) on the way to Ankyra (Ankara). In the 4C AD Cappadocia produced three saints from the area. These are St. Basil the Great from Caesarea, his younger brother St. Gregory of Nysa and St. Gregory Nazianzus. St. Basil the Great was the son of devout parents and received his higher education in Constantinople and Athens but renounced a promising career to become a monk. Impressed by the ascetic life, he settled as a hermit in Cappadocia where he was joined by Gregory of Nazianzus. Basil ably defended the Christian faith among the churches of Anatolia, which had suffered from divisions caused by the Arian controversy. In 370 he succeeded Eusebius as bishop. As a leader who had brilliant organizational skills, Basil established hospitals, fostered monasticism, and reformed the liturgy. His Rule, a code for monastic life, became the basis of eastern monasticism, and the liturgy of St. Basil, probably compiled by him though later revised, is still used on certain Sundays in Orthodox churches.

Anchorites of the Early Church, who sought refuge from the distractions of the world in wild and remote places, chose Cappadocia which led monasticism to develop in the area. They devoted their lives to prayer, penance and fasting, often living in man-made or natural caves. Martyrdom was the ultimate aim of a devout Christian.

After Christianity was accepted as the official religion by Constantine the Great in 330 AD, the days of martyrdom went and a peaceful and secure life did not satisfy these people. The geography of Cappadocia was suitable for people who preferred ascetic lifestyles.

In the 7 and 8C AD when the Arabs began to raid Anatolia, monastic communities had to hide themselves and, where it was geographically easy, dug their underground shelters. In time these shelters developed into large underground cities.

Churches of Cappadocia

It is estimated that there are more than 600 rock-cut churches in Cappadocia. These churches that people carved were similar in plan to the ones in the capital. Walls were covered with beautiful frescoes and they were also influenced by the Iconoclast period in the 8C and 9C. Most of the frescoes date from the 11C and 12C.

Two different techniques were employed for the frescoes, they were either painted directly on the rock or on a very thin coat of plaster. In churches where it was not plastered over, the painting became extensive. The predominant color of this style was red ocher.

In many pictures it is noted that eyes or faces of people are obliterated as it was believed that this action killed the painted subject in the Islamic period. In addition to this there are also many scratches of vandals' initials which is strictly forbidden today. The visitor should be reminded that the use of flash with cameras inside the churches is not allowed.

The simplest church had a rectangular vaulted nave with an apse covered by a projecting arch. There are many variations of the churches, some with triple apse and a dome, cross-planned and so on. Because the churches were carved into the rock, they did not need to be supported by columns. Therefore columns and vaults are only structural symbols. Names of the churches are based on their archeological style or decoration, for instance the Buckle or Sandal Church.

CAPPADOCIA [272]

The apses of the churches face different directions as they are carved in accordance with the natural formations and availability of suitable rock pieces.

In most churches there are many grave pits which are thought to have probably belonged to donors or the church dignitaries as this was the tradition.

NEVŞEHİR

Size	61st largest city in Turkey
Altitude	1260 m / 4133 ft
Industry	Textiles, flour, wine and fruit juice factories, carpet weaving, pottery
Agriculture	Grain (80%), sugar beet, potatoes, chickpeas, apples, grapes
Animal husbandry	Sheep
History	Byzantine, Seljuk, Ottoman, Turkish Republic

UÇHISAR FORTRESS, *Cappadocia* [273]

It was called *Muşkara* and the Grand Vizier of the Tulip Period in the Ottoman Empire, Damat İbrahim Paşa was from this city. He donated to his hometown many hans, kitchens, hamams, medreses and suchlike giving the town a new vision. Since then the town was called Nevşehir which means "new town". "Nev" in Persian means new. At the top of the hill there is a Byzantine castle which was restored many times during Seljuk and Ottoman periods.

UÇHİSAR (UÇHİSAR FORTRESS)

Uçhisar is the name of a town and the fortress in the town. The name of the town probably derives from the name of the fortress. *Uç* is "tip", *hisar* is "fortress" and *Uçhisar* is the "fortress at the tip (of the vicinity)" in Turkish.

This 60-meter-high (200 ft) fortress was not built but carved out of a natural hill dominating the area with a breathtaking view of all the surrounding Cappadocian formations. In the village directly below the fortress are dozens of tufa cones inside of which are hollowed out rooms. Many of these are still in use.

GÖREME AÇIK HAVA MÜZESİ
(OPEN AIR MUSEUM OF GÖREME)

Göreme museum consists of steep cliffs and many hidden churches dating from the second half of the 9C and afterwards. Some of the churches are passing through restorations once in a while. Therefore, not all of the churches have been included here.

Karanlık Kilise (The Dark Church) has just been opened, but it requires extra entrance fee.

CHRIST, ENTHRONED PANTOCRATOR WITH RIGHT HAND IN THE GESTURE OF BLESSING, *The Church of St. Barbara, Göreme Open Air Museum, Cappadocia* [274]

Kızlar Manastırı (Convent)

The convent to the left of the entrance of the museum is only a ruin today. However, in its heyday, it was a huge complex of more than five floors. The first two floors were used for the kitchen, refectory, nuns' parlor and storehouses. There was a chapel on the third floor. Large round stones at the gates on the fourth and fifth floors were used for security in times of danger.

The Church of St. Barbara

It is an 11C cruciform church with two columns, three apses and a side entrance. According to

ORTHOSTAT RELIEF FROM ASLANTEPE-MALATYA *depicting the Sky-God fighting against the dragon, Neo-Hittite period, Museum of Anatolian Civilizations, Ankara* [275]

some sources this church was believed to have come from the Iconoclast period. However considering its plan which is similar to 11C and 12C buildings, it can easily be concluded that this cannot be right. Its name derives from a legendary saint, Barbara. According to legend, Barbara, after becoming a Christian, was shut up and eventually killed by her father. Her father was later punished by being struck by lightning. Barbara was remembered as the patron saint of architects, stonemasons and artillery men. Her attribute is generally a tower with three windows representing the Holy Trinity. St. Barbara is depicted on the north wall.

In the apse Christ, pantocrator is shown enthroned with his right hand in the gesture of blessing. On the wall opposite the entrance are painted two soldier saints on the horseback, St. George and St. Theodore. These two equestrian figures battling against a dragon symbolize the fight between the divine heroes and the forces of evil. St. Theodore was a recruit in the Roman army who was burned to death for setting fire to the Temple of Cybele in Amasya.

The dark colored bird-like creature was believed to represent the evil.

The predominant color in the frescoes of the church is red which was obtained from ocher. The two pits to the left after entering are interpreted as being either baptismal or for wine production.

Yılanlı Kilise (The Church of the Serpent)

This 11C church has a single nave covered by a barrel vault and a small apse on the left after entering. An interesting feature in this church is that the frescoes are framed like icons. The name of the church derives from the serpent in one of the frescoes on the left above the apse. Here, like in the Church of St. Barbara, two soldier saints St. George and St. Theodore are fighting against evil forces in the appearance of a serpent. Next to them is St. Onesimus.

THREE SAINTS, St. Onophrius, St. Thomas and St. Basil the Great, Yılanlı Kilise (The Church of the Serpent), Göreme Open Air Museum, Cappadocia 276

On the right above the apse is another picture showing Constantine the Great and his mother Helena. They are holding the true cross. Constantine is very important in the name of Christianity as he is the emperor who declared Christianity the official religion in 330 AD. After her conversion to Christianity, she used her position to promote the cause of the faith. She is the subject of many legends and is said to have found the cross of Christ during a trip to the Holy Land after receiving a vision at the age of 80. In art her emblem is the cross.

On the wall opposite the entrance is Jesus Christ. The small figure next to him is probably either the donor of the church or the artist of the painting as found in Italian art.

Opposite the apse are shown three saints, St. Onophrius, St. Thomas and St. Basil the Great. St. Onophrius, with raised hands in a dismissive gesture, was a hermit who spent a life of solitude in the desert in Egypt. He used desert leaves for a loincloth and became the patron saint of weavers. Because of his breasts and the way he is dressed he became a subject of some apocryphal stories according to one of which he was originally a beautiful, lecherous girl who repented of her sins and prayed God to help her. Her prayer was accepted and she woke up one day as an ugly old man.

Refectory

In addition to churches, suitably to the monastic lifestyle, there was also a refectory, a dining complex, consisting of three rooms in line, a storehouse, a kitchen and a dining hall with a long table cut from the rock for about 30 people and an apsidal place for the father abbot at the top of the table.

Çarıklı Kilise (The Church of the Sandal)

This is a church with a cruciform nave, two columns, three apses and four domes (one central dome and three cupolas). Its frescos date from the 13C. The name of the church derives from a footprint below the Ascension fresco. The entrance to the church is from the north and the apse is directed to the east.

Frescoes of Çarıklı Kilise

Central dome; Christ pantocrator and archangels in medallions.

Pendentives; Four evangelists, Matthew, Mark, Luke and John.

Main apse; Deesis and Saints.

North apse; The Virgin Mary and Child.

North apse (lunette); Hospitality of Abraham.

South apse; Archangel Gabriel.

Cupolas; Three of the Archangels, Michael, Gabriel and Uriel.

Southern arch of the main dome; Ascension and the apostles.

Western arch of the main dome; Transfiguration, Adoration of the Magi.

Northern arch of the main dome; Entry into Jerusalem, Betrayal of Judas.

Southern wall; St. George, angels, the Virgin Mary and Child.

Western wall; Nativity and Donors of the church, Theognostos, Leo and Michael.

Northern wall; Crucifixion, Baptism.

Three donors are mentioned by their names in frescoes. The way they are dressed in the picture gives the impression that they were not from the upper class but they were probably rich peasants. The fact that there were many donors shows that financing a church was beyond the limits of a single person.

Tokalı Kilise
(The Church of the Buckle)

Tokalı Kilise, which for convenience is called the "**New Church**" is the most spectacular of all the rock-cut churches in

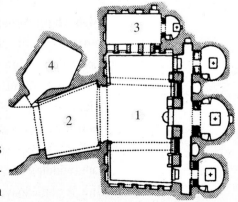

TOKALI KİLİSE (THE CHURCH OF THE BUCKLE); *(1)New Church, (2)Old Church, (3)Small Chapel, (4)Crypt* [277]

FRESCOES OF TOKALI KİLİSE (THE CHURCH OF THE BUCKLE), *Göreme Open Air Museum, Cappadocia (top) 278 (bottom) 279*

Cappadocia. The 10C church is different in plan to others in the vicinity, having a transverse nave (Mesopotamian type) with three apses and a narthex hewn out of an earlier church, known as the "**Old Church**". On the left of the transept is a **small chapel** and below the floor is a **crypt**. The most striking feature after entering the church is the dominant bright blue color used in the background of the frescoes. Because it was difficult to obtain, the color blue was very rare in Cappadocia. It was probably taken there from somewhere else which implies its cost. From this it is understood that the church was special among others. In the New Church, the niches in the walls of the nave serve to give a sense of depth and substance to the paintings.

Frescoes of the Old Church

Right (top); Annunciation, Visitation, Proof of the Virgin, Journey to Bethlehem, Nativity.

Left (top); Adoration of the Magi, Massacre of the Innocents, Flight into Egypt, Murder of Zacharias.

Right (middle); Flight of Elizabeth, Calling of John the Baptist, Prophecy of John the Baptist, Christ meeting John the Baptist, Baptism, Cana Wedding.

Left (middle); Miracles of wine, and fish, Calling of Apostles, Miracle of the loaves, Healing the blind, Raising of Lazarus.

Right (below); Entry into Jerusalem, Last Supper, Betrayal, Christ before Pilate (Roman governor of Judea).

Left (below); Way of the Cross, Crucifixion, Deposition, Entombment, Women at the tomb, Descent into Hell, Anastasis (Adam and Eve).

Saints are depicted below this panel, and above the entrance is the Transfiguration.

Frescoes of the New Church

North vault and north lunette
Visitation, Annunciation, Dream of Joseph, Journey to Bethlehem, Nativity, Adoration of the Magi.

West wall (below the vault - from left to right)
Presentation, Christ in the Temple, Calling of John the Baptist, Christ meeting John the Baptist, Baptism, Temptation of Christ, Calling of Matthew, Searching for fish, Cana Wedding.

Walls of the main apse
Healing of the blind, the leper, the widow's child, the withered hand, the possessed.

(from left to right)
Healing of the nobleman's son, Raising of the daughter of Jairus, Healing of the paralytic, Raising of Lazarus, Entry into Jerusalem, Last Supper.

South vault
Kings, Washing of the feet, Betrayal, Christ before Pilate.

Central apse
Crucifixion.

Both sides of the main apse
(left) Dormition of Mary,

(right) Transfiguration.

Center; Ascension, Benediction of Apostles.

A POTTER FROM AVANOS [280]

St. Basil and Emperor Valens, Prayer for Arians, Prayer of the Orthodox, Meeting of St. Ephraim and St. Basil, Absolution of the sinful woman, Funeral of St. Basil.

Also saint martyrs and bishop monks are depicted in different parts of the church.

AVANOS, pottery town, Cappadocia [281]

AVANOS (VENESSA)

It is a small town famous for its pottery and carpets. It is built along the banks of the Kızılırmak (Halys River), the longest river originating and ending within the borders of Turkey; 1,355 km / 842 miles. Halys means "salty river". It originates from the northeast of Central Anatolia (Kızıldağ 3,025 m / 9,920 ft.) after making a curve, flows into the Black Sea at Bafra Cape. Its water is colored by Cappadocia's rich deposits of clay, hence Kızılırmak, the Red River.

ZELVE AÇIK HAVA MÜZESİ
(OPEN AIR MUSEUM OF ZELVE)

Zelve was the name of a village which was inhabited until the 1950s in the Zelve Valley. The population of this settlement was moved further away to **Yeni Zelve,** and Zelve itself was made an open air museum because of the danger of collapse. The museum of Zelve consists of three canyons intersecting at the entrance of the museum. The first canyon on the right is entered through a pathway between the first two canyons passing by the *Geyikli Kilise* (the Church of the Deer) with paintings of a cross, fish and deer. Figures of fish are frequently used in churches of Cappadocia symbolizing the faithful who were called *pisciculi* and who became members of the church by being baptized in the piscina (fishpond in L). The acrostic of the Greek word for fish formed the phrase, Jesus Christ, Son of God, Savior. A cross in a circle with fish on both sides symbolized the faithful people who believed in Jesus Christ.

In the first canyon on the left there is a mosque which was converted from a church. Towards the end of the canyon, two rock faces are honeycombed with caves of dwellings, dovecotes, a monastery, storage rooms, chapels and tunnels leading to the second canyon. It is recommended that visitors not climb up these caves or pass through the tunnels.

A dwelling room with storage bins and stone wheels used for grinding grain and the *Üzümlü Kilise* (the Church of the Grapes) can be found in the third canyon. Grape juice here represents the blood of Christ.

YERALTI KENTLERİ (UNDERGROUND CITIES)

No one knows when the underground cities of Cappadocia were built, perhaps in Hittite times or as late as the 6C AD.

A TUNNEL IN AN
UNDERGROUND CITY,
Cappadocia [282]

There were certainly underground cities as early as the 5C BC. They are referred to by a 5 and 4C BC Athenian historian Xenophon in his Anabasis. So far 36 underground cities have been discovered some of them being very recent. It is also estimated that most of them are connected to each other. But it is difficult to identify these connections.

The ground consists of the same volcanic tufa. Cappadocians created vast cities which cannot be noticed from the ground level. They carved airshafts as deep as 85 m / 300 ft into the rock and then made holes laterally at different levels in all directions. They hewed an elaborate system of staircases and tunnels to connect all layers to the surface. They dug dwellings, bathrooms, kitchens, dining halls, storage rooms, wine cellars, chapels, graves and suchlike. In times of danger they provided security by rolling big round hard stones across strategic tunnels. Entrances at the surface were also camouflaged.

Today even from some of the modern houses there are man-made holes leading to underground passages most of which are used as cellars.

Kaymaklı Yeraltı Kenti
(Underground City of Kaymaklı)

It is one of the largest underground cities in Cappadocia with eight stories. It covers an area of approximately 4 km²

/ 1.5 sq mi. Visitors can see only about 10% of the city by going down a maximum of five floors. It probably is connected to nearby Derinkuyu. It was opened to visitors in 1964. The population of Kaymaklı is thought to have been about 3,000.

Derinkuyu Yeraltı Kenti
(Underground City of Derinkuyu)

The underground city of Derinkuyu which means "deep well", like Kaymaklı, is one of the largest. It was opened in 1965. It is 70-85 m / 230-300 ft deep with 53 airshafts. The original ventilation system still functions remarkably well. It is not recommended that visitors having problems of claustrophobia or restricted movement go inside since there are many passageways where one has to squat.

The first two floors under the surface housed a missionary school with two long rock-cut tables, baptismal place, kitchens, storehouses, living quarters, wine cellars and stables. Third and fourth floors were for the tunnels, places to hide and armories. The last floors had water wells, hidden passageways, a church, graves and a confession place.

NARLI GÖL (LAKE)

Location	On the way from Derinkuyu to Ihlara Canyon
Depth	65 m / 213 ft
Altitude	900 m / 2,950 ft
Formation	Crater lake
Water	Saltwater

Due to the existence of hot springs plans are being made to develop this as a geothermal area. Carp and frogs live in the lake.

Selime

N

Yaprakhisar

○ Ala Church
Belisırama

Direkli Church ○
Bahattin Samanlığı ○
Church
St. George Church ○

Karagedik
Church
○
Yılanlı
Church
Sümbüllü Church ○   ○
Ağaçaltı Church ○

Karanlıkkale
○ Church

Pürenliseki
Church   ○ ○ Kokar Church
○ Eğritaş Church

□
Museum
Entrance

Güzelyurt

Ihlara

IHLARA CANYON

IHLARA CANYON (PERISTREMA)

Ihlara Canyon is a deep, narrow river gorge cut through the tufa by the Melendiz River. The river running through the Ihlara Canyon at its lowest level is still contributing to the erosion of it. The canyon runs for 20 km / 12 miles offering one of the most enjoyable trekking routes to those people who can spare the minimum of half a day.

The canyon is approximately 150 m / 500 ft below the ticket office and reached by more than 300 steps. It has to be noted that the way back is not an easy climb. In the canyon there are about 60 churches, monasteries and cells of anchorites. There are a few major churches which are easier to reach.

Ağaçaltı Kilisesi (The Church under the Tree)

It is a cruciform church with two small aisles and an apse. Due to a few collapses the entrance to the church is from the altar section. In the dome there is a fresco of Christ in a *mandorla* being carried up to heaven by four angels. It is in primitive style, the faces orange and white with eyes unfocused and empty.

South; Annunciation, Visitation, Joseph, Nativity, Presentation. **North;** Flight into Egypt, Baptism, Dormition of Mary. **West;** Daniel in the lions' den.

Yılanlı Kilise (The Church of the Serpent)

It is a cruciform church with a horseshoe-shaped apse. It has a burial chamber in the north side. There is not enough light inside the church so the visitor might need a flashlight.

West wall; Christ, the judge, flanked by angels, is seated in a mandorla. Below him are the Forty Martyrs of Sebaste in oriental robes and the Twenty-four Elders of the Apocalypse. Below the west wall again, on the left, Day of Reckoning by weighing the Souls, a monster with three heads, and the body of a serpent devouring some of the damned representing the torments of hell. The name of the church derives from this painting. Next to it, on the right, naked women are being assaulted by snakes. One of them is in the coils of eight snakes probably because of her adultery. Another one's breasts are being gnawed by snakes because she left her children. Others guilty of disobedience and calumny are attacked on the ear and mouth.

To the right of the door of the burial chamber is Entry into Jerusalem. To the left is St. Onesimus.

Apse; Last Supper, Crucifixion.

East wall; At the top is a cross in a halo, on the inclined wall to the left is the Crucifixion (not well preserved) and Visitation. Top of the north face; St. John the Baptist, right hand raised and left hand holding an amulet. Top of the wall, east of the altar; Christ sitting on a rainbow, Christ dressed in red and holding a book surrounded by archangels Michael, Raphael, Gabriel and Uriel.

South wall; Michael and Gabriel on both sides. Below the window is the Dormition, near the cross is the fresco of Constantine and Helena.

Sümbüllü Kilise (The Church of the Hyacinth)

The name comes from the abundant hyacinths around the church. Sümbüllü Kilise has a domed single nave and was part of a two-storied monastery, the upper floor being living quarters. The arched doorways which are divided by pillars and linked with an architrave in the facade of the church carry the traces of Persian influence.

Central dome; Christ pantocrator. **North wall;** (next to the altar) St. George and St. Theodore. **West wall;** (in the niche) Constantine and Helena. **Altar section;** Gabriel and Michael. On the following wall Annunciation is depicted.

TUZ GÖLÜ (SALT LAKE)

Location	120 km / 75 miles to the south of Ankara, on the way to Cappadocia
Surface area	2nd largest lake in Turkey; 1,500 km² /

	580 sq miles. In summer the surface area might go down to 1,000 km² / 386 sq miles
Width	48 km / 30 miles
Length	80 km / 50 miles
Depth	1-2 m / 3-6 ft. 2.5 million years ago the water level was 100 m / 328 ft higher. In times of serious drought, the surface is covered by salt blocks up to 20 cm / 8 inches thick
Altitude	905 m / 2970 ft
Formation	Tectonic
Water	Saltwater

Tuz Gölü, also called *Tatta* in ancient times, is a closed lake with no way out, surrounded by plateaus on 4 sides. The sources feeding the lake are insufficient; Melendiz River (Aksaray) and Peçeneközü River (Şereflikoçhisar). In summer, because of the evaporation the lake dries out and a 30 cm / 12 in layer of salt forms. Under this layer is mud. In winter, water is collected again but at its deepest level is not more than 2 m / 6.5 ft. Although it is the second largest lake, there is not much water because of its shallowness.

It is among the lakes of the world with its very high salinity of 33%. Due to this high rate of salt it is impossible to grow crops around the lake.

Tuz Gölü is one of the richest salt beds in the world. The amount of salt which is obtained here is 300 thousand tons per year. This is 60% of the total salt production in Turkey.

Salt can only be taken from the lake from July through August. To ensure clean salt it is only collected from areas where the surface layer is more than 5-6 cm / 2-2.5 inches thick. The salt is dug, the dirty layer is removed and the clean salt is gathered into mounds and loaded manually onto the wagons of mini trains.

MOGAN LAKE

Location	25 km / 15 miles to the south of Ankara on the way to Konya or Cappadocia.
Width	125 m / 410 ft.
Length	4 km / 2.5 miles.
Depth	Maximum 5 m / 16 ft.

There are some beaches around the lake for the inhabitants of Ankara. Race competitions also take place there.

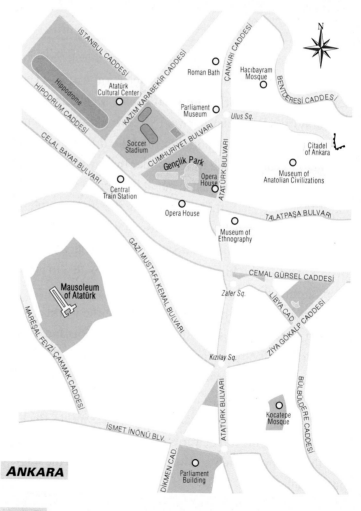

ANKARA

Size	When Ankara became the capital the population was only 25-30 thousand. Today it is the second largest city.
Altitude	850 m / 2,790 ft
Industry	Textiles, food, weapons, cement, tiles, beer
Agriculture	Most important after Konya; grain
Animal husbandry	*Tiftik keçisi (Angora goat)* is an Anatolian animal the name of which derives from the name of the capital city. The wool from this goat is also called angora, angora wool or mohair.
History	Hittites, Phrygians, Alexander the Great, capital of the Celtic Kingdom of Galatia and the Roman province of the same name, Persians, Arabs, Seljuks, Crusaders, Mongols, Ottoman Turks (1354), part of the Ottoman Empire (1413). Turkish nationalists established a provisional government in the city in 1920 and when the Republic of Turkey was proclaimed in 1923, it became the capital.

Ankara is the capital of Turkey. The city was formerly called "Ankyra" which meant anchor and later it was changed to "Angora".

As the capital city, Ankara can be regarded as the city of bureaucrats with the President's residence, the parliament building, government offices and foreign embassies. With students of Ankara University, METU, Hacettepe, Gazi, Bilkent and the Military Academies, Ankara is a planned modern city of students. Ankara is the only large urban center in the interior of Turkey with a European appearance.

Excellent roads and railroads and modern airline facilities connect Ankara with other cities of Turkey and with neighboring countries. The E5 road which connects Europe to the

KOCATEPE MOSQUE,
20C, Ankara [283]

Middle East, passes through Ankara. Esenboğa International Airport in Ankara is the second biggest in Turkey.

Anıtkabir (Mausoleum of Atatürk)

Unlike many famous leaders, Mustafa Kemal Atatürk never requested a monumental tomb for himself. But the adoration and respect shown to him by Turkish people would never have seen him buried in an ordinary place. An international project competition was held for the architecture of a monumental mausoleum for Atatürk after his death. The project of two Turks, Emin Onat and Orhan Arda, was finally selected.

The construction of a huge mausoleum similar to the Mausoleum of Halicarnassus, one of the Seven Wonders of the World, was started on the summit of Anıttepe, 6 years after his death in 1944 and finished in 9 years. On November 10, 1953 Atatürk was moved there in a gun carriage, from his previous grave at the Museum of Ethnography.

The Mausoleum was believed to represent the Turkish Nation under the name and personality of Atatürk. Therefore it included statues, inscriptions and reliefs on topics from Turkish history and Atatürk's life.

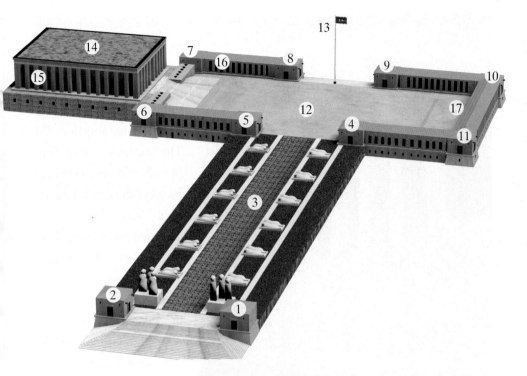

The richness of the Turkish Nation's mosaic is proven and symbolized once again with the materials and styles employed in Anıtkabir. The dominant theme is geometric simplicity. Anıtkabir, with all its surrounding parks covers an area of 15,000 m² / 3.7 acres. The main construction material is yellow travertine from Çankırı. The entrance to the complex is by way of a stairway located between two identical towers of (1) Independence and (2) Liberty. The tops of these towers are pyramidal, each having a bronze spear, as was the custom in old Turkish war tents. In front of these towers there are two group statues of people. On the left are three men, a soldier, a villager and a student each symbolizing in turn defense, productivity and education, the three pillars for the existence of a nation. The statues on the right are three women. The one at the back is crying silently symbolizing

ANITKABİR, MAUSOLEUM OF ATATÜRK, *1953, Ankara* [284]

MAIN BUILDING OF ANITKABİR (MAUSOLEUM OF ATATÜRK), *Ankara* [285]

people's grief for the death of Atatürk. The foremost couple are holding a wreath, the symbol of fertility, where the bowl also has the same function. (3) The pathway extending from the statues to the (12) Victory Square is called the Lions' Way. This path was designed to be especially long so as to create a sense of greatness in visitors' minds before reaching to the Mausoleum. On both sides there are 24 Hittite-style Anatolian lions indicating defense. There are altogether ten towers in Anıtkabir each having a simple look both from inside and outside. The other towers are (4) Mehmetçik, (5) Defense of Rights, (6) Republic, (7) Reform, (8) National Pact, (9) April 23 (10) Peace, and (11) Victory.

(12) The Victory Square is surrounded by colonnades on three sides and the remaining one side faces the main building. The transition from the square to the main section is via a 33-step stairway. To the left of the stairway is a big relief showing scenes from the Battle of the Commander-in-Chief. Atatürk's famous command from this battle is emphasized here: *"Armies, your first destination is the Mediterranean. For-*

ward!" The relief on the right depicts the Battle of Sakarya. Both battles were fought in the War of Independence against the Greek armies.

(13) The flag is the symbol of the Turkish Nation and the pole is a gift from a Turk who lives abroad. It is a single piece of steel, 5,000 kg / 11,000 pounds in weight and 33 m / 110 ft high. The crescent at the top is plated with 22-carat gold.

(14) The main building is called the Hall of Honor. It is 32 m / 105 ft wide, 60 m / 200 ft long and 20 m / 65 ft high. The ceiling is covered with gold mosaics, the floor and walls with colorful marbles from Bilecik. (15) The symbolic sarchophagus is a monolith marble and weighs 40 tons. The actual grave is downstairs. This is the first place where foreign statesmen and their delegations visit when they come to Turkey. (16) Next to the Sakarya Battle relief is the small Atatürk Museum with displays of his personal belongings, medals, gifts presented to him and his photographs. (17) İsmet İnönü, the second president of Turkey is buried between the Victory and Peace Towers.

ANADOLU MEDENİYETLERİ MÜZESİ (MUSEUM OF ANATOLIAN CIVILIZATIONS); *(1)Paleolithic, (2)Neolithic, (3)Chalcolithic, (4)Early Bronze, (5)Assyrian Trade Colonies, (6)Early Hittite and Hittite Empire, (7)Stone monuments from the Imperial Hittite period, (8)Neo-Hittite, (9)Phrygian, (10)Stone monuments from the Phrygian period, (11)Urartian, and (12)later periods* [286]

Anadolu Medeniyetleri Müzesi
(Museum of Anatolian Civilizations)

The museum of Anatolian Civilizations is one of the most beautiful and richest museums in the world with regard to its exhibits. The whole flow of civilizations of Anatolia is summarized in chronological order in this museum with many fine examples from the sites. The museum was begun in 1968 with the restoration of two 15C Ottoman buildings, Mahmut Paşa Bedesteni and Kurşunlu Han. The bedesten houses the exhibits while the han is used by the museum administration.

CEREMONIAL STANDARD, *Early Bronze Age, Museum of Anatolian Civilizations*
287

The exhibits are arranged chronologically, period by period: Paleolithic, Neolithic, Chalcolithic, Early Bronze, Assyrian Colonies, Hittite, Phrygian, Urartian and later periods until today. For detailed information about these periods see Ages in the History Section on page 25 of this book. Some examples of remarkable exhibits in the museum are as follows:

7.4 m / 24 ft-high **victory statue** standing outside the museum. It is thought to be a 13C BC Hittite statue for the cult area of Eflatunpınar, near Beyşehir. Reconstruction of a Neolithic **cult room** from Çatalhöyük. Neolithic **wall paintings**. Statuettes of **Mother Goddess** of Anatolia, generally depicted fat and with big breasts, giving birth, with two feline animals on both sides. **Painted pottery** of Chalcolithic period.

Early Bronze Age **stag statuettes**, ceremonial **standards** and **sun-discs**. Assyrian Colonies period **baked clay tablets,** important for the introduction of writing to Anatolia, and an **ivory statuette** of a nude female goddess. Hittite period **ceremonial vessels,** some of them in the form of bulls, the famous **İnandık vase** with a frieze of singers, musicians, priests, revelers and a couple engaged in sodomy. The central hall houses many **orthostat reliefs** from the Imperial, Neo-Hittite and Phrygian periods giving an account of life at the time. These scenes are of goats being taken to sacrifice, acrobats, priests in procession, hunts, and kings and queens in the act of pouring libations to gods. **Artifacts** from Gordion, the capital of the Phrygians and the reconstruction of the remarkable wooden chamber and funerary gifts of the **Midas Tomb** notable as the largest burial tumulus in Anatolia, 53 m / 174 ft in height. A 7C BC **bronze cauldron** is among the exhibits from the Urartian period.

A new hall is being prepared for the later period finds.

A CULT VASE FROM İNANDIK *depicting a couple engaged in sodomy which is interpreted as Hieros Gamos (Sacred Marriage) by Akurgal, Hittite period, Museum of Anatolian Civilizations, Ankara* [288]

ORTHOSTAT RELIEF FROM MALATYA-ASLANTEPE *depicting a Hittite King offering libation to four gods, Neo-Hittite period, Museum of Anatolian Civilizations, Ankara* [289]

BOLU

Size	51st largest city
Altitude	742 m / 2,434 ft
Industry	Lignite, marble, wood products, cement, tobacco
Agriculture	Grain (all), tobacco, potatoes, onions, sugar beets, flax, fruits, hazel nuts
Animal husbandry	Sheep, Angora goats
History	Roman, Byzantine, Ottoman, Turkish Republic

The name of the city derives from the Byzantine name "Claudiopolis". Turks called it *polis* for short which was later changed to *Bolu*.

YEDİGÖLLER (SEVEN LAKES)

Location	36 km / 22 miles to the northeast of Bolu
Depth	Büyük Göl; 15 m / 50 ft
Altitude	Lower level; 780 m / 2,560 ft. Upper level; 880 m / 2,890 ft
Formation	They were formed with the blocking of the valley

As its name bears it consists of seven lakes. Only 4 of the lakes are permanent. The other 3 generally dry out in summer. It was made a national park by the Ministry of Forests in 1965.

ABANT LAKE

Location	22 km / 14 miles to the junction of the highway which is 11 km / 7 miles after Bolu in the direction of İstanbul
Surface area	1.28 km² / 0.50 sq miles
Depth	Shallow

Altitude	1,298 m / 4,260 ft
Formation	It was formed by the blocking of a big valley
Water	Freshwater

SAKARYA NEHRİ (SANGARIOS RIVER)

A few km to the west of Adapazarı. It is the longest river after the Euphrates and the Kızılırmak with a length of 824 km / 512 miles. It originates from Eskişehir and flows into the Black Sea near Karasu.

SAPANCA GÖLÜ (LAKE SAMUNENSIS)

Location	25 km / 15 miles to the east of İzmit, on the way to Ankara
Surface area	47 km² / 18 sq miles
Width	6 km / 3.7 miles
Length	16 km / 10 miles
Depth	50-60 m / 164-196 ft. The deepest part is 61 m / 200 ft
Altitude	32 m / 101 ft
Formation	Tectonic. It was a part of the İzmit Bay, but because of the alluviums was blocked to form today's shape
Water	Freshwater

The excess of water is carried to the Sakarya river.

USEFUL TIPS

Electricity

It is standard; 220 V, 50 Hz all over Turkey.

Weights and Measures

The Metric & Kilo system is used.

Time

Local time is equal to GMT + 2 hours. Daylight Saving Time is applied during summer months. It is the same time zone all over the country.

Postal Services and Telecommunications

Turkey's postal services are comparatively organized and efficient. All post offices bear the distinctive yellow PTT sign (Post, Telephone, Telegrams). Larger and central offices are open from 08:00-24:00.

Telephone: All cities are linked by an efficient direct dialing system. Public telephones have two different systems. Some of them work with cards and some with tokens. They are both sold at PTTs. Tokens are called "jeton" in Turkish. Small jetons are only enough for local calls. Phone cards are in 3 different sizes and can be used more than once depending on the capacity of the card.

All over Turkey, phone numbers consist of two sections; area code (3 digits) and the number itself (7 digits).

During weekdays from 18:00 to 06:00 and on weekends calls are comparatively cheaper than the normal times as one can speak longer with the same amount of phone credit.

The telephone system in Turkey is good. The total number of the telephone lines is 7.5 million. In other words the ratio is 4 persons per telephone (1997). With this number Turkey lies seventh in Europe and fourteenth in the world.

Same area calls	just the 7-digit number
From area to area	0 + area code + number
International calls	0 + 0 + country code + area code + number

USEFUL TIPS

Monetary System

The unit of currency is the Turkish Lira (TL). Coins are 25,000; 50,000; 100,000 and bank notes are 100,000; 250,000; 500,000; 1,000,000; 5,000,000; 10,000,000.

Too many zeros can complicate life but are inevitable in a country where the annual inflation rate is about 70-100%. The cancellation of these many zeros is wondered about and suggested frequently by foreigners but, unless the inflation rate is reduced, it will have little effect and it cannot be repeated annually. Considering the possible psychological effects it has been discussed and in a very short time it will be implemented.

Banks and ATMs

Turkey boasts many banking companies and branches can be found everywhere. The big retail banks all have ATMs, some of which give cash advances against foreign credit cards. It should be noted that most ATM entry codes use numbers rather than letters / passwords.

Banks will exchange foreign currency and travelers checks with your passport as proof of identity. Commissions are charged at between 1 and 3% per transaction. Exchange rates change daily and can be checked in the press.

Banks are usually open between 09:30-12:00 and 13:30-17:00 on weekdays. On Saturdays and Sundays they are closed.

Changing Money

"Döviz" or exchange offices offer a fast service outside normal banking hours and at better rates than banks or hotels. They do not charge commission and only change foreign cash currency. Passports are not required.

Credit Cards

It should be noted that credit card commissions charged by the various credit card companies might sometimes be added to a client's bill—particularly if shopping in very touristic places. Also, with the rate of inflation affecting the daily exchange rate, the international rate used by the credit card company's banking agents may differ to that used by the vendor; clients may win or loose small amounts either way.

Food & Drinks

Turkish cuisine is considered to be among the best in the world. So many civilizations, so many styles and the abundant food supply contribute to today's cuisine.

"Afiyet olsun!" is an expression used to wish that a meal is enjoyed. Unlike many other languages it is used both before and after the meal.

When anybody wants to express appreciation about food prepared by somebody else, he says *"Elinize sağlık!"* which means "May God give health to your hands". When proposing a toast, the expression *"Şerefe!"* is used which literally means *"To honor!"*.

Restaurant Types

Lokanta

This kind of restaurant is typically Turkish and offers home-cooking style food. From a selection of meals, it is possible to go to the window and choose whatever you like. *Güveç* is any kind of meat prepared in a casserole. *Bulgur pilavı* is cooked crushed wheat. *Dolma* is stuffed vegetables, usually grape leaves, peppers, eggplants, cabbage leaves or mussels filled with rice, minced meat and raisins. Meatballs, vegetables or liver are among traditional Turkish food.

Kebapçı

This is the place where kebaps are sold. *Kebap* is a roast, broiled or grilled meat prepared in many different ways each of them called by adding a word to kebap; *döner kebap, şiş kebap, patlıcan kebap, etc. Döner kebap* is lamb meat roasted on a revolving spit. *Şiş kebap* is cubes of meat on skewers. *Köfte* is grilled or fried meatballs.

Farinaceous Food Restaurants

These differ from Italian pizza to Turkish farinaceous foods such as *börekçi, pideci, lahmacuncu, mantıcı, etc.*

Börek is a flaky pastry filled with cheese, eggs, vegetables, or minced meat, then fried or baked. *Gözleme* is a thin dough filled with cheese and parsley and baked on thin iron plate placed in wood or charcoal fire. *Pide*

A pideci preparing pide 291

is a thick dough base filled or covered with any combination of meat, cheese, eggs, etc. It is quite similar to pizza but served with butter and grated cheese. *Lahmacun* is a thin round dough base covered with a spicy mixture of minced lamb meat, onions, tomatoes and parsley. *Mantı* is a kind of pasta filled with minced lamb meat and served with yogurt and garlic.

Çorbacı

In the times before there was fast food, people went to these restaurants to eat tripe or chicken soup either for breakfast or after heavy nights of drinking. These places also sell a special food: *Kokoreç,* roast and grilled lamb intestines, also sold in push carts by peddlers in the streets.

USEFUL TIPS

Meyhane and Fish Restaurants

These restaurants are generally for proper dinner meals. First, a large variety of *soğuk (cold) meze,* (hors d'oeuvres) will be offered on a big tray among which you can choose a few, then you should sample a few *sıcak (hot) meze* before the main dish. The main dish is either fish or meat. After having desserts or fruit, it is time to drink a cup of Turkish coffee.

Soğuk meze: White cheese, olives, *lakerda* (salted bonito), *dolma* (stuffed vegetables), *cacık* (chopped cucumbers with yogurt and garlic), *piyaz* (beans salad), *Arnavut ciğeri* (spiced liver), *fava* (bean paste), *imam bayıldı* (stuffed eggplant), *pilaki* (white beans), *patlıcan kızartma* (fried eggplant), etc.

Sıcak meze: Fried mussels or squid, various kinds of *börek,* fried potatoes, etc.

Kestane şekeri (glacé chestnuts) of Bursa 292

Tatlıcı

This is a place where they sell different kinds of sweets. There are many of them like *baklavacı, muhallebici, dondurmacı, helvacı, etc.*

Baklava is thin layers of flaky pastry stuffed with almond paste, walnuts or pistachio nuts in syrup. Its name comes from the shape in which it is cut; lozenge-shapes. *Kaymak* is thick clotted cream eaten with most sweets as well as on its own with honey or jam. *Aşure* (Noah's pudding) is made from numerous types of dried fruits and pulses. *Sütlaç* is rice pudding. *Kadayıf* is shredded wheat in syrup. *Kestane şekeri* is glacé chestnuts. They are generally canned or kept in glass jars in syrup. It is common in Bursa. *Lokum* (Turkish Delight) is cubes of jelly like or gummy confection flavored with flower or fruit essences and dusted with powdered sugar. *Pişmaniye* is a sweet-meat made of sugar, flour and butter which resembles flax fibers. *Tahin-Pekmez* is a mixture of both *Tahin,* sesame oil and *Pekmez,* molasses or treacle (heavy syrup obtained from grapes). *Helva* is a flaky confection of crushed sesame seeds in a base of syrup. *Dondurma* is ice cream.

Drinks

Turkish coffee is a ritual rather than a drink. Although coffee is not grown in Turkey, it is called Turkish coffee because it was introduced to the western world by Turks during the Siege of Vienna in the 16C.

It is made by mixing an extremely finely ground coffee with water and sugar. According to your taste, you should let the waiter know in advance how much sugar you want in it: *sade* (without sugar), *az şekerli* (a little sugar), *orta* (medium sugar) or *şekerli* (with much sugar).

Turkish coffee is drunk in small sips after you've rinsed your mouth with a little water which comes in a glass together with the coffee. While drinking you should leave the coffee grounds at the bottom of the cup. Turkish coffee is drunk any time especially after meals but definitely not at breakfast. It is believed that after a heavy meal, one should either drink a cup of coffee or take a 40-step walk for digestion.

Çay (tea) is much more common. Especially at breakfast, but is also drunk anytime from small glasses and stirred with tiny spoons.

Boza is a fermented and sweetened drink made from corn or wheat.

Salep is a boiled milk flavored with orchis plant.

Ayran is a refreshing tangy drink of yogurt, water and salt whipped together.

Rakı (lion's milk) is the national drink; a 90-proof aniseed-flavored alcohol. To drink *rakı* properly, one needs two long and narrow glasses. One of the glasses changes its color from a clear liquid to a milky-white when it is filled with half rakı and half water. The other is for just plain water. The aim is to keep the levels of the two glasses more or less the same. *Rakı* is generally a drink that goes with a good meal. It is drunk cold, mostly with ice and requires some sort of food, the best accompaniment being some *meze*. The average number of glasses for one person is between 2-4.

Wine: There is a good variety of Turkish wine. They are comparatively reasonable in price and of good quality. Some selections are **Kavaklıdere** *Selection (red), Çankaya (white) and Muscat (white),* **Doluca** *Moskado (white), Villa Doluca (both red and white) and Sarafin.*

Drinking Water

Although water is considered safe to drink in most places in Turkey, chlorination and the different mineral contents of the tap water, particularly in the larger cities and tourist resorts, can sometimes cause problems for the visitor. It is therefore advisable to drink bottled water or mineral water as a safeguard.

Local people in major or touristic cities, especially in İstanbul, do not drink water from the tap. In fact, there are drinking water stations similar in organization to gas stations, where the locals go to "fill up" their water storage containers.

USEFUL TIPS

Smoking

"Either poor or penurious you feel,
Light a cigarette after each meal."

Turkey has the fourth place in the world with 22 million active and 22 million passive smokers. Unfortunately, people do not seem to care much for non-smokers. Recently however, there has been a tendency to prohibit people smoking in public places but this may take more time to gain acceptance.

Newspapers

Foreign newspapers are available one day after publication and only in big cities. **Turkish Daily News** is a good paper to keep up with daily events in Turkey.

Security Areas

Photography is not permitted in certain places; docks, airports, military establishments and frontier areas, etc. Check for signs or ask for advice if uncertain.

Baths and Toilets

Water has always been abundant enough to become part of the culture. Therefore, people of Anatolia have gotten used to running water. They always prefer washing themselves in running water (shower or Turkish bath) rather than sitting in bathtubs. If they have a bath, they would take a shower afterwards. Washing faces is the same; they would do it under running water rather than

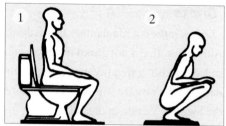

Toilets: (1) western style, (2) oriental style 293

in a washbasin filled with water.

Toilets may be oriental or western. They have separate sections for men and women. Near each mosque there are usually public toilets. Small water pipes coming from the back of the toilets are for water to cleanse with providing a simplified bidet. Toilet paper is used just for drying. Therefore, since paper is not thought to be absolutely necessary, you might not find enough in all public facilities.

Public toilets are always better in hotels and restaurants. On highways, toilets may be quite primitive. In most places both men and women have to pay to use public facilities.

Internet Cafes

Internet cafes are becoming popular in many cities. You can rent computers with internet access on hourly basis. It should be noted that the "ı" and "i" letters are not the same in Turkish keyboards.

Drugs

The illegal possession, sale or use of drugs such as hashish, heroin and cocaine, is strictly forbidden by Turkish Law.

Antiquities

From time to time genuine antiquities as well as imitations are offered for sale. Under no circumstance should these be purchased. The sale, purchase and possession are strictly controlled by Turkish Law and punishments are severe.

For instance, to take a used carpet or a piece of copper out of the country, one has to get approval from the directorate of an authorized museum.

Shops and Shopping

Shops are usually open between 8:30-19:00 and normally closed on Sunday.

Turkey, as a result of its geographical location, is a treasure-house of hand-made products. These range from carpets and kilims, to gold and silver jewelry, ceramics, leather and suede clothing, ornaments fashioned from alabaster, onyx, copper, and meerschaum.

When purchasing carpets, jewelry or leather products, it is advisable to consult your guide or do your shopping at a reputable store rather than in the street from vendors.

Carpets[72]

A carpet is more a work of art than an article which people step on for everyday use. 70% of the tourists coming to Turkey return to their homes with carpets because Turkey is a treasure-house of carpets.

To understand how valuable Turkish carpets are, it is better to go back to their origin. For a nomad who lived in a tent, home was a simple place; a combination of walls, roof and floor. The floor was not usually an elaborate structure, just a simple carpet laid directly onto the earth. The carpet was a bug-excluder, soil leveler, temperature controller and comfort provider all in one.

The texture of the material beneath one's feet was sensual proof that this was home and not the wild.

A geometrical carpet design [294]

As for the history of the carpet, various fragments exist from the 5-6C AD, but it is only from the Seljuk period in Anatolia that many more pieces have survived. Marco Polo, during his journey through Seljuk lands towards the end of the 13C reported that the best and finest carpets were produced in Konya.

Since a carpet is more of a work of art, the deeper meanings of each design cannot be neglected. A carpet can be likened to a poem; neither can tolerate any extra element which does not contribute to its wholeness

[72] Norman Roger, *Newspot*, 1995/2

and value. Therefore, just like in a poem, each pattern of a carpet is chosen for its beauty and motifs are carefully arranged to form *rhymes*.

Turkish carpets carry a wide range of symbols. For many centuries, Anatolian women have been expressing their wishes, fears, interests, fidelity and love through the artistic medium of carpets. Even so, there are typical repeated motifs changing from region to region; geometric designs, tree of life, the central medallion design, the prayer niches in prayer rugs, etc.

Turkish carpets are made of silk, wool or cotton. A silk pile gives a carpet the great brilliance. Cotton-warped carpets almost always have a more rigid and mechanical appearance than woolen-warped. Yarns have

A girl weaving a carpet 295

An Anatolian woman spinning yarn for carpets 296

been used in their natural colors or colored with dyes extracted from flowers, roots and insects.

Carpets are made on vertical looms strung with 3 to 24 warp (vertical) threads per cm (8 to 60 per in) of width. Working from bottom to top, the carpet maker either weaves the rug with a flat surface or knots it for a pile texture. Pile rugs use 5-7.5 cm / 2-3 in lengths of yarn tied in Turkish (Gördes) or Persian (Sehna) knots with rows of horizontal weft yarn laced over and under the vertical warp threads for strength. After the carpet is completely knotted, its pile is sheared and the warp threads at each end are tied into a fringe. The finer the yarn and the closer the warp threads are strung together, the denser the weave and, usually, the finer the quality.

The best-known flat-woven rug is the *kilim* which is lighter in weight and less bulky than pile rugs. It has a plain weave made by shooting the weft yarn over and under the warp threads in one row, then alternating the weft in the next row. The *sumak* type is woven in a herringbone pattern by wrapping a continuous weft around pairs of warp threads.

Taking a tour of a carpet production center is highly recommended in order to have firsthand experience of this art and to see a full range of the different designs exhibited.

Leather

Leather processing is a traditional handicraft in Turkey and was developed greatly during the Ottoman period. İstanbul's traditional leather manufacturing industry was concentrated in the district of Kazlıçeşme, where Sultan Mehmet the Conqueror had 360 tannery shops built to be rented out to leather craftsmen. Over the next 500 years Kazlıçeşme became a notorious eyesore which could be smelt long before it came into sight and the hundreds of small manufacturers have now been moved to a spacious modern industrial estate in Pendik.

Although it is a big industry, leather-wear is still very dependent on personal appeal and touch. It is also risky, time-consuming, laborious and therefore costly. It takes about 45 days to transform a skin into leather ready for dying and nearly 60 days from skinning to the finished garment. Also the volume of livestock in Turkey is not increasing at a sufficiently high rate to keep up with the industry's demand.

Despite all these difficulties, the leather sector comes after textiles in terms of export figures. The principal markets for Turkish leather goods today are the European Union countries led by Germany and then France.

When purchasing leather goods, one should be aware of the very wide range of products; different animal skins, baby lamb, lamb, suede, *nubuk*, *pelluria*, etc. and their differing qualities and prices.

Inter-city and International Transportation

Air

Together with some private airlines, Turkish Airlines (THY) has a domestic flights network covering seventeen Turkish airports, the first five of which are also international:

İstanbul, İzmir, Ankara, Dalaman, Antalya, Adana, Bursa, Denizli, Kayseri, Samsun, Erzurum, Erzincan, Malatya, Diyarbakır, Urfa, Elazığ, Kars, Van.

While Ankara is the major junction of the domestic air routes, İstanbul is the busiest airport and the principal terminus of international lines.

Domestic fares are quite reasonable, between 50-100 US Dollars one way to each destination.

Turkish Airlines has one of the newest fleets of aircraft and is among the youngest airlines in the world. THY has a capacity of 67 airplanes and 10,500 seats (1994).

USEFUL TIPS

Sea

As a country surrounded by sea on three sides Turkey should have been using much more sea transportation. Except for a few routes sea transportation is not very common. Turkish Maritime Lines is operating some routes from İstanbul to the Black Sea, Marmara Sea, Aegean Sea and the Mediterranean Sea.

Rail

Turkey's railway system extends approximately 10,200 km / 6,340 miles of which 2,300 km / 1,430 miles is within the framework of the International Main Railways European Charter and the Trans-European Railways (TER).

Turkish Railways employ 55,000 workers and the General Directorate replaces 300-500 km / 185-310 miles of track each year. There are 58 steam, 554 diesel and 58 electric locomotives in operation. 12% of the railways work on electricity and the remaining 88% are diesel. The number of passengers traveling by train per year is around 150 million, the amount of freight transported is 17 million tons.

Except for the route between Ankara and İstanbul and a few other routes extending to the eastern part of Turkey which provide comfort under severe climatic conditions, traveling by train is not usually preferred, because buses provide faster, cheaper and more comfortable services.

Bus

With a network of 368,677 km / 229,000 miles (1992) of roads, Turkey has excellent bus services. Many of the luxurious buses are manufactured in Turkey, therefore the number of buses is comparatively high. The ratio is 25 people per one public vehicle.

Because of the big competition among the private bus companies, the quality of services is high. In some destinations, services are as frequent as the airlines with cafe, bar and restaurant facilities on board. The fares are around 10-20 US Dollars to each destination.

City Transportation

Apart from public buses, trains and trams the most common means of transportation are taxis, ferry boats (İstanbul and İzmir), sea buses (İstanbul) and *dolmuş*.

Dolmuş

Dolmuş (literally full of passengers) is a kind of shared taxi which, sometimes takes the form of a large car, a station wagon, a regular taxi or a minibus. It follows a specific fixed route. Passengers pay according to the distance traveled and can get in and out whenever and wherever they want to by informing the driver. It is a very practical means of transport and much cheaper than a taxi. The dolmuş fares are determined by municipalities according to distances.

A ferry boat in İstanbul 297

Taxis

Taxis are numerous all over Turkey and are recognizable by their yellow color and lighted "taxi" signs on top.

Each taxi is metered and there are two different rates. After midnight (24:00) till morning (06:00) it will cost 50% more than the daytime fare. Additional expenses like ferryboat or bridge crossing fees are extra to passengers. Tipping is not necessary, however leaving the change or rounding up the fare is customary.

Ferry Boats (İstanbul and İzmir)

The busy city of İstanbul sits on the shores of Europe and Asia. Many of the inhabitants live on one continent but work, study or socialize on the other. Apart from the two bridges on the Bosphorus, ferry boats are the only means to connect the two continents and are therefore vital. It is different in İzmir where ferry boats provide an easy option with which to cross the Bay of İzmir.

The ferry service is reliable and peaceful operating throughout the day and until midnight.

Sea Buses (İstanbul)

With fewer boats than the ferry boat system these fast and smooth services by air conditioned power boats offer very efficient commuting from one point to another across İstanbul's Bosphorus. More expensive than the ferry boats they also offer light snacks and beverages.

1. TURKISH FLAG

Because the Turkish Republic was founded on the heritage of the Ottoman Empire, many things from that time, such as the Turkish flag, continued but sometimes with slight changes. The Ottomans used various flags of different colors at different times. In the 14C it was white, in the 15C it was changed to red. Once it was 3 white crescents with a green background. Each of the crescents symbolized a continent on which the Ottomans used to rule. As the Ottomans were associated with Islam, crescents might also have symbolized the sovereignty of Islam on those 3 continents. From then on, the crescent has been known as the symbol of Islam.

Later, in the 18C only one crescent together with an 8-pointed star on red background was used. The combination of the crescent and the red color came about, according to legend when one of the Turkish commanders while wandering around a battlefield, noticed the reflection of a star in the blood collected on the ground. That image so impressed the commander that he chose those symbols for the flag. Today, the red color is accepted as the symbol of blood. A heroic poem about the color says:

"What makes a flag is the blood and tears,
and what converts a land into a Nation is its martyrs."

After the foundation of the Republic, the Turkish flag was chosen to be a combination of a crescent and a 5-pointed star on a red background.

The fundamentals of the Turkish flag were laid down by the laws: Old, dirty or torn flags cannot be used. People cannot sit or step on them. In schools or official places it is hoisted at the weekends and on holidays. On Monday mornings, the new week starts with students saluting the national flag in schools.

All over the nation there are only two places in which the flag is kept permanently raised; the first is the parliament building, because here it symbolizes the continuity of the nation's existence, the second is at the Mausoleum of Mustafa Kemal Atatürk, the father of the Turks. Only on the day of his death, November 10, is the flag hung at half-mast as a sign of sorrow.

APPENDICES

2. THE NATIONAL ANTHEM

In a competition which was held in 1921, **"The March of Independence"** written by Mehmet Akif Ersoy was selected from among 724 poems. 24 composers participated in another competition arranged for the selection of a musical composition for the national anthem. The winner was Ali Rıfat Çağatay in 1924 and his music was sung for 8 years. Thereafter, the music of the national anthem was changed to an arrangement written by Zeki Üngör.

Turkish Flag 298

THE MARCH OF INDEPENDENCE

Fear not and be not dismayed,
This crimson flag will never fade.
It is the last hearth that's burning for my nation and
We know for sure that it will never fail.
It is my nation's star that ever forth will shine.
It is my nation's star and it is mine.

Frown not, fair crescent, for i
Am ready even to die for thee.
Smile now upon my heroic nation, leave this anger,
Lest the blood shed for the unblessed be,
Freedom's the right of this my nation,
Yes freedom for us who worship God and seek what's right.

APPENDICES

3. USEFUL TURKISH

Characteristics of Turkish

There are 29 letters in the alphabet and each of them has only one fixed sound. In pronunciation the stress is mostly on the last syllable. There is no **w**, **x** and **q** in Turkish, instead, there are additional letters: ç, ğ, ı, ö, ş and ü.

Vowels(8):

a, A as in "father"

e, E as in "get"

i, İ as in "seat", "feet"

ı, I as in "vowel", "farmer", "passenger"

o, O as in "ball"

ö, Ö as in "dirt", "earth"

u, U as in "bull"

ü, Ü as in French "Dupont"

Consonants(21):

All the consonants are as in English except for the following:

c, c as in "jam"

ç, Ç as in "church"

g, G as in "give"

ğ, Ğ It is silent. It only lengthens the proceeding vowel.

j, J as in "pleasure"

s, S as in "sit"

ş, Ş as in "sugar", "shake"

The sentence structure is not the usual subject-verb-object word order but subject-object-verb. Thus in English: "The people are eating food." becomes in Turkish: "(the) people food eating are."

Another interesting feature of Turkish is that it is an **agglutinative** language. In this way suffixes are used to express thoughts instead of phrases or sentences as used in some languages. For instance *"evdekiler"* is simple: *"those in the home"* But: *"tanıştıramadıklarımızdandırlar."* requires some more practice to form with ease: *"they belong to those whom we were unable to introduce."*

Common suffixes -ı, -i, -u, -ü, -sı, -si, -su, -sü like in Banka<u>sı</u>, Cadde<u>si</u>, Da<u>ğı</u>, Gö<u>lü</u> or Saray<u>ı</u> have the function of "of" in English. For example, *cami* means mosque and therefore "The Mosque of Sultan Ahmet" in Turkish is *Sultan Ahmet Cami<u>si</u>.*

Common words and phrases

hello	merhaba	restaurant	lokanta, restoran
good morning	günaydın	menu	menü
good day	iyi günler	bill	hesap
good evening	iyi akşamlar	VAT	KDV
good night	iyi geceler		
good bye	güle güle (said by	salad	salata
	the one who stays)	lemon	limon
good bye	hoşçakal (said by	vinegar	sirke
	the one who leaves)	oil	yağ
how are you?	nasılsınız?	salt	tuz
I'm fine	iyiyim	sugar	şeker
please	lütfen	bread	ekmek
thank you	teşekkür	hot, spicy	acı
Cheers!	Şerefe! (Literally		
	"to honor")	tea	çay
Good appetite	Afiyet olsun	apple tea	elma çayı
excuse me	afedersiniz / pardon	coffee	kahve
okay	tamam	instant coffee	neskafe
yes	evet	milk	süt
no	hayır	beer	bira
no, none	yok	whisky	viski
What is your name?	Adın ne?	gin and tonic	cin tonik
I/you/he, she, it	ben/sen/o	wine	şarap
we/you/they	biz/siz/onlar	red wine	kırmızı şarap
how much is it?	ne kadar?	white wine	beyaz şarap
how many?	kaç tane?	water	su
cheap	ucuz	bottled water	şişe suyu
expensive	pahalı	fizzy mineral water	soda
old	eski	soda water	maden suyu
new	yeni		
very nice, beautiful	çok güzel	cold	soğuk
this	bu	hot	sıcak
that	şu	ice	buz

spoon	kaşık	road	yol
fork	çatal	street	cadde, sokak
knife	bıçak		
glass	bardak	grandfather	dede
		grandmother	nine
entrance	giriş	mother	anne
exit	çıkış	father	baba
		sister	kızkardeş, abla
hospital	hastane	brother	erkek kardeş,
insurance	sigorta		ağabey
pharmacy	eczane	aunt (mother's sister)	teyze
medicine	ilaç	aunt (father's sister)	hala
		uncle (mother's brother)	dayı
post office	postane (PTT)	uncle (father's brother)	amca
letter	mektup		
postcard	kartpostal		
stamp	pul		
phone card	telefon kartı		
(phone/boat) token	jeton		
taxi	taksi		
ticket	bilet		
toilet	tuvalet		
woman	bayan / kadın		
man	bay / erkek		
Help!	İmdat!		
stop	dur		
lake	göl		
sea	deniz		
mountain	dağ		
hill	tepe		
river	nehir, akarsu		

Numbers

1	bir	20	yirmi
2	iki	21	yirmibir
3	üç	30	otuz
4	dört	40	kırk
5	beş	50	elli
6	altı	60	altmış
7	yedi	70	yetmiş
8	sekiz	80	seksen
9	dokuz	90	doksan
10	on	100	yüz
11	onbir	110	yüzon
12	oniki	200	ikiyüz

1,000	bin	1,000,000	milyon
2,000	ikibin	1,000,000,000	milyar

4. DISTANCES

			km	miles
İstanbul	Eskihisar		50	31
	Topçular	Bursa	90	56
Bursa	Susurluk		115	72
	Susurluk	Balıkesir	55	34
	Balıkesir	Soma	70	44
	Soma	Bergama	55	34
	Bergama	İzmir	105	65
Bursa	(Bergama)	İzmir	400	250
Bursa	(Akhisar)	İzmir	350	218
İstanbul	Tekirdağ		135	84
	Tekirdağ	Keşan	85	53
	Keşan	Gelibolu	70	44
	Gelibolu	Eceabat	45	28
İstanbul	Eceabat		335	208
Çanakkale	Troy		35	22
	Troy	Ezine	30	19
	Ezine	Troas	25	15
	Troas	Assos	60	39
	Assos	Ayvacık	20	13
	Ayvacık	Bergama	165	103
	Bursa	Denizkent	155	96
	Denizkent	Çanakkale	115	72
İzmir	Sardis		95	59
	Sardis	Akhisar	70	44
	Sardis	Alaşehir	45	28
	Alaşehir	Sarayköy	75	47
	Sarayköy	Pamukkale	25	15
İzmir	Selçuk		75	47
	Selçuk	Kuşadası	15	9
	Selçuk	Nazilli	100	62
	Nazilli	Aphrodisias	50	31

Aphrodisias	Tavas	40	26
Nazilli	Denizli	80	50
Denizli	Pamukkale	20	13
İzmir (Selçuk)	Pamukkale	275	171
Kuşadası	Pamukkale	215	134
Pamukkale	Dinar	120	75
Dinar	Afyon	105	65
Afyon	Kütahya	95	59
Kütahya	Bozüyük	75	47
Bozüyük	Bursa	100	62
Pamukkale (Dinar)	Bursa	495	308
Pamukkale	Tavas junc.	40	25
Tavas junc.	Tavas	20	13
Tavas	Muğla	125	78
Muğla	Marmaris	55	34
Pamukkale	Marmaris	220	137
Pamukkale	Dinar	120	75
Dinar	Burdur	55	34
Burdur	Bucak	65	40
Bucak	Antalya	60	37
Pamukkale (Dinar)	Antalya	300	187
Pamukkale	Salda	110	68
Salda	Korkuteli	100	62
Korkuteli	Antalya	70	44
Termessus	Antalya	35	22
Pamukkale (Salda)	Antalya	280	174
Antalya	Perge	20	13
Perge	Aspendus	20	13
Antalya	Aspendus	40	25
Aspendus	Köprülü Canyon	45	28
Antalya	Köprülü Canyon	85	53
Antalya	Side	75	47
Antalya	Manavgat	75	47
Manavgat	Alanya	60	37
Antalya	Alanya	135	84

Antalya	Kemer	45	28
	Kemer	Phaselis	15	9
Antalya	Demre	130	81
Antalya	Kaş	180	112
Antalya	Kurşunlu	Eğridir	155	96
	Eğridir	Fele	95	59
	Fele	Beyşehir	55	34
	Beyşehir	Konya	90	56
Antalya	Konya	420	261
	Konya	Sultanhan	105	65
	Sultanhan	Aksaray	40	25
	Aksaray	Ürgüp	85	53
Antalya	Cappadocia	650	404
Antalya	Kurşunlu	Isparta	125	78
Antalya	Akseki	Konya	330	205
Cappad.	Aksaray	85	53
	Aksaray	Konya junction	125	78
	Konya junction	Ankara	100	62
Cappad.	Ankara	310	193
Cappad.	(Avanos)	Boğazlıyan	80	50
	Boğazlıyan	Yozgat	100	62
	Yozgat	Hattusha	40	25
	Hattusha	Ankara	200	124
Cappad.	Ankara	420	260
Ankara	Gerede	140	87
	Gerede	Yeniçağa	20	13
	Yeniçağa	Bolu	30	19
	Yeniçağa	Mengen	20	13
	Mengen	Yedigöller	50	31
	Yedigöller	Bolu	45	28
	Gerede	Bolu	50	31
Ankara	Bolu	190	118
	Bolu	Abant	35	22
	Bolu	İstanbul	250	155
Ankara	İstanbul	440	274

5. GLOSSARY

Selection of the words in this section is directly related to Turkey and Turkish. For example, archeological expressions are from the archeology of Turkey or the birds in this section are the common birds in Turkey.

ARCHEOLOGY, ARCHITECTURE, HISTORY AND ART HISTORY

abacus	a slab that forms the uppermost division of the capital of a column
acropolis	Gr. *acr*, top + *polis*, city; uppermost city, the highest and most defensible part of an ancient city
acroterium	small statues or figures at the corners of a pediment
adak (Tr.)	votive offering
adyton	inner sanctuary of a temple
ağa (Tr.)	squire; village notable or landowner
agora	a public area where people gather for their political, commercial and social activities; see page 233
amphiprostyle	L *amphi*, around, both sides + Gr. *pro*, front + *stylos*, pillar; having columns at each end only
amphitheater	L *amphi*, around, both sides + *theatron*, theater; a kind of elliptical or circular stadium built by Romans for gladiator fights
amphora	a jar with a large oval body, narrow cylindrical neck and two handles
analemma	supporting wall at the side of a theater
Anastasis	Resurrection; Harrowing of Hell; Christ, who has just broken down the gates of Hell, stands in the middle and tries to pull Adam and Eve out of their tombs
andesite	dark grayish rock
andron	men's room in a temple or a house
ANZAC	Australian and New Zealand Army Corps
apotropaic	designed to avert evil
apse	a projecting part of a basilica or church building which is semicircular and vaulted

aqueduct	L *aqua*, water and *ducere*, to lead; a structure built to carry water from a source to a distant destination
architrave	*epistyle*; a main beam resting on columns
Assumption	Taking (Assuming) of the Virgin Mary bodily into heavenly glory when she died
atrium	court of a Roman house, center is open to the sky, sides roofed; entrance court of a church
auditorium	L *auditus*, act of hearing; the hearing place
ayazma (Tr.)	sacred fountain
barrel vault	ceiling or roof of a room which gives a semicircular cross section
basilica	a large, oblong building used particularly as a court of law and a place of public assembly; see page 248
bas-relief	F *bas*, low + *relief*, raised work; sculptural relief in which the projection from the surrounding surface is slight and no part of the modeled form is undercut
bedesten (Tr.)	an Ottoman shopping center built with equal domes
beşik tonoz (Tr.)	barrel vault
Bey (Tr.)	a lord, squire
birun (Tr.)	outer palace (Ottoman period)
boule	a legislative council of Hellenistic people consisting first of an advisory body and later of a representative senate
bouleterion	a public building that housed the *boule* (Senate House)
burç (Tr.)	bastion
caique	derives from Tr. *kayık*; a type of small boat
caldarium	late L *caldaria*, warm bath; the hottest section in a Roman bath
Caliph	Successor of the Prophet Mohammed
cami (Tr.)	mosque
capital	the part of a column crowning the shaft; it originates from stone pieces put on top of wooden columns to prevent rotting
cavea	L *cavus*, hollow; auditorium of a theater, so-called because originally it was dug out of the side of a hill
cella	*naos*; the inner sanctuary of a temple containing the cult statue
centaur	mythological half-man and half-horse creature who was said to dwell in the mountains

colonnade	a series of columns set at regular intervals supporting the base of a roof structure
Composite capital	a capital combining andular Ionic volutes with the acanthus-circled bell of the Corinthian
Corinthian	a bell-shaped capital enveloped with acanthuses
crepidoma	the stepped platform on which a temple stood
cresmographeion	a chamber in a prophecy center probably serving as an oracle office where prophecies are written out and delivered to people
cross vault	cross-shaped ceiling or roof of a room
cult	religious veneration, worship
cumba (Tr.)	bay window
cuneiform	wedge-shaped writing; see page 138
cuneus	wedge-shaped division in the cavea of a theater
çörten (Tr.)	gargoyle
Deesis	depiction of Jesus as the pantocrator flanked by the Virgin Mary and Saint John the Baptist who are shown interceding with him on behalf of mankind
defterdar (Tr.)	Ottoman finance minister
demos	Gr. *demos*, people; common people of an ancient city
dervish	(derviş in Tr.) a member of a Moslem religious order noted for devotional exercises
Diadochi	Gr. successors
diazoma	Gr. *dia*, through, apart; a horizontal passage separating the rows of seats in the cavea of a theater
dikilitaş (Tr.)	obelisk
dipteros	Gr. *di-* twice, double + *pteros*, wing; a temple surrounded by two rows of columns
dirlik (Tr.)	fief, a feudal estate
Divan (Tr.)	Ottoman administration and government
Dormition	falling asleep of the Virgin Mary
Enderun (Tr.)	Ottoman Royal School; inner palace (Ottoman period)
entablature	the stone work connecting columns, including *architrave* and *frieze*
epistyle	architrave; a main beam resting on columns

eyalet soldiers (Tr.)	*dirlik*-holding front line soldiers in the Ottoman army; see the Ottoman Army on page 74
ferman (Tr.)	edict or decree ordered by the sultan
forum	L *foris*, outside; open space in any Roman city where business, judicial, municipal affairs and religious activities were conducted
frieze	the middle division of a classical entablature, often decorated with carvings in low relief
frigidarium	L *frigus*, cold; the cold section of a Roman bath
gaza (Tr.)	holy war
gazi (Tr.)	fighter for the faith of Islam against the infidels
gendarme	soldier with the duties of a policeman in settlements smaller than towns where there are no police.
göbek taşı (Tr.)	(navel stone) a marble, heated table on which people lie in a hamam
gymnasium	Gr. *gymnos*, naked; a place where exercises are practiced by naked athletes
Hac (Tr.)	for Moslems visiting Mecca on a pilgrimage
hacı (Tr.)	Moslem pilgrim
hadis (Tr.)	recital and transmission of the words of the Prophet
han (Tr.)	caravansary; a building consisting of shops where same kind of merchandise is produced and places for people to stay
harpuşta köprü (Tr.)	Per. *har*, donkey + *püşt*, back, ridge; a hump-backed bridge which looks like the back of a donkey
has (Tr.)	a classification of land use in the Ottoman period; see the Ottoman land administration on page 73
hatip (Tr.)	preacher
harem (Tr.)	private sector of a Moslem household in which women live and work; see page 290
Hellenistic	of or relating to a Greek-Anatolian mixture of history, culture, or art of the period after Alexander the Great
heroon	a shrine dedicated to a deified or semi-deified hero
Hicret (Tr.)	Hegira, migration of Mohammed from Mecca to Medina in 622 AD which marks the beginning of the religious calendar.
hippodrome	Gr. *hipp*- horse + *dromos*, racecourse; places for chariot races wider than the horseshoe-shaped stadiums; see page 244

höyük / hüyük (Tr.)	mound, *Tell*
Iconoclasm	Gr. *eikon*, image + *klan*, to break; the practice of destroying religious images or opposing their veneration
Iconography	Gr. *eikon*, image + *graphia*, writing; the study of the subject matter, or content, of works of art, as opposed to their style
imam (Tr.)	prayer leader in a mosque
imaret (Tr.)	kitchens for the public, generally the poor
in antis	a type of temple with ante walls extended to form a pronaos
Islam	A *islam*, the act of committing oneself unreservedly to God; the religious faith of Moslems
janissary	*yeniçeri*, a soldier of an elite corps of Ottoman troops organized in the 14th century and abolished in 1826
Kaaba	a shrine in Mecca that had for some time housed the idols of the pagan Meccans, was rededicated to the worship of Allah and has become the object of pilgrimage for all Moslems
kapıkulu soldier (Tr.)	a class in the Ottoman army; see page 73
Kaptan-ı Derya (Tr.)	Commander in chief of the Ottoman fleet
kasır (Tr.)	summer palace
kathisma	royal box in a hippodrome
kazasker (Tr.)	Ottoman minister responsible for the military
kervansaray (Tr.)	Per. *kervan*, caravan + *saray*, palace; caravansary
kese (Tr.)	special gloves for rubbing the body in a hamam
kıble (Tr.)	the direction of Kaaba in Mecca faced by Moslems from all over the world during prayer
kırma çatı (Tr.)	hip roof
Koimesis	*Dormition*, falling asleep of the Virgin Mary
konak (Tr.)	mansion
Koran	Holy Book of the Moslems
kore	in sculpture, the female equivalent of kouros, always dressed in rich drapery enhanced by incision and color
kouros	in sculpture, the prototype of a standing boy figure with one foot advanced and the hands clenched to the sides
köşk (Tr.)	kiosk, summer residence, pavilion
kufi (Tr.)	a formal style in calligraphy with an angular character

kurgan (Tr.)	a grave similar to *tumulus*
külliye (Tr.)	complex of buildings
kümbet (Tr.)	domed or conical-roofed tomb
lahit (Tr.)	sarchophagus, a stone coffin
libation	pouring a liquid as a sacrifice to a deity
lunette	surface of the upper part of a wall filled by mural painting
lyrical poems	sentimental poems which were read with the music of lyres in ancient times
mahya (Tr.)	lights stretched on special occasions between the minarets of mosques with some figures, words or expressions
mandorla	meaning "almond" in Italian, the frame, generally round or oval in shape, that encloses the image of the enthroned Christ in art
mangal (Tr.)	brazier
martyrium	martyry, a shrine erected in honor of a martyr
maşallah (Tr.)	"god preserve him"
medrese (Tr.)	Islamic theological school
megaron	Anatolian house with long and rectangular plan
mescit (Tr.)	small mosque; a place to prostrate one's self in front of God
Mesolithic	Gr. *mesos*, mid + *lithos*, stone; transitional period of the Stone Age between the Paleolithic and the Neolithic
Mevlevi	a whirling dervish as a member of a mystic group who are followers of Mevlana Celaleddin Rumi
mevlit (Tr.)	place or time of birth
mihrab (Tr.)	*apse* in a mosque
minber (Tr.)	pulpit in a mosque
minare (Tr.)	minaret, tower in a mosque from which the müezzin calls people to prayer
Moslem, Muslim	believer of Islam
müezzin (Tr.)	somebody who calls people to prayer and assists imam during prayer in a mosque
naiskos	*cella* in modest proportions in a temple
nalın (Tr.)	wooden clogs
namaz	act of praying or set of prayers

APPENDICES

naos   *cella*; the inner sanctuary of a temple

nargile (Tr.)   hookah, waterpipe

narthex   a narrow vestibule in a basilica or church

nazar boncuğu (Tr.)   blue eye used to ward off evil influences from others

necropolis   Gr. *necr-*, *necro-* dead body + *polis*, city; city of the dead; large elaborate cemetery of an ancient city

Neolithic   Gr. *neos*, new + *lithos*, stone; New Stone Age

niş (Tr.)   niche

nişancı (Tr.)   general secretary of Ottoman administration

Nizam-ı Cedit (Tr.)   late Ottoman organized army, meaning the New Order

nymph   Gr. *nymphe*, bride; a mythological minor divinity of nature represented as beautiful maidens

nymphaeum   a place of nymphs; a structure with a pool for public use, fountain; see fountain on page 237

odeon   small Roman theater for musical performances, sometimes used as bouleterions

omphalos   a beehive-shaped stone at Delphi, designating that spot as the center or navel of the Earth

orchestra   Gr. *orcheisthai*, to dance; dancing place in an ancient theater

orthostats   upright slabs at the base of walls

pah (Tr.)   bevel, the slant or inclination of a surface

palaestra   Gr. *palaistra*, to wrestle; school or place of wrestling (in a gymnasium); exercise courtyard

Paleolithic   Gr. *palai*, ancient + *lithos*, stone; Early Stone Age

pantocrator   creator of all things and ruler of universe

paracclesion   funerary chapel

parados   space between the cavea and stage of a theater

paşa (Tr.)   pasha; an army officer of high rank

Pax Romana   200 years of peace during the reign of the Roman Empire Augustus (1C BC) when the Roman Empire was at its height with no rivals.

payanda (Tr.)   buttress

pediment   triangular gable of a two-pitched roof

peripteros	Gr. *per-* throughout + *pteros*, wing; a temple surrounded by one row of columns
peristasis	*peristyle*
peristyle	Gr. *per-* throughout + *stylos*, pillar; columns surrounding a building or open court
peştemal (Tr.)	a piece of cotton cloth worn when in a hamam
phyale	bowl used for pouring libations to the mother goddess during the Phrygian period
pithos	a large jar for storing oil, grain, etc.
podium	Gr. *pod-* foot; a platform serving as a foundation
porch	covered entrance to a building with a separate roof
portico	L *porta*, gate; a sheltered walkway; *colonnade*
prohedria	Gr. *pro-* front + *hedra*, seat; special seats for high officials at a theater
pronaos	Gr. *pro-* front + *naos*, cella; porch in front of a temple
propylon	Gr. *pro-* front + *pylon*, gate; entrance gate to a sacred area
proskene	Gr. *pro-* front + *skene*, stage building; front of the building forming the background for a dramatic performance, proscenium
prytaneion	the administrative building in a city; see page 236
pseudodipteros	Gr. *pseudes*, false + *dipteros*, a temple which looks like a dipteros temple
pseudoperipteros	Gr. *pseudes*, false + *peripteros*, a temple which looks like a peripteros temple
Ramazan (Tr.)	*Ramadan*, the 9th month of the Moslem year observed as sacred with fasting practiced daily from sunrise to sunset
revak (Tr.)	*colonnade*
Rum (Tr.)	Christian Greeks of Anatolia
saçak (Tr.)	eaves
sahın (Tr.)	nave (in a mosque)
sancak (Tr.)	standard, banner or flag representing the Caliphate of the sultan
sanduka (Tr.)	coffin
saray (Tr.)	palace
sarcophagus	Gr. *sarc-*, flesh + *phagein*, to eat; flesh-eating stone (probably comes from local Assos stone), a stone coffin

savat (Tr.)	*niello*, the art of decorating metal with incised designs filled with niello (usually an alloy of sulfur with silver)
sema	rite of communal recitation practiced by the Mevlevis
semahane (Tr.)	hall in which sema is performed
sericulture	cultivation of silk worms for industry
Shamanism	a religion characterized by belief in an unseen world of gods, demons, and ancestral spirits responsive only to the shamans who are priests using magic
skene	Gr. *skene*, temporary shelter, tent building forming the background for a dramatic performance; the stage building of a theater
sofra (Tr.)	a tray or table on which meal is eaten
son cemaat yeri (Tr.)	outer narthex of a mosque in the courtyard for latecomers to the prayer
sorguç (Tr.)	plume
spina	barrier or the central axis of a Roman amphitheater or hippodrome
stadium	Gr. *stadium*, a unit of length equal to 185 m / 606.95 ft.; a structure specifically designed for sporting contests and other spectator events originally one stadium in length; see page 244
stele	an inscribed or carved upright stone slab or shaft that served as a monument, memorial, or marker
stoa	Gr. *stylos*, pillar; colonnaded walkway; see page 234
sünnet (Tr.)	whatever the prophet does or says in Islam; circumcision
synthronon	semicircular rows of seats for the clergy in a church
şadırvan (Tr.)	ablution fountain
şerefe (Tr.)	minaret balcony
şeriat (Tr.)	Canonical Law (Islamic)
şeyhülislam (Tr.)	authorized head of religious matters in Ottoman Empire
tekke (Tr.)	dervish monastery
tellak (Tr.)	hamam attendant who does the **kese** work
temenos	a sacred area in which stand one or more temples
tepidarium	L *tepidus*, warm; lukewarm section of a Roman bath
terra-cotta	type of hard-baked clay or earthenware produced by means of a

	single firing
tetrapylon	Gr. *tetra-* four + *pylon*, gate; monumental gateway with 4 columns
theatron	Gr. *theatron*, act of seeing; theater building (the seeing place); see page 240
thyrsus	staff surmounted by a pine cone or by ivy leaves with grapes
tımar (Tr.)	a classification of land use in the Ottoman period; see the Ottoman land administration on page 73
toga	loose outer garment worn by ancient Romans
tonoz (Tr.)	vault, an arched structure of masonry used to form a ceiling or roof
transept	L *trans-* across, beyond + *septum*, enclosure, wall; the part of a cruciform church that crosses the main body of the church at right angles
trident	three-pronged spear
tuğra (Tr.)	monogram of a sultan
tumulus	grave formed by piles of soil
tülü (Tr.)	a special breed of a wrestler camel
türbe (Tr.)	a domed tomb; see page 205
ulufe (Tr.)	salary paid to Ottoman soldiers
vakıf (Tr.)	trust, foundation
vitray (Tr.)	stained glass
vomitorium	L *vomitus*, disgorge; section used for disgorging the spectators; vomitory; covered exit in a theater, stadium or amphitheater
XP	a monogram consisting of the first two letters of the Greek word for Christ
yalı (Tr.)	Waterfront wooden house or villa on the Bosphorus
yeniçeri (Tr.)	Tr. *yeni*, new + *çeri*, soldier; see *janissary*
zaviye (Tr.)	multi-functional mosque with inverted "T" plan
zeamet (Tr.)	a classification of land use in the Ottoman period; see the Ottoman land administration on page 73

VEGETABLES

artichoke	enginar
beet	pancar
broad / fava bean	bakla
cabbage	lahana
celery	kereviz
chickpea	nohut
eggplant	patlıcan
flax	keten
gherkin	salatalık (turşusu)
gourd	kabak (usually seen in Cappadocia)
Jerusalem artichoke	yer elması
leek	pırasa
lentil	mercimek
lettuce	marul
nettle	ısırgan otu
okra, lady's finger	bamya
opium	afyon
opium poppy	haşhaş
parsley	maydanoz
pea	bezelye
purslane	semiz otu
radish	turp
sesame	susam
shallot	küçük soğan
sugar beet	şeker pancarı
sugar cane	şeker kamışı
zucchini / marrow	kabak

Purslane 299

HERBS

allspice	yeni bahar
aniseed	anason
bay leaf	defne
black cumin	çörekotu
cinnamon	tarçın
clove	karanfil
coriander	kişniş otu
cress	tere
cumin	kimyon
dill	dereotu tohumu
ginger	zencefil
henna	kına
linden / lime	ıhlamur
mint	nane
mustard	hardal
nutmeg	Hindistan cevizi
orchis	salep
oregano, marjoram	mercanköşk
paprika	kırmızı toz biber
red pepper	kırmızı biber
rocket leaf	roka
rose hip	kuşburnu
rosemary	biberiye
saffron[73]	safran
sage[74]	adaçayı
soapwort	çöven
sumach	sumak
thyme	kekik
vanilla	vanilya

[73]In Anatolia, it grows only in Safranbolu and it is accepted as the most expensive herb in the world.

[74](Salvia officinalis) In Latin salvia means savior; and it is used for the treatment of sterility.

FRUITS

almond	badem
apricot	kayısı
bergamot	bergamut
cherry	kiraz
date	hurma
fig	incir
lime	misket limonu
loquat	Malta eriği, yeni dünya
medlar	muşmula
mulberry	dut
pear	armut
persimmon	Trabzon hurması, cennet elması
plum	erik
pomegranate	nar
quince	ayva
raspberry	ahududu, frambuaz
sour cherry	vişne

DRIED FRUITS

chestnut	kestane
currant	kuş üzümü
ground nut	yer fıstığı
hazel nut	fındık
peanut	yer fıstığı
pistachio nut	Antep / Şam fıstığı
raisin	kuru üzüm (çekirdekli)
sultana	kuru üzüm (çekirdeksiz)
walnut	ceviz

GRAINS

barley	arpa
corn	mısır
grain	tahıl
oatmeal	yulaf unu
oats	yulaf
rye	çavdar
semolina	irmik
wheat	buğday

FISH

anchovy	hamsi
bass	levrek, sudak
bluefish	lüfer
bonito	palamut / torik
bream	mercan
carp	sazan
crawfish	kerevit
gilt-head	izmarit
horse mackerel	istavrit
mackerel	uskumru
mussel	midye
pike	yayın balığı
red mullet	barbunya
salmon	som balığı
sardine	sardalya
sea bream	çipura
sea urchins	deniz kestanesi
shrimp	karides
sole	dil balığı
spanish mackerel	kolyoz
squid	kalamar
sturgeon	mersin balığı
trout	alabalık
tuna fish, tunny	ton balığı
turbot	kalkan
whiting	mezgit

BIRDS

budgerigar	muhabbet kuşu
buzzard	şahin
canary	kanarya
cormorant	karabatak
crane	turna
crow	karga
curlew	çulluk
duck	ördek
egret	beyaz balıkçıl
falcon	doğan
finch	ispinoz
goose	kaz
gull	martı
heron	balıkçıl
ibis	kelaynak
kingfisher	yalı çapkını
kite	çaylak
magpie	saksağan
nightingale	bülbül
owl	baykuş
partridge	keklik
peacock	tavus kuşu
pheasant	sülün
pigeon	güvercin
quail	bıldırcın
raven	kuzgun
sparrow	serçe
sparrow hawk	atmaca
squab	güvercin yavrusu
starling	sığırcık
stork	leylek
swallow	kırlangıç
swan	kuğu
tern	deniz kırlangıcı
thrush	ardıç
vulture	akbaba
wagtail	kuyruk sallayan
woodpecker	ağaçkakan

ANIMALS

badger	porsuk
beaver	kunduz
chamois	dağ keçisi
gazelle	ceylan
hedgehog	kirpi
heifer	düve
hyena	sırtlan
leopard	pars
lynx	vaşak
marten	sansar
mole	köstebek
red deer	geyik
roe deer	karaca
squirrel	sincap
stag	erkek geyik
vole	tarla sıçanı
weasel	gelincik

PLANTS AND FLOWERS

anemone	dağ lalesi
asphodel	çiriş otu
azalea	açalya
baby's breath	müge
begonia	begonya
basil[75]	fesleğen
bougainvillea	begonvil
broom	katır tırnağı

[75] In Anatolia people grow it especially in the windows to keep mosquitoes far away from houses. It was a sacred plant belonging to Mother Goddess.

carnation	karanfil
castor (oil-plant) bean	kene otu
clover	yonca
crocus	çiğdem
daffodil	fulya
dahlia	dalya
daisy	papatya
geranium	sardunya
heath	funda, süpürge otu
hollyhock	gülhatmi
honeysuckle	hanımeli
hyacinth	sümbül
hybiscus	japon gülü
ivy	sarmaşık
jasmine	yasemin
lavender	lavanta
lilac	leylak
lily	zambak
liquorice, licorice	meyan kökü
moss	kara yosunu
mushroom	mantar
narcissus	nergis
oleander	zakkum
passion flower	çarkıfelek
rose	gül
rose / lemon geranium	ıtır
seaweed	deniz yosunu
snapdragon	aslanağzı
snowdrop	kardelen
sunflower	ayçiçeği
thistle	deve dikeni
tulip	lale
violet	menekşe
water lily	nilüfer

TREES

acorn	meşe palamudu, pelit
beech	kayın
carob (locust)[76]	keçi boynuzu
cedar	sedir
chestnut	kestane
cypress [77]	selvi
ebony	abanoz
fir	köknar
holly	çoban püskülü
hornbeam	gürgen
Judas tree[78]	erguvan
juniper	ardıç
laurel, bay	defne
lime	ıhlamur
magnolia	manolya
mahogany	maun
maple	akça ağaç
mulberry	dut
myrtle	mersin
oak	meşe
oleaster, Russian olive	iğde
palm	hurma, palmiye
pine	çam
plane	çınar
poplar	kavak
willow	söğüt

[76]Carat, a unit of weight for precious stones, derives from carob beans which were used for the same purpose.

[77]This is usually a cemetery tree for its roots go deep into the earth vertically.

[78]Originally this tree had white flowers. However, after betraying Jesus Judas hung himself from this tree. It is said that the flowers from then on became red because of their shame.

MUSICAL INSTRUMENTS

çevgan / felek	jingle bell
kanun	zither
kaval	duct flute
keman	violin
kemençe	spike fiddle
kudüm	double kettle drum
lavta	lute
mızrap / pena	plectrum
ney	end blown flute, reed flute
rebab	a stringed instrument similar to violin
saz	a stringed instrument similar to banjo
tambur	long lute
tef	hand drum
tulum	bag pipe
ud	short lute
zil	cymbal
zurna	shawm

PRECIOUS STONES

agate	akik
amber	kehribar
ambergris	esmer amber
coral	mercan
diamond	elmas
ebony	abanoz
emerald	zümrüt
ivory	fildişi
jade	yeşim
jet	kara kehribar, oltu taşı
meerschaum	lületaşı
mother-of-pearl, nacre	sedef
pearl	inci
ruby	yakut
sapphire	safir
turquoise	firuze

INSECTS

bee	bal arısı
cicada	ağustos böceği
dragonfly	kız böceği
gadfly	at sineği
hornet	eşek arısı
leech	sülük
moth	güve
praying mantis	peygamber devesi
snail	salyangoz
wasp	arı

6. ANCIENT GREEK ALPHABET & ROMAN NUMBERS

While traveling in Anatolia, it is highly likely that people will encounter old inscriptions carved on stones or marbles, etc. As Anatolia has a very rich history of different civilizations, these inscriptions are diverse dating from different periods; from Hittite cuneiform or hieroglyphs to modern Latinized Turkish alphabet.

The following table is given here to shed light on only some parts of history for those interested.

ANCIENT GREEK ALPHABET

A	α	Alpha	a	N	ν	Nu	n
B	β	Beta	b	Ξ	ξ	Xi	x
Γ	γ	Gamma	g	O	o	Omicron	o
Δ	δ	Delta	d	Π	π	Pi	p
E	ε	Epsilon	e	Π	ρ	Rho	r
Z	ζ	Zeta	z	Σ	σ,ς	Sigma	s
H	η	Eta	è	T	τ	Tau	t
Θ	θ	Theta	th	Ψ	υ	Upsilon	ü
I	ι	Iota	i	Φ	φ	Phi	f
K	κ	Kappa	k	X	x	Khi	k
Λ	λ	Lambda	l	Ψ	ψ	Psi	ps
M	μ	Mu	m	Ω	ω	Omega	ò

Examples

ΣoΦIA	:	SOPHIA	:	Wisdom
AΠETH	:	ARETÈ	:	Valor
ENNOIA	:	ENNOIA	:	Thought
EΠIΣTHMH	:	EPISTÈMÈ	:	Knowledge

ROMAN CARDINAL NUMBERS

I	unus	1	X	10	C	100
II	duo	2	XX	20	CC	200
III	tres	3	XXX	30	CCC	300
IV	quattuor	4	XL	40	CD	400
V	quinque	5	L	50	D	500
VI	sex	6	LX	60	DC	600
VII	septem	7	LXX	70	DCC	700
VIII	octo	8	LXXX	80	DCCC	800
IX	novem	9	XC	90	CM	900
X	decem	10	C	100	M	1000

APPENDICES

7. MYTHOLOGICAL GODS AND GODDESSES

Gods and goddesses	Roman counterparts	Associations	Symbols
Asclepius	Aesculapius	god of medicine and healing	snakes
Aphrodite	Venus	goddess of love	myrtle, dove
Apollo	Apollo	god of prophecy, medicine, the fine arts, archery, flocks and herds	tripod, omphalos, lyre, bow and arrows, laurel wreath, palm tree, wolf, hawk, crow and fawn
Ares	Mars	god of war	spear, vulture and dog
Artemis	Diana	goddess of the hunt, mistress of wild things and protectress of youth and women	bow or quiver
Athena	Minerva	goddess of war, wisdom, reason and intellect	shield with Medusa head, helmet, spear; owl; sometimes with Nike
Demeter	Ceres	goddess of earth and fertility	wreath
Dionysus	Bacchus	god of fertility, ritual dance and mysticism	drinking cup and *thyrsus* (staff), deer
Eros	Cupid, Amor	young, playful god of love	winged, carrying a bow and wearing a quiver of arrows
Hades	Pluto	god of the dead and underworld	
Hephaestus	Vulcan	god of fire	anvil and hammer
Hera	Juno	goddess of marriage, women and childbirth	apple, pomegranate and peacock
Heracles	Hercules	courage and strength	naked with his athletic body, lion's skin, staff
Hermes	Mercury	god of merchants, commerce, science, thieves and travelers	winged hat, sandals, herald's staff, ram, lyre and shepherd's staff
Hestia	Vesta	goddess of the hearth, security and hospitality of the home, family	
Nike	Victoria	goddess of victory	winged, standing on a globe holding a laurel and a palm branch
Poseidon	Neptune	god of the sea and of earthquakes	trident, three-pronged spear, bull, horse and dolphin
Tyche	Fortuna	goddess of fortune	ship's rudder, cornucopia
Zeus	Jupiter	god of sky, thunderbolt and lightning	eagle

8. WEIGHTS AND MEASURES CONVERSION TABLE

TEMPERATURE

°C →°F	multiply by 9, divide by 5, and add 32
°F →°C	subtract 32, multiply by 5, and divide by 9

LINEAR MEASUREMENT

1 centimeter	0.3937 inch
1 meter	3.280 feet
1 kilometer	0.6214 mile
1 inch	2.54 cm
1 foot	0.3048 m
1 yard	0.9144 m
1 mile	1.609 km

MASS

1 gram	15.43 grain
1 kilogram	2.205 pound
1 ton	2204.62 lb.
1 grain	64.8 mg
1 ounce	28.35 g
1 pound	0.4536 kg
1 stone	6.350 kg

CAPACITY MEASUREMENT

1 milliliter	0.00176 pint
1 liter	1.76 pint
1 fluid ounce	28.41 cm^3
1 US gallon	3.785 liter

SQUARE MEASUREMENT

1 sq centimeter	0.1550 in^2
1 sq meter	10.766 ft^2
1 hectare	2.471 acres
1 sq kilometer	0.386 sq mile
1 square inch	645.16 mm^2
1 square foot	0.0929 m^2
1 square yard	0.8361 m^2
1 acre	4047 m^2
1 square mile	2.59 km^2

CUBIC MEASUREMENT

1 cubic centimeter	0.06102 in^3
1 cubic meter	1.308 yd^3
1 cubic inch	16.39 cm^3
1 cubic foot	0.02832 m^3
1 cubic yard	0.7646 m^3

9. THE ORDERS OF ARCHITECTURE

DORIC

-There is a *crepidoma* with 3 steps

-No column bases

-Columns get narrower as they rise

-Columns have flutes separated by sharp arrises

-Doric capitals

-Plain *abacuses*

-Architrave is one block

-Acroteriums

IONIC / CORINTHIAN

-Number of steps changes; 8, 10 or 12

-There are column bases

-Straight columns

-Columns have flutes separated by blunt arrises

-Ionic capitals with volutes / Corinthian capitals

-Ornate *abacuses*

-Architrave consists of 3 blocks

-No acroteriums

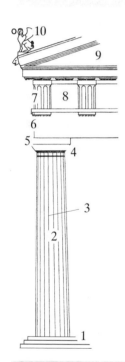

Doric Order

(1)crepidoma

(2)column

(3)sharp arrises

(4)Doric capital

(5)abacus

(6)architrave

(7)triglyphs

(8)metopes

(9)pediment

(10)acroterium

Ionic Order

(1)crepidoma

(2)column

(3)blunt arrises

(4)Ionic capital

(5)abacus

(6)architrave

(7)frieze

(8)pediment

(9)column base

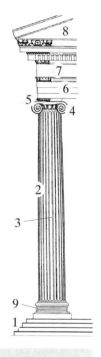

CAPITALS

| Doric | Ionic | Composite | Aeolian | Corinthian | Ottoman | Stalactite |

10. TYPES OF THE HELLENISTIC AND ROMAN TEMPLES

a) In antis temple
b) Amphiprostyle temple
c) Dipteros temple
d) Pseudodipteros temple
e) Peripteros temple
f) Pseudoperipteros temple

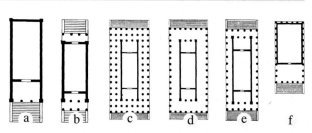

Parts of Temple

a) Walls
b) Crepidoma
c) Cella (Naos)
d) Porch (Pronaos)
e) Ante walls
f) Columns

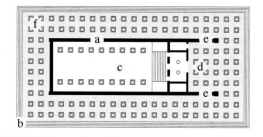

11. ANCIENT THEATERS

Hellenistic Theater
-Built on hillsides
-Orchestra more than semicircle
-Performances in orchestra
-No prohedria
-Spectators can see outside, *skene* was not very big or did not exist at all
-Seeing is concentrated; theatron

Roman Theater
-Freestanding structures
-Semicircular orchestra
-Performances in proskene
-Prohedria
-Skene and cavea are unified

-Hearing is concentrated; auditorium

Parts of Ancient Theaters

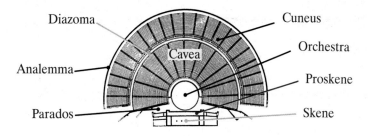

Diazoma
Cuneus
Analemma
Cavea
Orchestra
Parados
Proskene
Skene

CHRONOLOGY

BC	Anatolian Events	World Events	Periods
600000			
	Neanderthal man Homo Sapiens		Paleolithic
10000			Mesolithic
8000			Neolithic
5500			Chalcolithic
3000		Wheel discovered 3500	
		Egyptian Pyramids erected 2500	
		Papyrus used 2400	
		Mesopotamian Epic of Gilgamesh 2000	Bronze
	Introduction of writing to Anatolia 1950		
		Stonehenge built in England 1600	
		Moses	
	Trojan War 1300		
	Treaty of Kadesh 1284		
1200	Panionic League 800		Iron
	King Midas (Gordion), Homer (Smyrna) 700		
700	First coin in Sardis 640		Dark
	King Croesus, Lydia 560		
		Democracy in Athens 508	
490	Historian Herodotus 484		Classical
	Earliest town planner Hippodamus (Miletus) 450		
		Socrates 420	
	Alexander the Great 356-323		
300		Great Wall of China 200	Hellenistic
	Library of Pergamum 190		
133			

Map labels:
Alacahöyük
Hattians ?-2000
Afrodisias
Hacılar Çatalhöyük

Troy 3000-1260
Hattusha
Hittites 2000-1200
Hurrians

Gordion Pazarlı
Urartians 860-580
Ephesus Phrygians 750-300
Ionians Neo-Hittites 1200-650
From c.1100

Sardis Phrygians 750-300 Persians 550-333
Lydians 650-546
Carians c.7C-129 Lycians c.7C-? Cilicia

Bithynia Pontus
Cappadocia
Pergamum
Caria Roman

AD	Anatolian Events	World Events	Periods
		Birth of Jesus Christ	0
Roman	**Constantinople became capital**		330
		Roman Empire divided	395
395			
		Göktürks, Central Asia	500
		Birth of Mohammed, Mecca	571
	The Battle of Manzikert		1071
	First Crusade		1096
Byzantine	**Fourth Crusade**		1204
		Venetian explorer Marco Polo was born	1254
	Osman's Principality		1299
	Bursa, Ottoman Capital		1326
	Edirne, Ottoman Capital		1364
		German Johann Gutenberg's printing	1440
		Columbus was born	1451
1453			
	Conquest of Constantinople		1453
	Rise of the Ottoman Empire		1453
		Protestant Reformation leader Martin Luther	1483
		Colombus discovered America	1492
	Decline of the Ottoman Empire		1699
Ottoman	**Ottoman Reform attempts**		1789
		Darwin was born	1809
	Atatürk was born		1881
	Overthrow of the Ottoman Empire		1908
		World War I	1914
	Çanakkale Battles		1915
		Treaty of Sévres	1920
		Treaty of Lausanne	1923
1923			
	Reforms of Atatürk		1923
Republic	**Atatürk died**		1938
		World War II	1939-45
	Turkey joined NATO		1952
Today			

Roman Anatolia

• Byzantium

• Bursa

Ottomans 1324-1922

Republic of Turkey 1923

• Ankara

BIBLIOGRAPHY

1. Akurgal Ekrem, *Anadolu Uygarlıkları*, Net, 1987
2. Akurgal Ekrem, *Ancient Civilizations and Ruins of Turkey*, Haşet, 1985
3. Akurgal Ekrem, *The Art of the Hittites*, 1962
4. Akyıldız Erhan, *Taş Çağı'ndan Osmanlı'ya Anadolu*, Milliyet, 1990
5. Altun Ara, *Turkish Architecture in the Middle Ages,* Arkeoloji ve Sanat Yayınları, 1990
6. *AnaBritannica*, Ana Yayıncılık, 1988
7. *Anatolian Civilizations Museum, the*, Ankara
8. Aslanapa Oktay, *Türk Sanatı,* Remzi Kitabevi, 1984
9. Atasoy Nurhan Dr., *Splendors of the Ottoman Sultans,* Wonders, 1992
10. *Atlas* No. 20, Hürriyet, 1994
11. Ayyıldız Uğur, *Cappadocia*, Net Turistik Yayınlar A.Ş., 1989
12. Ayyıldız Uğur, *The Kariye Museum, İstanbul*, Net Turistik Yayınlar A.Ş., 1988
13. Balaman Ali Rıza, *Gelenekler Töre ve Törenler*, Betim, 1983
14. Bayatlı Osman, *Bergama Tarihinde Asklepion*, Bergama Belediyesi, 1993
15. Bayburtluoğlu Cevdet Prof., *Arkeoloji*, Kültür ve Turizm Bakanlığı, 1982
16. Bayhan Suzan, *Priene, Miletus, Didyma,* Keskin Color, 1989
17. Bayrak Orhan M., *Türkiye Tarihi Yerler Kılavuzu,* Remzi Kitabevi, 1982
18. Bayral Mete, *Secret Ephesus*, Ofis Ticaret Matbaacılık, 1985
19. Belge Murat, *İstanbul Gezi Rehberi*, Tarih Vakfı, 1993
20. Berlitz, *The Travelers Guide to Turkey*, 1993
21. *Birds of Britain and Europe*, The, Collins, 1972
22. Blake C. Everett, Edmonds G. Anna, *Biblical Sites in Turkey*, Redhouse, 1990
23. Boratav, Pertev Naili, *100 Soruda Türk Folkloru*, Gerçek, 1984
24. Brosnahan Tom, Turkey, *A Survival Kit*, Lonely Planet, 1985
25. Buckler McKay Hill, *A History of World Societies*, Houghton Mifflin, 1988
26. Campbell Joseph, *Creative Mythology*, Penguin, 1968
27. Cimok Fatih, *Cappadocia*, A Turizm Yayınları, 1987
28. *Cornucopia in Turkey*, Issue III, Volume I, 1992 / 93
29. Croutier Alev Lytle, *Harem: Peçeli Dünya*, Yılmaz Yayınları, 1990
30. *Cumhuriyet Dönemi Türkiye Ansiklopedisi*, İletişim, 1983
31. *Çağdaş Liderler Ansiklopedisi*, İletişim, 1986
32. Çuhadar Mehmet, *Cappadocia*, Panda, 1988
33. Demir Neşat, *Valley of Ihlara and its Rock Churches*, Simge
34. Doğramacı Emel, *Türkiye'de Kadının Dünü ve Bugünü*, İş Bankası, 1992
35. Donagh Mc Bernard, *Blue Guide Turkey*, A & C Black, 1989
36. Donagh Mc Bernard, *Blue Guide Turkey*, A & C Black, 1995
37. *Dünden Bugüne İstanbul Ansiklopedisi*, Tarih Vakfı, 1993, 1994
38. *Encarta, The Complete Interactive Multimedia Encyclopedia*, Microsoft, 1995
39. *Encyclopedia Britannica*, 1995
40. *Encyclopedia of Archeology*, Larousse, 1972
41. *Encyclopedia International*, Grolier, 1975
42. Engelhart Aysun, *Notlar*, 1995
43. Ercan Nural, *Notlar*, 1995
44. Erhat Azra, *Mitoloji Sözlüğü*, Remzi, 1984
45. Eyice Semavi Prof. Dr., *Ayasofya*, Yapı ve Kredi Bankası, 1984
46. Eyüboğlu İsmet Zeki, *Anadolu Uygarlığı*, Der, 1991
47. Freely John, *Blue Guide İstanbul*, A&C Black, 1987
48. Freely John, *The Western Shores of Turkey*, John Murray, 1988
49. *From Ephesus to Pamukkale,* Boyut Publishing Group, 1990
50. *Gezi Türkiye Tatil Rehberi 95*, Ekin Yazım Merkezi, 1995
51. Graves Robert, *The Greek Myths 1, 2*, Penguin, 1990
52. Greenhalgh Michael, *Turkey: Classical Architecture & Sculpture*
53. *Grolier Electronic Publishing*, Inc., 1992, 1993
54. *Guide News*, June 1994
55. Gülersoy Çelik, *A Guide to İstanbul*, Director General of the Touring and Automobile Club of Turkey, 1978
56. Güleryüz Naim, *The History of the Turkish Jews*, 1992
57. Güvenç Bozkurt, *Türk Kimliği*, Kültür Bakanlığı, 1993
58. *Hayat Küçük Ansiklopedi*, Hayat Yayınları, 1968
59. *Hürriyet*, 11 June, 1994

60. *Insight Guides, Turkey*, APA Publications, 1990
61. *İstanbul, Turkey*, Knopf Guides, 1993
62. *İl İl Büyük Türkiye Ansiklopedisi*, Milliyet
63. *İlgi Dergisi*, Shell, Aralık 1973, Summer 1994
64. İzbırak Reşat, *Türkiye*, MEB, 1984
65. İzer Müheyya, *Baharatın İzleri*, Redhouse, 1988
66. Kekeç Tehvit, *Pergamon*, Hitit Color, 1989
67. Kinross Lord, *Atatürk, The Rebirth of a Nation*, Rustem, 1990
68. Kuşoğlu Mehmet Zeki, *Mezar Taşlarında Huve'l Baki*, 1984
69. *Longman Dictionary of Contemporary English*, 1985
70. Longman-*Metro Büyük Sözlük*, 1993
71. Lloyd Seton, *Ancient Turkey*, University of California Press, 1989
72. Mandıracı Sabri, *Notlar*, 1994
73. *Milliyet*, 17-18 November, 1994
74. *Nasreddin Hoca*, Minyatür Yayınları
75. Necatigil Behçet, *100 Soruda Mitologya*, Gerçek, 1969
76. *New Larousse Encyclopedia of Mythology*, Hamlyn, 1978
77. *New Perspectives on Turkey*, Vassar College, 1992
78. *Newspot*, 1993 / 19, 22, 26, 1994 / 3, 7, 8, 9, 15, 17, 18, 1995 / 2, 3, 4, 5, Ankara
79. *Oxford Dictionary of Quotations The*, Oxford University Press, 1992
80. Önder Mehmet, *Konya Rehberi*, TTOK
81. Önder Mehmet, *Mevlana and the Mevlana Museum*, Akşit, 1985
82. *Örf ve Adetlerimiz*, Türk Kültürüne Hizmet Vakfı
83. Özcan İsmail, *İslam Ansiklopedisi*, Milliyet Yay., 1991
84. Perek Zeki Faruk, *Latince Grameri*, Edebiyat Fakültesi. Basımevi, 1968
85. Radt Wolfgang, *Pergamon, Archeological Guide*, Türkiye Turing ve Otomobil Kurumu, 1984
86. Rogers Jean Scott, *In Search of St. Paul*, Arthur Barker Ltd., 1964
87. Sevin Veli, *Anadolu Arkeolojisinin ABCsi*, Simavi, 1991
88. Sözen Metin, Tanyeli Uğur, *Sanat Kavram ve Terimleri Sözlüğü*, Remzi, 1986
89. Stoneman Richard, *A Traveler's History of Turkey*, Interlink Books, 1993
90. Soytürk Işık, *Myra-Demre: The Home of Santa Claus*, İlgi, Issue 79, The Shell Company of Turkey, 1994
91. Tanilli Server, *Uygarlık Tarihi*, Say, 1981
92. Taşlıklıoğlu Zafer, *Grekçe Gramer ve Syntaks*, Edebiyat Fakültesi Matbaası, 1968
93. Tavernier Jean Baptiste, *Topkapı Sarayında Yaşam*, Çağdaş Yayınları, 1984
94. Toker Biltin, *Spot on İstanbul*, P.P.I., 1986
95. *TPAO Annual Report*, 1992
96. Tunay İ Mehmet, *Sanat Tarihi Ders Notları*, Yeni Gün, 1977
97. Tuncer Ömer, *İşte Anadolu*, Arkeoloji ve Sanat Yayınları, 1993
98. Tuğlacı Pars, *Türkçe - İngilizce Sözlük*, 1973
99. *Turkey-A Country Study*, The American University, 1979
100. *Turkey, A Phaidon Cultural Guide*, Phaidon Press Limited, 1989
101. *Turkey-A Times Bartholomew Guide*, 1990
102. *Turkey*, Directorate General of Press and Information, 1993
103. *Turkey Magazine*, Hilton, No 1, 1994
104. *Turkey, The Real Guide*, Prentice Hall Press, 1991
105. *Turkish Musical Instruments*, Net Group of Companies, Calendar, 1995
106. *Türkiyemiz Kültür ve Sanat Dergisi*, No 64, Akbank, 1991
107. Türkoğlu Sabahattin, *Efes'in Öyküsü*, Arkeoloji ve Sanat Yayınları, 1986
108. Türkoğlu Sabahattin, *Pamukkale (Hierapolis)*, Net Turistik Yayınlar A.Ş., 1989
109. Türkoğlu Sabahattin, *The Topkapı Palace*, Net Turistik Yayınlar A.Ş., 1989
110. *Türsab*, July, 1994
111. Uluaslan Hüseyin, *Gallipoli 75th Anniversary*, Çanakkale Seramik, 1990
112. Umar Bilge, Prof., *Lydia*, Ak Yayınları, 1981
113. Unger Merrill F., *Archeology and the New Testament*, Zondervan Publishing House, 1962
114. *Yıllık Ekonomi Raporu*, T.C: Maliye Bakanlığı, 1994,
115. Yurtbaşı Metin, *Turkish Proverbs*, Turkish Daily News, 1993
116. *Webster's New Collegiate Dictionary*, 1979
117. Wiplinger Gilbert, Wlach Gudrun, *Ephesus, 100 years of Austrian Research*, Österreichisches Archaologisches Institut, 1996
118. Wycherley R. E., *Antik Çağda Kentler Nasıl Kuruldu?*, Arkeoloji ve Sanat, 1991

INDEX

TURKISH IDENTITY
Variety in Unity;
Unity in Variety!

Bozkurt Güvenç[79]

[79] Güvenç Bozkurt,
Türk Kimliği, (Turkish Identity)
Kültür Bakanlığı, 1993